To my mentor, Andrew Needham, without whose support and guidance this project would never have been possible.

To my father of blessed memory and my mother for their kindness, wisdom, and love, for which I am forever indebted.

And to my life partner, Stephanie Brianne Wortel-London, and our children, Samuel and Eva. God only knows.

The Menace of Prosperity

 Historical Studies of Urban America

Edited by Lilia Fernández, Timothy J. Gilfoyle, and Amanda I. Seligman

James R. Grossman, Editor Emeritus

RECENT TITLES IN THE SERIES

A. K. Sandoval-Strausz, ed., *Metropolitan Latinidad: Transforming American Urban History*

Alexander Wood, *Building the Metropolis: Architecture, Construction, and Labor in New York City, 1880–1935*

Leslie M. Harris, *In the Shadow of Slavery: African Americans in New York City, 1626–1863, With a New Afterword by the Author*

Tim Keogh, *In Levittown's Shadow: Poverty in America's Wealthiest Postwar Suburb*

Nicholas Dagen Bloom, *The Great American Transit Disaster: A Century of Austerity, Auto-Centric Planning, and White Flight*

Sean T. Dempsey, *City of Dignity: Christianity, Liberalism, and the Making of Global Los Angeles*

Claire Dunning, *Nonprofit Neighborhoods: An Urban History of Inequality and the American State*

Tracy E. K'Meyer, *To Live Peaceably Together: The American Friends Service Committee's Campaign for Open Housing*

Mike Amezcua, *Making Mexican Chicago: From Postwar Settlement to the Age of Gentrification*

Arnold R. Hirsch, *Making the Second Ghetto: Race and Housing in Chicago, 1940–1960, With a New Afterword by N. D. B. Connolly*

William Sites, *Sun Ra's Chicago: Afrofuturism and the City*

David Schley, *Steam City: Railroads, Urban Space, and Corporate Capitalism in Nineteenth-Century Baltimore*

Rebecca K. Marchiel, *After Redlining: The Urban Reinvestment Movement in the Era of Financial Deregulation*

A complete list of series titles is available on the University of Chicago Press website.

The Menace of Prosperity

New York City and the Struggle for Economic Development, 1865–1981

DANIEL WORTEL-LONDON

The University of Chicago Press
Chicago and London

The University of Chicago Press, Chicago 60637
The University of Chicago Press, Ltd., London
© 2025 by The University of Chicago
Published 2025
Printed and bound by CPI Group (UK) Ltd, Croydon, CR0 4YY

34 33 32 31 30 29 28 27 26 25   1 2 3 4 5

ISBN-13: 978-0-226-84109-0 (cloth)
ISBN-13: 978-0-226-84111-3 (paper)
ISBN-13: 978-0-226-84110-6 (e-book)
DOI: https://doi.org/10.7208/chicago/9780226841106.001.0001

Library of Congress Cataloging-in-Publication Data

Names: Wortel-London, Daniel, author.
Title: The menace of prosperity : New York City and the struggle for economic
   development, 1865–1981 / Daniel Wortel-London.
Other titles: New York City and the struggle for economic development, 1865–1981 |
   Historical studies of urban America.
Description: Chicago ; London : The University of Chicago Press, 2025. |
Series: Historical studies of urban America | Includes bibliographical
   references and index.
Identifiers: LCCN 2025008160 | ISBN 9780226841090 (cloth) |
   ISBN 9780226841113 (paperback) | ISBN 9780226841106 (ebook)
Subjects: LCSH: Economic development—New York (State)—New York—
   History—19th century. | Economic development—New York (State)—
   New York—History—20th century. | New York (N.Y.)—Economic conditions—
   19th century. | New York (N.Y.)—Economic conditions—20th century.
Classification: LCC HC108.N7 W67 2025 | DDC 338.9747/100904—dc23/eng/20250417
LC record available at https://lccn.loc.gov/2025008160

♾ This paper meets the requirements of ANSI/NISO Z39.48-1992 (Permanence of Paper).

Contents

Introduction

The roots of the city's failures are not in the necessity of earning its keep but in how that impulse gets translated into action.

STANLEY ELKIN[1]

"If we can find a bunch of billionaires around the world to move here, that would be a godsend, because that's where the revenue comes to take care of everyone else."[2] This statement, spoken by New York City mayor Michael Bloomberg in 2013, captures how most American cities pursue economic development today: by enticing and retaining the wealthy. To attract this quarry, local governments lavish public subsidies on their behalf ranging from tax-exempt apartments bordering tax-financed parks, to municipally financed highways routed to gated communities, to swollen police budgets and seductive branding campaigns, and much more besides.[3] But no matter what form this strategy takes, its rationale remains consistent. Without the taxes and jobs generated by wealthy firms and households, we are told, our communities cannot survive.[4]

But what if the costs of elite-driven growth outweighed its benefits? What if the wealthy were not the fiscal saviors of American cities, but their assassins? What if relying on the rich to "take care of everyone else" was neither politically nor financially sustainable?[5] And what would all this mean for how our communities *should* develop economically?

These questions are not new. Between the 1870s and 1960s, a wide range of urbanites connected local fiscal crises to the greed, waste, and other "externalities" of the wealthy. Economist Richard T. Ely stated in 1888 that "many of our growing cities have become embarrassed by expenditures made at the solicitation of land owners" and "not, as popularly imagined, by the moneyless rabble."[6] Muckraker Henry H. Klein argued in 1916 that New York's "largest private fortunes," far from saving the city's economy, were wrecking it.[7] And public finance specialist A. M. Hillhouse declared the use of "municipal credit in aid of real estate speculation and overdevelopment" to be a "veritable master key to an understanding of the financial collapse of hundreds of areas in the early 1930s."[8] Local elites, in short, produced local catastrophe.

To avoid this fate, many activists and ordinary citizens called for a radical reconstruction of local economies. From Henry George and Lewis Mumford to Rexford Tugwell and Jane Jacobs, urbanites theorized how their communities could be made economically viable without the poisoned largesse of the wealthy. Their strategies encompassed cooperatives and public housing, land-value taxation and regional planning, public utilities and community-owned enterprises, and much more. Some of these policies were successfully passed; many were not. Yet all centered on the needs and capabilities of ordinary residents as the basis for prosperous *and* just local economies.

By the 1960s, however, local policymakers and much of the public had forgotten these campaigns. No longer was elite-driven growth seen as a major cause of local fiscal strains, or worker-oriented development strategies looked to as alternatives. Rather, local officials looked to the wealthy to fund social programs, provide employment, and for fiscal salvation more broadly. To attract such saviors, they relied upon the same failed strategies Ely and others warned against more than a century ago—using public funds to attract high-income private firms and households. And even when a wave of fiscal crises engulfed cities across the country during the 1970s, local policymakers—liberals and conservatives alike—continued clinging to the failed paradigms which helped generate those crises in the first place.

This book is a history of modern urban economic development told through stories of struggle over the costs of elite-driven growth in New York City. It recounts how generations of New Yorkers fought for viable and democratic local economies following waves of wealth-induced fiscal crises. It reveals how layers of subsidies and burgeoning white property ownership narrowed the constituency for local economic reform. And it argues that advocates of elite-driven growth strategies dominated postwar New York not by *delivering* economic development but by *obscuring* both its burdens and its alternatives. In this way, *The Menace of Prosperity* upends our understanding of urban growth, urban crisis, and urban politics more broadly—and, in doing so, suggests ways we can build local economies that work for all of us.

Diversifying the Economy

If we are to recognize the damage inflicted by elite-driven growth and to identify alternative economic development strategies, we must first challenge our assumptions on what "the economy" is and what it can be. Two concepts can help us accomplish this: "social costs" and "fiscal imaginaries." "Social costs" are the harm any economic activity imposes upon third persons or the community at large.[9] This concept covers far more than textbook "externalities" wherein the costs of economic activity are rare, visible, and easily addressed. Rather, social costs encompass deep, omnipresent, and often unquantifiable damages: emotional (the psychic effects of harsh working conditions), physical (the adverse effects of unaffordable health care), ecological (the destruction of biodiversity, the extraction of resources beyond environmental carrying capacity), and much more. It is one thing to suggest that smog is an externality; it is another to suggest that *poverty* is. But such is the framework of social costs.[10]

"Social costs" have economic consequences. Every economic activity—every aspect of investment, production, and consumption—depends on a deeper layer of resources. These resources range from natural materials to uncompensated emotional labor.[11] To the extent that an activity depletes these resources, that activity is uneconomic—and its increase represents what Herman Daly called "uneconomic growth."[12] To the extent that actors pass on the costs of "cleaning up" this uneconomic growth to others—such as the public sector—their actions can strain local budgets and lead to fiscal crisis.[13] And such social costs are in addition to the fiscal burdens borne by local governments to promote such "uneconomic growth" in the first place.[14]

The concept of "social costs" provides scholars with a paradoxical but powerful fiscal lens. It suggests that fiscal crises and economic underdevelopment derive not only from economic growth's absence but often from its *presence*. It suggests that policies meant to reduce social costs, such as welfare spending, can be fiscally dependent on the very economic activities producing those costs.[15] And it discloses the self-destructive logic by which actors often promote growth strategies—for the sake of "paying off" the costs of earlier growth stratagems.

But if the concept of "social costs" reveals the hidden wastage of elite economic activity, the concept of "fiscal imaginary" helps us find alternatives to it. The economy, as Karl Polanyi noted long ago, is not a limited set of activities and actors (such as profit-seeking privately-owned firms) governed by a particular way of thinking (such as rational self-interest). Rather, the economy comprises *all* the ways people "interchange with [their] natural and social environment" in order to acquire "the means of material want-satisfaction."[16] "Wants" can be cultural or educational, individualistic or social, but as long as material or energy is necessary for their realization, they all possess an economic dimension. Similarly, interchange—how we interact with natural and social forces to achieve our material wants—can take the form of barter, mutual aid, theft, cooperative enterprise, and other expressions of what feminist geographer J. K. Gibson-Graham has called the "diverse economy."[17] All this implies that understanding "the economy" requires us to understand how the economy—as a set of material wants and a set of means for achieving them—is defined by different people. Or defined for them.[18]

Here is where the notion of "fiscal imagination" comes in. "Fiscal imagination" refers to the range of alternative strategies people use to define and pursue their material wants.[19] By recovering the range of concepts past actors used to describe the economy, we can trace the broadening or narrowing of a group's "fiscal imagination" over time. And by comparing rival fiscal imaginaries we can provide new contexts for explaining conflict between different groups: for what appears wasteful to one group—production for use rather than profit, the public ownership of profitable enterprises, etc.—can appear self-evidently efficient to others. Such rival fiscal imaginaries, perceiving different types of social costs, form the foundation for rival economic development strategies.[20]

Historians, urbanists, and activists alike can enlist these concepts to better understand the inner workings of political economies. We can trace why certain economic activities, and not others, are validated as "profitable" or "investments." We can map these activities and their social costs within the urban landscape, revealing hidden flows of profit and plunder across what I call a city's "fiscal geography." We can see how these costs have deepened inequalities while wrecking urban economies. And we can see how different groups have contested these costs with alternative development strategies of their own. The concepts of social costs and fiscal imaginaries, in short, help us understand urban fiscal crises as grounded in failed "bets on growth" while giving us tools to imagine alternative development strategies.

Changing the Narrative

Using the concepts of social costs and fiscal imagination to broaden our understanding of the economy also allows us to rewrite one of the central historical narratives of our era: that the social and political ills of our time are largely due to our failure to sufficiently generate or tax elite-driven growth. This narrative takes two forms. On the right, pundits and policymakers blame an excess of taxation and regulation for stifling growth and repelling wealthy taxpayers. On the left, scholars blame an inability or unwillingness to tax the wealthy to begin with.[21] They disagree on whether this tendency, often described in terms of "neoliberal" ideology and statecraft, is the result of a structural shift in technology and economic operations since the 1970s, a political outcome determined by opponents of the redistributive welfare state, an improvised bipartisan response to that decade's fiscal tumult, or an extension of far longer patterns of wealth-deferment in our politics. But the explanation for our ills—and according to many narratives, the unravelling of twentieth-century liberalism more generally—remains the same: the rich no longer pay their fair share.[22] Unfortunately, this focus on wealth taxation can inadvertently reinforce a deeper assumption that the presence of the wealthy is a prerequisite for economic and fiscal vitality.

This "tax-oriented" narrative is also prevalent in our accounts of American urban history. Before the 1970s, according to mainstream narratives, local governments were able to tax locally bound wealth while enjoying robust transfers from state and federal bodies. This redistributed revenue provided cities with the fiscal leeway needed for relatively robust, decommodified public services. By the 1970s, however, the flight of wealthy firms and households from urban jurisdictions placed cities under severe fiscal strain. Facing economic collapse from within and denied state or federal revenue from without, cities adopted more "entrepreneurial" strategies to survive—strategies that stressed subsidies on behalf of the wealthy without commensurate taxation.[23] Again, scholars disagree whether this shift was structural, political, improvised, or overdetermined in general.[24] Underlying them all, however, is a similar causal narrative behind both urban fiscal strains and modern inequality: that policymakers are either unwilling or unable to adequately attract and tax the wealthy and their enterprises. Ironically, this narrative mirrors a broader bipartisan consensus that elites, whatever their tax burden, are essential for local fiscal health.[25]

While undeniably just and accurate in many ways—tax avoidance by the wealthy is indeed a serious problem—this narrative rests on two incomplete assumptions. First, it assumes that the social costs of the wealthy and their firms *does not outweigh their benefits*, no matter how well-taxed. Financing progressive policies through levies on a regressive economy, in other words, has its limits.[26] Second, it overlooks the possibility of alternative forms of economic activity that are *just and viable the first time around*. And such assumptions come with both practical and intellectual costs. On the one hand, reducing "the economy" to modern capitalism obscures economic alternatives to capitalism while rendering "social" policies further dependent on it for financing.[27] On the other hand, such assumptions distort our historical understanding by obscuring how the social costs of the wealthy, our fiscal reliance on them for social programs, and our unwillingness to envision alternative economic models—an unwillingness often shared by both opponents *and* proponents of wealth taxation—have also contributed to inequity, instability, and domination in our time.[28]

Here is where the concepts of social costs and fiscal imaginaries come in. By using these concepts, we can change the way we understand urban economies and urban crises—and in so doing, change our political narratives. We would characterize our era not as an "economic age" (in the words of Tony Judt) but as a profoundly *un*economic age in which the gross inefficiencies and costs of mainstream growth strategies are largely absent from public discourse.[29] We would recognize how depending upon elites for public revenue can lead to public bankruptcy and underdevelopment.[30] And we would ask: at what times have actors recognized the costs of elite-driven growth, and what can we learn from their efforts to build more democratic and sustainable routes to prosperity?

Some scholars have begun asking these questions. Historians of populism and Black Power have traced how citizens have challenged the purpose, ownership model, and scale of the modern corporate economy.[31] Historians of economic knowledge have shown that the rise of modern capitalism was a messy and contested affair.[32] And activists around the world are demonstrating that elite-oriented growth is not the only feasible development strategy for communities and countries—demonstrations that have scholarly as well as practical import.[33]

And while these scholars show the potential of heterodox economic development, others demonstrate the way mainstream growth strategies have failed on their own terms. Urbanists uncover how a "healthy business climate" can *contribute* to the fiscal difficulties of American cities.[34] Scholars of post-development detail the costs of extractive and neocolonial growth on the economic well-being of entire populations.[35] And historians have traced how local governments have been thrown into debt and crisis due to private realty speculation and public subsidies on its behalf.[36]

Still, there are few studies that analyze local economic alternatives and local fiscal crises together. And this is a missed opportunity. Studying whether actors were willing to replace economic development strategies during moments of recession and fiscal crises—moments when these strategies were tested *on their own terms* and found wanting—can reveal how America's fiscal imagination has broadened or narrowed over time.[37] But to glean these new insights, we must ask new questions. What does it mean that American cities were often thrown into fiscal crisis due to failed "bets on growth" before the 1970s? In what ways did urban residents view these crises and the social costs that produced them? How and why did they launch campaigns for local economic reform? What might these campaigns tell us about the vexed fortunes of modern liberalism and social democracy during the twentieth century? And what can we learn from these struggles in our efforts to build more equitable and sustainable economies today?

Argument, Method, and Structure

The Menace of Prosperity seeks to answer these questions. It does so by examining how New Yorkers perceived and reacted to the social costs of different growth strategies in their city. It demonstrates that after New York's fiscal crises of the 1870s, many residents consistently campaigned for alternative economic strategies. It traces how, by the time of New York's 1970s fiscal crisis a century later, many citizens ceased demanding or even perceiving such alternatives. And it argues that this shrinkage of New York's fiscal imaginary occurred largely due to the cumulative weight of prior growth strategies: strategies whose outcomes empowered their white and wealthy beneficiaries, whose "sunk costs" weighed heavily upon the public sector, and whose operations both obscured and shifted those costs in a way that fragmented the constituency for radical fiscal reform.[38] These material effects, together with a broader narrowing of economic thought among liberal policymakers and public finance officers, profoundly limited the fiscal options and fiscal imagination of New York City by the time of its 1970s fiscal crisis. In this way, rather than signaling the triumph of "economic thought" over social concerns, New York's 1970s fiscal crisis—and the neoliberalism it helped entrench—both reflected and deepened the long-term decline of urban America's fiscal imagination.

I have chosen New York City between the 1870s and the 1970s as this study's context both for its generalizability and its singularity. Like thousands of other cities, New York experimented with multiple paradigms of economic growth between the late nineteenth and mid-twentieth centuries. Like thousands of other cities, New York experienced multiple waves of fiscal crises during this period, thus providing scholars with a moving window into how contemporaries responded to the social costs of these strategies. And the city's diversity and national stature provide a uniquely comprehensive lens into these commonly shared tensions: a further advantage.

Above all, recasting New York City's economic history helps us challenge broader narratives built around Gotham's experiences. New York's retreat from redistribution following its 1970s-era fiscal crisis—"from welfare state to real estate," in the words of one scholar—often serves as a synecdoche for larger political phenomena: the fall of urban liberalism, social Keynesianism, European social democracy (as inflected through the New Deal), and much more.[39] In nearly all these cases, most scholars view a single culprit: the inability or refusal of policymakers to tax wealth.[40] Yet this focus overlooks how elite-oriented development strategies themselves made postwar redistributive policies both politically and fiscally fragile. By showing how New York's finances were often wrecked and not aided by the wealthy—that is, by showing the limits of wealth taxation—we can begin to rewrite the larger political narratives and policy goals we have built around it.

To tell this tale, *The Menace of Prosperity* adopts a three-part structure. Each part focuses on a different period of fiscal crisis in New York City: the

1870s, the 1930s, and the 1970s. Each chapter describes the fiscal imaginaries held by a particular group, examines how they mobilized to translate these imaginaries into policy, and identifies how the rules and resources implemented by these policies accelerated and "legitimated" different growth strategies. By tracing how one era's growth policies established the political and material terrain for subsequent fiscal reform movements—via new expectations, expensive "sunk costs," or similar mechanisms—*The Menace of Prosperity* traces how the fiscal imagination of America's largest city expanded and contracted over time.[41]

Part 1 focuses on debates over what actors New York should rely upon for revenue between the late nineteenth and early twentieth century. Following New York's fiscal crisis of the 1870s, radicals ranging from Henry George to William Randolph Hearst argued that the public ownership of profitable enterprises or the confiscatory taxation of land would democratize and unleash New York's economy. These fiscal imaginaries, however, were eclipsed by a rival one that stressed growing land values, via "rational" regulation and public subsidies, as the guarantor of both local finances and local economic development.

Part 2 examines how New Yorkers debated their city's realty-based growth strategy during the interwar period. During this time, local policymakers promoted both peripheral homeownership and central-city redevelopment on behalf of white property owners and speculators. Public debt on behalf of this program contributed to New York's Depression-era fiscal crisis, prompting critics like Catherine Bauer and Lewis Mumford to promote new development paradigms stressing stability over expansion using tools such as public housing. By the 1940s, however, domestic realty operators and federal programs on their behalf had largely buried this paradigm. Boosterism survived the Depression battered but alive.

Part 3 traces how New York's postwar development strategy, built around the needs of white-collar enterprises, maintained its hegemony even after the city's 1970s-era crisis. Changing theories of urban growth in the 1940s stressed income as the source of urban prosperity, rather than growing land values alone. Public and private financial officers built on this theory to claim that large corporate firms were the necessary and sufficient "economic base" of urban centers. Black advocates of community autonomy and neighborhood activists like Jane Jacobs contested this claim, arguing that the well-being of ordinary New Yorkers constituted the true economic health of New York. Most liberal policymakers, however, chose to pair corporate-centric growth with redistributive welfare mechanisms rather than rethink their growth strategies. Lacking a strong vision or constituency for local economic alternatives, policymakers responded to the 1970s-era fiscal crisis by accelerating their city's white-collar stratagem—without compensatory welfare policies.

The Menace of Prosperity thus shows how the liberal embrace of elite-led urban growth strategies helped erode the imagination and coalition necessary for economic alternatives—and robust redistributive policies—well before the ascent of "neoliberalism" in the 1970s.

Before commencing, a brief overview of local public finance is in order. Local governments generally receive revenue from three sources—taxes, profits, and debt. Taxes can derive from both local sources, often in the form of levies on real estate, and transfers from other jurisdictions. Debt is achieved by selling municipal bonds, often to private financiers eager for repayment of principal and interest. Profit, comparatively paltry as a revenue source in most American cities, derives from publicly owned enterprises.[42] What fiscal instruments a local government has available to it are, in the United States, often decided at the state level rather than locally. Federal and state assistance can supplement local finances, of course, but as we shall see, such assistance can come at a heavy price when used on behalf of misguided growth strategies.

A number of definitions are also useful for the sake of clarity and consistency. "Economic growth," or simply "growth," represents the expansion of a particular economic activity. It can be represented through the monetary value of final goods and services as indicated by GDP, the value of land and structures as represented by property values, and other indexes. By contrast, "economic development" is the improvement of a community's well-being *through* the growth (or simply maintenance) of different economic strategies. But while growth is often equated with development, this is not the case: many scholars have demonstrated how different growth strategies can inflict social costs in ways that undermine development more generally.[43] Whether a community can identify these costs depends on their fiscal imagination. Whether they can undo these costs depends on their power.

The reader will also find, throughout this book, terms of my own invention such as "fiscal republican" or "fiscal corporatist." These terms refer to groups of people who share a similar fiscal imaginary. For example, in chapter 4, I refer to the small homeowners, developers, and elected representatives who sought subsidies on behalf of outer-borough real estate as "developmental populists." While I am careful to delineate the diversity and tensions that existed within this and similar bodies, as a means of comprehension, I have found it useful to refer to them via this shorthand insofar as they shared a broadly similar economic agenda. I also refer frequently to "liberal" policymakers across these chapters, the most relevant characteristics of whom are (a) a commitment to "public" goods and services, including (among more radical liberals) robust welfare state policies, and (b) a commitment to financing these services via taxes drawn from "private" individuals, property, and the conventional for-profit sector.[44] As we shall see, liberals in New York have often been more active in developing new forms of social expenditure than in reimagining the economic activity financing them.

One final note: I write this book amid the greatest ecological crises humanity has ever faced. As thinkers from Herman Daly to Donella Meadows have long pointed out, the "social costs" of extractive growth are directly to blame for declines in biodiversity, rises in CO_2 emissions, and the other calamities of our time.[45] On these grounds, a growing number of activists call for "steady-state," "postgrowth," or "degrowth" economies more attuned to the needs of humans and the boundaries of the earth.[46] Much of this work, however, proceeds without a robust knowledge of how previous activists have sought to place the human economy on more just and resilient foundations.[47] By investigating the "fiscal imaginaries" of prior activists and recounting their struggles in one city, it is my hope that this book can provide some insights into how we might forge better economies on our one planet.

PART I

Taxation and Its Discontents, 1870–1913

"Monstrous Growth"

In 1891, George Ashton Black, a professor of political science at Columbia University, published a history of public landownership in Manhattan. Reviewers lauded the book as pathbreaking, with one admirer describing it as "the first scientific contribution towards an economic history of an American municipality."[1] The book's conclusions, however, were decidedly conventional. Public ownership of land, Black concluded, was "unprofitable" and "unfavorable to improvements." "Exclusive private ownership," on the other hand, "has this advantage, that under the stress of its competition, those who are in general best able to improve the land get it." For this reason, he argued, it was in the interest of New York's government to quickly dispose of public land in order to spur real estate growth, raise property values, and "benefit the community generally."[2]

Black's faith in private property and competitive markets as the bedrock of local prosperity reflected a fiscal imaginary shared by many nineteenth-century realty owners and local officials.[3] Its prevalence stemmed from a complex conjuncture of ideological animus against public landownership, fiscal arrangements tying local budgets to local property values, and politically mobilized private realty owners themselves. But through these myriad pressures and their translation into public policies such as the public land sales Black recommended, the notion that "exclusive private ownership" of land led to public prosperity was well established in New York by the 1890s.

Or so it seemed. In fact, by the time Black published his book—indeed, decades earlier—private realty's fiscal reliability had been deeply discredited. The immediate cause was New York's fiscal crisis of the early 1870s, a crisis that many New Yorkers saw as deriving from irresponsible real estate owners and expensive public subsidies on their behalf. A concurrent wave of local

fiscal crises across the nation further discredited antediluvian urban development theories. And in the policy void left by these crises, and amid a broader
upsurge in radical thought and political mobilization, private realty owners
were unable to prevent alternative strategies of economic development from
emerging and gaining support.

This chapter examines how New York's local government became dependent on realty owners for revenue during the early nineteenth century, and
how the city's fiscal crisis of the 1870s led many New Yorkers to question these
owners—and public subsidies on their behalf—as a reliable "base" for local
economic development. It begins by reconstructing the fiscal imaginary of
precrisis real estate developers and public policymakers—an imaginary in
which white male property ownership and competitive real estate markets
ensured local prosperity. It examines how this imaginary was translated into
public policy in the form of new fiscal arrangements and public land sales.
And it traces how local policymakers questioned and curbed these subsidies
following New York's fiscal crisis of the early 1870s, helping create a policy
vacuum that would shortly be filled with more radical theories of urban economic development by figures such as Henry George.

In stressing the fractured and fragile nature of nineteenth-century developmental statecraft, this chapter modifies prevailing arguments stressing
"privatism" as an entrenched growth strategy within American cities. Scholars
have long argued that practices of associational statecraft and public-private
partnerships dominated local public policy in the nineteenth century.[4] These
accounts, however, ignore the confusion and disillusionment evident in the
wake of New York's 1870s fiscal crisis—of widespread movements to restrict
rather than promote debt on behalf of real estate, and of even the *New York
Times* complaining of unprincipled real estate speculation. Recovering this
crisis of faith helps explain why radical proposals for local economic reform
grew in popularity after the 1880s—and why older verities would survive only
after further struggle.

Property

White male property ownership within a competitive real estate market—up
until the 1870s, most New York policymakers assumed this schema generally
led to growing public budgets and private prosperity. Such a fiscal imaginary
was a contingent product of the constrained fiscal powers of the city, the ideological context of the early republic, and the political mobilizations of property owners themselves. But through the conjuncture of these political ideas

and activities, by the 1850s, New York largely "identified its collective interest as aggregate economic growth and placed the (private) real estate market at the center of local economic expansion," in the words of Elizabeth Blackmar.[5] And to promote this market, New York officials implemented a suite of policies ranging from land sales to street platting to debt-financed public improvements. Such generous policies, however, would have unforeseen fiscal repercussions in the 1870s.

While private landowners had enjoyed outsized political influence in New York since its days as an unprepossessing port colony, "real estate" was not treated as a commodity on a large scale until the early nineteenth century. Until then, land was generally used by its occupiers for farming or other productive purposes, land sales were conducted through informal personal networks, and land itself was relatively cheap and in seemingly plentiful supply: roughly 70.5 percent of New York taxpayers owned land in the early 1700s.[6] By the late eighteenth century, however, a new class of entrepreneurial landowners took up real estate as a business—that is, as a commodity to rent out or sell for profit. And as New York's population and land values grew in the late eighteenth century, the "product" of these landlords became ever dearer and harder to acquire. By 1790, only 46.9 percent of New York's electorate owned land, a number that would decline to 19.6 percent by 1821.[7]

And yet the political and economic significance of private landownership continued to grow in early nineteenth-century New York. Partly this was due to simple political power: only property owners were allowed to vote in New York State until 1821.[8] Partly it was due to belief: many republican-minded New Yorkers believed private property ownership connoted civic virtue and saw the distribution of land through open markets as an antidote to unjust hierarchy. But private ownership's significance was further reinforced through New York's fiscal structure as expressed through its reliance on a particular fiscal instrument: taxation.

This was a somewhat recent development: during the colonial era, the Corporation of New York generated revenue itself via public ownership rather than relying on taxes drawn from private owners. Acting as a developer-capitalist, the local state had leased land, operated profitable ferry franchises, and engaged in other entrepreneurial ventures. As late as 1820, 9 percent of the city's publicly held lands were devoted strictly to revenue-producing purposes.[9]

By the early nineteenth century, however, a series of court and legislative decisions divested the City of New York of the right to own profitable property. Nominally this shift was intended to bring the city's colonial-era powers in alignment with the republic's more recent city charters. But underpinning this shift was a broader republican animus against investing governments with "property rights" to begin with, rather than private persons.[10] And this belief was grounded, in turn, by a broader economic claim: that the self-interest and initiative of private property owners was a superior guarantor of local prosperity.[11] Public purposes would be achieved not by entrusting the government to pursue profits directly but by harnessing the fruit of private sector growth via taxation. Such campaigns against profitable public ownership continued through the mid-nineteenth century, culminating in an 1844 ordinance that authorized the municipal corporation to sell any property held for purposes of "mere revenue."[12] And pressures for such sales continued well after: during the 1860s, for example, the Citizens' Association—made up of larger merchants and realty owners—argued that the city should sell its municipal markets because "business will not reach such a stage of development as it would in the hands of private individuals."[13]

But not all individuals. Married women were legally prohibited from owning land in New York until 1848, their contributions to the local economy given no credence from local boosters. Black citizens of all genders were largely excluded from participating in the city's property market as well, giving white men even more of a monopoly access to the landed wealth of their city.[14] And Indigenous Americans like the Munsee Lenape and the Canarsee, who generally did not practice private landownership before the arrival of European colonists, had been brutally displaced from the region for decades. Such exclusions within the "private sector," however, coexisted with the broader exclusion of the public sector from earning revenue via rents or profits on its own accord. The city was thus cast as a dependent—with all the racialized and gendered meanings white men ascribed to that term—reliant upon taxes earned by others for revenue.

And the most important of these taxes was the "property tax"—a tax that generally fell upon private structures and land, thus creating a legal (if not logical) relation between the city's fiscal health and the value of private real estate. As a Dutch colony, New York had enforced levies on real property as early as 1654, and by the mid-nineteenth century, most municipal revenue derived from this tax. And because the city required permission from New York's state legislature to develop new forms of taxation—permission the rural-dominated legislature was largely unwilling to provide—New York would remain largely dependent on that tax for decades. Such fiscal dependence on the property tax, in turn, provided property *owners* with a great deal of leverage—or what a later planner called a "strategic position"—in New York's financial and hence political life. They would exploit this position well.[15]

Policy

Landowners did not merely assert that private property ownership was economically beneficial for New York: they translated this belief into policy. And while this translation began with the primal act of auctioning public land for to private purchasers, it did not stop there. Property owners insisted on additional support from their state: street platting, public services, debt-financed public improvements like parks, and other amenities that could increase the value of their property (figure 1.1). And New York's policymakers—desirous of the tax revenue such realty development could bring and often possessing realty investments of their own—were easily persuaded.

The most important implementation of New York's pre-1870s fiscal imaginary into policy was the selling of public land to private developers. During the colonial era, New York had owned numerous tracts of land in central and upper Manhattan. By the late 1700s these began to be sold off, at first via small-scale auctions conducted as the city's financial needs required, and increasing in size and frequency as the century wore on, until by 1865 New York had sold off the bulk of its estate.[16] New York also sold off rights to provide services to this land: local officials routinely granted franchises to private omnibus and water companies, ferry companies and streetcar lines, electric and gas companies, and other entities. While these services might indirectly benefit local coffers through enhanced realty values, New York was barred from profiting directly from them. Profits, in service as in real estate, were a private concern.

What powers city hall retained, it often used on behalf of raising realty values, due in no small part to the pressure of property owners. New York's gridded street layout of 1811 was famously designed, at least in part, to "facilitate the buying, selling, and improving of real estate," in the words of one surveyor.[17] But such logic also extended to cleaning streets and widening roads, which both expedited traffic and raised the selling value of land.[18] This rationale was captured by the statement of one alderman in 1836, who declared that his "proposal for widening the street" was motivated by the fact that "property in the neighborhood has been in a very low and depressed situation."[19] Efficiency was not even proffered as a rationale—raising property values was. City officials also provided revenue for new parks, such as Union Square and Madison Square, in the hope of attracting wealthy residents and developers. Indeed, even the design of these parks was justified in fiscal terms, with Frederick Law Olmsted defending the "natural" beauty of Central Park as a draw for visitors and property values alike. "The increase in beauty and influence on the imagination of the one," he declared, "increase[s] the value of the city's property—the amount of the city's income—in the other."[20]

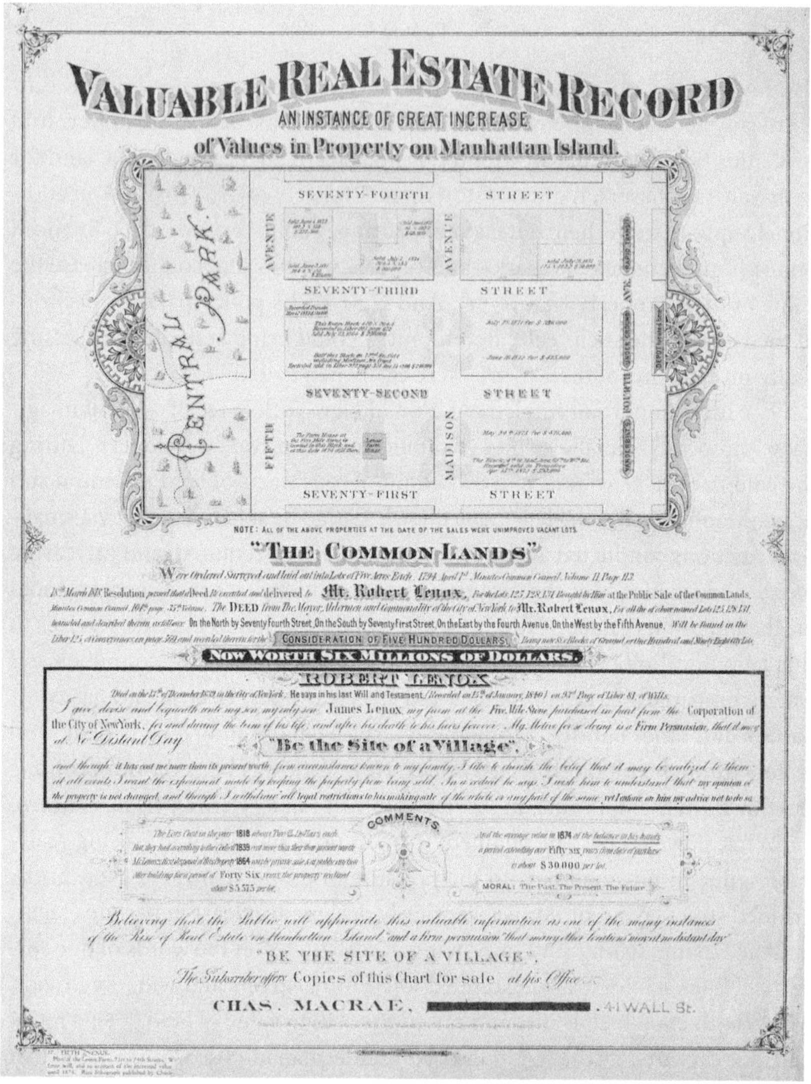

FIGURE 1.1. *Valuable Real Estate Record, an Instance of Great Increase of Values in Property on Manhattan Island*, 1874. Unknown creator, Museum of the City of New York (29.100.1360G). This image conveys how public policies, ranging from the selling of "common lands" to private owners to gridded street plans to the establishment of Central Park itself, contributed to increasing property values in mid-nineteenth-century Manhattan.

Above all, New York policymakers promoted realty growth through debt-financed public improvements: grand works of infrastructure ranging from new streets carved from Manhattan schist to great parks dynamited out of former meadows. In some ways this was a surprising development: in theory, New York and other cities utilized a system of "special assessments" intended to ensure that public services were paid for strictly by the property owners who benefited from them, and not by the municipality as a whole.[21] Municipal debt limits similarly prohibited the city's spending decisions from burdening future generations. Such limits, however, posed challenges for developers of large-scale projects that could not be financed by a single neighborhood or generation. Particularly frustrated were the city's larger merchants and financiers, whose dreams of an "Empire City" entailed expensive boulevards and grand parks.

To convince city residents to embark on these projects, boosters claimed that the economic benefits of one large project would ultimately benefit the city as a whole. Speaking of Central Park, for example, one advocate declared that citywide levies and debt financing for the park would be "fairer and more equitable" than levies upon the park's immediate neighbors, as the "enhanced values" wrought by the park would belong "not to the neighboring owners" in the present alone, but to the "city itself."[22] New York's chief financial officer, the comptroller, agreed: "The increase in the amount of taxes accruing to the city, in consequence of the enhancements in the value of real estate situated in the upper parts of the island" as the result of the park, he argued, would pay back the project's debt many times over.[23]

Such citywide debt measures grew rapidly after the 1840s. New York City floated its first securities in 1812 and issued a series of additional bonds for the Croton Aqueduct in the late 1830s. Once state investment in canals, turnpikes, and other internal improvements declined following the depression of 1837, however, New York and municipalities across the country increased their debt correspondingly. Municipal debt in the United States increased tenfold between 1840 and 1860. Whereas municipal debt was only one-tenth the size of state debt in 1840 across the country, by 1870, it was more than a third larger.[24]

While increasing the city's debt was generally a bipartisan affair, it reached its greatest height in New York under a faction of the city's Democratic Party: Tammany Hall. In 1868, state senator William "Boss" Tweed united the city's chamberlain and county treasurer, comptroller, and comptroller's auditor into a single "ring" controlled by Tammany. This consolidation, combined with the strength of the Democratic Party in city hall and the judiciary, allowed Tammany legislation to be quickly passed and easily funded.[25] Between the

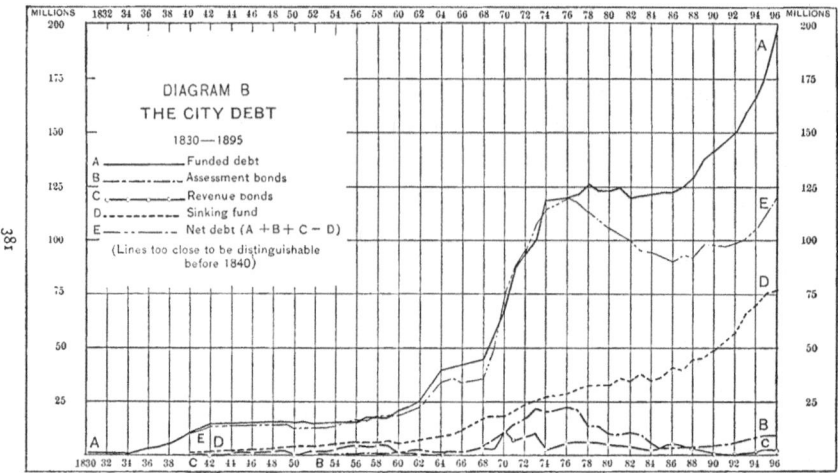

FIGURE 1.2. "The City Debt," in Edward Dana Durand, *The Finances of New York City* (New York: Macmillan, 1898), 381. A chart indicating changes in New York's debt levels between 1830 and 1895. Note the rapid increase in funded debt between 1868 and 1874, followed by a period of relative stability between 1874 and 1886. The earlier increase in debts was largely on behalf of realty expansion; the subsequent era of fiscal stability was, in part, a reaction to the fiscal crisis to which that earlier debt had led. Division of Art, Prints and Photographs.

close of 1868 and the overthrow of the ring in 1871, New York's total funded debt nearly doubled from $44 to $81 million (figure 1.2).[26]

Despite this rapid increase, however, the ring's spending patterns generally followed rather than deviated from the city's earlier fiscal commitments to real estate. Of the $41,724,624 worth of new debt issues produced by the city between January and September of 1871, the four largest issues were for street improvements (totaling $5,635,139). This was followed by issues for expanded water supply on behalf of the city's projected future growth ($2,536,000), construction of and repairs to public buildings ($1,881,000), and that grand magnet of real estate improvement, Central Park ($1,041,600).[27] Other expensive initiatives, such as the Brooklyn Bridge and plans for waterfront boulevards, were also developed under Tammany auspices.

Real estate entities applauded such increased spending and debt on their behalf. The *Real Estate Record and Builders' Guide*, the paper of record for the city's realty industry, noted that Tammany leaders were "champions" of the "real estate movement." Property owners, for their part, were "jubilant" at the boulevards and street improvements the machine had wrought.[28] Such calls for improvements by landlords were partly driven by the "stress of competition" with their rivals, including those of other cities: if New York should fall behind in public improvements, population and investment would shortly move elsewhere. As the *Record* declared in 1873, "New York cannot stand still, it must go forward in the work of improvement. To remain stationary is to retrograde."[29] Fear of decline, not only hopes for expansion, thus prompted calls for realty growth: a rationale speaking to the larger fiscal dependencies—particularly the need to pay back mortgage debts—that seemingly compelled Gotham to grow.

In all these ways, New York policymakers translated their faith in "exclusive private ownership" into public policy through debt-financed projects, land sales, and other initiatives. Physically, at least, their actions were transformative. By the 1870s, New York was no longer the humble port of the early republic, a heap of red brick rowhouses and winding streets clustered near the tip of a largely forested island. Now it was a metropolis of nearly a million, boasting broad avenues thrusting miles north into the heart of Manhattan: those near the island's center flanked with costly residences, those near the waterfronts lined with smoky factories, and those in between a bewildering mix of brownstones, townhouses and tenements. By all appearances, the city's economy was resilient and thriving.

Appearances, however, could be deceiving—for debt was growing as fast as buildings in New York, threatening to lead the prosperous city into bankruptcy once the realty bubble burst. And when that happened, when even the boasts of the *Record* were unable to dispel the scale of the city's crisis, New York policymakers soon demanded drastic cuts in municipal aid to the developers whose speculations had spawned that crisis.

"No One Had Any Idea of Value"

Nineteenth-century New York property owners and their political allies were—as least as compared to their twentieth-century successors—relatively vulnerable. They lacked the professional unity and intellectual hegemony that could help insulate their theories from public criticism. They lacked the large homeownership constituency that would later provide electoral weight to their defenses of property. And they lacked the kind of federal subsidies that could restore their industry in the wake of fiscal catastrophe. These weaknesses were all displayed following the city's fiscal crisis of the 1870s: a crisis that led opponents of Tammany to curtail subsidies and debt on behalf of realty owners. What should replace those owners and subsidies as instruments of local economic development, however, remained unclear.

New York's post–Civil War real estate boom, accelerated by debt-financed public spending, abruptly ended in 1873. The occasion was the bursting of the Wall Street railroad-investment bubble, which led to a collapse of banks

and businesses across the country, drying up both mortgage funding and demand for new construction for much of the decade. An article in *Banker's
Magazine* later recalled that the "panic of 1873 stopped building construction
for at least six years"—and even after construction resumed, New York land
values would not reach their mid-1870s high for another twenty years.[30] Even
as real estate stagnated, however, New York still needed to pay back the debt
it had spent on realty's behalf: municipal debt service quadrupled during the
decade, and nearly a third of the city's budget went to the payment of interest
alone in 1876. Such levies were drawn ultimately from New York taxpayers—
many of whom with little sympathy for Tammany. Their political response
would be swift and sure.[31]

Opponents of Tammany seized the initiative to critique the ring for their
"wasteful" spending, which they believed had contributed to the city's debt
crisis.[32] As befitting such partisan attacks, many of their critiques were limited to the location of the city's debt-financed improvements, rather than the
fiscal "logic" underlying it. Much of Tammany's spending, for example, was
directed toward the northern districts of the island where cheap land was
easier to acquire than in the city's lower wards: those with investments or ties
to the older districts of Manhattan did not look favorably upon much of this
uptown spending, particularly when carried out by their political rivals. Andrew H. Green, a firm opponent of Tammany and an investor in downtown
real estate, complained in 1875 that the city would be better served providing for infrastructure in districts "where people actually live and transit their
business."[33] The *New York Times* echoed this claim a year later. "The idea
that [uptown] 'improvements' have repaid the City by enhancing the value
of property, and so widening the area of taxation," it declared, "is a totally
fallacious one."[34]

A more profound argument levied by Tammany critics, however, was
that real estate speculation *anywhere* was a threat to city finances everywhere. This claim was made in a remarkable 1871 editorial published near the
height of New York's fiscal crisis. Addressing claims that the ring's downfall
would mean a decline in realty values, the *New York Times* responded in the
affirmative—"without deploring it." If "corrupting speculation in real estate,
which has been carried on by the plunder of the Ring, and which has reached
so gigantic a scale, be stopped," the paper wrote, "we, for one, shall not be
graved."[35]

The *Times* was not alone. Roughly one out of every five municipalities in
the United States were in default during the early 1870s, and many citizens
cast blame upon the local interests they believed had brought them to that
point.[36] An 1878 commission in Pennsylvania, for example, squarely blamed

pressure by realty interests for local fiscal crises. Local governments, it wrote, had been "besieged" by "men of wealth" until "they have been driven into making appropriations to open and improve streets and avenues largely in advance of the real necessities of the city." It concluded that "the undue accumulation of debt in most of the cities of the State of Pennsylvania" had resulted largely from "speculation on the part of owners of property themselves."[37] A later study of precrisis municipal defaults confirmed this sentiment: 35 percent of all such defaults were for public bonds on behalf of private railroads (themselves key drivers of realty values), 9 percent were for bonds on behalf of "improvements," yet another 9 percent were for street construction, and 4 percent were for miscellaneous aid to private enterprises.[38] And few such initiatives, it seemed, had added to the economic resilience of communities.

"Owners of Property" and their political allies, for their part, were unable to counter these criticisms as effectively as they later would be.[39] Partly this was because they lacked the kind of robust professional associations or bureaucratically insulated planners who would later deflect blame for urban fiscal crises. But it was also because they lacked a well-developed body of theory to explain real estate growth or decline at all. Looking back from the 1920s, one economist compared the state of real estate economics in the nineteenth century to "the medieval practice of alchemy."[40] This was, of course, an exaggeration: individuals such as David Ames Wells and Frederick Law Olmsted possessed well-developed theories of what provided value to land, and there existed a prolific "booster" literature from the Midwest and elsewhere.[41] But such theories were generally not codified and promulgated to a corps of institutionally embedded professionals.[42] And what theories of value were held during the mid-nineteenth century tended to dissolve under the pressure of competition and speculation (figure 1.3). As one 1860s New York City realtor summarized in an unintended double entendre, "No one had any real idea of value."[43]

The same naivety applied to public finance officers, who generally had little sustained interest in why real estate values rose or declined—much less in how urban economies as a whole did.[44] The Central Park Commission, for example, argued that their park was *entirely responsible* for all valuation increases in the three wards adjacent to it between 1857 and 1881. This calculation, of course, ignored how any number of additional factors—such as new boulevards or new sewer lines—could have contributed to these increases. In fact, a recent scholar found that Central Park added only $735,146 to local property values every year: *seven times less* than the commission's estimations.[45] And the Central Park Commission was considered a "professional"

FIGURE 1.3. "Glimpse of Change," *Illustrated London News*, September 27, 1856. Wallach Division Picture Collection, New York Public Library. This image of a realty auction and the accompanying caption convey something of the raffishness associated with realty speculation in the mid-nineteenth century. Original caption: "The fever of speculation is at its height in Wall-Street—one of the numberless offshoots from Broadway. A sketch we give of 'a glimpse of Change' affords a faint notion of the shrewd money-making community and of their 'cute'-looking physiognomies. The auctioneers, who have stalls all round the interior of the Exchange, decorated with print advertisements of the property they are to dispose of, are bellowing at the top of their voice and taking the bid. We took this sketch on the sly, as the profane non-commercial man is not supposed to enter these precincts; we entered the place, however, utterly unconscious of the veto."

civic body—one can only imagine the fiscal assumptions carried by figures like Tammany comptroller Richard "Slippery Dick" Connolly.

A sense of the disrepute to which local real estate and public finance practices had fallen after the fiscal crisis of the 1870s is revealed by how the first generation of "professional" economists wrote of them.[46] Herbert Adams, a founder of the American Economic Association (AEA), wrote that "the mention of the words real estate suggests another reason why ambitious cities are so willing to incur heavy indebtedness," as "any public work that indicates what businessmen call 'enterprise,' will be apt to prove more persuasive than the boast of a 'slow town' that her finances have been conservatively managed."[47] Summarizing, Adams declared that "as far as debt accumulation was concerned . . . owners of property need more protection against themselves than against the non-property-holding class."[48] Richard T. Ely, a cofounder of the AEA, concurred. American cities, he wrote, were routinely "embarrassed by expenditures made at the solicitation of landowners, particularly on the occasion of 'booms,'" and "not, as popularly imagined, by the moneyless rabble."[49]

Rethinking Subsidies

By the time Ely wrote those words in the 1880s, however, a broader backlash against publicly subsidized realty speculation had begun. Local Republicans and chastened Democrats—facing a fiscal crisis, aware of the costs that public debts on behalf of realty had inflicted upon their city, and lacking many other fiscal alternatives—responded to their city's crisis by curtailing the subsidies they had previously lavished upon property owners. Retrenchment, however, was not a positive program, and in the labor and agrarian struggles of the 1870s and 1880s, theorists like Henry George would soon find an audience for alternative theories of economic development.

This "backlash against boosterism" was launched by Andrew H. Green, a foe of Tammany who gained control over the city's comptrollership in 1871. Once in power, Green denied local petitions for increased park and boulevard spending. In dismissing one such proposal in 1875, Green wrote, "It is not difficult to discover the impelling motives to this step. The influence of real estate speculators combine at this juncture with the necessities of politicians for places for more men before elections."[50] A year later, he denied requests for additional park space in the city's northern stretches, declaring that "we have expended millions enough for the present in paying the most monstrous prices for uptown lands."[51] Green's Tammany successor, "Honest" John Kelly, similarly curtailed efforts to levy capital funds for the city's peripheral development. Altogether, New York's public works budget declined by some 25 percent during the 1870s.[52]

Local governments placed analogous limitations on municipal debts. An 1871 commission assembled by New York Governor Tilden to inquire into the "monstrous growth" of municipal debts and taxation recommended

a constitutional amendment limiting local indebtedness to 5 percent of the
city's assessed property values. A referendum promoting this measure was
ultimately passed in 1883 with a broad majority. And even as land values in
Manhattan recovered and rose through the later 1870s and 1880s, the city's debt
levels remained conservative in comparison to the heady days of the Tweed
era. By 1885, the city's debt was more than a quarter lower than it had been ten
years earlier.[53] Such limitations were echoed in cities across the country, contributing to a broader wave of fiscal retrenchment that would last more than
twenty years.[54] Per capita county debt in America decreased from $4.86 in 1870
to $2.30 by 1890, and local debt more generally saw a decline in this period as
well.[55] And this is not counting actions by local property owners across the
country to simply accept municipal default rather than see their taxes used to
pay for wasteful improvements and their "vampiric" bondholders.[56]

   And such popular animus against aiding speculators extended to other
forms of subsidy. One-fifth of all municipal bankruptcies in the 1870s, for
example, were tied to municipal investment in private railroads—railroads
that were often undercapitalized or never built in the first place.[57] By the end
of the 1880s, twenty-four states had restricted the right of cities to invest in
railways, and twenty-five were barred from investing in private corporations
outright.[58]

   In some ways this retrenchment represented, as David Scobey has argued,
a retreat from activist government analogous to broader political developments of the era—such as the defeat of Radical Republicanism, a turn towards laissez-faire jurisprudence, a Mugwump distrust of the electorate and
public bodies.[59] But it also represented an act of popular self-defense against
"corrupt bargains" with the wealthy in ways analogous to the emergent agrarian and labor movements of the era. It is telling that while an 1877 New York
referendum proposing to limit universal male suffrage was roundly defeated,
an 1883 New York referendum to limit local debt received an "almost unani-
mous popular vote."[60] Both were justified by their defenders as means to prevent local fiscal crises: the one by restricting the capricious electorate, the
latter by restricting debt that, as we have seen, was largely on behalf of realty
speculation. And it was the latter policy that was enacted.

   These restrictions on public aid on behalf of private expansion also reflected a broader, if brief, questioning of reckless economic expansion during
the depression of the 1870s. Robert P. Hough's seminal 1877 *Report on Forestry*, for example, warned that depleting natural resources could imperil national prosperity, a warning amplified by groups like the Appalachian Moun-
tain Club and the American Forestry Association. Journals like the *Atlantic
Monthly* complained that factories were producing for "imaginary markets"

in a fit of greed and competition; only restricted production could stabilize America's economy.[61] Such questioning of growth was suffused with hypocrisy, of course, with the "protection" of Yellowstone through the exclusion of its Indigenous population and the welcoming of robber baron tourists being only one example.[62] But such questioning of growth, coming in the midst of a depression, nonetheless provided a broader context for the fiscal retrenchment taking place in New York and other cities.

This is not to say, of course, that realty speculation and subsidies on its behalf entirely ended after 1873, or even temporarily. New York's local government continued to erect debt-financed public improvements and continued to award public powers to private franchise holders through the late nineteenth century. Even the 1898 amalgamation of New York (what was then Manhattan and the Bronx) with what would become the boroughs of Brooklyn, Staten Island, and Queens represented, among other things, a boosterish faith that opening new terrain for development would bring prosperity along with it. But the discrediting of realty and subsidies on its behalf wrought by the urban fiscal crises of the 1870s—together with the broader labor and agrarian uprising of that decade—helped establish the conditions for new and far more radical theories of urban development to emerge as the nineteenth century drew to a close.

Conclusion

The prevalence of private landownership and property taxes in New York by the early nineteenth century created a fiscal precedent that structured—if not constrained—New York's development for decades.[63] But their prevalence was not "natural," as we have seen. Rather, they were established through the political mobilization of property owners imbued with market-republican beliefs, entrenched through New York's fiscal structure, and aided through generous public policies ranging from public land sales to debt-financed public improvements.

But this fiscal order was not invulnerable. New York's fiscal crisis of the 1870s seemed to demonstrate the unreliability, if not unwisdom, of subsidizing private speculators to achieve public prosperity. And while many policymakers curbed such subsidies merely to punish their partisan opponents, New York's fiscal crisis—and the broader economic tumult of the 1870s—also sparked a broader reimagining of how American cities should best prosper. And as we shall see, such reimaginings—taken up by artisans and "professionals" alike—would vastly expand the fiscal imagination of urban America. Private property ownership and property taxation would be questioned; new policy tools like public utility ownership and land-value taxation would be developed. And for forty years, these policies would be fought for by grand populist campaigns led by figures like Henry George, helping raise the "urban question" to the ranks of the "social questions" and "labor questions" then transforming American life.

For a moment, these questions remained open—and contested.

"Who Created It? Who Gets It?"

"Monopoly, the result of special privilege, rather than Capital or Production, which are the creation of individual effort, should be the primary source of public revenue." Thus declared the Association for the Public Control of Franchises, formed in 1897 by a coterie of New York worthies ranging from the treasurer of the American Longshoreman's Union to the borough president of Brooklyn. Private franchises in power and transit, the association argued, derived their market power from state-backed charters—and were thus obligated to compensate that state for their privileges. And if they refused to do so, that community was obligated to take control of those franchises and their profits through municipal ownership (figure 2.1). In either case, placing the burden of local finances upon monopolistic franchises rather than productive workers or investors would spur New York's economic development.[1]

Seven years later, another organization took aim at another "natural monopoly" standing in the way of New York's prosperity: private landownership (figure 2.2). The New York Tax Reform Association, formed in 1891 by followers of Henry George, argued that high rentals charged by landlords and high taxes on property were driving away "capital engaged in production or trade" from the city. Confiscatory taxes on land, however, could lower these rentals and unleash Gotham's economic potential while sparing the productive "farmer" and "worker" from paying more onerous taxes.[2]

These two alliances were participants in a fierce political struggle—a struggle to place America's cities on more democratic and resilient fiscal footing. Prompted by the apparent failure of local development strategies in the wake of the fiscal crises of the 1870s, a wide variety of urbanites—artisans and small homeowners, political reformers and press barons, business associations and professional planners—accused local governments of undermining

Reproduced from Klein's Weekly News, July 26, 1913

Vast Profits from City Franchise Went to Swell the Already Swollen Fortunes of Only a Few Men

FIGURE 2.1. "Vast Profits from City Franchises Went to Swell the Already Swollen Fortunes of Only a Few Men." From Henry H. Klein's *Bankrupting a Great City (The Story of New York)* (New York: Henry H. Klein, 1916), 82. Note how both the broke white taxpayer (on the right) and the city's emblem, Father Knickerbocker, are depicted as standing to benefit from taxing—or appropriating via public ownership— "private interests" in the form of the owners of public utilities and franchises.

local economies by wastefully subsidizing monopolists at the expense of "productive" enterprises. Such accusations were particularly fervent in New York City, where ties between real estate firms and local machines had seemingly brought the city to the brink of fiscal collapse during the 1870s.

As an alternative, these activists—whom I call "fiscal republicans"—stressed productive citizens and firms as the ultimate source of urban prosperity. Political economists like Henry George declared that local tax policies should encourage entrepreneurship and industry by lifting the rent burdens oppressing them. Parties like the Municipal Ownership League argued that by seizing control of profitable franchises through public ownership, cities could generate revenue without burdensome taxation.[3] And in making these claims, some fiscal republicans proffered an even more radical proposal: that cities need not rely on wealthy enterprises for prosperity at all but were *themselves* cooperative enterprises fully capable of ownership and management by their citizens.[4]

This chapter examines how urban activists campaigned for alternative economic development strategies between the 1870s and 1910s. It examines how a wide variety of urbanites came to see private monopolies as obstacles to local economic development. It examines the electoral campaigns and policies by which these urbanites sought to dismantle or gain public control over these monopolies. And it examines the ambivalent consequences of this political movement, which both opened new policy horizons and entrenched older assumptions around race, gender, and the nature of economic

WHO PAYS THE TAXES?

When the trunk is tapped each branch is drawn upon for its due proportion of sap.

FIGURE 2.2. "Who Pays the Taxes?" New York Tax Reform Association, *New York Tax Reform Association Platform* (New York: New York Tax Reform Association, 1902), 5. This cartoon conveys the Georgist belief that taxing nonproductive real estate values would spare the income, wages, and business capital of more "productive" workers and enterprises.

growth—assumptions that would limit the constituency for radical fiscal reform in subsequent decades.

In charting the career of fiscal republicanism in New York City, this chapter reinterprets the fiscal context behind Gilded Age and Progressive-era urban reform. While many historians have traced the rise of public ownership and Georgist tax-reform initiatives, most have understood their popularity in terms of the social or civic benefits they would deliver.[5] While undoubtedly true, these narratives underplay the *economic* possibilities of these proposals: possibilities that shone all the more given the economic turmoil engulfing many cities during the 1870s. And it was these concrete economic benefits that helped account for the wide variety of groups—taxpayers and renters, commercial firms and labor organizations—attracted to the fiscal republican cause in the early 1900s.[6] Recalling this history can thus provide a model for contemporary activists seeking to reform urban political economies.[7]

There were, however, unresolved tensions at the heart of this movement. Was it possible for publicly owned utilities to generate profits for the metropolis as well as provide adequate service for its citizens? Which citizens were included or excluded from the populist construction of the "people"? And above all, was the goal of fiscal republicanism to *discourage* monopoly or merely to *collect* its proceeds? The way fiscal republicans answered these questions, as we shall see, would ultimately narrow both the constituency and possibility of economic reform in New York City for decades.

Fiscal Republicans

The tumult of post-1870s urban economic thought mirrored the era's broader social unrest. Knights of Labor and Grangers, Greenbackers and populists—all sought answers for how to build a more just and prosperous economy in a time of growing inequality, harsh working conditions, and frequent unemployment.[8] And underlying these campaigns was a relatively well-formed fiscal imaginary, one that stressed productive labor and enterprise as the best source of local prosperity. This belief, with all its strengths and biases, informed the drives by many workers to undo the monopolies they believe threatened urban economies and their own livelihoods.

Fiscal radicalism found its largest constituency, between the 1870s and the 1900s, among New York's white artisans and so-called skilled labor. By 1890 these workers, largely native born and Northern European in background, comprised 21.2 percent of the city's male workforce and made up most of its unions.[9] Holding to the ideals of the male producer as the foundation of national prosperity and civic virtue, many of these workers were radicalized by the depressions of the late nineteenth century. A quarter of New York's labor force endured unemployment in the winter of 1877, and urban workers across the country routinely faced similar economic instability.[10] Shorn of public aid and lacking much personal property of their (only 9.63 percent of all New York City households owned real estate in 1870), Gilded Age workers were both vulnerable to economic calamity and arguably more receptive to radical prognoses for such calamity than they would be in an age of the welfare state and mass homeownership.[11]

To make sense of the era's tumult, many white artisans applied their labor-republican framework to questions of local economic development. Where productive workers and firms provided jobs and services to their communities, they believed, speculative financiers and state-backed monopolists posed distinct threats to local prosperity.[12] These monopolies, ranging from railroad corporations to Standard Oil, used corrupt ties with state officials to saddle a rentier economy upon the nation, extracting wealth from communities while burdening producers with high prices. Wall Street ties among these corporations further yoked the fortunes of communities to the speculative whims of an outside elite. This division between state-backed and parasitic speculators versus "independent" producers and workers formed the core of the fiscal republican imaginary.

And while many of these fiscal republicans continued to pay homage to private property as an antidote to monopoly, others increasingly placed their faith in an alternative form of property—worker-owned cooperatives.[13] Such cooperatives, they believed, would witness no wasteful conflicts between management and workforce, no outflow of productive profits to the idle wealthy, and no crisis of competitively propelled over- or underproduction. Cooperative banks would invest honestly earned savings back into further productive enterprises, rather than economy-wrecking financial speculation. Altogether, the "cooperative commonwealth" would, in the words of one advocate, "lift the burdens and weight from labor and the productive industries of the country."[14] Such efficiencies would allow worker-owners more time and income to purchase goods, thus furthering economic development. And local ownership would ensure that such firms would face no incentives to burden communities with the social costs of low wages or the threat of displacement.

By the 1880s, the "cooperative commonwealth" was being built in communities across the nation. A total of 334 worker-owned cooperatives, ranging from factories to mines, were established in that decade alone.[15] Western farmers associated with the Grange established similar enterprises, while many Black citizens set up mutual aid and cooperative initiatives of their own.[16] These movements continued to see economic development as their ultimate end: as one cooperative aficionado declared, "No action of the work-ingmen will ever mar the progress of the new town."[17] Nonetheless, what their vision of what progress entailed—"the organization of production without the intervention of the capitalist," as one advocate put it—was quite different than the prewar boosters had in mind.[18] Such enterprises, and the network of newspapers and local political figures who supported them, provided mate-rial evidence that another economy was possible.

Even in New York, home of Wall Street, the cooperative commonwealth was taking form. One of its primary champions was Victor Drury, author of the influential 1876 pamphlet *The Polity of the Labor Movement* and staunch advocate of worker cooperatives. Drury helped found Assembly 49 of the Knights of Labor six years later, which went on to organize several coopera-tives in New York over the decade—eight in a single year at one point.[19] To-gether, Victor and Assembly 49 represented one of the more radical branches of the Knights of Labor, rumored to be more influential than the organiza-tion's president himself.

For all their speeches and writings, however, most fiscal republicans gave little attention to the *urban* as a distinctive site of economic development. They largely did not discuss how the key problematics of urban life, particu-larly real estate, might foster or enfeeble this development. But this would soon change. In 1879, a journalist named Henry George published a book translating the issues of urban America into fiscal-republican terms: a book that would shape the course of fiscal radicalism in New York for a generation.

Progress and Poverty

"Unfortunate as have been some of the phases of the agitation of Henry George," wrote the economist Richard T. Ely in 1888, "I cannot but think that the world owes him a debt of gratitude for placing in a clear light before the masses the fact that land is a natural monopoly."[20] That competitive markets neither could nor should apply to urban land would have been seen as rank heresy by most urbanites thirty years earlier. Intervening fiscal crises and the writings of Henry George, however, had by then convinced many urbanites— particularly politically restless workers and an ascendant class of professional planners—that unrestricted private landownership could wreck even the mightiest cities' finances. Government subsidies on behalf of land values for the sake of economic growth were apparently worse than immoral—they were self-defeating.

Henry George was born to a lower-middle-class family in Philadelphia, moved to California in the 1850s, and worked for some time as a printer and later a writer for the *San Francisco Times*. While he honed his radical voice through an exposé of the corrupt practices of national railroad monopolies in the late 1860s, it was in the early 1870s that he identified what he believed to be a far deeper source of inequality and poverty in America: private landownership and speculation. And in 1879, George published a treatise explaining why this was so and what the solution to it was: *Progress and Poverty*.

Urban economic development, George believed along with many fiscal republicans, ultimately depended on productive enterprises—but such enterprises and their workers required affordable land. High land values maintained by speculative landlords repelled manufacturing and commercial firms from cities. When landlords did sell to industries, they demanded an "unearned increment" in return—rent—which cut into the incomes of capitalists and workers alike. And this was on top of the boom-and-bust cycles that realty speculation promoted, wrecking the investments of institutions and individuals alike while undermining local economies more broadly.[21] It was on these grounds that Henry George subtitled his treatise *An Inquiry into the Cause of Industrial Depressions and of Increase of Want with Increase of Wealth*.

George's work directly challenged the assumption underlying many cities' pre-1870s development strategies: that growth was cost free. "What we call an industrial depression," he summarized, was "merely an intensification of phenomena that always accompany material progress." And insofar as local governments promoted this "progress" —at least, as defined as increased land values—they were contributing to the economic suicide of their communities. In words that could have described New York City, George asked, "Where do we find the deepest poverty, the hardest struggle for existence, the greatest enforced idleness? Why, wherever material progress is most advanced. That is to say, where population is densest, wealth greatest, and production and exchange most highly developed."[22] Growth, in other words, could be *uneconomic*, and no amount of private wealth could obscure the public want that accompanied it.

George's solution to unlocking the economic potential of cities was to reduce the price of land. While the most direct way of accomplishing this was through public landownership, George advocated for a more subtle strategy: shifting the object of property taxation from structures *upon land* to the *land* itself. Through the late nineteenth century, one later Georgist argued, there had been a "long and well-recognized custom" that land should only be assessed at 30 percent of its value. Tax assessors preferred, instead, to base their assessments on the highly visible structures upon the land itself—a system that, for Georgists, penalized the city's "productive" enterprises and new construction more broadly, even as it rewarded idle speculators holding land vacant in the hope of a later sale.[23]

By taxing land at 100 percent of its value, however, the public could make it profitless for speculators to maintain high land prices. This would force landlords to either lower land prices in the hope of attracting productive enterprises to their property and making some kind of profit, or to sell their land to those who would. Either way, a heavy tax on land would liberate urban real estate markets from the distortions of the speculator and rentier, making it easier to establish businesses and freeing cities to reach their economic potential.[24] As one advocate later declared in the late 1880s, "If city lots are taxed on all that they are worth . . . instead of discouraging enterprise, it will encourage it; for it will make it harder for speculators to withhold the land from those who wish to improve it."[25]

Building a Constituency

There was an audience for George's theories: *Progress and Poverty* was sold in increasing numbers through the last decades of the nineteenth century. While partly a symptom of the late nineteenth-century "boom" in utopian thinking, it also reflected a more specific dissatisfaction among a wide range of constituencies: a dissatisfaction with the economic crises that speculators and rentiers had seemingly inflicted on American cities. Artisans furious at lower wages and unemployment, homeowners and manufacturers angry at high taxes and the high cost of land, public officials seeking a more effective source of revenue, manufacturers chafing against high taxes, professional economists and planners aghast at the sheer inefficiency of private speculation in land: all saw in George's theories a seemingly simple explanation of and solution for their troubles.[26] The property tax, after all, was already an instrument within the control of cities: why not use it to increase prosperity rather than poverty?

George's first great political constituencies were urban artisans and small entrepreneurs: his book's vision of ethically acquired prosperity aligned perfectly with the fiscal republican vision. When New York's Central Labor Union decided to run an independent candidate for mayor in 1886, the union chose to nominate Henry George. He accepted, less in anticipation of victory than in hopes that his campaign would further publicize his "single-tax" campaign.[27] For a moment, the ranks of the urban "cooperative commonwealth"— Knights of Labor, union members, artisans, and many more—seemed to have found their champion.

While George lost the election of 1886, his campaign for land taxation grew in breadth and depth in the following decades, particularly in New York City. Home builders like the Metropolitan League of Savings and Loan Associations and the New York State League of Savings and Loan Associations lobbied for higher taxes on land, seeing it as a boon to their industry.[28] Taxpayer bodies like the East Flatbush Taxpayer Association and the Wyckoff Heights Taxpayer Association similarly mobilized to lower taxes on housing and raise them upon land.[29] In 1906, a man with the remarkable name of Cornelius Donovan founded the Tenants Union as a vehicle for advocating land-value taxation among renters, arguing that tenants too "paid the tax" in the form of rent increases brought about by high taxes on the structures of their landlords.[30] And the indefatigable Georgist planner Benjamin C. Marsh established the Society to Lower Rents and Reduce Taxes on Homes, which helped mobilize thirty-six thousand signatures—6 percent of New York's electorate—in support of a version of Georgist land-value taxation in the early 1910s.[31]

Even groups that were not explicitly Georgist, like the New York Tax Reform Association, were able to garner support for higher taxes on land from commercial and manufacturing executives seeking relief from high property taxes. As its secretary, Lawson Purdy, later stated, "It was our policy that we wanted the association backed financially by people who would not give to promote the policy of Henry George." Ultimately, the association would receive much of its "chief financial and political support . . . from individual and corporate taxpayers," in Purdy's words.[32] Indeed, into the 1920s, a "Manufacturers & Merchants Tax League" demanded higher land taxes as a means of relieving fiscal burdens from their enterprises.[33]

Finally, a new generation of "professional" housing reformers and planning officials—inspired less by labor republicanism than ideals of efficiency and rationality—believed that land-value taxation would, in the words of Marsh, "encourage the logical and economic development of cities."[34] For these planners, looking at the current urban landscape and seeing naught but chaos, taxation served as both a culprit and a solution. As it was, low taxes on land encouraged landlords to keep their property vacant, thus denying opportunities for homeownership while creating a "sporadic and irregular" pattern of growth as wasteful as it was ugly (see figure 2.3). By keeping land vacant on the periphery and expensive in the core, landlords forced the working class to rent their shelter in narrow, congested tenements—and such high rentals and poor conditions caused immiseration at a scale that inevitably translated into higher costs for the city in the form of police and hospital

THIS CONDITION WILL EXIST—

—Courtesy of "The Great Adventure," Los Angeles, Calif.

—SO LONG AS THIS CONDITION LASTS

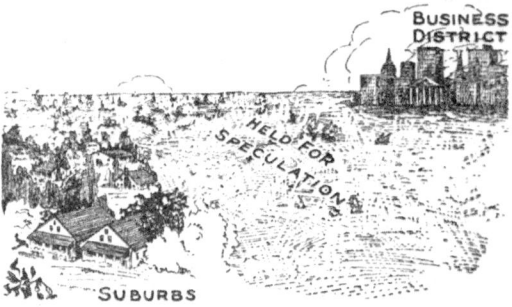

FIGURE 2.3. "This Condition Will Exist—so Long as This Condition Lasts," from Emil O. Jordensen, *The Next Step Toward Real Democracy* (Chicago: Chicago Single Tax Club, 1920), 66. This image depicts the costs of land speculation according to Georgist city planners. Because speculators held land around central-city districts vacant, citizens were forced to travel further outside those districts to build or purchase homes. This increased the cost of homeownership (due to limited supply), added to the congestion of central cities, and forced local governments to spend additional funds on streets, sewer lines, and other services serving far-flung neighborhoods. Taxing land values, however, would encourage landlords to build upon their property outside the city center, thus creating a more compact, efficient, and salubrious cityscape.

services. In all these ways, as Marsh growled, "American city planning in the main has been a method of rewarding speculation in land at the expense of the taxpayer."[35]

Lowering land values via taxation, however, would solve two seemingly antithetical planning problems at once. On the one hand, it would make land affordable to working-class homeownership, thus ensuring that "each family (would) have its healthful home, set in its garden," in the words of Henry George.[36] On the other hand, it would create a more condensed and efficient cityscape by reducing land vacancies.[37] The result would be a city at once decentralized and urbane: one where, in the words of one proponent, home-ownership was plentiful, "the mansion had been turned into public art galleries," and "there was not one tenement to be found on the East Side."[38] This vision, later be formalized by garden city planners like Ebenezer Howard, was also captured well by Georgist advocate Felix Adler:

> I see the people, there are five million, or ten million, spread out over the great area beyond the rivers, dwelling in peace and contentment in homes that are worthy of the name . . . I see not one city hall, the business section of the city in one place, and the living sections round about it; I see many townhalls. Each of them shall be surrounded by a cluster of buildings—a public library branch, a branch of the public museum, one of the minor court houses, and halls where the people of that district may meet for political and other purposes, the great club of the democracy.[39]

And as bold as this planning vision was, some advocates of full land-value taxation forwarded an even bolder economic proposition: that local government's wealth ultimately derived from its ordinary residents. Every "babe that is born, every immigrant hastening to the city to adopt it as his home," in the words of one fiscal republican, added to the value of urban land. *Every* citizen was thus a taxpayer and a stakeholder in urban wealth.[40] Such a belief was held tightly by many Georgists and their sympathizers: a 1913 committee charged with developing new sources of municipal revenue in New York City, for example, promoted higher levies on land on the grounds that the fiscal burden of local government should be placed "on those forms of property which represent values largely created by the community itself"—namely, real estate.[41]

And if this was true, then so was the corollary: that community-derived wealth needed to be returned to the community in the form of tax-financed improvements, not siphoned into the hands of private rentiers and speculators.[42] But this was precisely what was happening. As it was, New York's land was more than $3.5 billion in 1904—more than adequate to service city hall's $100 million budget.[43] But Gotham's government generally assessed that land at only 30 to 60 percent of its "market value." The rest went to private hands.[44] To allow this to happen, to enable private rentiers to steal wealth from the community that produced it, was, in one Georgist's words, to deny citizens "the best use of our common heritage."[45] Or as a Georgist-inflected public exhibition declared in 1908 when depicting the assessed value of Manhattan's land value ($2,707,862,301), "Who created it? Who gets it?"[46]

Even as many New Yorkers fought to win their city's wealth back from the land monopolists, however, others were combating another monopolistic foe: the public franchise utilities which were committing similar fiscal abuses against the urban commonwealth.

Fighting the Franchise Monopolists

New York's public franchises—private corporations with state-backed privileges to provide services such as transportation or energy transmission—were at the center of political controversy in Gilded Age New York. While some of these controversies revolved around poor service and political corruption on the part of these "public-private partnerships," many fiscal republicans levied a deeper charge: of bankrupting New York's government and undermining its economy. And while taxpayers and small businesspeople initially limited their remedies to taxation, by the 1880s, many fiscal republicans believed a more radical policy was required: public ownership.

While New York had long dispensed franchises to private companies for everything from water provision to streetcar service, the scale of such franchises—and the scale of their abuses—grew drastically in the 1870s and 1880s. Elevated railroad companies built tracks above public streets, showering passersby with cinders and their passengers with extortionate fares. Electric trollies hurtled through crowded intersections, driven by conductors required to meet high trip quotas, killing and maiming hundreds every year. Power utilities like the Edison Electric Light Company and the Consolidated Gas Company raised prices on consumers while delivering poor-quality service.[47] Such major and minor abuses had, by the late nineteenth century, united a wide range of consumers, commuters, and property owners against the franchises and the "corrupt bargains" that created them.

But public franchises were not only endangering private citizens' health, many critics charged—they were also endangering the finances of the city itself. Such damage began with the low or nonexistent fees they paid for their incorporation. As early as 1868, the well-heeled Citizens' Association complained that streetcar companies "enjoyed the public streets for their business as a monopoly; they make large profits, and should pay for the privileges they possess."[48] But they rarely did. In 1881, local officials charged the Metropolitan Telephone and Telegraph with paying the city a mere one cent per foot for the privilege of installing electric cables under public streets, while, until 1882, no gas company in New York paid any public compensation whatsoever for their franchises.[49] In the sardonic words of one scholar, when city hall awarded public franchises, "the purpose of deriving the greatest possible income for the city is by no means in every case the sole or even the paramount motive."[50]

Public franchises also avoided paying their fair share of taxes, thereby adding to the tax burdens of other households and businesses. In 1882, state legislators passed a bill reducing the taxes of the powerful Manhattan Railway Company, and in 1894, the court of appeals relieved it from paying any property taxes whatsoever on its Third Avenue line.[51] As one scholar wrote in 1890, "The beggarly sums derived from the sale of railway franchises and from the taxation of transportation companies and other quasi-public corporations such as gas companies are proverbial."[52]

By the 1880s, these abuses were inspiring criticisms by many commercial and taxpaying organizations, their favored journals accusing franchises of adding to the tax burdens of "responsible" property owners. The *New York Times* complained that "if the public received what private owners would charge for the use of the streets for the private profit, the relief of tax-payers would be very considerable."[53] Even the *Real Estate Record and Builders' Guide*, resentful of the tax burdens that franchises were shunting onto property owners, argued that "if the money that corporations ought reasonably to pay for privileges granted to them by the city were in the municipal treasury, New York could be steadily improved and beautified in a measure that is impossible at the expense of the already well-burdened taxpayer."[54]

Collecting utility revenue, however, was an arduous process. It was not until 1879 that street railways were regularly taxed by the city and not until 1884 that streetcars were required to pay a fixed amount for the use of public streets.[55] And franchises were able to avoid these taxes by overcapitalizing and "stock watering" their industries, claiming low earnings while disbursing dividends to investors.[56] In 1895, a New York State Assembly committee to investigate street railways found "a great deal of flagrant over-capitalization, covering up exorbitant profits."[57] In the cynical words of one fiscal republican, "The requirement that public service corporations shall make sworn returns" had only "encouraged perjury among corporate officials (who needed no such encouragement)."[58]

Frustrated by franchise evasions, by the 1890s, many fiscal republicans pressed for a more direct strategy of wringing justice from the city's utilities: public ownership. Economists inspired by encounters with German *Kathedersozialismus* joined a surprisingly broad coalition of taxpayer associations and labor groups in arguing for the economic utility of municipal enterprise.[59] Profits, rather than taxes, would save New York's budget and the city's economy. Advocates of profitable municipal ownership generally gave three economic rationales for their proposal. First, cities would be able to raise large sums of revenue without the political liabilities of taxation. Albert Shaw, a liberal British journalist and editor of the *Review of Reviews*, declared

in 1889 that "the great difficulty of municipal finance has been that it has relied far too much upon [taxes] and a [tax] is always an unpopular means of
raising money." On the other hand, "if . . . the community kept the monopolies of service in its own hands, it would be able to, in many cases, ultimately
raise a magnificent revenue without laying on a rate at all."[60]

Second, municipal enterprise would reduce taxes on New York's ultimate
source of prosperity: its productive enterprises. As mentioned earlier, many
fiscal republicans feared that high tax rates were driving industry from the
city. Relying on profits rather than property taxes could reduce these taxes and
prevent such an industrial exodus from taking place. As economist Richard T.
Ely asserted, "The full and complete utilization of all natural monopolies for
the benefit of the public" was "the way, and the only way, to reduce taxes."[61]
Already, European cities like Cologne had seemingly displaced "taxes" as a
source of revenue through widespread municipal ownership. Many reformers in New York and other American cities were enchanted by similar results
in their own communities (figure 2.4). New York's private utility companies
in 1905, for example, were worth $450 million—$50 million more than the
city's total indebtedness.[62] Appropriating such wealth could lessen the city's
reliance on other, more regressive sources of revenue.

Finally, public ownership would allow citizens to better direct utilities toward the development of the broader metropolis. For example, private transport franchises in New York generally refused to extend their services for fear
of diluting their profits, leading to costly congestion in central districts, or
carelessly spread new lines and routes into remote districts, thus forcing the
city to pay for additional infrastructure costs. In either case, private greed was
thrusting social costs upon the public. By gaining public control over these
franchises, however, the public could spur urban expansion where and when
it was needed.

And much like many advocates of land-value taxation, proponents of
public ownership celebrated profit making as a rightful activity of local governments—and looked to European cities as models of such initiatives. In
Germany, Frederic C. Howe noted, cities "generally make a charge for many
services that in this country are rendered free. There are admission fees to the
zoological and palm gardens, the museums, baths, and concerts. The German city tries to make as many services self-supporting as possible, while
many activities realize an increasing profit with which the burdens of taxation are being reduced."[63] In contrast, most American public services were
provided *gratis* to the private sector. In 1914, 66.9 percent of urban debt in
the United States was incurred for unprofitable sewers, public buildings,
park construction, and street openings. Only 33.1 percent was delegated to

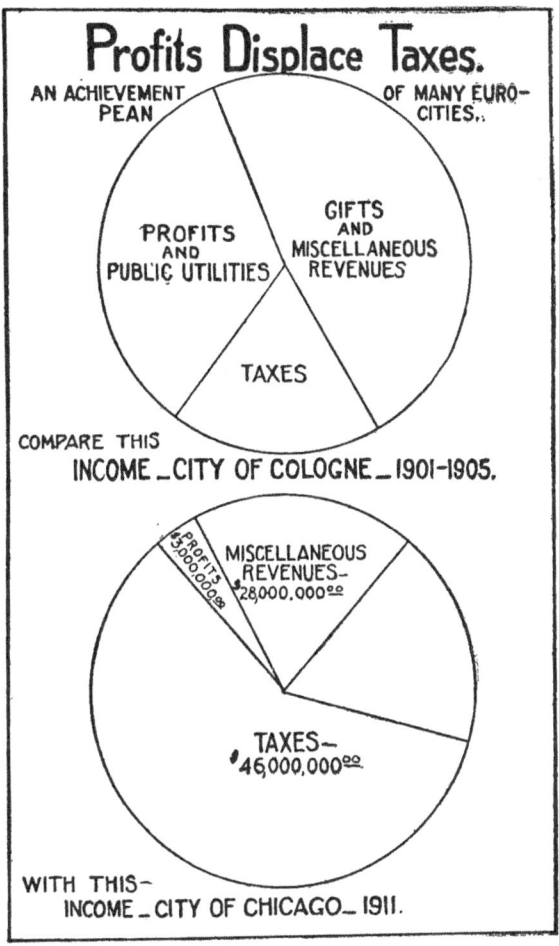

IN EUROPE PROFITS DISPLACE TAXES

FIGURE 2.4. "In Europe Profits Displace Taxes," from Anna E. Nicholes, "How Women Can Help in the Administration of a City," in *The Woman Citizen's Library* (Chicago: Civics Society, 1913), 11:2169. This chart, originally developed by planner John Nolen, illustrates the role of profitable public ownership in supplementing local revenue in European cities. Note how the attainment of profits as a high proportion of municipal revenue is labeled an "achievement" within this chart. Public ownership, Nolen believed, would allow cities to control their own economic destiny while lowering taxes on its productive citizens and enterprises.

potentially profitable enterprises such as docks, gas supply systems, wharves, and ferries (figure 2.5). In many European cities, however, this ratio was reversed. "Judged by the standards of commercial enterprises," one commentator summarized, "American cities incur debt in larger proportions for nonproductive purposes than do the European cities."[64] This was both a waste and a crime: as one municipal ownership advocate declared, "Capital is too

218   EUROPEAN CITIES AT WORK

TOWN	POPULATION	TOTAL DEBT	FOR PRODUCTIVE UNDERTAKINGS	OTHER PURPOSES
Berlin.....	2,001,032	$99,254,000	$64,767,000	$34,512,000
Elberfeld...	168,000	13,595,000	7,252,000	6,392,600
Halle......	176,798	9,500,000	2,877,000	4,612,000
Solingen...	50,961	3,285,000	2,257,000	1,029,000
Magdeburg.	247,358	15,005,000	7,775,000	7,503,900
Remscheid.	69,700	3,930,000	2,790,000	1,147,000
Düsseldorf.	284,439	28,585,000	22,260,000	6,327,000

A similar table of the indebtedness of seven American cities shows the amount as well as the distribution of indebtedness between productive and unproductive agencies.[1]

TOWN	POPULATION 1910	INDEBTEDNESS 1909	FOR PRODUCTIVE PURPOSES	FOR OTHER PURPOSES
Philadelphia..	1,526,383	$99,355,026	$30,776,642	$68,578,384
Cleveland....	538,374	37,304,908	5,613,684	31,691,224
Minneapolis..	294,330	14,927,202	1,933,424	12,993,778
Indianapolis..	228,690	4,790,401	22,000	4,768,401
Denver......	207,112	5,814,419	329,200	5,485,219
Omaha......	122,187	8,598,997	......	......
Grand Rapids	110,060	3,184,612	1,137,500	2,047,112

[1] Financial Statistics of Cities, 1909. Bureau of the Census.

FIGURE 2.5. Tables from Frederic C. Howe, *European Cities at Work* (New York: Charles Scribner's Sons, 1913), 218. Howe described "productive" debts as those that returned revenue directly to the city by their operations through fares or other charges. "Unproductive" debts were those, such as parks, sewer lines, or roads, that at best added value to another source of local revenue—property values. Surprisingly, American cities were far more likely than European cities to incur debt on behalf of "unproductive" than "productive" purposes—a result, he believed, of their dependence on taxation for revenue and their refusal to form profit-making enterprises on their own accord.

valuable to society to be wastefully destroyed. . . . If we destroy it, we are destroying that which ultimately belongs to the community."[65]

Such rationales for public ownership were synthesized in the work of Henry H. Klein, an irrepressible muckraker and sworn foe of the city's franchises. In his newspaper, *Klein's Weekly,* and in publications like *Bankrupting a Great City*, Klein exposed the connections among private franchises, public infrastructure, and urban finances (figure 2.6). Costly infrastructure on behalf of realty speculation, paid for by municipal bonds whose interest was directed into Morgan banks; piers built for luxury steamships at the city's expense; private franchises pillaging the public—all this and more was exposed by Klein.[66] In article after article, Klein drove home his argument that there was only one way New York and other cities could avoid the fiscal calamity its monopolists were foisting upon them: to "own their own public utilities or derive most of the profits therefrom, to provide for public need." Lamenting how the city had shortsightedly sold off its rights to profitable property and landownership during the nineteenth century, Klein called for New Yorkers to restore their city as a propertied, self-directed municipal corporation. "THE CITY'S FINANCIAL RESTORATION," he declared in capital letters, "COULD BE ACCOMPLISHED ONLY BY A RESTITUTION OF PUBLIC PROPERTY."[67]

Klein was not alone. Many commuters and taxpayers, frustrated with a lack of progress in adequately taxing or regulating the franchises, were becoming receptive to public ownership as a remedy. As Governor Theodore Roosevelt noted in 1899, "Where they [the utility companies] have escaped taxation as in Detroit, Toledo, and Chicago," the "citizens generally join in

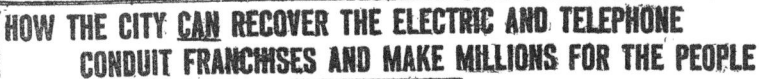

FIGURE 2.6. From Henry H. Klein, *Bankrupting a Great City (the Story of New York)* (New York: Henry H. Klein, 1916), 118. This sampling of headlines from muckraker Henry H. Klein speaks to the broader themes adopted by advocates of municipal ownership: how privately owned utilities promoted both waste and corruption, and how profitable public ownership could bolster urban finances.

such a revolt that they have swung to the opposite extreme of municipal ownership and have forbidden the granting of any franchise."[68] But what Roosevelt called "extreme," others simply called good business sense. When the *New York World* inveighed against tax-resisting franchises in 1905, it asked, "What would a private corporation, served by a capable executive, do if confronted by such extortion in a matter absolutely within its control?" It summarized, "The city is, or should be . . . a business corporation."[69] And to secure the profits of this corporation and its citizen-shareholders, a generation of New Yorkers attempted to translate the fiscal republican cause into policy.

Mobilization

Klein's call for a "restitution of public property" was taken up by growing numbers of New Yorkers in the early 1900s. Republican stalwarts like Samuel Seabury and Lawson Purdy, Democrats like Bird S. Coler and Edward M. Grout (both elected comptrollers of the city in 1898 and 1905 respectively), mavericks like William Randolph Hearst: all waged campaigns against local land and franchise monopolies. Artisans mobilized by newspapers like *Klein's Weekly*, property owners assembled in organizations like the New York Tax Reform Association, and "progressive" professionals disgusted by the inefficiencies and corruptions of realty speculation and franchise abuses all mobilized to support them. They were, of course, unsuccessful in establishing a "cooperative commonwealth" in the metropolis. But at their height, the scale of their campaigns and the scope of their victories seemed to herald a fundamentally new fiscal imaginary for New York City.

The first great policy victory for New York fiscal republicans was the Ford Franchise Bill of 1900. This measure aimed to tax special franchises not only on the basis of their physical structures but on what one supporter called the "infinitely more valuable" *right* to a franchise in the first place.[70] The coalition behind this amendment ranged from the Central Federated Labor Union and the Real Estate Board of Brokers to the West End Taxpayers Association. Republican senator John Ford, the main sponsor of the bill, celebrated the act's passage by declaring, "Were the cities in the full enjoyment of the revenues derived from (public franchises) alone, the municipal tax rate would be cut nearly in two, and the whole population—for it is the rent-payer, not the landlord, who is the real-taxpayer—would be proportionally benefited."[71] The *Brooklyn Eagle* agreed, stating that "tremendous revenues come from franchises. The list of privileges worth millions a year is an exceedingly long one. The conviction that they have been free from assessment long enough has crystallized."[72] Summarizing the prevailing mood, the state tax commissioners in 1901 declared that "no enactment of modern times is more popular with the people of this state."[73]

Subsequent amendments, however, quickly undercut the bill's effectiveness. The state legislature removed franchise assessment authority from local governments and lodged them in Albany—due, growled Ford, to the fact that local taxes were "undodgeable."[74] Other franchise owners questioned the constitutionality of the law itself and took their cause to the Supreme Court, tying up $25 million of public revenue in the process.[75] And assessments under the Ford Franchise Bill still tended to lag behind the true value of the franchises.[76] "We may endure with comparative equanimity the spectacle of the elected representative of the people selling himself to a piratical corporation," the *Evening Post* complained in 1905, "but the most apathetic of us resents having his pockets picked to pay someone else's dividends on watered stock."[77]

Such resentment quickly soured into political revolt in the form of the Municipal Ownership League. The party was largely organized and financed by William Randolph Hearst, a newspaper publisher well known for mixing muckraking with jingoism. His New York papers had led the charge against Consolidated Gas's high rates in the spring of 1899, and Hearst supported Comptroller Bird S. Coler (himself a municipal ownership advocate) in his successful campaign to prevent a franchise "steal" by the Ramapo Water Company in 1904.[78] In 1905, following additional reports of tax evasion by the city's utilities, Hearst organized the Municipal Ownership League to compete in that year's municipal elections.

The party's platform declared its commitment to municipal ownership of utilities, with their profits "devoted to comfort and lower fares, the lowering of taxes and better pay and shorter hours for the employees."[79] The party's mayoral nominee, none other than Hearst himself, declared that municipal ownership would lessen the burden on "the home and the store" by appropriating the profits of utility monopolies.[80] These references to the "home" and the "store" spoke to the Georgist-inflected coalition Hearst assembled—a combination of skilled workers and what his Tammany opponent later called the "white-collar proletariat . . . clerks, small employees, and small shopkeepers."[81] Hearst also tapped into the resentment of transportation utility companies felt by the city's streetcar and elevated commuters in the "outer boroughs" of Brooklyn and Queens—in a 1906 interview with Lincoln Steffens concerning his vision of the class he most appealed to, Hearst stated that "the Commuter is about it."[82] While Hearst ultimately lost the election by a slim (and possibly corrupt) margin, his electoral strength led many opponents to concede that municipal ownership was becoming a vital growing political force. The Tammany candidate beat Hearst by less than 1 percent—3,485 votes out of a total vote of 609,000—and Hearst won both Brooklyn and Queens outright. Bird S. Coler even won borough president of Brooklyn under the Municipal Ownership ticket.

Similar advances were made in campaigns for land-value taxation. Following years of pressure from the New York Tax Reform Association and similar Georgist organizations, in 1902, New York reformed its assessment practices to fully assess the city's land at 100 percent of its value. Although Manhattan's borough president warned that the plan would "alienate the propertied classes," the reform administration of Seth Low ceded to the association's arguments that the measure would bring in more revenue, more efficiently, than the present system.[83] Within a year, this policy enhanced the city's tax revenue by an extraordinary 42 percent, or $1.5 billion.[84] This not only freed up the city for additional capital improvements but reduced taxes upon both small homeowners and landlords—and, by extension, their tenants. As one newspaper noted, "Taxes . . . have been decreased, and decreased most largely in the poorer sections of the city, which were, as a rule, the worst sufferers from the old system of assessing property."[85]

This victory was followed by others. In 1906, New York's mayor appointed the Tax Reform Association's secretary, Lawson Purdy, as president of New York City's Tax Department. Another Georgist was soon afterward appointed registrar of deeds in Bronx County. In 1909, a Municipal Commission on Congestion argued for a land-value tax as a means to both encourage new housing construction and raise municipal revenue. In 1911 and 1912, bills for this measure were presented and supported by well-established reform associations like the Citizens Union and City Club, labor groups such as the Women's Trade Union League, and progressive social-reform bastions such as the People's Institute and the Neighborhood Workers Association.[86] Finally, in 1913, New York City mayor William Gaynor appointed a Commission on New Sources of City Revenue to investigate land-value taxation as a possible solution—for which the commission gave their blessing.[87] The "real estate interests of New York," glumly reported the *Real Estate Record and Builders' Guide*, "have been very much disappointed by the report of the Mayor's Commission on New Sources of Revenue."[88]

Fiscal republicans found similar successes in other states. Nearly a quarter of all cities in the United States owned profitable electrical plants by 1906, and others moved to municipalize street railways, gas plants, docks, and even theaters.[89] And by 1916, the cities of Pittsburgh, Scranton, and Everett had each replaced taxation upon improvements with taxation upon land, and many more cities elected Georgists to reform their assessment policies.[90]

By the early 1900s, then, fiscal republicans had made deep inroads in transforming the fiscal imagination of New York and other cities. This was not so much because their policies had laid a new fiscal foundation for cities— far from it—but because they had repoliticized local development strategies in a way that was at once radical and practical. As the *Real Estate Record* warned in 1910, campaigns for the land-value tax would "derive strength from the practical necessity of municipal revenue."[91] They had succeeded in drawing attention to how private ownership, in the absence of public controls, could damage the finances of cities as a whole: an argument that even defenders of private ownership were beginning to take to heart. And above all, their arguments seemed to resonate with a surprisingly large constituency willing to mobilize politically. As the *Record* grudgingly stated in reference to Hearst's calls for municipal ownership, "it is a program which will, we believe, eventually triumph in substance if not in the form which it receives in Mr. Hearst's platform."[92]

Narrowing the Subject

As much as fiscal republicans had expanded notions of economic development policy in New York, however, they also succeeded in deepening certain inherited beliefs around what—and who—made up economic growth. Such assumptions, once translated into politics and policy, would ultimately *narrow* the constituency for radical fiscal reform in New York in the coming decades.

First, many fiscal republicans reproduced the gender and racial exclusions of previous booster theories. Many white workers, fearing competition with Black Americans and "undesirable" immigrants, barred them from unions and cooperatives. Women, too, were estranged from the "cooperative commonwealth" by both franchise exclusion and prejudice against female employment.[93] Instead, many fiscal republicans saw the prosperity of cities as depending on white men and policies on their behalf. Bird S. Coler, first comptroller of Greater New York and fervent municipal ownership advocate, announced his proposal for increasing local debt on the grounds that "the Anglo-Saxon race has never moved backward."[94]

In addition, many fiscal republicans ignored how groups in their favored categories—the "taxpayer," the "homeowner," and the "producer"—could cause their own share of economic havoc (figure 2.7). Their fiscal imaginations generally could not accept that homeowners could be a source of fiscal strain or that "productive" property owners could generate their own share

FIGURE 2.7. Original caption: "The public should bear in mind that 95 per cent of the city's annual expenditure is borne by the taxpayers: This includes the rentpayers who must pay their share of the land-lords' burden." From Henry H. Klein, *Bankrupting a Great City (the Story of New York)* (New York: Henry H. Klein, 1916), 94. The "besieged taxpayer" was a trope of fiscal republican rhetoric. And while some fiscal republicans sought to expand the category of "taxpayer" to include tenants, the category's boundaries remained largely white, propertied, and male. This narrow constituency would ultimately abandon fiscal republicanism as alternative—and less radical—routes to property ownership and tax reduction were made apparent.

of social costs. Fiscal republicanism was thus a bold economic strategy with a remarkably narrow political subject—white "producers" and "homeowners" whose claims to whiteness and property bound them with less with their fellow workers than their rentier "foes."[95] And as white artisans increasingly *became* property owners in the early twentieth century through large-scale homeownership, they would further retreat from challenging private property's hold on the city's finances—or from forming alliance with the nonwhite and women workers who were bearing the brunt of private property's social costs.

But there was another assumption that many fiscal republicans carried over from older theories: that real estate growth was an index of local prosperity. While this sounds counterintuitive, it must be remembered that while many Georgists opposed speculation in land, they had little opposition to structures being erected *upon* that land. As such, many fiscal republicans considered themselves allies of "honest" developers and were perfectly willing to encourage the growth of property values through public policies. As a 1916 report by Pittsburgh's Georgist-inflected Committee on Taxation declared, if a city was to "raise practically all its revenues by taxing real estate values, steps must be taken to prevent the needless destruction of those values and to stabilize and promote their increase in every way possible."[96] A nineteenth-century booster could barely have expressed it better.

In this way, fiscal republicans entrenched both white male property ownership and real estate growth in the urban fiscal imagination, obscuring alternative principles of developing local economies. There remained much that was just and radical in their critique of private ownership's excesses, particularly as regards to land and utilities. But the political constituency for this critique would be weakened once opponents of fiscal republicanism provided alternative policies for acquiring property ownership and achieving local growth. And by the early 1900s, these opponents were beginning to mobilize.

Conclusion

Fiscal republicanism emerged from the municipal bankruptcies, labor unrest, and economic turmoil that swept through late nineteenth-century America. A wide range of Americans—labor unions and economists, farmers and small homeowners—debated what fiscal policies and ownership arrangements could best unleash urban prosperity. Solutions ranged from worker-owned cooperatives and land-value taxation to outright public ownership of local utilities. Uniting them all, however, was the view that productive property was the economic foundation of local prosperity—and that the social costs of privately owned monopolies threatened this prosperity. Such debates were particularly fervent in New York City, where organizations ranging from the Knights of Labor and single-tax clubs to Municipal Ownership Leagues mobilized to place Gotham's economy on a more resilient and profitable footing. By 1905, they seemed poised to transform New York's economic policy.

Even as these fiscal republicans won successes, however, their opponents were counterattacking. Rather than reduce land values for the sake of strengthening local economies, a new generation of fiscal "experts" declared that cities should *increase* those values for the sake of greater tax revenue. Rather than own private utilities for the sake of profits, a new class of municipal finance "professionals" claimed that cities should *subsidize* those corporations for the sake of service. And such arguments were gaining increasing weight in city halls across the country, setting the stage for a conflict whose outcome would shape the fiscal imaginary of American cities for decades.

3

"That Privately Owned Land
May Be Put to Its Best Use"

When Lawson Purdy stepped up to address the banquet of the Real Estate Board of Brokers in 1906, he might have expected a hostile reception. A confirmed Georgist since the late 1880s, Purdy had consistently lobbied for heavier taxes upon land as secretary of the New York Tax Reform Association throughout the past decade.[1] Only the previous year, he had been appointed to president of New York's tax board—not exactly the most beloved municipal post among real estate associations. That his address was entitled "The Best Taxed City in the World" could only seem a deliberate provocation to the landed gentry assembled before him in the Waldorf Astoria ballroom.

Nonetheless, Purdy assured his audience that public finance officials such as himself had only the best interests of the realty industry at heart. "We have on Manhattan Island," he declared, "the finest business blocks and the most costly hotels and dwellings in the world."[2] Where Henry George might have decried such conspicuous symbols of inequality, Purdy saw such edifices as valuable sources of public revenue via the property tax. And Purdy believed that his department encouraged such construction by assessing land at higher rates than the structures upon them, thus incentivizing property owners to build grand edifices. "The splendid growth and improvement of our cities in this country and of our city of New York," Purdy asserted, "is due to the fact that it does not pay to hold land idle too long."[3] And Purdy's commitment to raising and taxing realty values went beyond strategic tax measures. During his eleven years as president of the Tax Department, Purdy promoted debt-financed public improvements as a means to raise real estate values, encouraged city planning measures as a means of directing those values, and advocated for zoning measures as a means of stabilizing and protecting those values.

Purdy's career reflected a broader convergence among municipal finance officers, planning officials, and private realty organizations during the early 1900s. Supporters of private landownership but increasingly skeptical of the laissez-faire market, these groups—whom I collectively label "fiscal corporatists"—believed urban prosperity could be achieved not by expropriating large land and utility owners but by supporting them through public subsidies and wise regulation.[4] And where Georgists had seen real estate's "progress" as causing poverty, these corporatists believed taxing such "progress" would help *reduce* poverty through the new public expenditures it enabled.

This fiscal imaginary, with its virtuous fiscal cycle of subsidy, growth, taxation, and public-spirited expenditure, was at the core of the modern liberal statecraft then emerging in American politics.[5] Fiscal corporatists translated this imaginary into local development strategies with private real-estate at their center. And through the ceaseless political mobilization and intellectual output of figures like Purdy, this imaginary would be promulgated through economic textbooks, converted into budgetary practices, and implemented in city-planning policies ranging from zoning to publicly subsidized transit lines across the country. Together, such actions elevated the pursuit of land's "highest and best use" as the dominant development strategy in American cities for decades, marginalizing the radical alternatives that had emerged during the Gilded Age. But by continuing to view profit accumulation as the sole prerogative of private owners, these fiscal corporatists rendered New York's economy vulnerable to the social costs of these owners: a vulnerability that contributed to New York's fiscal crisis of the 1930s.

By reconstructing the convergence of municipal finance officials and real estate organizations during the early 1900s, this chapter reinterprets the broader origins of modern city planning and budgetary reforms. While earlier Georgists and municipal ownership advocates had developed and advocated for reforms such as zoning, they complemented these reforms with robust anti-monopoly measures—measures that fiscal corporatists refused to pursue. In this way, modern city planning and public finance both emerged and departed from more radical fiscal rationales. While fiscal corporatists would soon debate over *which* private owners the city should promote, the broader assumptions behind their fiscal imaginary would not be broadly challenged until the Great Depression.

This chapter also demonstrates how new theories of public finance underpinned early twentieth-century planning policies and the inequalities they structured. During this period, land economists like Richard T. Ely, mortgage officials like Richard Hurd, and Georgists like Lawson Purdy all argued that

local property taxes were progressive and largely sufficient sources of revenue. In depending on this revenue source, however, local governments found
themselves fiscally dependent on the furnishers of this revenue: property
owners themselves. This chapter thus suggests how seemingly innocuous efforts to tax wealthy actors for local revenue can have dangerous downstream
consequences. As far as local finances are concerned, the power *to be* taxed
can be the power to destroy.[6]

Fixed Principles

At the core of New York's fiscal corporatist coalition was the city's real estate industry, which sought to place their industry on more respectable and
"scientific" footing during the early twentieth century (figure 3.1).[7] In doing
so, they were attuned to the mainstream progressivism then transforming
American politics. A flood of earnest middle-class professionals, ranging
from settlement house workers to social scientists, sought to treat economic
ills without radically altering relations of power and property.[8] Grand organizations like the National Civic Federation, philanthropies like the Russell
Sage Foundation, the moderate reformism of newspapers like the *New York
Times*: all believed that a broader "public good" could be achieved by making
private ownership "responsible." And by this time, New York's realty industry,
recovering from the doldrums of the 1870s, was quite ready to proclaim their
industry's responsibility—and fiscal indispensability—to the city.

   Realty's renewed confidence partly derived from the revival of their industry. The highest prices fetched for realty in 1873 were finally summited, after
a twenty-year lull, in 1893.[9] And these numbers continued to grow—between
1900 and 1914, Manhattan's land-value index (the average price of land in a
given year) rose from $100 in 1900 to a peak of $202 in 1914, while the value
of real estate in the city as a whole tripled from $2.5 billion to $8 billion.[10]
The city itself was larger now, having consolidated with neighboring villages
and cities to form Greater New York in 1898, and hundreds of current and
would-be-landowners besieged city hall to convert the new territory into private wealth. New financial devices such as the mortgage bond expressed the
confidence placed in urban land values by the city's largest financial firms.[11]

   The realty industry was also more organized than before. Grand associations such as the Real Estate Board of New York (formed in 1896) brokered no
doubt that the city's real estate was, in the words of one pamphlet, "The Safest
and Most Profitable Investment in the World."[12] Such organizations were used
by realty practitioners for sharing information, raising collective standards—
and coordinating assaults against the Georgists who threatened their wealth.

FIGURE 3.1. William D. Hassler, *Interior View of Crowds Assembled for the Loretta Sale*, 1918. Glass plate negative, nyhs_PR83_6545, William D. Hassler Photograph Collection, New York Historical Society. This depiction of a 1918 real estate auction, as compared with the 1858 auction depicted in figure 1.3, conveys something of the "orderly" and "respectable" face the real-estate industry was presenting to the public by the early twentieth century.

And they were largely successful. In 1914, for example, realty groups across the five boroughs, such as the Allied Real Estate Interests, the Harlem Property Owners' Association, and the Bedford Park Taxpayers Association, wrote and rallied consistently against a proposed land-value tax. The *New York Times* noted that their opposition marked "The First Time That a Successful Effort Has Been Made to Unite the Taxpayers' Organizations of the Greater City."[13]

But realty's political revival was also due to their success in the battle of ideas. In a host of magazine articles and textbooks, the realty industry portrayed itself not as the scurrilous and speculative trade of Gilded Age stereotype but as a sober and "scientific" enterprise.[14] As the assistant secretary of the American Real Estate Company declared in the *Banker's Magazine*, "Land values are not in the last analysis the creatures of chance, speculation or promotion; they are based on the fixed principle of use and demand."[15] And in adopting the language and procedures of "science," realty was able to align itself with the "scientific" ethos of the emergent professional class struggling for power in city halls across the country—groups who would become powerful allies in the political mobilizations to come.

Perhaps the most important figure to establish realty's intellectual bona fides was Richard M. Hurd, head of the mortgage department of the US Mortgage and Trust Company. In 1895, Hurd had sought a guide on what he called
the "science of city real estate as an aid in judging values." Finding no such
reference text, he created one of his own—a work that would, in his words,
"eliminate the power of chance" in buying, selling, loaning on, or "in any way
dealing with city real estate."[16] The result, seven years later, was *Principles of
City Land Values*: a work that would inform the practice and political goals of
the realty industry for decades.

For Hurd, the "intrinsic" value of land was the income or revenue that
could be capitalized from its use. The use of a land parcel that garnered the
maximum possible revenue was what he called its "highest and best" use.
Different parcels of land contained different potentials for "highest and best"
uses, and landlords therefore charged different premiums—rent—for its use.
What determined the "highest and best" use of land, however, was ultimately
the amenities of the land itself. As Hurd declared, "That buildings create land
values is to reverse the truth, buildings being the servants of the land and of
value only as they fulfill its need."[17]

And if the value of property was determined by land, the value of land was
determined by its location—and by location, Hurd meant *accessibility*: the accessibility of a parcel to different land uses ranging from markets to parks (see
figure 3.2). As Hurd summarized, "Since value depends on economic rent,
and rent on location, and location on convenience, and convenience on nearness, the intermediate steps may be eliminated and say that value depends
on nearness."[18] Transportation was therefore key to unlocking urban growth,
Hurd believed, as it enabled a given parcel to be accessible to—and therefore
available for—the "highest" amount of "uses."[19] This rule applied not only
to increasing the value of individual buildings but to increasing the value of
neighborhoods and entire cities. And as the value of land rose, those who
owned it would be encouraged to convert structures upon it to "higher and
better" uses—trends that Hurd believed would begin in the accessible core of
a metropolis and spread radially along its street and transit lines.

Hurd's book was celebrated as a groundbreaking work of applied scholarship, establishing a paradigm of urban growth that shaped both the theory and
policy objectives of realty for decades. His stress on accessibility as driving up
land values informed subsequent realty campaigns for transit and highway
infrastructure. The concept of "highest and best use," which he originated,
came into common parlance.[20] Summarizing his influence, a 2014 article on
urban land valuation produced by the American Enterprise Institute declared
that "after 110 years, Hurd's annunciated principles still inform property

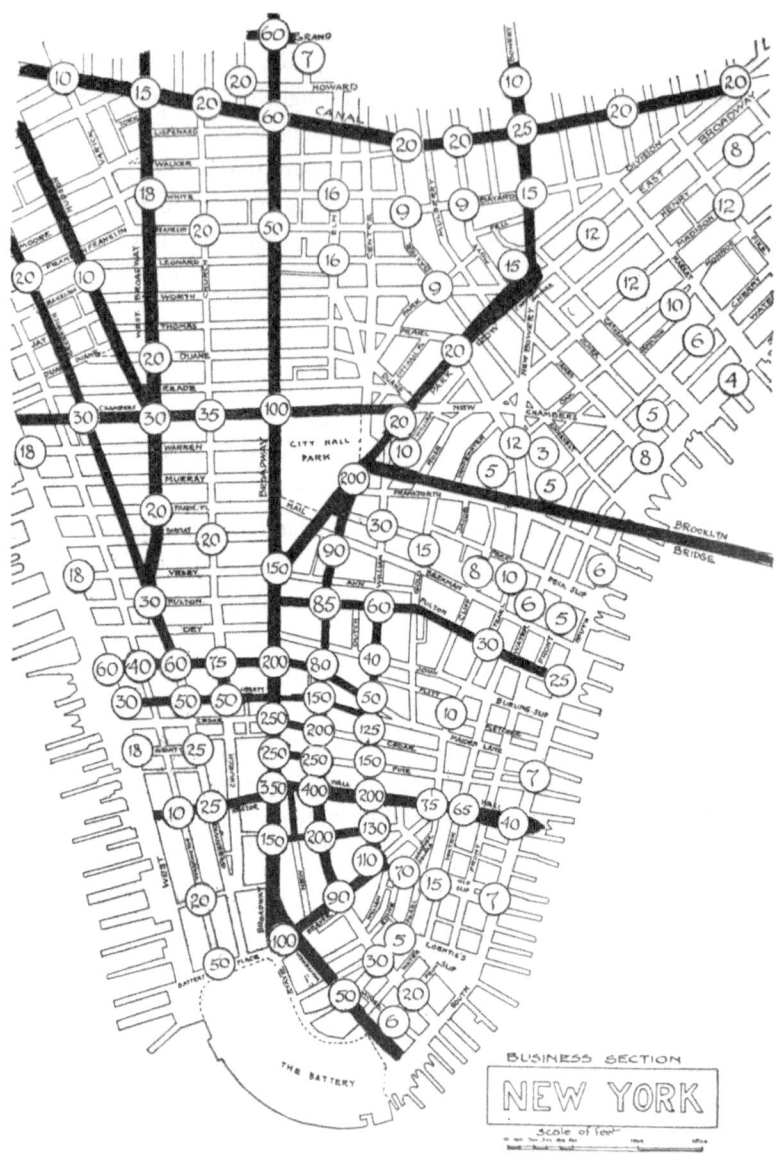

FIGURE 3.2. Map from Richard M. Hurd, *Principles of City Land Values* (New York: Record and Guide, 1903), 158. A map of land values from Hurd's seminal treatise on urban economics. Note how property values are higher at larger streets and intersections. Hurd's theory of land valuation placed a premium on accessibility as the determiner of land's value. And as land values rose, he believed, those who owned it would be encouraged to convert properties upon it to "higher and better" uses.

valuation theory and practice today."[21] And as his principles were promulgated, so were his gendered and racial prejudices. For example, Hurd asserted that "business property is elected by the man from an economic standpoint, and residence property by the woman from a social standpoint." And Hurd shared many of his contemporaries' racism in viewing "negro ownership" of "shabby and repulsive" structures as a threat to local property values.[22] And while such prejudices were prevalent before Hurd's work, they were now fortified with a "scientific" imprimatur and systematically disseminated.

The spread of such theories, however, foreclosed alternative understandings of urban economics and how they developed. Specifically, they countered earlier arguments by Georgists that land speculation—or private landownership itself—was economically harmful to cities. But if "scientific" theories promulgated by the realty industry were obscuring the social costs of private property, so too were new theories of municipal finance promoted by public finance officers within local governments. Together, this urban "scientific revolution" would significantly narrow urban America's fiscal imagination.

Highest and Best

During the early 1900s, public finance officers in New York City and elsewhere developed what they believed to be "rational" techniques for understanding and developing urban economies.[23] The use of advanced statistical methods, the growth of professionally trained civil servants to deploy them, the employment of financial officers with impeccable private sector backgrounds to oversee them: all this gave banks and liberal policymakers greater confidence in local finance decisions than in the days when Richard "Slippery Dick" Connolly was comptroller. But this confidence was also buttressed by the "scientific" new theories of urban land economics these officers espoused—theories that saw the growth of taxable urban land values as the key to financing New York's growing public sector and social expenditures.

Perhaps the most important individual to bring fiscal corporatism within local governments was Lawson Purdy, president of New York City's Tax Department from 1906 to 1918.[24] During the 1890s, Purdy had been a confirmed Georgist, serving as secretary of the single-tax-tinged New York Tax Reform Association. In that role, he helped the association successfully press New York to levy higher tax assessments on land in 1902. But where Henry George and others had viewed such measures as a means of *curtailing* what they saw as wasteful land values, Purdy defended these taxes as a means of ultimately *raising* them.

Purdy saw an intimate and ultimately mutually rewarding connection among public fiscal policy, private real estate, and urban growth more generally. When put to its "highest and best use," realty could furnish adequate revenue for cities—and high tax rates on land could help encourage such uses.[25] In public speeches and articles like "The Influence of Taxation upon the Prosperity of Cities," Purdy professed his faith. "Land," he summarized, "ought to pay the bill and can well afford to pay it."[26]

If Purdy shared the optimism of many Georgists over the upward trajectory of urban land values, however, he differed from them over whether those values should be confiscated or accelerated by the state. For orthodox Georgists, the chief purpose of land-value taxation was to reduce land's value—not to raise it. High land values, they argued, made it more difficult to establish productive enterprises or build small homes within the metropolis.[27] For them the land-value tax was less a means of garnering revenue than a means of wholesale economic transformation.

Other Georgist-inflected tax reformers, however, believed that the land-value tax should be used to *collect* the proceeds from rising land values—not reduce them. While the "unearned increment" was illegitimate if it was siphoned into the private sector, it could benefit the metropolis if it was taxed and distributed equitably. In 1906, Frederic Howe stated that land-value taxation would enable the city to "retain the benefits *and the unearned increment* of the city's expansion."[28] Or in the words of another Georgist, "The rent of land blesses neither him that gives nor him that takes, *unless it falls into the public treasury*."[29]

But if some Georgists vacillated on the wisdom of growing "unearned increments," fiscal corporatists like Purdy had no such hesitation. While the immediate effect of higher taxes on land was to lower them, Purdy claimed, the resulting growth in real estate would ultimately raise them—a cycle that, while somewhat contradictory, would nonetheless rebound to the city's benefit through both development and increased taxes. "The higher land is taxed," he asserted, "the easier it is to get, the lower the taxes on other things, and the greater is the stimulus to growth and improvement; this, in turn, increases land values. The further this policy is pursued, then, the more rapidly will the source of revenue increase."[30] And landlords stood to benefit from this cycle as well: as early as 1891, a prescient critic in the *Financial and Mining Record* noted that placing heavier taxes on land and reducing them on "productive" enterprises would stimulate economic activity, improvements, and population growth in the territories that implemented them—thus raising land values in the end. In this way, "large real estate owners" would find that "even if personal property taxes are abolished and all the burden placed upon real estate . . . they will be gainers through the resulting increased value."[31]

This virtuous fiscal cycle of taxation and improvement was, of course, perfectly in keeping with the liberal fiscal reform movements of the 1900s—one
that sought to tax the wealthy for the sake of public service rather than expropriate them for the sake of more "millenarian" ends. Such a cause informed
campaigns for tax reform at every level of governance, campaigns epitomized
by shifting the rationale of taxation from "benefits received" to "ability to
pay."[32] In an essay on New York's finances in 1915, prominent economist E. R. A.
Seligman declared that "the trouble is not with our expenditures" but the city's
"absurd and inadequate system of revenue," which spared the "rich man" at
the expense of its middle class.[33] Where some Georgists might have doubted
whether "rich men" were actually necessary for a thriving local economy, Seligman and other fiscal corporatists were happy to draw from them as needed.

Similarly, the faith liberal reformers held in tax-financed public spending
as sufficient to counter the ills of private ownership had not been shared by
earlier Georgists. Any attempt to alleviate the symptoms of poverty through
measures like public libraries or transportation, Henry George had declared,
would be temporary as long as landownership remained concentrated—for
all such measures would merely increase the value of land, thereby enabling
landowners to charge residents and businesses more for the privilege of using
it.[34] "If you made the East Side a garden," he noted, "only the millionaires could
live there."[35] Fiscal corporatists like Purdy, however, believed in public-spirited
reform (he would later serve as the chair of the Tenement House Committee
of the Charity Organization Society), and he and many others genuinely believed that wise regulation and public services like parks, transit, or even welfare services could alleviate social misery without needing to expropriate the
wealthy.[36] And if promoting local real estate was necessary to help build a state
wealthy enough to provide such services, fiscal corporatists were quite willing
to do so. As Seligman declared, "The problem is not to reduce desirable social
services, but to mobilize the resources of the community so as to make a development of these expenditures possible."[37] Private development for the sake of
public expenditures: a perfect encapsulation of the liberal fiscal imagination.

These assumptions, moreover, were being transmitted to large corps of
"professional" civil servants prepared to implement them. Purdy alone served
as vice president of the National Tax Association (1907–1912), president of the
National League of Cities (1916–1919), and president of the National Conference on City Planning (1920). Such organizations would help consolidate,
disseminate, and enforce the beliefs of fiscal corporatists around the country,
further narrowing the fiscal imaginary of civil servants and the governments
they worked for. And once installed in government, these officials developed new budgetary practices that would further insulate their theories from

critique. While this was partly due to a faith in expert direction held by fiscal corporatists themselves, it was also a consequence of their very efforts to tax wealth: as R. Rudy Higgens-Evenson states in *The Price of Progress*, "In exchange for the financial support of the business community [during the early 1900s], city and state governments had to adopt business methods of management to make their costs more acceptable to taxpaying business owners."[38]

Partly this was accomplished through bureaucratic centralization. New York's capital spending decisions—perhaps the most consequential for the city's economic development—were lodged in the city's Board of Estimate, dominated by borough- and citywide officers rather than the more representative City Council. This was for the best, for in the opinion of one comptroller (the city's chief financial officer), "the rights of the people of the city are always safer in the hands of a capable and conscientious Mayor and Comptroller, endowed with ample power . . . than they can possibly be when left to the care of a multitude of irresponsible office holders." In this way, direct democratic oversight into the policy and politics of economic development was minimized (see figure 3.3). True, there was the danger of corruption and hubris at the top—but the comptroller assured the public that "it would be preposterous to say that a thief, or even a man of questionable character, could be elected Mayor or Comptroller of the city."[39]

But gestures toward transparency by municipal finance officers also obscured the social costs of private ownership. Organizations like the New York City Bureau of Municipal Research, for example, organized "budget exhibits" so that the public might better gauge the city's fiscal health.[40] Lawson Purdy developed a similar initiative by publicizing "tax maps," assuring the public that property values were both flourishing and fairly assessed.[41] But many Georgists of the old school saw the transparency effected by these measures as false, obscuring deeper sources of fiscal strain that city-aided speculators were wreaking on municipal finances. Henry H. Klein accused the Bureau of Municipal Research of accepting donations from the same banking interests that were robbing the city with high interest rates.[42] Benjamin C. Marsh argued that any "adoption of business methods" by local budget offices should be preceded by confiscatory land taxes and other Georgist measures.[43]

Most of New York's realty industry, however, approved of Purdy and the privileged place they held in his fiscal imagination. Middle-class professionals and private financial officers could concur with the city's comptroller that "everywhere there is a promising tendency toward thorough business methods in the conduct of the affairs of cities."[44] Such allies would help public finance officials like Purdy translate their beliefs into public policy, including and especially those related to city planning.

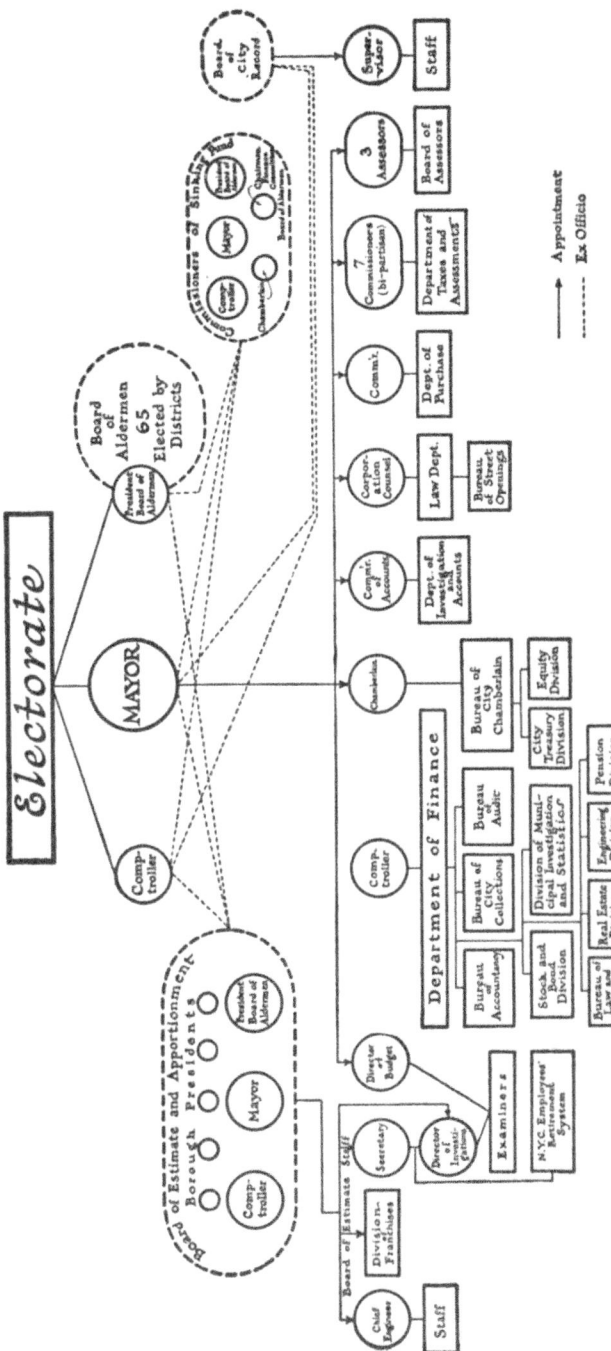

ADMINISTRATIVE UNITS DEALING WITH THE CITY'S FINANCES

FIGURE 3.3. Chart from Herbert H. Lehman, *The Finances and Financial Administration of New York City* (New York: Columbia University Press, 1928), 5. This diagram of New York's financial bureaucracy, much of which was established by progressive reformers in the early twentieth century, suggests how insulated the city's spending and investment decisions were from popular oversight and control. Such an abstruse fiscal structure helped "depoliticize" New York's developmental strategies during the early twentieth century.

Zoning

Purdy defined city planning as "arranging streets and public places that privately owned land may be put to its best use."[45] Buried in this definition, of course, was the assumption that privately owned land was *necessary* for urban flourishing: an assumption that fiscal corporatists firmly held. Still, turn-of-the-century local finance officers and realty owners were not entirely ignorant of the social costs that private landownership could place on the city. Heightened to the sources and fragility of property values through the work of land economists like Hurd and the decades-long mobilization of Georgists, fiscal corporatists were less willing than their nineteenth-century predecessors to leave such values to the chaos of the private market. And to regulate this chaos in the collective interest of property owners and the city at large, fiscal corporatists looked to city planning policies like zoning. Such policies would embed Purdy's goal of growing land values into New York's very structures and streets, generating benefit for some—and social costs for others.

Zoning, of course, cannot be fastened to any one political tendency. Left-wing Georgists like Benjamin Marsh consistently lobbied for use and height restrictions on private property during the early 1900s. They did so, however, largely to *reduce* land values rather than raise them. Such restrictions, Marsh argued, would prevent landlords from erecting an excess of tall buildings in one place, thus rendering that land affordable for small home and factory construction. Nonetheless, Marsh demanded that confiscatory land taxes be implemented *before* zoning measures were applied in order to prevent any "unearned increment" from accruing to landlords under the new restrictions. "The change in the tax system which we advocate should precede the zoning of the city," he stated, to prevent a "rapid increase in (the) selling values of land."[46]

Purdy, by contrast, was more concerned with the social costs of land's *uses*—smoke, air, laborers—than with the costs of high land *values*. "Concerned as I have been with the value of real estate," Purdy stated in 1917, "I have seen during these last fifteen years many sections of the city of New York decline in value" and "buildings worth hundreds of millions of dollars become worthless."[47] Partly he blamed realty declines on speculators building an excess of tall buildings, thus concentrating land values at individual points rather than dispersing them. But he focused his enmity largely on the *physical* consequences of "poor" land uses, such as skyscrapers casting shadows on their neighborhoods and factories casting soot upon their surroundings. For example, Purdy joined with the Fifth Avenue Association in worrying that "the intrusion of the garment industry"—and by extension, the presence of its Jewish and Italian employees—"was playing havoc with the land values in that district."[48] While individual landowners could ignore these "social costs" as long as the landlord made a profit individually, a tax official concerned with the aggregate values of the city could not.

Purdy's efforts to encourage zoning were for some realtors as threatening as land-value taxation. Landowners in peripheral districts did not wish their transit-induced values to be curtailed by tight height and use restrictions. Skyscraper owners chafed at Purdy's suggestion that their properties could threaten neighboring land values.[49] Looking back from 1948, Purdy recalled the opposition that his zoning proposals engendered among many property owners. "We had little success in Queens because the real estate interests there controlled politics," he declared. "Those men couldn't see what was good for them."[50]

Nonetheless, by 1916 many of the larger real estate firms and local chambers of commerce looked to zoning as a means of securing their investments from "noxious uses" and other ills. Regulation, they perceived, could indeed be "good for them." That year, Purdy served as an officer on the city's first Zoning Commission and was later elevated to vice chair of the second Commission. This commission would ultimately produce the city's first zoning ordinances—ordinances expressly designed, in the words of Purdy, to "enhance the value of land throughout the municipality."[51]

But zoning was only one instrument in New York's planning repertoire—so was transportation. And Purdy's reference to "land throughout the municipality" spoke to the Greater New York that had come into existence in 1898 and featured hosts of landlords and speculators "hover[ing] like a Parthian army on the outskirts of the city," in the words of one critic.[52] This army wanted public improvements—specifically the subway—that would spur development and property values in their districts. And now they had allies like Purdy in city hall, eager to deliver this subway for them in the name of higher tax revenues.

Subway

New York's promotion of the subway during the early 1900s, exemplified by the Dual Contracts of 1913, embodied the fiscal corporatist belief that powerful economic actors could provide for the public good under the right regulations and incentives. Such faith in "public-private partnerships" ran counter to those of Georgists and municipal ownership advocates, who saw both land speculation and privately owned franchises as threats to the city's finances. But these advocates were unable to defeat the wide coalition of policymakers, realty groups, and municipal finance officers who mobilized on behalf of private subway expansion. And this subway expansion, once passed into law, would subsequently weigh the city down with social costs for generations: not only with the debts accrued for its construction but with the speculative realty development it unleashed.

Real estate groups mobilized in earnest to expand New York's subway during the early 1900s. While realty boosters had called for underground rapid transit since at least the late 1880s, memories of the previous decade's fiscal collapse had died hard. Not until 1894, after years of attempting and failing to secure private aid to construct and operate the transit system, did New York State pass a referendum enabling local governments to construct rapid transit lines with subway operations themselves leased to private companies.[53] But little progress had been made by the early 1900s. And by then, real estate organizations were becoming insistent in their calls for a subway that would link Manhattan and the "outer boroughs" of Brooklyn and Queens, an insistence born by the revival of their industry, the expanded borders of the city waiting for transit-driven colonization, and new theories of land economics placing high premiums on accessibility.[54] The assistant secretary of the American Real Estate Company, for example, declared in Hurd-ian language that an expanding subway would carry "a tremendous increase along the line of the proposed improvements in every direction."[55]

Realty groups were not alone in calling for a subway. Labor unions saw the promise of jobs wrought by both the subway and the building boom that would attend it. Tenants in the city's crowded central districts saw the subway as a route toward homeownership in the city's periphery. Opponents of Tammany saw an opportunity to weaken the machine's base by turning them into "propertied voters"—even as Tammany saw the subway as a means of expanding their organization's influence within the outer boroughs. And social reformers saw the subway as a means of decongesting the city's crowded central districts while providing tenants with salubrious homes. As the *New York Times* moralized, "An adequate system of rapid transit through the length of the city" would help "relieve the congestion and greatly simplify the problem of providing better homes for the poor, or, what is infinitely more desirable, enabling them to provide better in every way for themselves."[56]

Most realty associations, however, were not inclined to wait for private operators to expand transit lines on their own volition. The city's main subway operator, the Interborough Rapid Transit Company (IRT), refused to dilute its profitable Manhattan lines with unprofitable routes through sparsely-settled Brooklyn and Queens.[57] As the president of the liberal City Club complained in 1908, the IRT would "extend these lines into the outskirts as rapidly as they find it profitable to do so."[58] Only higher fares or congested lines could guarantee those lines, both of which were unacceptable to many of New York's housing reformers.

Rather than trust subway expansion to "market forces" alone, many advocates of a large and affordable subway demanded the city construct additional transit infrastructure while leaving the operation of the subway to private actors. But to build such infrastructure, realty interests needed to remove an impediment: municipal debt limits. Such limits, considered a vital safeguard to municipal finances when they were first installed, were by the early 1900s seen by the *Real Estate Record* as "an insuperable obstacle to any proper provision for the future growth of the city."[59]

Some Georgists were skeptical of these calls for subsidized and debt-financed transit expansion. Such expansion, they feared, would render land values prohibitively expensive for single-family homes if confiscatory land taxes or municipal landownership did not accompany the new lines.[60] Under these conditions, well-intentioned demands for low subway fares by housing reformers would only increase speculative land values without increasing homeownership. "Charitable Experts," Benjamin Marsh wrote, "have suggested that transit in that city of high land values and exorbitant rents should be as free as walking in the streets." "Naturally," he continued, "the land speculator cheerfully pronounces his benediction" upon this policy "because he makes money from the passengers coming and going."[61] Inexpensive transit was thus a device for enhancing land speculation in the guise of social reform.

Advocates of municipal ownership similarly feared that debt on behalf of privately owned transportation companies would simply funnel money into the same financiers wrecking the city's economy. Henry H. Klein railed against the "Morgan" and "Rockefeller" interests who owned shares in both banks and transit companies, while Benjamin C. Marsh spoke of the "unholy alliance between the land and the loaning interests" to which "an entire third of New York's revenue" would be channeled should the city construct additional lines.[62] While certainly not adverse to transit expansion, Marsh insisted that such lines only be expanded when warranted. "The unused capacity of existing transit facilities in every American city," he insisted, "should be availed of before more transit at the cost of the citizens at least is suggested."[63]

Most New Yorkers, however, refused to delay transit expansion until land-value taxation and municipal ownership were accomplished facts. Conditions in the overcrowded subway were, as one critic wrote, "scandalous."[64] Would-be homeowners saw the subway as a more expedient route toward property ownership than waiting for the land-value taxation to pass.[65] And speculators sought to grow the value of newly acquired property quickly—and before their mortgage loans were called in.

In the face of this pressure, calls for fiscal restraint were drowned out. In response to a suggestion that the city build the subway incrementally as the city's debt limit allowed, the president of the Allied Real Estate Interests argued instead for building several lines simultaneously via an expanded debt limit. "Do you believe that the piecemeal construction of such subways, as and when the debt limit permits, is going to satisfy the transit needs of this growing City?" he exclaimed. "You are asking that the City start a subway now, working so long as the debt limit permits, and speculating on the possibility of additional available debt margin next year and the year following and so on until the subway is completed"—a proposition that "a sane business man would not entertain for one moment."[66]

Acquiring the public debt needed for this expansion would be a long and grueling process—with Purdy at its center. As tax commissioner, Lawson Purdy worked to expand the city's debt capacity—which was pegged at 5 percent of the city's assessed values—by simply raising assessments on the city's land. As mentioned earlier, the New York Tax Reform Association (with Purdy serving as secretary) had successfully lobbied for the assessment of city real estate at 100 percent of its market value in 1902. Surprisingly, the *Real Estate Record and Builders' Guide* hailed the result: an expanded debt capacity for the city. "Every one of the large number of improvements, which are now underway," it stated, "will be a direct benefit to real estate. The new Subways and Bridges will be a clear gain to the propertied interest." And "scarcely any" of these projects "could have been undertaken had it not been for the administration policy of full real estate assessments."[67] Purdy was soon appointed president of New York's Tax and Assessment Board, where he continued to raise assessments for the sake of the subway, assuring local taxpayers that the transit lines wrought by the higher assessments would ultimately increase the value of their property.[68]

It would not be enough simply to expand the city's debt margin to build the subway, however—the limits themselves would have to be broken. Breaking those limits represented a departure from the city's relatively conservative post-1870s fiscal policies—but drastic means, public officials asserted, were necessary. In 1908, Comptroller Metz drafted a state amendment to exempt subway construction from the state-imposed debt limit. "Without this exemption," he declared, "I have little hope for the undertaking and accomplishment of our subway . . . improvements."[69] A report that same year from an Advisory Commission on Taxation and Finance recommended that the state expand the city's debt-incurring powers to support additional subway service, assuring legislators that it would present "no burden upon the taxpayers."[70] "It is . . . the poorest economy," concurred New York's commissioner of docks in 1909, for the state to "tie the city's hands as to prevent it from securing the best transit possible continuously."[71]

New York State passed the debt-expansion amendment in 1909—and voters approved the measure overwhelmingly in a referendum. A glance at supporting organizations reflected the coalition that had been won over to the fiscal corporatist cause. These included the Merchants Association, the New York Board of Trade, and a committee of bankers including J. P. Morgan Jr. and F. A. Vanderlip of the National City Bank.[72] Real estate bodies in both the center and periphery of the city, from the Greater New York Taxpayers Conference to the Association of Long Island and Queens Property Owners, advocated for its passage.[73] And Tammany Hall representatives joined hands with outer-borough Republicans and Democratic rivals for its passage, eager for the contracts, construction, and constituencies an expanded subway would bring them.[74] Even the president of the largely rural Borough of Richmond (Staten Island), which the subway manifestly did not run to, asserted that the subway would help provide the kind of "separate houses for each family" that "normal home life requires" while enhancing taxable land values throughout the city.[75]

The city would have to expend more than just debt to ensure the expansion of its subway system, however. While the city had lifted the debt restrictions needed to construct subway lines into the city's periphery, private operators were still unwilling to operate in areas where ridership remained small.[76] After years of fruitless negotiations, in 1911, the city offered a new round of incentives to encourage the IRT and the Brooklyn Rapid Transit Company (BRT) to expand into New York's periphery. The resulting agreement, the "Dual Contracts," offered public subsidies to the private sector in exchange for doubling the city's track mileage from 296 to 618 miles.[77] New York City would pay the majority of construction costs—$226 million out of a total cost of $300 million—which would be eventually repaid via transit company revenues. Such repayment, however, would only take place once the subway companies recovered the interest costs and sinking fund expenses for their own share of capital construction. The BRT would also receive a yearly lump sum and fare revenues equal to their current profit rate as a reward for building outlying rail lines.[78]

The terms of the Dual Contracts revived the cause of municipal ownership and Georgism—at least momentarily. The promise of municipal subsidies on behalf of a select group of landlords, transit monopolists, and financiers seemed a return to the worst of Gilded Age excesses. Hearst's *Evening World* declared that "Tammany would not dare give any corporation what these eminently respectable gentlemen are giving to Morgan and Belmont and this traction monopoly."[79] Or as another critic wrote, "The public officials of 1913 are still thinking in the grooves of 1875."[80]

But the political context of 1913 New York was different from that of 1875—and the differences were in favor of fiscal corporatists. New York's expanded City Council and Board of Estimate gave greater representation to land-owners on the city's periphery than had the preamalgamated government. Property owners and realty investors were better organized and better positioned to advocate their policies through the language of science and public service. Creditors were more willing to dispense loans to local governments than in the years following Tweed's ouster, convinced that house cleaning by "professional" civil servants like Purdy had rendered local finances more trustworthy. Regulatory state bodies like New York's Public Service Commission seemed to furnish adequate public safeguards for public franchises in the minds of most middle-class progressives. And where 1875 was a year of national depression, revealing the dangers of debt-financed realty speculation and leading to decades-long fiscal retrenchment, rapid urban growth in the years leading up to 1913 convinced many public finance officers that the future could take care of itself. As an executive committee member of the National Conference on City Planning sanguinely stated the following year, "the resources of a city increase with its needs."[81]

Calls by critics for the profitable ownership of the subways were also in the minority, opposed by reformers who saw the public sector's role as providing regulation or service—not earning profits. Some social reformers worried that profit-seeking municipal owners would be as contemptuous toward public service as profit-seeking private owners.[82] Others argued the public sector had neither the right nor the ability to earn profits as effectively as the private sector. In either case, the responsibility of the local state was not to profit from public transit but to subsidize private lines so as to raise land values and, by extension, property taxes. As the president of the National Tax Association argued in 1907, the most useful "tax" to place on transit lines was to "extend their service lines beyond present paying limits, thus causing them to serve as a factor in improving and building up the ever-widening limits of the municipality."[83]

In the end, New York's Board of Estimate approved the Dual Contracts in March of 1913 (see figure 3.4). The *New York Times* hailed it as "the best terms . . . evidently the only terms, upon which new subway construction can be had."[84] Perhaps not: municipal ownership advocate Delos F. Wilcox lambasted the terms, arguing that the public subsides it guaranteed would be drawn from productive enterprises on behalf of private shareholders, undermining the city's fiscal health in ways impossible under public ownership.

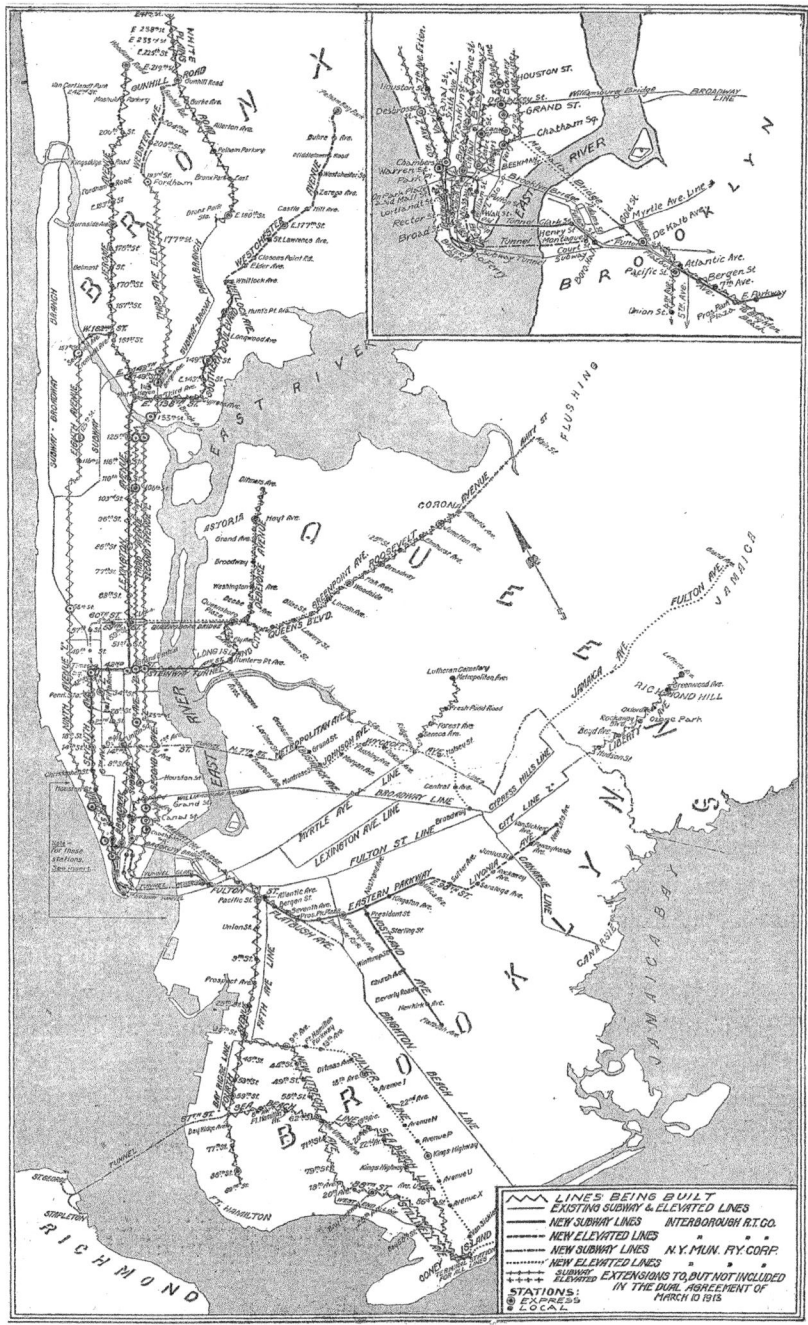

FIGURE 3.4. "Official Map of Dual Subway Showing Lines and Stations," *New York Times*, April 26, 1914, XX1. Before the Dual Contracts were signed in the early 1910s, the majority of the city's subway lines were confined largely to Manhattan. The Dual Contracts extended New York's subway lines far into the hinterlands of Brooklyn and Queens, growing land values in their wake. But the real estate developments that followed these subway lines would soon foist their own costs upon the metropolis.

"New York," he complained, "rejects profits as if they were plebeian."[85] For its defenders, however, such profits were insignificant compared to the land values that the subway would soon unleash. As Mayor Gaynor declared, subway-enhanced property values would make the profits rendered through municipal ownership "comparatively immaterial to the city."[86]

Time would tell how "immaterial" the city's sacrifice of profits would be.

Sunk Costs

The subway expansion launched by the Dual Contracts was just one prominent example of the broader policy successes fiscal corporatists achieved in the 1910s. The growth of debt-financed public improvements, the growing influence of "professional" planners and public finance officers, the spread of zoning policies—all this represented the commitment of local governments to promoting land's "highest and best use." Together, these developments would transform the financial and geographic landscape of American cities for decades—while considerably narrowing the fiscal imagination of their inhabitants.

The most immediate sign of fiscal corporatist success were the growing debts cities now accrued on behalf of land-enhancing public improvements. Between 1898 and 1914, New York City's debt more than tripled, from \$237,366,000 to \$942,204,000, much of it on behalf of promoting realty growth in the city (see figure 3.5). Indeed, \$300 million of debt was sunk into new transit construction alone, and much of the rest—street openings, bridge construction, and so forth—was of similar benefit to property owners.[87] And New York was not alone. Between 1890 and 1902, total municipal debt grew from \$926 million to \$2 billion, nearly regaining its 1870s level. Whereas per capita municipal debt among cities with more than thirty thousand residents was \$16.37 in 1880, it had doubled to \$35.81 in 1912—and even these numbers would soon be eclipsed.[88]

But New York was now not only indebted to bond purchasers for these improvements; it was indebted to the New Yorkers who used them. Between 1920 and 1930, Brooklyn's population increased by half a million, while Queens more than doubled in population to slightly more than a million.[89] The subway had helped populate New York's periphery—and now New York would have to service these populations with costly new schools, new roads, new sewers, and much more besides. The growth of New York's subway thus begat further expenditures: just one of the many "sunk costs" that would burden local budgets following the construction of debt-financed public improvements (see figure 3.6).

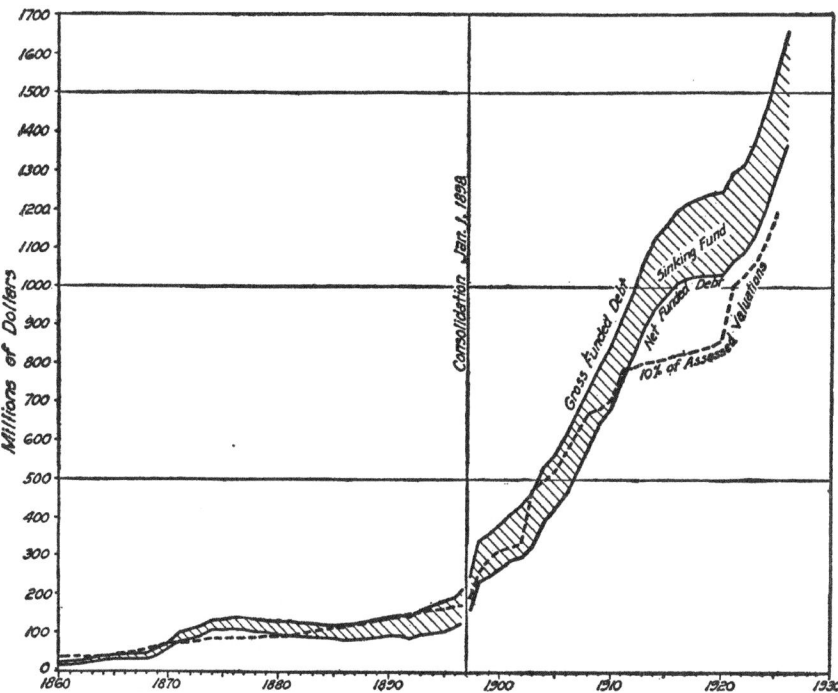

FIGURE 3.5. Chart from Herbert H. Lehman, *The Finances and Financial Administration of New York City* (New York: Columbia University Press, 1928), 189. Note how the thirty-year stability of the city's post-1870s debt level rose dramatically in the early 1900s, starting a trend that would continue well into the 1930s. Much of this debt was incurred for "public improvements" on behalf of promoting real estate values, including subways and bridges.

The social costs of growth, however, would be largely expelled from the thought of early 1900s public finance officers and planners: a narrowing of the fiscal imagination that marked another fiscal corporatist legacy. While planners might seek to alleviate some symptoms of growth, the more radical critiques of rent and land speculation that had motivated Henry George were largely excised from planning and public finance theory. Through new planning and public finance textbooks, through "professional" bodies like the National Association of Comptrollers and Accounting Officers, and through prominent realty-funded think tanks like the Institute for Research in Land Economics and Public Utilities (whose head confessed a "desir[e] to get away from presuppositions and, indeed, prejudices which are connected with the term rent when used as denoting an unearned income"), planning and public finance thought was thoroughly consolidated under the fiscal corporatist banner.[90] This consolidation, together with the broader suppression of

THE CITY'S MILLIONS POURED OUT FOR PROFITLESS BRIDGES

TWENTY-TWO MILLION DOLLARS for a bridge, the cost of which was originally estimated at $14,000,000. The NET income from ALL the bridges was less than their laboring cost of maintenance, not counting about $3,000,000 a year interest on bonds issued for their construction.

FIGURE 3.6. Image from Henry H. Klein, *Bankrupting a Great City (the Story of New York)* (New York: Henry H. Klein, 1916), 45. Klein's papers critiqued debt-financed infrastructure like bridges and subway tunnels on the grounds that they benefited realty speculators and the Wall Street firms that financed them at the expense of New York's citizens and economy more broadly.

suppression of radical thought after World War I, further obscured the costs of growth from American planners and finance officers.[91]

And if the cause of ending the land monopoly was in abeyance, so too was the cause of profitable public ownership. The spread of public authorities after World War I, to be sure, provided the public sector with a limited public mechanism for generating revenue. Such revenue, however, was generally recycled directly into the authority's infrastructure and services—both of which were generally meant to promote private sector growth rather than wean the city off its fiscal dependence on the private sector more generally.[92] The latter was no longer seriously entertained by most professional civil servants; more prevalent was the notion that earning profits was for the private sector. While the public sector could regulate such actors, they were strictly barred from earning revenue on their own accord. As the mayor of Boston declared in 1910, "Municipal Corporations are organized not to make money, but to spend it; their object is government, not profit."[93] This was an arrangement that would be quite satisfactory to the private sector.

In all these ways, fiscal corporatists helped obscure both the costs of real estate growth and alternatives to that growth. And while later planners like Lewis Mumford would rediscover these costs, undoing them would be another matter. For once the debt was accrued, once the concrete was laid, once hopes of future growth were generated, trying to limit future growth would be physically and financially difficult—and politically nearly impossible.

Conclusion

During the early 1900s, real estate practitioners and municipal finance officers converged on a single fiscal imaginary: one built around promoting "highest and best" use of private land in the name of increased tax revenue. This imaginary, promulgated by figures like Lawson Purdy and transmitted through influential professional associations, was soon translated into policies such as zoning, public-private partnerships like the Dual Contracts, and debt-financed public improvements on behalf of real estate expansion. Such policies, together with the consolidation of planning and liberal public finance thought, marginalized the influence of more radical Georgist and municipal ownership advocates—while obscuring the social cost of speculation and private ownership that those radical theorists had perceived.

But these costs would not stay concealed for long. The subway-driven growth of New York's outer boroughs was creating new neighborhoods whose inhabitants would soon demand costly public services. And many of these inhabitants, particularly white homeowners, had little inclination to pay for them in full. The more the city grew, it seemed, the more costly it became to grow. But this troubling thought could be banished as long as future growth could be relied upon to pay the costs of yesterday's growth. And for most of New York's realty industry and public finance officers, their cities' prospects during the 1920s seemed bright indeed.

PART II

On What Grounds, 1913–1945

"Homes Are More Important than Skyscrapers"

When Republican and self-titled "friend of the homeowner" George U. Harvey campaigned for Queens borough president in 1928, he righteously declared that he would not "give" the borough's homeowners anything—as "no public officials ever gave you anything." This was, to put it mildly, untrue.[1] Since the beginning of the decade, New York policymakers of both parties had showered Brooklyn and Queens property owners with subsidies ranging from tax exemptions to tax-financed infrastructure to debt-financed subway lines (figure 4.1).[2] Only four years earlier, Mayor John Hylan, Democrat and proud scion of the outer boroughs, stated that "I have been accused of spending large sums to develop the outlying sections of the City. I plead guilty."[3] And Harvey himself, upon winning his race, would continue to spend "large sums" on behalf of his property-owning constituency.[4]

Harvey's statement, however, spoke to his audience's self-perception: that they were "taxpayers," put-upon citizens who contributed more than they received from their city. Such beliefs helped obscure, in their own minds and the minds of others, the role white property owners played in undermining the city's finances through the speculative developments they lived in and the subsidies they demanded. And even those who perceived such costs were generally willing to countenance them for the sake of increasing white property ownership. In this way, New York continued to spend debt and treasure on behalf of white property owners—homeowners and skyscraper owners alike—throughout the 1920s. And even after the social costs of these subsidies threatened New York's finances in the 1930s, their beneficiaries would fight fiercely—and largely successfully—to retain them.

This chapter examines how a coalition of outer-borough property owners, developers, and policymakers campaigned to subsidize white real estate

FIGURE 4.1. *Dezendorf's Delightful Dwellings*. Photograph by Joseph Smith, LC-USF344-000877-ZB, Prints and Photographs Division, Library of Congress. While this image of a subdivision in Queens conveys the scale of New York's peripheral expansion during the 1920s, a closer look reveals how such expansion was only made possible through inequitable public finance policies. The sign on the right for "Dezendorf's Delightful Dwellings" advertises the projects as tax exempt: new subdivisions like this one were provided with property tax exemptions within New York City as a matter of policy, foisting greater tax burdens upon the city's older districts—and, by extension, their tenants. The sign advertising "two family homes" on the left, meanwhile, advertises paved streets as part of their subdivisions' amenities—streets that were paved by municipal tax dollars, much of which were also drawn from the city's older and poorer districts. In both these ways, New York's peripheral expansion during the 1920s reinforced fiscal discrimination—and fiscal instability—within the city.

and homeownership on the urban periphery during the 1920s. This group, whom I call "developmental populists," believed that promoting the city's outward expansion was in the broader city's economic interest (as well as their own). Well-organized homeowners and developers translated this fiscal imaginary into policies by lobbying tax exemptions, debt-financed subway lines, and other expensive subsidies. And policymakers, many with realty investments of their own and desirous of the taxes realty development could furnish, largely obliged. But as fast as the outer boroughs grew, debt on behalf of that growth grew faster—even as the city's Black and working-class tenants were denied services freely granted to white property owners.[5] The result was a public finance strategy as unjust as it was unstable—and whose collapse during the Depression would reignite debates over how the city should grow.

By examining the rise and success of developmental populists during the 1920s, this chapter reinterprets the political origins and economic consequences of mass white homeownership in America.[6] As this chapter shows, increasing homeownership during this decade was accelerated by local public subsidies—even as these property owners were hailed as revenue-positive "taxpayers" by their representatives. Insulated from fiscal critique, urban property owners and their defenders ignored the broader social costs they imposed on cities. And when these costs threatened to bankrupt their local governments, these taxpayers would insist upon continuing those subsidies at the expense of the urban budgets and their most marginalized citizens. The onset of large-scale homeownership thus established a set of fiscal expectations among America's white property owners that would both accelerate and obscure economic instability in American cities for many decades.[7]

A New Constituency

New York's subway system, vastly expanded thanks to the Dual Contracts of 1913, brought swaths of home seekers to the "outer boroughs" of Brooklyn and Queens during the 1920s. And many found what they were looking for. Where 36 percent of Queens residents owned their own homes in 1920, 45 percent did by the decade's end. Where 19 percent of Brooklynites owned homes in 1920, 26 percent did by 1930. Altogether, one out of five New Yorkers owned their own home by 1930—a rate that would not be met again until 1960.[8] Altogether, the number of owned homes in Brooklyn and Queens catapulted from roughly 130,000 in 1920 to nearly 285,000 in 1930.[9] A new urban landscape and political constituency had been created: one that was not shy in demanding additional public policies that could support their dreams of stable homeownership.

Among the most eager home seekers in New York were the city's white workers and artisans. The most radical of these groups had, in the past, supported Georgist and municipal ownership campaigns as a means toward property ownership, that old labor-republican dream. With subway expansion now an accomplished fact, however—and with radical politics at a more general low ebb in the United States following World War I—many of these workers were content to take advantage of the city's private transit lines and realty markets in order to purchase or build homes of their own.[10]

Partly these workers were motivated by financial gain, a hope to acquire a piece of rising land values. But many also saw homeownership as their only escape from the burdens of congested tenements and rapacious landlords (figure 4.2).[11] The description of one former tenement inhabitant, Thomas F. Malone, described these motivations well when speaking of southern Queens at a public meeting. "It is a section of the city," he said, "where thousands are coming down from the commonest, lowest-priced tenements of Manhattan, Bronx and Brooklyn, and all they can afford to pay is ten dollars down on their lot. They come and buy a lot of secondhand lumber and no title to the property and sticking up what you and others call a shack. But Mr. Mayor, every one of them is a home and it harbors a family and the door is open to take care of those people."[12]

But Thomas F. Malone was not just a former tenement dweller living in southern Queens—he was also a real estate developer in southern Queens and therefore had vested interests in attracting new residents to his community. For him and thousands of other builders in New York's outer boroughs, the city's subway-driven expansion was an opportunity to profit from renting and selling both commercial and residential property. And many of these builders, like many of the city's home seekers, hailed from relatively humble backgrounds. As early as 1917, the Socialist editor Abraham Cahan noted how "small tradesmen of the slums, and even working-men, were investing their savings in houses and lots. Jewish carpenters, house-painters, bricklayers, or instalment peddlers became builders of tenements or frame dwellings, real estate speculators."[13]

The inhabitants of the homes Malone built were often immigrants and the children of immigrants, with a high amount hailing from lower-middle or working-class backgrounds. In Brooklyn, 28.31 percent of foreign-born families owned homes in 1930, as compared to only 22.77 percent of native-born families, while in Queens the ratio was 47.79 percent to 43.29 percent.[14] One subdivision builder claimed to "advertise only in newspapers read largely by definite racial groups formerly concentrated in the older boroughs."[15] A cost of living survey from 1926, meanwhile, found that "policemen, firemen, letter carriers, mechanics and industrial workers have bought [houses] in Queens."[16] Commenting on the report, the *New York Times* noted that "the moderately incomed men of the educated classes of our people are not building homes of their own in large numbers as the laboring man . . . according to building statistics."[17]

The world these builders and homeowners made was fundamentally unlike the world of tenements, villages, and shtetls they had left behind (figure 4.3). It was a world of bungalows and mock Tudors, orderly subdivisions and scraggly clusters of frame houses, waves of new homes overtaking the meadows of eastern Queens and southern Brooklyn down to the bay.[18] It was

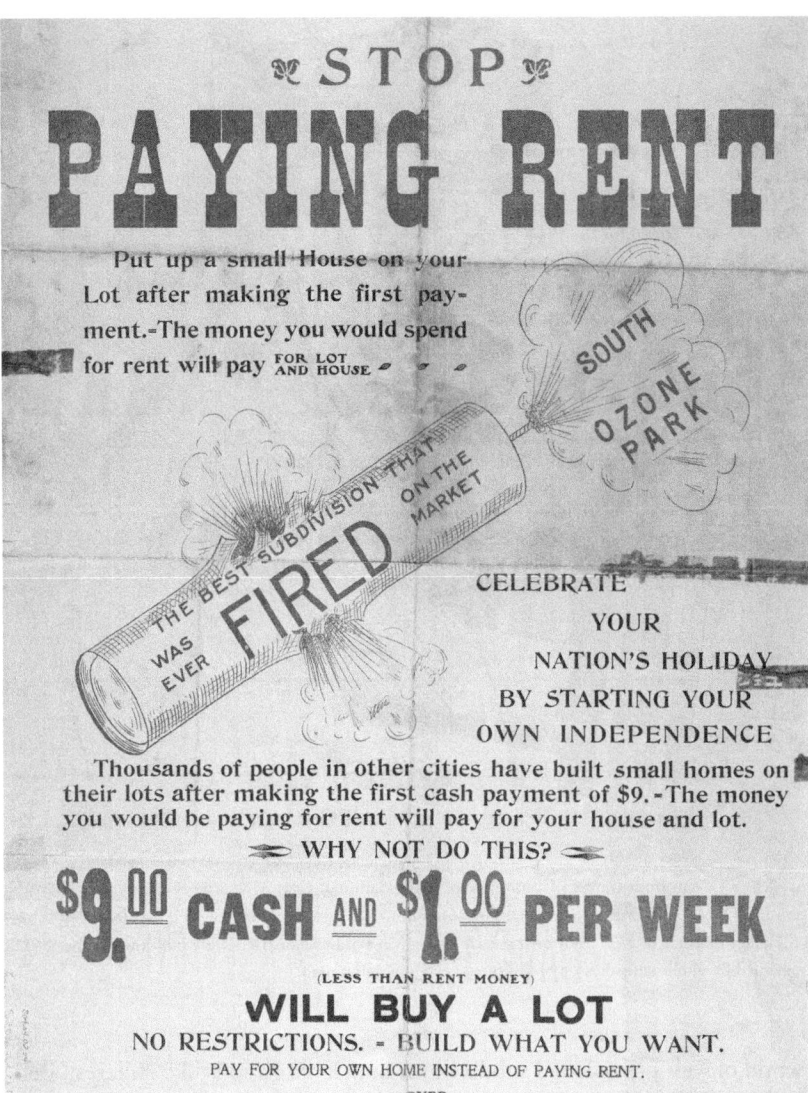

FIGURE 4.2. David P. Leahy Realty Co., "Great Sacrifice Sale of Fine Building Lots in South Ozone Park." Courtesy Maps Collection, Archives at Queens Public Library. This advertisement for building lots in southern Queens, with its imperative to "stop paying rent" and build one's own "small home," conveys how New York's tenants were encouraged to own property on the city's periphery during the early 1900s.

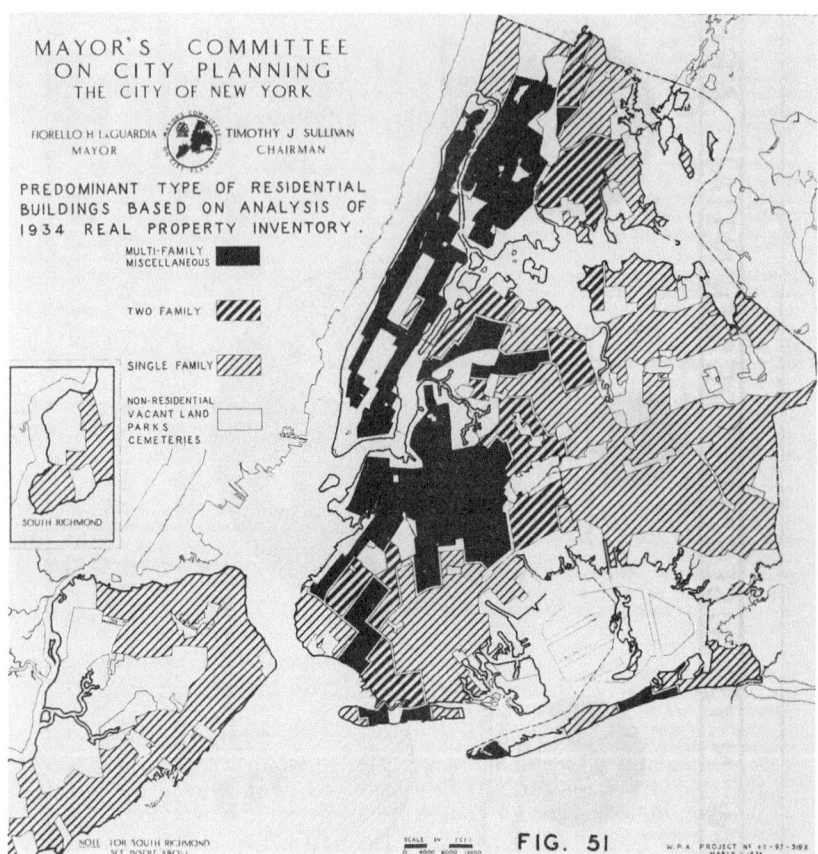

FIGURE 4.3. Map from Mayor's Committee on City Planning, *City Wide Studies* (New York: Mayor's Committee on City Planning, 1940), 1:82. This map shows the prevalence of one- and two-family housing in the outer districts of New York by the early 1930s. Most of these districts were built during the 1920s, accelerated by public subsidies on behalf of real estate development.

a world of well-provisioned subdivisions in neighborhoods like Hillcrest, Bellaire, Jamaica Estates, and Hollis in Queens; Flatbush and Manhattan Terrance in Brooklyn; and Allerton and Wakefield in the Bronx. And it was a world of barely accessible spreads of jerry-built homes in the Bronx's Clason Point, in Ozone Park and Laurelton in Queens, and in Gerritsen Beach, Bergen Beach, and Canarsie in Brooklyn.[19] For Manhattan-bound planners, such a landscape could seem tasteless and raw. But for many of their inhabitants, this landscape represented the kind of comfort and security they had long sought.

Or so they thought. In fact, many working-class homeowners found that owning property came with costs—costs that they were often ill equipped to pay. Partly these were the costs of maintaining and repairing houses, the quality of which was often sacrificed by speculative builders. Partly these were the costs of repaying mortgages, which funded nearly 60 percent of residential construction financing by the late 1920s.[20] And partly these were the costs of paying the property taxes these new homeowners were obliged to pay—and which they were not always able to. In 1926, otherwise a very good year for real estate, a total of $108 million in taxes in New York were outstanding—much of it in the outer boroughs.[21]

To pay back mortgage debts, pay off taxes, and still make a profit on their "investment," New York's small homeowners demanded additional assistance in the form of lowered tax assessments, increased public improvements, and other variations on the subsidy. And real estate investors and developers in the outer boroughs demanded additional assistance for similar reasons. These two groups, homeowners and developers, joined with other outer-borough interests like commercial associations and banks to form what I call the "developmental populist" coalition. While this coalition occasionally experienced internal tensions—particularly between tax-averse homeowners and improvement-seeking merchants—the presence of public subsidies on behalf of both groups helped smooth tensions between them in New York.[22] Together, these groups argued that subsidizing homeownership and real estate development on the city's periphery would benefit the economy and budget of New York more broadly. And policymakers, many with agendas and investments of their own in the outer boroughs, were quite convincible.

Public Assistance

New York's outer-borough homeowners, together with innumerable chambers of commerce, real estate boards, and neighborhood improvement associations, quickly organized to demand additional subsidies that could secure and raise the value of their property. And many policymakers quickly acceded, motivated by a drive to expand both their constituency and investments. But to secure these improvements on a large scale, New York's developmental populists needed to justify such expenditures as being in the *entire* city's best interest, and not simply in the interests of its component boroughs. And this they did, with gusto.

"Three people meet out there in Queens and they form an association," Mayor O'Dwyer joked in the 1940s.[23] He knew of what he spoke—there were hundreds of civic associations in Queens alone by the late 1920s, and such associations lobbied for public improvements practically as soon as they were formed. Homeowners also pressed their demands through the political clubs that followed the course of suburban settlement. By 1930, Queens possessed

108 Democratic clubs and 86 Republican clubs, while Brooklyn featured 239 Democratic clubs and 77 Republican clubs.[24] In these clubs, homeowners could be sure of finding a hearing for their pleas, often from a familiar face: many of the city's migrating homeowners maintained their original partisan affiliations, with all the ties of reciprocity and patronage that implied.[25] As the Democratic chair of the Bronx asserted in the 1940s, "The influential people in most of [the outer boroughs] had originally lived in New York County (Manhattan) and had followed the general drift to the outer counties of the city; their original political allegiance had been to the Tammany organization. We succeeded in capitalizing on this fact."[26]

But local policymakers had their own reasons to support local home-owners and home builders. Many had landed investments in the city's outer boroughs, stakes in local construction companies, or interests in other enterprises that stood to benefit from local construction. These policymakers were thus quite supportive of efforts by civic associations to steer more municipal funding toward their districts—indeed, many were instrumental in forming such associations in the first place.[27] And even those who lacked a direct financial incentive to "boost" their districts certainly had an electoral one: any policymaker who shirked the opportunity to meet the demands of well-organized property owners was in danger of being replaced on election day.[28] The end result was that "aid to property owners, though entirely just in many cases, probably exceeds in actual value the relief offered proletarians," as political scientist Roy Peel summarized in the early 1930s.[29]

Much of this aid took the form of lowered tax assessments, which local officials were generally happy to receive in exchange for a vote—the outer-borough equivalent of a Tweed-era Thanksgiving turkey handout. In 1929, Lewis Mumford asserted that New York appraised the value of new residential areas at only 50 or 60 percent of their actual value, whereas the housing economist Arthur C. Holden claimed that Queens property owners were assessed at less than 50 percent of their property's market price—far short of the 100 percent required by law.[30] In 1938, the president of New York's tax board complained that that the borough of Queens had been "under-assessed" in the 1920s because "Tammany desired to give to the 'home owning Borough' reductions where they were not warranted, so as to increase votes."[31]

These same property owners also sought expensive public improvements—paved streets, lit sidewalks, refurbished schools, and other amenities. And New York's borough presidents were able to provide such improvements through their positions on the city's chief budgetary and financial body, the Board of Estimate. By the late 1920s, a tacit policy of "borough autonomy" allowed every borough president to attain support for capital projects concerning their own jurisdiction. And these presidents could also initiate public improvements on their own, including approving street extensions, street paving and repairs, and sewer construction. This ensured a constant stream of new improvements on the city's periphery, as well as what New York governor Al Smith tactfully called "a reasonable amount of patronage."[32]

And when public improvements could not be financed through existing tax revenue, civic associations and developers insisted that the city construct them through debt. Debt for bridge construction, debt for street construction, debt for sewer construction, debt for subway construction, and debt for much more besides was insisted upon by the city's taxpaying bodies. At a single meeting of the Board of Estimate in 1924, the Benedict Taxpayer Association, the Taxpayers of Clason Point, the Clairmont Heights Property Owners Association, and the Taxpayers Civic Welfare League of the Eastern District joined forces to insist the city incur an additional $300 million in debt for the purpose of constructing new subways.[33] They were successful.

But advocates of such debt-financed improvements insisted that these projects would ultimately benefit the entire city, largely thanks to the property values they would raise. As Hylan declared, "The resources of a City are chiefly its taxable values. I set out to develop these values in the interest of the corporation which is the City of New York." This rationale was used to justify any number of public improvements. Street platting, for example: as one critic wrote in 1930, "It is common to hear most municipal tax officers speak against any attempt to restrict the pace at which raw land is being converted into building sites, on the ground that the development of new land creates new taxable values for the city."[34] But "increased property taxes" was also the cry behind other amenities, ranging from parks, schools ("will stimulate the growth of the borough beyond anything we have yet seen"), highways (would add greatly to the "real estate and tax values of a great commercial city"), and above all, the subway.[35] Perhaps the bluntest boosterism came from the city's transportation chair, who declared in 1930 that *all the city is benefited by every addition to its transit facilities.*"[36]

And since subsidizing peripheral growth benefited the city, developmental populists felt perfectly justified in placing the costs of those subsidies upon the city as a whole. Nominally it was a policy of New York to pay for local improvements through local or "special" assessments on the properties benefited by them.[37] But New York did not, for the most part, avail itself of this tool: in 1926, for example, New York received only 3 percent of its revenues from special assessments. As a later report stated, "It is not the practice in New York City . . . to meet the costs of repaving or of various services such as street cleaning, streetlighting, etc., by the special assessment method."[38] And

New York's elected officials were proud of this fact: as late as 1930, New York's comptroller wrote a tract explaining how the city's "system of city-wide and borough assessments . . . to cover the costs of local improvements" was "fair, equitable, simple and direct, and has proven to be eminently successful." The title of that tract was *Why New York City Can Never Become Bankrupt.*[39]

Center versus Periphery

Not all private property owners, however, agreed that peripheral growth was to the greater city's benefit. Many developers and investors in the city's older districts worried that subsidies on behalf of the city's outer boroughs were drawing property values and population away from their own districts. And groups who sought to develop the city's economy as a whole—most notably, the Regional Plan Association of New York (RPNY)—lamented the parochial goals and wasteful results of the city's outward growth. Such tensions over the proper location and scale of realty development threatened, at times, to break out into what the *New York Times* called a "civil war" between the boroughs.[40]

Owners of real estate in the city's older and denser districts were occasionally wary of allowing their property taxes to be used on behalf of improvements benefiting distant Queens and outer Brooklyn. Despite entreaties by their outer-borough equivalents, real estate owners and developers in Manhattan and downtown Brooklyn sometimes evinced skepticism that growth in the urban periphery would benefit their territory.[41] The city's larger realty interests, who generally had little opinion of immigrant "curbstoner" developers in the outer boroughs, were similarly resistant to citywide subsidies for Brooklyn and Queens. The mighty Real Estate Board of New York (REBNY), for example, demanded at one point that the administration "abandon the practice of placing a large part of the cost of local improvement proceedings on the boroughs and the city and say to the applicants you can have this if you will pay for it yourselves."[42]

Organizations with a "citywide" planning ambit critiqued peripheral boosters as well, accusing them of reducing not just downtown's property values but the city's values as a whole. The most detailed of these criticisms came from the RPNY, formed in 1922 with aid from the Russell Sage Foundation and featuring directors hailing from some of the city's most powerful financial institutions. Their national perspective on the sources and function of New York's economy provided them with a distinctive view of how the city should finance its growth: one that was frequently critical of outer-borough boosters.

For the outward-facing RPNY, the most appropriate geographic scale upon which to plan public improvements was not the borough or even the city, but the region. On these grounds, much of the RPNY considered the city's developmental policies to be utterly wasteful. Rather than promote the grand bridges, docks, and airports that could increase the accessibility—and hence value—of New York as a whole, the city was wasting its capital on paltry sewers servicing disheveled subdivisions. The bankers and brokers supporting the RPNY had no need for such projects and were not afraid to invoke the term *speculation* when criticizing them. "The financing of local improvements by the city," complained an RPNY research survey in 1929, "involves an increase in the borrowings of the city—and means, in too many cases, that the city is providing capital for the benefit of many who are nothing more than speculators in real estate."[43] That local policymakers were supporting such spending based on a short-term electoral timetable rather than the city's long-term interests (as the RPNY defined it) only added to the RPNY's disdain.

Not even the physical form of the city's new subdivisions passed the muster of some professional planners. "Scattered homes in scattered subdivisions," they feared, were incapable of paying for the improvements benefiting them. In 1914, the president of New York's Public Service Commission warned that "areas given over to private houses, each with its own grass plot and garden, cannot furnish a sufficient population to support a subway."[44] But not only was New York encouraging this wasteful form of housing—it was locking it in through zoning ordinances. And few politicians had the incentive to challenge them. Lawson Purdy later recounted how Hylan, confronted with the sight of homeowners protesting a proposed apartment complex in their district, exclaimed, "This zoning business is loaded!"[45] The proposal was defeated.

In Debt to Growth

For all their conflicts, however, developmental populists and their critics converged on many points during the 1920s. Growing land values across the city convinced many realtors that peripheral expansion and central-city prosperity were complementary. Grand public improvements seemed to meet the needs of regional planners, outer-borough realtors, and private bond purchasers alike. And small property owners, shielded from the cost of these improvements by low assessments, welcomed the new sewers and paved streets being built on their behalf. The result was an upsurge in municipal debt in New York and cities across the country, creating a shared investment—and dependence—upon future growth that would soon lead to disaster.

Any criticisms downtown developers might have held toward peripheral growth were mollified by the high volumes of Manhattan office and residential construction during the decade. Office space in Manhattan expanded by 30 million square feet between 1921 and 1929, and plans were laid for another 30 million square feet of construction for the following decade.[46] Indeed, some city officials and real estate owners believed that the city's upward and outward growth complemented each other. On the one hand, outer-borough subways made New York more attractive to potential home-seeking employees.[47] On the other hand, the outflow of downtown workers into the outer-boroughs districts expedited the conversion of their districts into "higher and better" uses like expensive residences and skyscrapers. Thus, housing reformer Arthur C. Holden argued that downtown realty's support for outer-borough improvements was "not done with the high-minded purpose of helping the newer districts" but "because 'business' and the older sections like to see the city grow."[48]

The perceived need for additional public improvements also united interests in the core and periphery of the city. While the RPNY shied away from endorsing many of the city's projects, they nonetheless saw virtue in some debt-financed initiatives. As one of the RPNY's reports announced, "Projects based on a bold vision and requiring large expenditures of capital may be sounder from an economic point of view than those that are easier and cheaper to carry out."[49] The RPNY thus joined with smaller realty firms in lobbying for debt-financed projects—debt-financed bridges linking Manhattan to New Jersey, 630 miles of debt-financed water and sewage infrastructure, and numerous other works.[50]

The ability of New York to pay back such debt, of course, depended on the continuation of its growth—but this was not in doubt to most sober urban planners. George McAneny, architect of the Dual Contracts and then-president of the RPNY, declared in 1928 that "when I speak of expansion, I have in mind, as I am sure you must, the fact that our present rate of growth is not likely to slacken."[51] And underpinning this faith was that New York's land values, which had grown ever higher for more than seventy years, had not yet reached their peak. As the vice president of one prominent realty firm declared in 1929, "New York can never be overbuilt, which means it can never be overproduced in a permanent way. . . . As a particular piece of real estate lies in the line of population growth, whether residential, business or industrial, it is inevitable that its value must be enhanced."[52]

Thus, a variety of New Yorkers, confident in real estate's growth and certain that public improvements would expedite that growth, pressed their cities for debt-fueled spending on behalf of realty growth during the 1920s. And they were largely successful (figure 4.4). New York's total funded debt grew from $1.21 billion in 1918 to more than $1.968 billion in 1930—and this

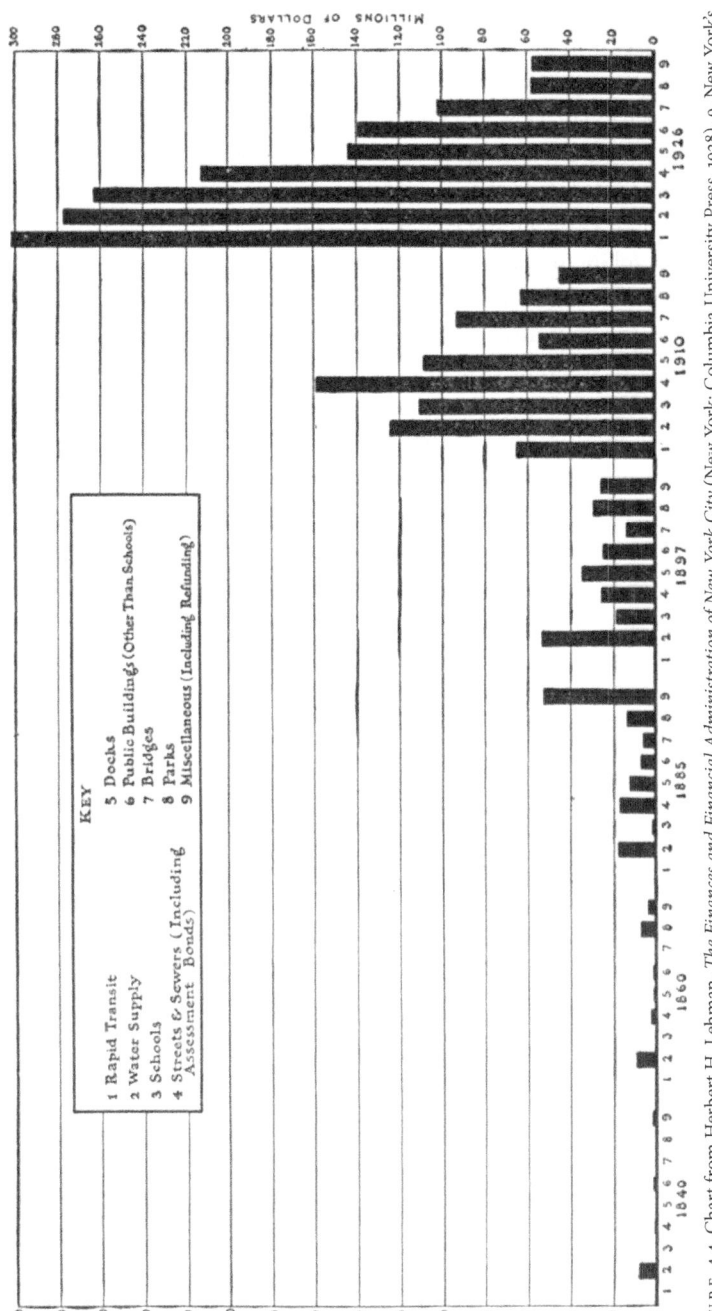

FIGURE 4.4. Chart from Herbert H. Lehman, *The Finances and Financial Administration of New York City* (New York: Columbia University Press, 1928), 9. New York's total funded debt grew from $1.21 billion in 1918 to more than $1.968 billion in 1930. Such debt was largely on behalf of improvements intended to raise real estate values in the city's core and periphery. These improvements represented "sunk costs" that would burden the metropolis for many decades afterwards.

number would increase by nearly an additional half a billion over the next six years. Interest and redemption payments on this debt grew as well, from $64 million per year in 1922 to $143 million per year by 1930. Overall, debt service and interest comprised roughly a third of each year's budget. Interest alone comprised 16 percent of New York's budget in 1929 when capital spending made up 22 percent of the city's budget.[53] And New York was not alone: per capita municipal debt grew from $71.32 in 1922 to $269.70 in 1933 in cities across the United States, and yearly interest payments on that debt grew from $129 million in 1915 to $366 million in 1929—at which point it would climb even higher.[54]

Such debts made on behalf of future growth, however, made these cities further dependent on future growth to repay them. For now growth was not simply a matter of attaining benefits but of avoiding default and bankruptcy. New York was thus "locked in" to financing infrastructure on behalf of massive theoretical cities: New York's water supply expansion project assumed a future urban population of 9,700,000 in 1950, while the city's sewage expansion system assumed an urban population of nearly 12 million by 1960.[55] These futures would not come true: New York's population would be less than 8 million in 1950 and would still be less than 8 million by 1960. But the city's debt on this future growth would remain, constraining the city's fiscal options well into the future.

But this debt—and specifically, New York's way of paying for this debt—was creating another kind of "sunk cost" for New York. For by sparing white property owners the costs of financing projects on their behalf, and placing this burden upon working-class and Black tenants, New York reinforced the fiscal privileges of white property owners in ways that would make reforming New York's development strategies far more difficult than in the past.

Assessing Whiteness

Growing debt for public improvements, low assessments for new homes, and citywide financing for local projects: all represented, in part, the faith many developmental populists held in New York's future growth. But they also represented a desire to support white homeowners, regardless of or even *despite* the fiscal costs of these subsidies. While this further narrowed the fiscal imagination of many New York policymakers, it also reinforced a racist fiscal geography whereby working-class and Black tenants were made to pay for policies on behalf of white homeowners. These homeowners, however, were generally unwilling to see such subsidies as costs upon the greater city and proudly claimed the title of "taxpayer" that policymakers flattered them with. Such a title obscured the fiscal privileges they enjoyed and the fiscal burdens they imposed on the city. And when later reformers attempted to lift these burdens by curbing realty subsidies, this vast population of new homeowners would be among their fiercest and most influential foes.

The white homeowner had long been valorized in American political rhetoric, and this tradition continued in New York—both despite and because of the relative paucity of homeowners in the metropolis. For labor republicans the home was a locus of civic virtue, for conservative republicans it was a politically moderating device, and for Georgists it was a means of evading the specter of rent.[56] Such valorization continued well into the 1920s: Mayor John Hylan hailed a state law exempting new residential structures from taxation on the grounds that it would "swell the ranks of the small home owners of whom there can never be too many in a growing city."[57] And this was in addition to the nearly ubiquitous "Own Your Own Home" campaign of the time, promoted by both the National Association of Real Estate Brokers and federal agencies like the Department of Commerce.[58]

With this degree of support behind it, public subsidies—even "wasteful" ones—were seen by a broad swath of New Yorkers as being justified if they to an expansion of homeownership. The Citizens Union, a fiscal watchdog group that complained of wasteful subsidies toward the outer boroughs, nonetheless agreed that aid to homeowners was warranted. "People are more important than buildings and homes are more important than skyscrapers," a representative from the union stated. "Small homeowners in Brooklyn and the other boroughs should not be denied essential improvements because they cannot pay on such a scale as the great enterprises in Manhattan which they help to maintain."[59] And at a 1923 hearing over whether the city's tax-exemption measure should be overturned, the New York Times uncritically reported on how "thousands of men and women in moderate circumstances—firemen, policeman, city employees, clerks and mechanics"—declared that canceling the exemption would mean "ruin and loss of their homes, in which many of them have invested their life savings."[60] The exemption was maintained.

Such sympathy, however, was generally not expressed for those who would need to take up the fiscal slack opened up by outer-borough tax exemptions: the city's working-class and Black tenants. Tax exemptions and low assessments on white homes placed greater fiscal burdens on districts spared such benefits, particularly the city's older and poorer districts.[61] Arthur C. Holden claimed that while Queens homes were typically assessed at less than 50 percent of market price, Manhattan properties were assessed at up to 40 percent *in excess* of market price.[62] And tenements in poor districts were assessed at even higher rates: a later study found that "the properties of higher value . . . tend to be assessed at a lower level of sale price than the properties of lesser value."[63]

The result was growing tax burdens on landlords in working-class districts—which translated into reduced maintenance and higher rents for their working-class tenants. As the New York State Communist Party later complained, "Tenement propert[ies] in crowded sections of the city" were "assessed at a very high value" with "a disproportionate tax burden . . . put on the slum-dwellers."[64] But with the city's peripheral districts refusing to pay their fair share of taxes, New York's government continued to fiscally press on the city's poorest neighborhoods. As housing reformer Charles Abrams later wrote, "Against the social welfare of its inhabitants, the city [is] compelled to weigh the tax-income that flowed from large areas of slums."[65]

And if central-city landlords were unable to squeeze enough rent from their tenants to pay off discriminatory assessments on behalf of the outer boroughs, many were willing to replace those tenants—and their tenements—with a wealthier clientele living in denser, taller (i.e., "congested"), and more profitable structures. As Arthur C. Holden complained, New York was "beset by two extremes of policy. In the center they encourage and insist upon congestion as a necessity for tax purposes in order that land on the outskirts may be developed more rapidly than would be possible were they required to pay their own way."[66] Manhattan's vertical growth—one might even call it "gentrification"—was thus both a result and an accelerator of the city's outer-borough growth (see figure 4.5). But the congestion and displacement wrought by this central-city development only increased demand for more "spacious" development on the urban outskirts—thus repeating the vicious cycle.

And if tenants in general were being plundered for the sake of white homeowners, Black tenants were especially so. As early as 1918, Mayor Hylan received a letter asking whether "the same basis of appraisal of property be used in colored sections as in other sections of the city."[67] It would not—in 1930, a landlord complained that many buildings in Harlem were "assessed at more than double than the city said they were worth thirteen years ago" in "spite of the fact that nothing more than ordinary improvements have been made by landlords."[68] And when Harlem landlords hiked rents and delayed repairs as a result of these high assessments, their Black tenants were the ones who suffered. During one public hearing in the mid-1930s, a member of the Consolidated Tenants League complained that "the landlord tells you that the property depreciates when Negros take possession. Then taxes should go down if the property depreciates and rents still go up higher. Have you any judgement whether the city in assessing property is putting too great a burden on the landlord?" The municipal official glumly responded that "in some instances the assessments are . . . higher and not fair."[69]

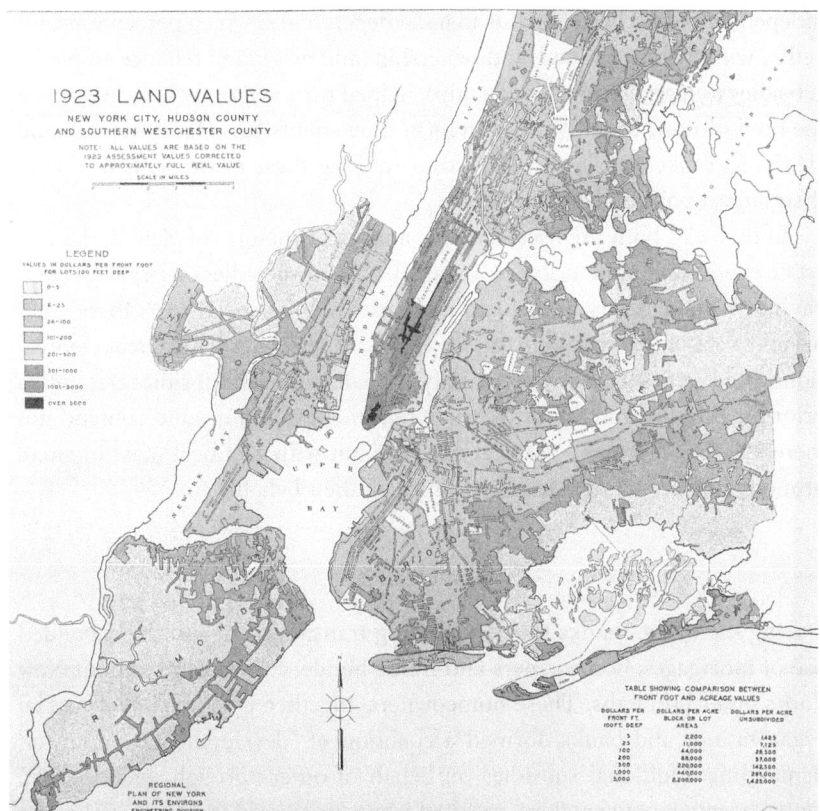

FIGURE 4.5. Image from Harold M. Lewis, Wayne Heydecker, and Raymond A. O'Hara, *Land Values: Distribution within New York Region and Relation to Various Factors in Urban Growth* (New York: Regional Plan of New York and Its Environs, 1927), 31. During the 1920s, New York subsidized growth on the city's periphery—which contained largely low land values—through taxes drawn from the city's older areas possessing higher land values. These high taxes (and the broader hope that central-city property was increasing in value) encouraged landlords in the central-city to build denser and taller buildings. This further increased land values and rent burdens on central-city tenants, leading those who could move to the city's periphery, spurring further development there and repeating the fiscal cycle.

This plunder of Black tenants on behalf of white property owners, however, was obscured by the city's fiscal structure. The tax revenue raised by central-city tenants paying their share of their overassessed landlord's property taxes did not appear on any tax bill or municipal budget. Rather, white homeowners were considered, and considered *themselves*, the city's sole "taxpayers"—not the city's Black tenants who helped pay for their improvements.[70] And because only 6 percent of Black New Yorkers owned their own homes, due to both discrimination and lack of capital, many whites could make the slippage that white property owners had a special claim to fiscal independence and Black tenants to fiscal dependence.[71] Such perceptions, together with their newfound landownership (and newfound reliance on public subsidies to maintain that ownership), helped turn white workers away from the kind of transformative fiscal reform movements that Henry George and Hearst had taken up in the past—thus robbing these movements of one of their largest political constituencies.

In this way, both the fiscal strategy and fiscal rhetoric of New York's real estate expansion in the 1920s—growing debts and subsidies on behalf of "taxpaying" white citizens—deepened and obscured the social costs these "taxpayers" were unloading upon the city. Only at the height of the Great Depression would critics have an opportunity to challenge such subsidies But unlike prior fiscal radicals in the 1870s, these reformers would need to contend not merely with a disgraced political machine but with a critical mass of small property owners—and federal assistance on their behalf.

Conclusion

During the 1920s, thanks to an expanding transit system and the expanded use of mortgages, homeowners and home builders spread throughout New York's outer boroughs. These homeowners, together with local commercial organizations and banks, formed a coalition of "developmental populists" demanding additional subsidies on behalf of outer-borough development. Outer-borough policymakers, many of whom possessed their own real estate investments, swiftly acceded to their demands for lowered tax assessments, additional municipal services, and debt-financed public improvements.

The result was a massive growth in municipal spending secured through an unstated but active process of plunder: of tenants by homeowners, of older boroughs by newer boroughs, of Black by white. Dependent on future growth to pay back current debts, unwilling to combat or even perceive the social costs that new realty development was foisting upon local budgets, by the late 1920s, New York's finances were as fragile as its fiscal imaginary was narrow.

This could not and would not be sustained. During the early 1930s, New York's finances collapsed, both despite and because of the millions of dollars the city had poured into speculative real estate the previous decade. And just as the city's crisis in the 1870s led to a subsequent fiscal reckoning, so Depression-era New York would witness another movement to reform the city's pre-crash developmental policies. Whether this movement could dislodge the fiscal expectations that had been established during the 1920s, however, was far from certain.

5

"Private Gains at Public Cost Cannot Be Tolerated"

"One-third of the budget of the city of New York would be saved if New York had been built for the accommodation of its people instead of having been built for the accommodation of landlords and bankers."[1] Baruch Charney Vladeck—Socialist manager of the *Jewish Daily Forward*, former City Council member, and soon-to-be member of the New York City Housing Authority (NYCHA), spoke these words in 1934. His argument was threefold. Sanitary public housing could help city hall relieve itself of the "social costs," such as crime and poor health, that tenements and their banker-owners were foisting upon public budgets. New construction would furnish revenue to local businesses. And lower rents would mean more spendable income in the hands of working-class people. All this made public housing not merely a moral prerogative but an economic "investment" that would redound to the city's prosperity.[2]

But if public housing was an investment, Vladeck and other members of the NYCHA warned, promoting housing for "landlords and bankers" was a waste. First, demand for upper-income housing was utterly saturated—any further construction on their behalf would transfer rather than create new realty values. And second, promoting such construction would only fuel further real estate speculation in the city—speculation that had already led the metropolis into fiscal crisis and was still burdening it with debt, useless infrastructure, and vacant subdivisions. Only by *restricting* and not subsidizing such elite speculation, Vladeck argued, could New York recover from its fiscal crisis. And only by building for its working people could New York recover from the Depression.

This chapter traces how a diverse group of housing advocates like Vladeck, social critics, and urban planners attempted to transform New York's approach toward economic development during the city's fiscal crises of the 1930s. Gotham's finances would be restored, figures like Lewis Mumford and Rexford Tugwell argued, not by subsidizing realty speculation on behalf of perpetual expansion but by meeting the existing needs of the city's residents with the city's existing resources.[3] Taking advantage of the policy space opened by the shock of the Great Depression and Fiorello La Guardia's reform administration, this group—whom I call "fiscal stabilizers"—were able to translate many of their ideas into policies ranging from robust city planning measures to public housing initiatives. Nonetheless, these planners lacked both the mass constituency that fiscal radicals of the past such as Henry George had enjoyed and a vision for what new forms of job-creating enterprises the city should cultivate. Both these weaknesses would undermine the position of fiscal stabilizers once additional actors started to come to the aid of local speculators—such as the federal government.

By exploring the local economic reform movements of the 1930s, this chapter provides a new context for one of the decade's boldest policies: public housing. While scholars have generally viewed public housing as motivated by social rather than economic ends, we cannot understand the breakthrough of public housing during the 1930s without understanding its fiscal context and rationales.[4] Redundant office towers, unneeded apartments, and sprawling subdivisions: all these, many local finance officers believed, were wrecking urban finances. Low-income housing, by contrast, promised to reduce social costs, serve existing demand, and—through the device of the public authority—pay back their costs. Amid the more general wreckage of the private realty market, such fiscal rationales were a key factor behind the growth public housing and other "decommodified" public services in 1930s New York, paralleling how "productivist" concerns helped drive the establishment of social-democratic welfare states in Britain and Scandinavia around the same time.[5]

Nonetheless, these "fiscal stabilizers" were less interested in fully reconstructing New York's economy than earlier radicals such as Henry George. Based largely in the housing and planning professions, they lacked both the large constituency and interest in economic production that earlier fiscal reform movements possessed. And holding little sympathy for the city's *existing* economy or land uses, these planners rarely considered which *forms* of commerce were most beneficial to the metropolis. Such sins of omission and commission would come to weigh heavily on the city's economy by the time of New York's next fiscal crisis.

"Growth Penalizes Itself"

The present economic scheme of the big city depends upon the expectation of a stable income from an investment, public and private, that becomes ever more speculative, unstable, and insecure. The growth of such a city means an increase of insecurity: to ensure such growth, to subsidize it, to attempt to freeze this obsolete structure in the effort to maintain the financial values that have been attached to it is to exhibit an ungovernable antagonism to prudence and good sense.

                              LEWIS MUMFORD[6]

"Fiscal stabilization" as a goal of local economic reform during the Depression had its immediate roots in the work of the Regional Planning Association of America (RPAA), formed in 1923 by a small but influential coterie of heterodox architects, housing advocates, and urban planners. The members of this group, including such luminaries as Lewis Mumford, Clarence S. Stein, and Catherine Bauer, drew their beliefs from fields as diverse as ecology, Georgism, Deweyan pragmatism, and Socialist political economy. Uniting the RPAA members, however, was a strong conviction that rapid urban growth was neither sustainable nor desirable—a belief stemming less from an ingrained "anti-urbanism" than from anger at the subsidized speculation they saw as driving that growth.[7] While their articles and scattered policy initiatives had little influence in the 1920s, their prescient sallies against overheated realty growth—and hopes for a more socially just and ecologically balanced economy—would receive a more receptive hearing during the Great Depression.[8]

The problem with urban finances, RPAA members argued, was not that urban growth wasn't regulated: it was that urban growth was expected. The problem began with the shared interests of financial actors and public bodies in raising the value of land. All through the 1920s, insurance companies and savings banks had accelerated their realty loans and purchases.[9] Where bank-backed mortgages generally constituted less than half of construction funding in the pre–World War I years, by 1926 they supplied nearly two-thirds of such financing.[10] To recoup such investments, these firms encouraged local governments to promote debt-financed improvements that would service their new construction. And local governments, dependent on property values for revenue and banks for loans (and informed by the fiscal theories of tax officials like Lawson Purdy, we recall), were more than happy to oblige.

But such municipally backed growth, the RPAA members believed, was self-defeating. The more cities grew, the more expensive land became and the more other costs accelerated: the cost of transit, the cost of housing, the cost of business, and the costs of public services more generally. A 1923 study by New York's Commission on Housing and Regional Planning found that the doubling of urban populations increased per capita fiscal burdens by 13 percent.[11] A study by the RPNY found that traffic congestion alone was costing the city $500,000 a day.[12] To alleviate such congestion, cities were forced to spend additional debt and interest on new infrastructure projects—further increasing the land values that were driving congestion in the first place (figure 5.1). For most liberal policymakers, of course, this was not a problem: the revenues raised by growth would be sufficient to pay for the public services needed to address the physical and social "externalities" of growth. But the RPAA members were not so sure. As Lewis Mumford later wrote, "[One] may say definitely that beyond a certain point, which varies with regional conditions and culture, urban growth penalizes itself. Too large a part of the capital outlays and annual income of the city must be spent in devices for increasing congestion and mechanically relieving its worst results."[13]

But if cities could not afford to continue growing, neither could they afford to cease it. Too many actors—banks and their depositors, landowners, municipal governments—possessed what Frederick Ackerman called a "stake in congestion": that is, a stake in growing land values and in order to pay back the debt and interest they had incurred.[14] These groups now pursued growth not only to secure benefits, but to avoid catastrophe. And to cease expenditures on behalf of land-value growth, or to question whether further growth was inevitable or even desirable, was to invite such a catastrophe. And so developers continued to boost, and cities continued to spend.[15]

But cities, the RPAA believed, were destined to lose this gamble. Demand for urban space would saturate. Population growth would plateau. Rising land values would repel new enterprises. Advances in transit and communication would undercut urban land's monopoly value as a site for production and consumption.[16] And all this would mean that urban land values *themselves* would eventually level off, spelling disaster for the urban financiers, enterprises, and governments that had gambled on their indefinite expansion. Already, the trajectory of urban land-value growth was slowing; while urban mortgage debt grew by 208 percent between 1922 and 1929, the total value of urban real estate over that same period rose only 14 percent.[17] And without such values increasing, private and public actors alike would be unable to pay back the enormous debts they had accrued. Ackerman stated the matter starkly: "We are not likely to avoid the collapse that will follow the deflation of values when our cities reach the saturation point and stability succeeds the fever of expansion."[18]

There was, however, an alternative. If communities could avoid the trap of growth, if they could see maturity as a goal rather than a threat, than an entire

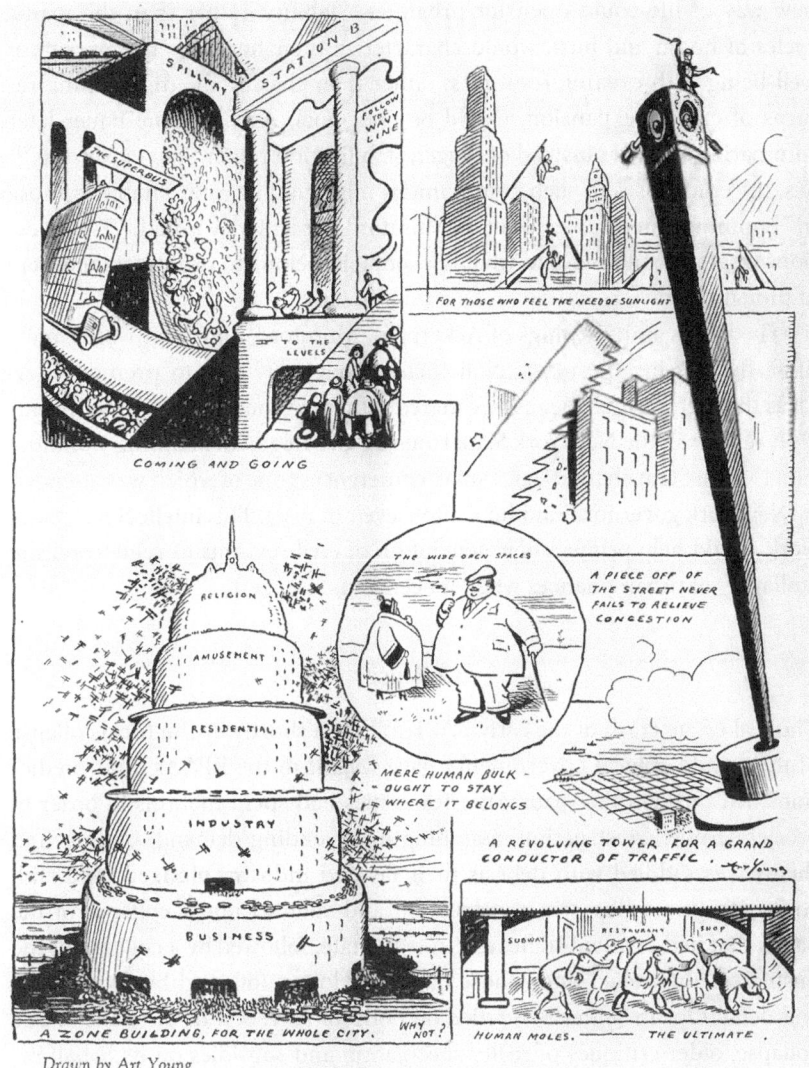

FIGURE 5.1. Art Young, "Boost the Big City!," *Survey Graphic* 54 (May 1, 1925), 142. The Regional Planning Association of America's vision of the big city's future, featured in a special "regional planning" issue of the reform journal *Survey Graphic*. Real estate speculation at the urban core was creating more and more congestion while real estate speculation at the urban periphery was requiring more and more debt-financed infrastructure to service. All this, RPAA members believed, was making for an unlivable—and economically unsustainable—metropolis.

new way of life could open for urbanites. Stability, rather than the manic cycles of boom and bust, would characterize their finances. The pursuit of well-being with existing resources, rather than chasing the diminishing returns of endless expansion, would be their goal. As Catherine Bauer later summarized, "Better instead of Bigger, stabilization rather than expansion."[19] Yes, the enterprises in such communities might not be as profitable as those in "booming" metropoles—but as Mumford perceptively noted, "The questions what is 'economic' and what is 'profitable' belong to two different orders of thought."[20]

The hopes and warnings of Ackerman, Mumford, and Stein were largely unheeded during the 1920s. Nonetheless, they were able to promote their ideas through various means—scattered articles in the *Survey Graphic* magazine, reports in the New York State Housing and Regional Planning Commission (which Stein chaired), and small conferences (one of which was attended by New York governor Franklin D. Roosevelt in 1931). This intellectual spadework would help prime a new generation of civil servants to reinterpret the "collapse" of urban finances when it occurred.

Collapse

The real estate crash of the early 1930s, followed shortly by the fiscal collapse of thousands of local governments, gave weight to the RPAA's dour predictions. All through the 1920s American cities had spent millions in order to accelerate new construction, assuming never-ending demand, only to find themselves saddled with debt as their favored industry plunged off a cliff. And with this collapse in construction and values came a collapse of the banks that had invested so heavily in real estate, followed by a collapse of the businesses that relied upon those banks for loans, followed by fiscal strain and default for the cities that relied on both for solvency. In the wake of this collapse, older critiques of realty speculation and subsidies on its behalf received a renewed hearing.

"Perhaps never before in the history of the nation," lamented Detroit mayor Frank Murphy in 1933, "has the problem of the cities been as distressing as at present."[21] The early 1930s were anni horribilis for America's real estate industry. Nonfarm residential construction fell 90 percent between 1926 and 1933. Chicago's land values fell by 50 percent between 1928 and 1932, while those of Manhattan fell by 75 percent.[22] And nowhere was this collapse more visible than in New York. All through Manhattan were new, gleaming, and vacant structures ranging from quarter-empty residential towers to half-finished office buildings. A full 30 percent of the city's offices were vacant in 1933: "There is not a skyscraper in the city of New York that won't be foreclosed this year," lamented the head of the United Real Estate Owners Association.[23] On the city's periphery were 148,000 vacant lots, 148,000 barren yards facing streets "improved" at municipal expense for nonexistent residents. In between was what writer James Agee called a "hopeless desolation" of "criminally-made row houses in the middle of nowhere," vast stretches of foreclosed mock Tudors, and other evidence of a boom gone bust.[24]

This collapse was both consequence and cause of the broader Depression: as the economist A. M. Hillhouse wrote, "The collapse of real estate values is itself an integral part of the depression and cannot therefore be discussed separately."[25] Widely overestimating demand for their structures, realtors in the late 1920s found themselves with unwanted property and unable to pay back their creditors. In 1934, half of the Lower East Side's property was in debt to some $2.50 per square foot, even as their "real" value was worth barely $1 per foot.[26] The result was mass default and a cascade of financial failure: fifty title companies with outstanding mortgage guarantees of over $2.5 billion defaulted in New York alone during the early 1930s.[27] And the ripples from such shocks soon enveloped the commanding heights of America's financial economy. As the economist Herbert Simpson declared in 1933, it was "real estate, real estate securities, and real estate affiliations in some form have been the largest single factor in the failure of the 4,800 banks that have closed their doors during the past three years . . . it becomes increasingly apparent that our banking collapse during the present depression has been largely a real estate collapse."[28] And with this banking collapse came the loss of thousands of businesses that relied on them for loans—and with business collapse came unemployment.

Collapsing realty values thus endangered local finances in several ways: it eviscerated tax revenue, increased demands for social services due to growing unemployment, and gave little room for liquidity-challenged creditors to bridge the fiscal gaps through loans.[29] The result was municipal austerity across the nation. Real spending by large American cities fell by 15 percent on average between 1931 and 1934, and sixteen slashed their budgets by more than 30 percent.[30] And how deeply a city cut was in proportion to how deeply in debt they were: for every additional 10 percent an American city was in debt in 1929, it generally cut an additional 1.3 to 2.3 percent on protective services, health services, and sanitation on behalf of its citizens.[31] The city's most vulnerable were thus made to suffer for the debt made earlier on behalf of the city's property owners. And for cities unable to cut costs sufficiently, there was only one other option in the early 1930s: default. Nearly 12 percent of all cities with more than thirty thousand inhabitants defaulted during the early 1930s—310 communities in all—in addition to 16,056 smaller localities.[32]

The net result of these cuts and defaults was a vast increase in human misery—less municipal soup kitchens for the poor, less public works projects for the unemployed, and less public services for all who relied on local governments in any way.[33] Such was the bitter fruit of subsidized speculation: as the economist A. M. Hillhouse declared in 1936, "Municipal credit in aid of real estate speculation and overdevelopment" was a "veritable master key to an understanding of the financial collapse of hundreds of areas in the early 1930s."[34]

The Tragedy of Waste

Once again, local aid on behalf of real estate had contributed to a wave of local fiscal crises—and once again, a new generation of fiscal radicals insisted that cities rethink their canons of economic development to avoid such catastrophes in the future. Spearheading this critique were RPAA members who had evinced discomfort with overheated urban growth even during the boom years of the 1920s and who now seized America's urban crisis as an opportunity to place local finances on a more resilient, less speculative basis.[35] In the words of Clarence Stein, "If land subdividers and speculative real estate developers will not put an end to their obsolete methods . . . the municipalities must do so in self-defense."[36] Joining them was a new generation of economist-planners, awake to the waste that heedless growth generated and well embedded within Franklin Roosevelt's administration. And perhaps most importantly, America's municipal finance officers and bondholders—shocked by the scale and speed of realty's collapse—were for a moment willing to countenance curbs on local growth in the name of stability.

It is famously difficult, of course, to characterize the New Deal as embodying any one political or economic philosophy. RPAA Lewis Mumford and Keynesian economist Alvin Hansen—political opposites in many ways—perceived confusion if not contradiction among the goals pursued by Franklin Roosevelt.[37] But if promoting and subsidizing private growth was one tendency of the New Deal, as we shall see, another strain—particularly in its early years—was an attentiveness to the risks of overheated growth. When presidential candidate Franklin Roosevelt declared in 1932 that the nation's task was no longer of "producing more goods" but of " administering resources and plants already in hand . . . of adjusting production to consumption, of distributing wealth and products more equitably," he was reflecting a current of thought that was shared by many during the dark days of the early Depression. It was a current that would be translated into some of the New Deal's most prominent policies. And it was a current which would be manifested in

fiscal reform movements in cities across the country—including and especially New York.[38]

The "conservation strain" of the New Deal was grounded partly in Roosevelt's policy background and partly in new strains of economic thinking
within his "Brain Trust." Imbibing the "sustainable yield" ethos of Gifford
Pinchot and recognizing the threat that overextraction could place on the
state's natural resources, Roosevelt had passed robust reforestation and soil
conservation policies as governor of New York. As president, he continued
to promote conservation as both an environmental and economic measure
through initiatives such as the Civilian Conservation Corps and the Soil Ero-
sion Service.[39] At the same time, "Brain Trust" economists like Adolf Berle
and Rexford Tugwell argued that heedless overproduction was threatening the nation's economy and that in a "mature" economy, restrictions on
production—enforced by the state planners if necessary—were necessary to
compensate for imbalances.[40] And such restrictions were indeed carried out
in the early New Deal by agencies such as the National Resource Administration and the Agriculture Adjustment Administration.[41] Tellingly, nearly all
the major RPAA members featured in one or more of these initiatives.

Such efforts to place restrictions on growth, to be sure, were usually
couched in terms of achieving "efficiency" and avoiding "waste" rather than
the more agonistic terms of Henry George. The goal was not to expropriate the landlord and speculator but to plan and regulate growth in order to
achieve long-term prosperity: a goal befitting the "professional" background
of many of these fiscal stabilizers in planning and economics. Nonetheless,
the assumptions underlying these efforts were in some ways even more radical than George's had been: for where George had ultimately sought to promote productivity and economic growth through his policies, by the 1930s,
some Depression-era policymakers doubted that rapid private sector growth
was *even possible* in a "mature economy." The National Resource Planning
Committee, composed partly of veteran urban planners, insisted that America reexamine its "expectation of continuous and unlimited growth."[42] Alvin
Hansen, the "American Keynes," asserted that slowing population growth and
a slowdown of technological innovation would permanently stagnate private
sector growth rates in America. While these commentators might have dis-
agreed over whether the public sector could or should revive that sector, as
we shall see, they nonetheless reflected a broader concern with unwarranted
growth conveyed in everything from economist Stuart Chase's bestseller *The
Tragedy of Waste* to ecologist Paul Sears's searing treatment of rural overhar-
vesting, *Deserts on the March*.[43]

FIGURE 5.2. Nelson Lee, "Housing Harmful or Beneficial?," *Land Usage*, September 1935, 2. An image featured in a magazine edited by Arthur C. Holden in the mid-1930s. As the city government (as embodied by Father Knickerbocker) expands into the city's periphery, it is burdened by the expensive subways, sewers, highways, and public utility costs it must provide for these districts. Holden and many other housing advocates would later urge Father Knickerbocker to direct these services and funds toward the city's older districts in the interest of both efficiency and social justice.

This broader attentiveness to the "tragedy of waste" provided the context for more local revolts against unrestricted growth during the early 1930s—spearheaded by the same municipal finance officers and commercial organizations who had supported the industry prior to the crash (figure 5.2). While these groups would still promote *individual* realty developments during the 1930s, as we shall see, they were more than willing to blame the industry in more general terms for their cities' fiscal strains—at least in the early years of the Depression. Officials at the National Municipal Finance Conference declared in 1933 that "real estate subdividers and their bankers who indulged in land speculation during the pre-depression period are ... largely responsible" for the "the alarming increase in public debts" of their time.[44] Private organizations like the New York Chamber of Commerce and new "fiscal watchdog" groups like the Citizens Budget Commission, while sparing the realty speculator, nonetheless blamed local governments for improvidently subsidizing improvements on their behalf.[45] And at least some of these groups admitted their own culpability in promoting such debt: a New York State finance commission complained in 1936 that the "misuse of municipal credit" to service land developers had been "the source of unbearable tax delinquencies for both communities and ultimately households."[46]

Real estate developers and their lenders, too, were (temporarily) prepared to accept a period of stability rather than growth. Empty skyscrapers and vacant subdivisions pointed to an excess of demand; as the president of the Central Savings Bank declared at a meeting of the National Security Trades Association in 1939, "There was no more need for the Empire State building in this city than one and one-half World's Fairs at the present time."[47] The first vice president of the Emigrant Savings Bank, in a *New York Times* article declaring an "ERA OF STABILITY FOR REALTY SEEN: Speculative Booms Probably Never Will Occur Here Again," concurred. Greater reticence on the part of lenders to promote construction, he stated, would "stabilize real estate values," thus creating a market with "less dazzling peaks in the real estate market, but also fewer valleys of desolation."[48] And a 1931 article in the *Harvard Business Review* made the connection between local overproduction and national production especially clear. "Lenders, meaning the large life-insurance companies, savings banks, etc.," William Wheelock wrote, "have come to the conclusion that there is overproduction of space, as there has been of every other commodity, and they scrutinize with unusual care the proposals which come to them to invest in new enterprises." Altogether, then, "there is no likelihood of any considerable amount of new construction taking place in our cities; in fact, *it must be discouraged.*"[49]

And if realty lenders were counting the costs of growth, so too was an even more important group as far as local finance officials were concerned—municipal bond purchasers.[50] During the 1920s, banks and other bond buyers had eagerly promoted New York's debt accumulation: as economist Lindsay Rogers later recounted, "So long as New York City's obligations could be sold, the bankers were not greatly concerned over whether the city was living beyond its means."[51] Once banks were facing fiscal jeopardy themselves, however, they became more cautious in promoting municipal debt—particularly on behalf of real estate. Frederick Bird, the director of financial research firm Dun & Bradstreet, complained that during the 1920s, "municipal credit became the bolstering ally of high-pressure real estate promotion. Municipal bonds carried the load for many a shoestring subdivider; realtors ran many local governments, in fact, sometimes were local governments."[52] Creditors, he argued, could no longer allow cities like New York to go without a financial strategy broader than supporting the "shoestring subdivider."[53]

Just as in the 1870s, then, New York's Depression-era fiscal crisis led to calls for curbing municipal aid on behalf of realty growth from a variety of public and private actors. And like that earlier period, a "reform" administration—in particular, that of Mayor Fiorello La Guardia—would be the political vehicles to implement these curbs. But whether these policies would place the entire city's economy on new footing, as fiscal radicals like Henry George insisted in the wake of the earlier crisis, depended on the will and influence of the planning and housing professionals who would carry them out. And for a time, such professionals were willing to go quite far.

A Place of Stability

New York's experiment in fiscal stabilization began in 1933, when the city's creditors and many of its larger commercial bodies insisted that metropolis develop a public planning body to regulate its future growth. The result was the City Planning Commission (CPC), formed in 1938 and headed by economist and "Brain Truster" Rexford Tugwell. Under his direction, the CPC would pursue a new paradigm of planning for the city: one not devoted to continual growth as promoted by private boosters but to stability in the name of the public good. As the CPC's inaugural report declared, "Private gains at public cost cannot be tolerated."[54] Established at a time when "planning" was enjoying a vogue it had never enjoyed before, the CPC seemed to herald a new paradigm of development for the city.

In 1933, New York submitted to requirements by its largest bondholders for additional credit in exchange for budget and capital spending cuts.[55] The bankers paired calls for retrenchment, however, with an insistence that the city establish a new capital spending strategy based on long-range planning. The mayor who would implement this strategy was Fiorello La Guardia, a progressive Republican who had won the previous year's election with support from an unsteady amalgamation of fellow liberal Republicans, independent Democrats, and outer-borough homeowners who blamed Tammany for growing tax burdens.[56] La Guardia pledged to place the city's fiscal house in order and took up the cause of planning as an instrument of doing so.

The CPC's form and function was developed by the Mayor's Charter Reform Commission in 1935.[57] The commission, whose members largely shared La Guardia's liberal-progressive politics, stated forthrightly that "the greatest waste and extravagance in the City Government did not arise from over-staffing of departments or over-payment of employees" but "from improvident, badly timed, poorly planned, and extravagant public improvements."[58] To curb such improvements, the CPC was granted the power to establish an annual capital budget and develop a five-year capital spending schedule. Individual departments would present their requests to the commission, which would have the power to approve or reject disbursements based on the budget. Such powers were complemented by other provisions of the charter, which constrained the use of citywide assessments for local improvements and the power of borough presidents to unilaterally initiate them.[59]

These restraints were welcomed by many of the city's influential public officials and commercial organizations, particularly those hailing from the older and denser districts in the metropolis. No longer convinced that the growth of the outer boroughs redounded to their districts' benefit, the borough presidents of Brooklyn and Manhattan endorsed the charter and the CPC it proposed.[60] Citywide groups like the New York Building Congress and the Citizens Budget Commission similarly lobbied for the charter along analogous lines. And while the representatives of Queens and Staten Island opposed the charter for the curbs it threatened to place on their growth, they were ultimately unsuccessful: the new charter was adopted in 1936 by a margin of 344,000.[61]

The commission, however, was to be far more controversial—and radical—than its early supporters had expected. Much of this controversy related to the CPC's outspoken chair, Rexford Tugwell. A Columbia economist before being appointed to Roosevelt's Brain Trust, Tugwell abhorred the waste produced by unregulated private ownership and sought to undo its waste through national planning measures. His term as undersecretary of the United States Department of Agriculture and later as director of the Resettlement Administration revealed him as both committed to this task and extraordinarily impolitic at carrying it out. By the late 1930s, hounded from Washington by opponents of the Resettlement Administration and bored from a stint in the business world, he sought to apply his vision of balanced growth to the most prestigious public administration that would hire him. La Guardia—wanting to signal his liberal bona fides to the newly formed American Labor Party, seeking someone with White House contacts in preparation for his own potential candidacy, and hoping to benefit from the insight of an experienced planner—saw Tugwell as a natural choice for the CPC's chair.[62] It would be a short but eventful post.

Tugwell's heterodoxy was embodied by a statement he made to the *New York Times* in 1939: that "New York's paid growth in the past does not assure us of its continued growth."[63] Long-term declines in birth rates and immigration, the transit-driven decentralization of industry and population outside urban cores, and other *longue durée* factors meant, for Tugwell, that urban economies could no longer expect the kind of expansion they had experienced earlier. And Tugwell's theories were taken up by his CPC: the commission's annual report of 1940 baldly stated that "the optimistic expectations of the 20's that the city would continue to grow at a fairly rapid rate are not likely to be realized."[64] Rather than plan around such expectations, Tugwell argued, cities needed to be planned strictly "in accordance with the known prospect for population and for business or industrial expansion"—no matter how large or small.[65]

If New York was to limit its growth to what was reasonable, however, it needed to curb the unreasonable subsidies that individual realtors were receiving. While citywide subsidies for local improvements might be rational under more propitious times, to implement them in a period of stability was simply to enrich one district—and one set of speculators—at the expense of other districts and the broader metropolis.[66] This could not be allowed to stand: as the CPC declared in its inaugural report, private citizens—even "those who speculate in realty"—must "become reconciled to the superior power and interest of the city itself."[67]

Such rhetorical sallies by the CPC were met with concrete policies. Aside from scrutinizing proposals for capital improvements with greater care, Tugwell set the CPC to limit new construction through zoning reform. As it stood, New York City had zoned the metropolis under the expectation that the metropolis's growth was unlimited: 77 million people and 344 million workers could fit in the city if residences and workplaces were built to their maximum legal density. Zoning thus acted as a public sanction for speculative building—and the costly public improvements that promoted it.[68] Restrictive zoning, however, could curb both these sources of fiscal instability: a cause Tugwell took up by attempting to downzone lower Manhattan and implementing floor area ratio limits in 1940 (an idea that was first developed by RPAA member Frederick Ackerman).[69]

The most ambitious policy pursued by the CPC, however, was its master plan of 1940. The plan was premised on the assumption that New York's population was in the process of stabilizing. "If the city were to continue its physical growth as in the past" under these new population conditions, the report declared, it would lead to "underdevelopment, if not complete uselessness, for substantial portions of its area."[70] To prevent needless further expansion, the plan called for much of the city's remaining vacant land—nearly one-third of the city's area—to be reserved as parks, designed as much to prevent costly subdivisions as to provide places of recreation for New Yorkers (figure 5.3).

What accounts for the CPC's radicalism during this period? Partly it was the personality of Tugwell, partly the broader attentiveness to growth's costs as discussed earlier. But it was also a matter of fiscal timing: the CPC was

FIGURE 5.3. "Diagram C," from the City Planning Commission, *Master Plan Land Use-Second Stage*, 1940. Courtesy Municipal Archives, City of New York. Tugwell's Master Plan of New York. Note how much of land on the city's periphery is reserved here as park land as a means of restricting wasteful realty speculation.

envisioned during the early 1930s, a period when New York still relied predominantly on property taxes for revenue and federal aid had yet to arrive en masse. Facing a fiscal crisis and lacking other fiscal options, planned retrenchment in the wake of fiscal crisis seemed the city's only option to many professional planners. But where later retrenchment measures were based on cutting services to New York's poor, the CPC's retrenchment focused on cutting subsidies to the city's private speculators, whom they believed had brought the city to its crisis. As the CPC's annual report of 1939 declared, "The present fiscal difficulties of cities in general and, of course, of New York," it declared, "are due not to the multiplication of services for citizens but rather to the spreading process which has followed real estate speculation in outer areas. Real estate interests have only themselves to blame."[71]

The Costs of Central-City Speculation

But speculators in "outer areas" were not the only realty actors undermining New York's economy—those in the city's "central districts" were as well. For decades, landlords and financiers had purchased tenements in New York's central districts in the hope they would blossom into skyscrapers and expensive apartments. Such absentee owners placed the social costs of their neglected properties—the fires, disease, and other ills that ravaged their tenements—onto the public purse (see figure 5.4). But as the Depression came and demand for high-grade structures collapsed, many housing reformers argued that an alternative and more "economic" use for the city's central districts existed: public housing. And just as Tugwell was able to wage his war against speculation through the CPC, so other reformers would have their opportunity through another public agency—the New York City Housing Authority.

All through the 1920s, speculators had purchased property in low-income districts with easy access to Manhattan and Brooklyn's downtowns and office districts. They did so not "because of their present use or the income derived from it," in one housing reformer's words, "but because they believe that is destined, sooner or later, with the growth of the city, to be in demand for high-grade business, on account of its proximity to the center of the town."[72] This hope, promoted by private planning bodies like the RPNY and spurred by new upper-income developments like the Fred R. French houses, also led savings banks, commercial banks, trust companies, and life insurance companies to purchase mortgages in these districts. Altogether, banks held 45.8 percent of first mortgages in the Lower East Side and 36.6 percent of mortgages in Harlem.[73] And New York's government, eager for additional tax revenue, encouraged this speculation by zoning these districts for tall buildings and assessing them at the same high rates private landlords sought to sell them for.[74]

High tax assessments, however, hid the costs of central-city speculation in the metropolis. While waiting to sell their property, investors and landlords forwent maintenance and improvements to save money. The result was decaying housing stock, and districts suffering from this neglect were deemed "blighted" by many housing reformers—distinguished from "slums" in that their decay was driven not by the poverty of their tenants but by the speculative expectations of investors and landlords.[75] And this speculation-induced neglect led to expensive social costs, such as the health costs of congested housing, the fire costs of poorly designed structures, and the costs of immiseration wrought by landlords "sweating" their tenants with high rents. As Vladeck later stated, in "blighted" districts, "the municipal government is

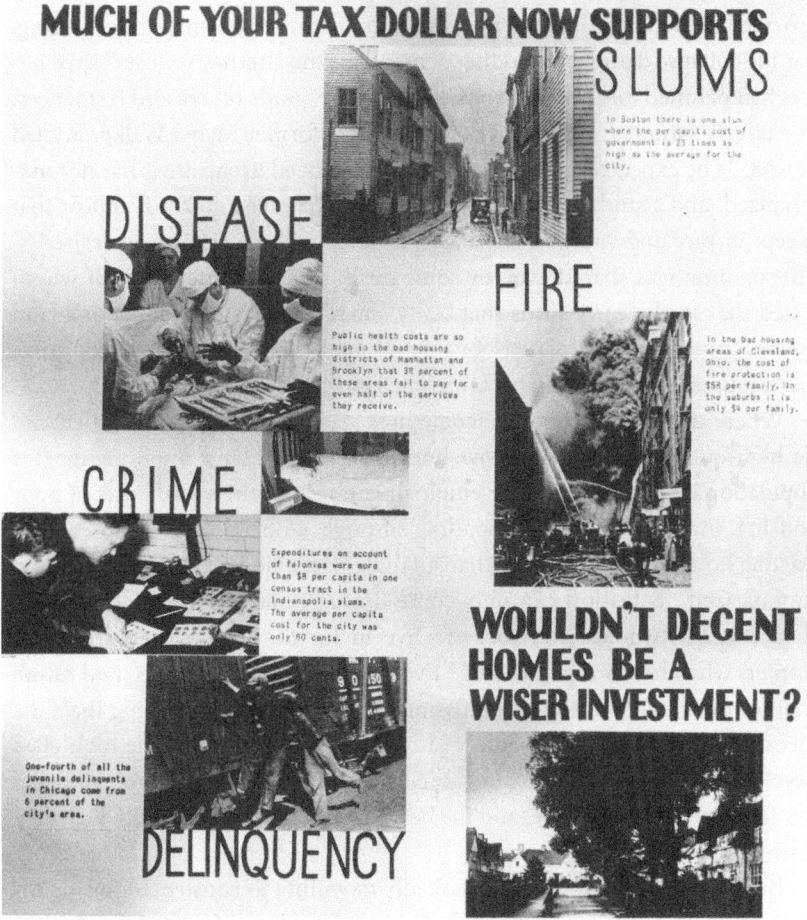

FIGURE 5.4. Suburban Resettlement Administration Record Section, *Can We Afford It?*, 1935. Miriam and Ira D. Wallach Division of Art, Prints and Photographs: Photography Collection, New York Public Library Digital Collections. This 1935 poster produced by Rexford Tugwell's Resettlement Administration summarizes many of the fiscal costs that New Deal planners ascribed to "slum" conditions. Whereas this poster advocates for suburban resettlement as a solution, planners and housing officers like Langdon Post saw public housing as a means of eroding these costs.

compelled to spend larger amounts of money on protection of life and property . . . the city is compelled to spend in slum areas ten times the amount of
its income from the same areas." Such areas, he summarized, "have become a
great danger to the financial solvency of our municipalities."[76]

But while housing reformers had critiqued New York's "tenement districts" on economic grounds for decades, the realty collapse of the early 1930s
provided an opportunity for a novel solution to this problem: public housing.
For the collapse demonstrated that demand for the alternative "uses" speculators had planned for these districts, such as high-grade offices and residences,
was utterly saturated (figure 5.5). As housing reformer Mabel Walker argued
in 1938, "The expected market for many high-priced urban areas has not ma-
terialized, and a study of the economic factors involved makes it appear that
except in rare and sporadic instances, it never will materialize as desired."[77]
This opinion was shared even by some disillusioned builders, one of whom
stated that in the early 1930s that "only small portions of Manhattan's land
now occupied by depreciated housing are likely to be in demand for commercial uses or for housing high-income families."[78]

Where demand for upper-income uses was saturated, however, demand
for high-quality but less expensive housing remained large. Building for this
population could help generate employment, reduce the social costs of poor
housing, increase consumer spending through reduced rents, *and* serve an
existing housing market rather than an imaginary one. As Edith Elmer Wood
summarized, "Salvation can only come through making the blighted areas
attractive and wholesome places to live in for the low-income groups of
workers who already reside there."[79] Even private realty developer (and future
chair of the City Planning Commission) James Felt agreed, writing that "the
theory that the Lower East Side will become the center of some high class
development" was "a wild dream. . . . I believe the East Side will remain what
it is for many years to come, and the best that can come of it would be decent
[low-income] housing."[80]

But private developers were markedly *un*willing to construct housing for
a low-income market, no matter how large. The lure of speculative profits
and the need to pay back interest-heavy loans, many housing reformers believed, both encouraged and forced developers to construct exclusively for
upper-income clienteles. While New York State had tried to lure developers into providing such housing through tax exemptions and other subsidies
during the 1920s, only eleven such corporations had been launched by the
mid-1930s.[81] "The building industry," the New York State Board of Housing
drily noted in 1933, "was too busily engaged in other directions during the period of prosperity to explore a field which was distinguished for the absence

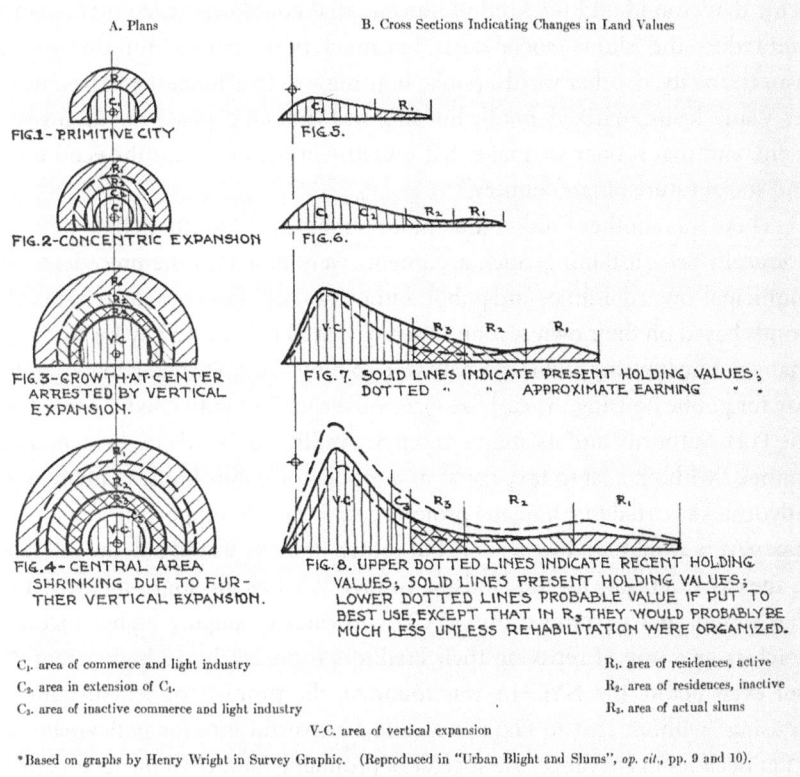

A. Plans   B. Cross Sections Indicating Changes in Land Values

FIG.1- PRIMITIVE CITY   FIG.5.

FIG.2-CONCENTRIC EXPANSION   FIG.6.

FIG.3-GROWTH·AT·CENTER ARRESTED BY VERTICAL EXPANSION.   FIG.7. SOLID LINES INDICATE PRESENT HOLDING VALUES; DOTTED " " APPROXIMATE EARNING " ·

FIG.4- CENTRAL AREA SHRINKING DUE TO FUR-THER VERTICAL EXPANSION.   FIG.8. UPPER DOTTED LINES INDICATE RECENT HOLDING VALUES; SOLID LINES PRESENT HOLDING VALUES; LOWER DOTTED LINES PROBABLE VALUE IF PUT TO BEST USE, EXCEPT THAT IN R_3 THEY WOULD PROBABLY BE MUCH LESS UNLESS REHABILITATION WERE ORGANIZED.

C_1. area of commerce and light industry R_1. area of residences, active
C_2. area in extension of C_1. R_2. area of residences, inactive
C_3. area of inactive commerce and light industry R_3. area of actual slums

V-C. area of vertical expansion

*Based on graphs by Henry Wright in Survey Graphic. (Reproduced in "Urban Blight and Slums", *op. cit.*, pp. 9 and 10).

FIGURE 5.5. Figure from George Herbert Gray, *Housing and Citizenship: A Study of Low-Cost Housing* (New York: Reinhold Publishing, 1946), 146. This graph, originally produced in the early 1930s, illustrates how speculative hopes fueled central-city housing decay and "blight" in the views of housing reformers. Landlords owning property adjacent to the highly valued urban core (i.e., in the "r3" areas) hoped to sell their land once it was needed for "higher and better" uses like offices and high-class residential towers. While waiting to be bought out, they kept their properties in disrepair while "soaking" their tenants with high rent. By the mid-1930s, however, many housing reformers believed that demand for core-adjacent land—at least for expensive offices and residences—was utterly saturated. Only low-rent housing, built by the public if necessary, constituted the "highest and best" use of these districts. But such rehabilitation could only take place if both tax assessors and property owners were willing to end their hopes for increased land-value growth in these districts.

of the glamour of speculative profits."[82] By continuing to build for imaginary markets, however, these developers were doing nothing for the city but adding unnecessary structures to it.[83]

And this is where public housing advocates made their fiscal rationale. The public sector, they argued, was not as committed to pursuing speculative profit as the private sector and could thus build for lower-income populations than the latter was willing to. The public sector was thus the only actor that could build the kind of housing that could meet existing demand *and* reduce the "slum's" social costs. For much of the land within the typical American city, in other words, public housing *was* the "highest and best use." As Vladeck summarized, public housing was "not an expense but an investment, and that sooner we make that investment the better for the economic and social future of our country."[84]

There was another fiscal argument for public housing—they could be economically self-sustaining. Such arguments were based on the precedents of municipal-owned utilities and public authorities, which were able to pay back bonds based on their own revenue stream. Just as tolls could pay for bridges, many public housing advocates believed, so rents—despite being low—could pay for public housing. As early as 1926, Governor Al Smith cited the work of the Port Authority and its ability to sell $14 million of bonds for bridges and tunnels "without cost to taxpayers" as a model for public housing financing. Advocates asserted that housing projects could "be self-supporting" such that "tax payers would not lose a cent" but rather "tenants would pay the bill just as the car-riders pay for the Hudson Tunnel."[85] It was this logic, incidentally, that would later encourage the NYCHA to cater to slightly higher income brackets as a way of repaying their creditors more easily via higher rents.[86] But even before the NYCHA was founded, the promise of self-sustaining housing "without cost to taxpayers" was a powerful lure for policymakers. After decades in abeyance, the specter of profitable municipal ownership had returned to New York. As the first general counsel of the NYCHA, Charles Abrams, declared, "We must abandon the position that government must never make a profit from its operations"—a phrase that would have warmed the heart of prior municipal ownership advocates.[87]

Such fiscal justifications for public housing, coming at a time of massive unemployment and private realty collapse, helped draw additional support for this policy in the early years of the Depression. Acting in concert with unions like the Amalgamated Clothing Workers of America and mainstream reform organizations like the Welfare Council of New York, housing reformers demanded that La Guardia implement a public housing program after his election.[88] The result was the New York City Housing Authority, formed in 1934 as the first of its kind in America. And in a 1936 court case challenging the NYCHA's power, fiscal arguments were front and center. In its final ruling, the New York Court of Appeals argued that "slums" had caused "enormous economic loss" to the city due to high service costs and tax reductions. But the court was equally clear that the private sector was unwilling to erect the kind of housing that was necessarily to rebuild these districts on an economic basis. As the ruling continued, "to eliminate the inherent evil (of unsanitary tenements) and to provide facilities at low cost—the two things necessarily go together"—it was necessary to promote housing through "the ownership and operation by and under the direct control of the public itself."[89] The ruling was public housing's magna carta—and fiscal arguments had helped deliver it.

"Break Them"

To actually construct housing, however, the NYCHA needed to address the same issue Tugwell was facing at the CPC: speculative land values and those who profited from them. Such high values made land purchases expensive for the NYCHA, even as they reproduced the kind of speculation that led to slum formation in the first place. For this reason, many NYCHA members joined Tugwell in arguing that speculative land values needed to be reduced—a further challenge to pre-crash development strategies.

The issue of high land prices faced the NYCHA from the very beginning. Landowners often raised their sales prices to prohibitive levels as soon as the NYCHA began to secure options in their district. Whereas housing economists believed that the city could only afford to put up low-cost housing at prices of $2 per square foot of land, Harlem land was often priced at five times that amount, while speculators on the Lower East Side generally held out for $7 to $8 per square foot.[90] By ceding to such prices, some housing advocates feared, the NYCHA risked validating the kind of real estate speculation that public housing was meant to combat. Nathan Straus, the mayor's special housing commissioner, worried that in matching such prices, the NYCHA would "bolster up inflated real estate values and confirm other owners of slum properties in their determination to hold out for similar high prices."[91]

But how to reduce those values? For some housing reformers, the answer lay in constructing public housing on the urban periphery where land was cheap. By building outside "blighted" districts and siphoning off their working-class population, these developments would help lower land values in the city's central districts sufficiently to enable construction there.[92] As Straus summarized, building housing "on vacant land, and draining into these projects some or superfluous customers for slums will gradually make possible for public agencies to acquire slum properties at reasonable prices."[93]

Perhaps the most radical NYCHA gesture made in this direction was the Clason Point development in the Bronx. Opened in 1941, the project was located on peripheral land and housed a tenant constituency that directly matched that of private sector landlords in central districts. For example, only 33.2 percent of residents in the project hailed from the Bronx itself—the remainder came from other boroughs, 59.2 percent from Manhattan alone.

Moreover, 36.5 percent of residents belonged to blue-collar professions such as truck drivers and factory machine operators, while another 16.5 percent were clerical or semi-professional workers. Only 9.8 percent of the residents made less than $800 annually, and only 10.9 percent were dependent upon any form of public assistance.[94] Such a constituency directly competed with private landlords—indeed, by 1943, the Real Estate Board of New York could complain that high vacancy rates in Manhattan's tenement districts could partly be linked to "the presence of low rent public housing facilities in this and other boroughs" such as Clason Point.[95] And where vacancies were, Straus and his allies believed, lowered land value generally followed.

Most housing advocates in New York, however, believed construction on the city's periphery would only replicate the fiscal damage wrought by 1920s suburbanization.[96] NYCHA director Alfred Rheinstein wrote to Mayor La Guardia stating that he "insisted on constructing housing developments in . . . slum areas, not only because they tear down actual slum buildings" but because they helped "to maintain real estate and tax values in deteriorating neighborhoods and sav[ed] the city from the expense of new schools, fire houses, hospitals, sewers and other services."[97] Indeed, it was on the grounds of economic stabilization that some local housing groups demanded public housing for their communities. The chair of the housing committee of the Brownsville Neighborhood Council, for example, worried that if "public housing . . . is not brought to our community, or should, for some reason, be further delayed, it will cause further considerable depreciation in property values in the community."[98]

But although the many public housing advocates were willing to build in central-city districts, they were no less committed to lowering land values in those districts through zoning and other means. Such commitment was revealed by NYCHA director Langdon Post at a housing panel following the Harlem uprising of 1935. Post blamed the uprising's immediate cause on poor housing conditions—but claimed that the cause behind those conditions was speculation. Landlords, he argued, neglected their properties and "sweated" their tenants in "anticipation and hope that some day Harlem will become an area of skyscrapers and property will increase tremendously in value." The city's tenants—and ultimately, the city—paid the price for these futile hopes. Only by "breaking" those values, he claimed, could sanity be restored to the city's realty market, justice provided to its tenants, and solvency returned to its budget.[99]

The NYCHA thus joined the CPC in claiming that growing land values was neither desirable nor possible for New York. Moreover, both groups cast doubt on the idea that catering to the wealthy, particularly regarding housing, was a viable economic strategy for the city. Langdon Post declared in 1938 that if "high-income families move from the area in which they are now living" into newly improved districts in the city's periphery or center, there "would be a collapse of real estate values and mortgage holdings in the areas where they now live."[100] And as late as 1943, City Planning Commission member Cleveland Rodgers asserted that "New York cannot be rebuilt with high-rental apartments for the simple reason that there are not enough people in that income group to fill them."[101]

Cleveland was speaking at a profound inflection point in New York's economic history: a moment in between the office boom of the 1920s and the white-collar boom of the postwar era. The notion that realty could continue in its old pattern was, for a moment, doubtful. In 1934, the newly elected Mayor La Guardia had stated in a press conference that "I don't think even the youngest of you reporters will live to see another skyscraper go up in New York."[102] Even the city's future as a capital of wealth was in doubt: as late as 1942, the president of the Emigrant Savings Bank complained that "wealthy persons no longer find it necessary to flock to New York as to a financial, cultural, and social capital."[103] A new era of the city's development seemed to be at hand—with the CPC and the NYCHA in the vanguard.

Sins of Omission

For all their radicalism, however, New York's fiscal stabilizers shared many of their opponents' prejudices. They had little concern for or awareness of the distinct issues facing New York's Black population.[104] They believed much of the city's existing housing stock, particularly in "blighted" districts, needed to be torn down and replaced. And while they had numerous thoughts on how New York's realty market should be restructured, they had little concern with how the productive *economy* of New York should be reformed. New York's fiscal stabilizers thus reinforced as well as challenged pre-crash developmental practices in ways that would narrow the city's fiscal imaginary well into the postwar period.

While NYCHA members like Langdon Post might have sympathy with New York's Black tenants, they generally ignored or underplayed the distinct issues of racism and segregation that distinguished their plight from those of white tenants. This was evident in Post's discussion of race at the 1935 Harlem housing panel. "There is no question in my mind," Langdon stated at the panel, "that the colored people have been exploited by the landlords, over a period of years, and by our economic system and our economic approach to the question of land values."[105] But Langdon was equally certain that segregation itself was not contributing to Harlem's neglect. During the same panel, the secretary of New York's Urban League asked if Post thought "we should concentrate on legislation which would break down the barriers" hemming in Black citizens. Langdon responded in the negative. His answer to the problem of housing people of low income—"including the negro"— was direct government subsidy and zoning laws. The unique challenges facing Black Americans—the obstacles these challenges placed on the broader economic development of American cities—were generally not addressed by fiscal stabilizers.[106]

And if the NYCHA had little sympathy for the distinct issues facing Black tenants, they had little awareness of the distinct virtues represented by the city's existing built environment. Large-scale planning and homogeneous zoning laws were considered inherently more "efficient" than the city's mixed cityscape. This was the belief of even the most radical of the RPAA members: Catherine Bauer, for example, insisted that the future New York could only emerge through the "complete re-planning and reconstruction . . . of entire districts now occupied by dreary tenements and flats, narrow old houses." She continued, "It's too late, if indeed it ever was possible, to think of 'saving' the old city centers in their congested nineteenth-century form."[107] And Tugwell's master plan proposed not only a green belt but highway belts running across the city. Despite his aversion to realty speculation, Tugwell had few doubts that catering to automobiles could be a "higher use" than preserving the city's older and poorer neighborhoods.

Fiscal stabilizers also tended to promote an expertly derived and citywide "public good" over the needs of individual neighborhoods and the participation of citizens. This was partly by design, of course: planners like Tugwell accused the city's myopic developers of putting their individual profits before the general welfare. But these celebrations of managerial autonomy, however well intentioned, would nonetheless further insulate economic development decisions from ordinary New Yorkers—both obscuring the costs of growth for planners and impeding the ability of ordinary New Yorkers to contest those costs.

But perhaps the most consequential oversight of the early fiscal stabilizers was their failure to present an *alternative* model of urban economic development: one that provided not only restrictions on real estate speculation but job-creating enterprises for its citizens. There was, to be sure, an expansion of cooperative enterprises during the 1930s that mirrored the great boom of the 1880s. Federal aid for cooperatives also blossomed, with agencies like the Tennessee Valley Authority, Farm Security Administration, and the Rural Electrification Administration providing loans and assistance to thousands of cooperatives—twenty-five thousand by the FSA alone.[108] And some fiscal stabilizers approved of these new forms of democratic ownership: such enterprises, Lewis Mumford enthused, would eliminate the "wasteful duplications, ruinous competitive salesmanship, ballyhoo, and profit for absentee investors" that afflicted privately run enterprises.[109]

For the most part, however, fiscal stabilizers were more focused on *limiting* unnecessary growth than on spurring development through changes in economic ownership, as Georgists and municipal ownership advocates had attempted before. Indeed, they generally had little thought on what the economy of cities *should* consist of—whether the best livelihood for urban citizens was manufacturing, trade, or some other sector. Halting unwarranted growth was their priority—not reconceiving it. And when they did think of the urban economy, as we shall see, it was white-collar enterprises that they celebrated as being the urban economic "base," thus joining many of their opponents in promoting the deindustrialization of New York.

All this is not to gainsay the radicalism of the early CPC and the NYCHA. At their most ambitious, these entities promoted a truly radical understanding of municipal well-being: one based not on meeting the whims of the wealthy through debt but on meeting the needs of the city's working people through its existing resources. Meeting these needs, to be sure, might require deflating the speculative expectations and property values that had accrued in more irrational times. But the reward of this deflation would be abundance: cheaper land would enable more sanitary low-income housing, restrictions on development would enable more green spaces, and all this would, in the end, save New York from the instability and social costs that "prosperity" had inflicted upon it. As Lewis Mumford wrote of New York during this period, "Life-values came back to the city only after financial values had been deflated. From the standpoint of decent metropolitan living one might well speak of the 'menace of prosperity.'"[110]

But public housing and city planning do not an economic development strategy make. While fiscal stabilizers had helped draw attention to the social costs of growth and the economic benefits of social provisions like public housing, they did not work to establish *new* forms of enterprise that could meet the needs of New York's unemployed and underemployed—and for whom the "menace of prosperity" was less pressing than the "menace of poverty." Unlike the Knights of Labor and the populists, New York's fiscal stabilizers did not strive to envision and build an alternative "cooperative commonwealth" that could sustain a local economy around worker ownership. Rather, most fiscal stabilizers left the job of defining New York's future economy to their opponents: a failure that would haunt the finances of New York for decades to come.

Conclusion

During New York's fiscal crisis of the 1930s, a group of public officials, housing advocates, and urban economists presented the city with a chastened development strategy. Only by *restricting* subsidies on behalf of the well-off, they argued, could Gotham and other cities balance their budget and prosper. Taking advantage of a moment when New York's creditors were making demands for similar fiscal restraint, reformers like Tugwell and Post were able to translate their strategy, at least in part, through new city planning and public housing measures.

But the opponents of these "fiscal stabilizers" were not idle during this period. While many of the city's property owners and public officials no longer expected rapid land-value growth, neither did they want those values further reduced. To retain them, these actors looked once again to public subsidies— and if local government was no longer in a position to furnish such aid, many in the federal government were more than happy to provide them.

"Actual Conflict"

In October of 1934, a Staten Islander by the name of Anne Juppe wrote Mayor La Guardia with a request. She asked the mayor to help her apply for a housing loan from the Home Owners Loan Corporation, a federal agency formed earlier that year. This loan, she argued, would enable her to pay off her back taxes and so support her local government. "You will see," she stated, "that I do not want the money for myself, but it is for the government, and why should they refuse me when it is for their own benefit?"[1] A month later, Juppe wrote another letter with a sharper tone. "Why is the government planning a gigantic housing program," she asked, "and yet turning their back on people who are trying to pay them their taxes, which they are not all modest in levying, together with their assessments[?]"[2]

But a confidential letter written two years later revealed that small homeowners like Anne Juppe were not the only ones to throw fiscal stones. The letter came from James S. Taylor, associate director of economics and statistics at the Federal Housing Administration (FHA). It was addressed to Philip Cornick, a Georgist land economist who had studied the fiscal costs of unregulated peripheral development. Privately, the director agreed with Cornick's accusations. "Although we might never want to mention the matter outside," the administrator stated, "I think we might give some consideration to the allegation that families living in houses costing less than $4,000 or $5,000 do not, as a group, pay property taxes commensurate with the direct cost of services rendered to them."[3] In this remarkable document, an FHA economist admitted that small single-family homes–whose construction was one of the FHA's very purposes—could cost cities more than it benefited them.

That aid on behalf of private actors could ultimately impoverish the public sector was, of course, not the intention of the FHA or other federal programs during the 1930s. Funds on behalf of infrastructure projects, housing insurance, or urban renewal projects were all predicated on the assumption that private wealth would translate into public (financial) health. For critics like Cornick, however, such policies threatened to reproduce the unsustainable patterns of growth that they were attempting to control on the local level. As New York's City Planning Commission complained in 1939, there was a "lack of cooperation, if not an actual conflict, between federal agencies . . . and the city itself regarded as a whole."[4]

This chapter traces how local actors like Anne Juppe and federal officials like Frederick Taylor accelerated subsidies on behalf of real estate during the New Deal. During this period, many local property-owners and their elected representatives mobilized against fiscal-reform bodies like the City Planning Commission, seeing its efforts to restrict local real estate growth as threatening the city's prosperity. Through their electoral weight and the city's dependence on property values, by the early 1940s, they were successful—not only in winning back pre-crash forms of subsidy but in gaining additional state and federal aid in the form of urban redevelopment legislation and programs like the FHA. But while these programs might have bolstered private profits in the short term, in the longer term, such "outside" aid both accelerated and obscured the kind of local realty speculation that had long undermined the city's economy.

By recounting the fiscal politics of New Deal–era New York, this chapter challenges assumptions that federal assistance was necessarily beneficial to the long-term economic outlook of cities. This is not a mainstream perspective: most scholars argue that federal programs such as grants-in-aid and financing for infrastructure were and are necessary for communities to maintain solvency and ultimately expand their economic health.[5] Recounting New York's Depression era through the lens of social costs and fiscal imaginaries, however, challenges this view. For critics like Tugwell and Post, federal assistance merely *reproduced* and accelerated the waste of pre-crash land development, rendering cities more rather than less fiscally fragile. And by framing the origins and solutions to local fiscal crises strictly in national terms, aid-seeking policymakers both obscured the local sources of urban fiscal strain—that is, realty speculation and its abettors—and marginalized the importance and possibility of reforming local economies based on democratic *local* ownership. This chapter thus builds off Noam Maggor's insight that "New Deal work relief and public works programs . . . acted as a surrogate for urban fiscal reform."[6] To be sure, after the Depression, many New Yorkers took such aid as a signal that their city's development pattern needed to be fundamentally rethought, but with fiscal radicalism temporarily in abeyance, such rethinking would occur along lines far less egalitarian than many earlier reformers had sought.

Domestic Resistance

While figures like Tugwell and Post raged against "excessively" high real estate values during the 1930s, their efforts were largely frustrated by three sets of local opponents. The first was the city's existing property owners, of whom there were more than ever before thanks to expanded homeownership in the 1920s. The second was their elected representatives: public officials who sought to raise rather than reduce land values. And the third were liberal professional organizations like the Citizens Budget Commission, who sought to regulate realty growth rather than curb it outright. Together, these groups would prove stubborn obstacles to fiscal reform in New York City.

Although many property owners in New York recognized their city's fiscal straits during the Depression, few were willing to curb expensive subsidies on their behalf for the city's greater benefit. As Rexford Tugwell later stated, while his City Planning Commission "received a good deal of praise from conservative citizens" for its "budgeting efforts," such praise was bestowed only so long as the commission's "proposals were made in general terms." "In general," he noted sardonically, "all would seek to be the exception" as far as constraints on their own landed investments were concerned.[7] And there were more of these investments than ever—not only through financial devices like the mortgage bond but through the vast expansion of homeownership that had taken place in the past decade.[8] Such small property owners, together with the city's larger realty owners and investors, would fight fiercely to maintain their "private gains" regardless of whether they came at "public expense."

Most local officials were similarly set against curbing speculative land values. New York's expenditures and debt capacity rested on the high valuations it had placed on property. To curb these valuations, either through assessment reform or by restricting subsidies on behalf of property, was to threaten both property owners and New York's finances. As one prominent Georgist wrote at the time, since New York "could not abolish speculative values and still collect taxes on speculative values . . . many city officials would rather collect than abolish."[9] For this reason, as Tugwell later stated, the "city's officials became the most ardent defenders of real estate speculator's gains."[10]

But even "responsible" critics of realty speculation were generally wary of curbing realty growth in toto. Liberal professionals ensconced in institutions like the Citizens Budget Commission (CBC), the *New York Times*, and the RPNY all believed realty expansion could be made responsible through regulation rather than curbed outright. As such, these groups too "ridiculed suggestions of stability," in Tugwell's words.[11] Even too-general critiques of realty were disapproved of: the *New York Times*, for example, chided Tugwell's deriding of realty speculation in 1940 as "unfortunate"—"all that can be meant is that an economic mistake has been committed."[12] That there were financial incentives for private actors to make such "mistakes" was not discussed.

This is not to say that the Depression did not contribute to a more general rethinking of urban economics. As we shall see, the collapse of land values during the early 1920s, despite all the treasure and policies dispensed on its behalf, would prompt many realty groups and economists to consider new sources of urban prosperity. Such rethinking, however, coexisted with a determination to hold on to what benefits and subsidies these groups already enjoyed. For example, municipal reformer William Harvey Allen recounted telling a group of savings bank presidents about how some of their properties were escaping tens of thousands of dollars a year in assessments, which their other clients had to pay in excess of their fair share. The next morning, Allen recalled, another one of the presidents called him and stated, "As I watched your face I feared you were misreading the interest we presidents manifested when you showed up inequities of assessing. You know we are about as hard-boiled a bunch as there is. You apparently thought we wanted to stop the inequities. On the contrary we were thinking: 'How can I get my bank's share of inequities? If melons are being cut I want big slices.'"[13]

And behind all these obstacles to local fiscal reform was a broader pressure: the city's "sunk costs" in the form of debt-financed projects inherited from the pre-crash era. New York's water supply had been presented during the 1920s on an assumed growth of the city at a rate of 15 percent per decade, with a population of 9,700,000 in 1950. The city's sewage system was developed in 1931 on an assumption that the city's population would be 11,900,000 in 1960. To anticipate population stability, and hence realty stability, was to threaten the legitimacy and financing of these projects. As a member of the "fiscally conservative" Citizens Budget Commission asserted, "The theory of a stabilized population is quite inconsistent with the Plans now being carried for great public works."[14] Growth was not only desirable; it was necessary.

Tugwell and other fiscal radicals thus faced numerous fiscal and political obstacles within their city. What was more, they lacked the relatively broad constituency prior radicals like Henry George and Hearst had enjoyed, when many white artisans had joined them in grand campaigns to expropriate landlords and utility magnates. Now many of the city's better-off workers owned property of their own and had little incentive to see the value of that

FIGURE 6.1. A group of homeowners en route to Albany to protest a new tax program, 1939. Bettman/ Editorial Imagespopu via Getty Images. During the Depression many New York homeowners, whose numbers had greatly expanded during the 1920s, mobilized against efforts by planning bodies like the CPC to place greater restrictions on citywide subsidies for local improvements. Such restrictions, these homeowners feared, would force them to pay for services that had been paid for by the city as a whole— and, by extension, by working-class and Black tenants—during more prosperous times. In this way, the "small homeowner" and "small taxpayer," in whose name many campaigns for fiscal equity had been launched in the early twentieth century (see figures 2.1 and 2.7), had by the 1930s become electorally significant forces for preserving fiscal privileges.

property decline—or see their own taxes rise once the City Planning Commission cut citywide subsidies on their behalf (see figure 6.1). Neither did many local officials, convinced that New York literally could not afford to curtail revenue-enhancing growth. "If property fails, the City fails," declared Mayor James Walker in 1932. "Let us understand that."[15] And fiscal radicals— confined to a base of heterodox planners and housing officials ensconced in a few municipal departments—had little capacity to beat back these opponents once they began to counterattack.

Subsidizing the Periphery

The mobilization against fiscal reform in New York took place on many fronts—through electoral pressure, through opposition within departments like the Board of Estimate, and through lobbying efforts by large and small civic bodies alike. Many of these campaigns targeted the CPC, whose power to curtail public expenditures was resented by many property owners and their representatives. By the early 1940s, these campaigns had succeeded not only in defeating many of the CPC's more radical proposals but in forcing the resignation of its head, Rexford Tugwell.

All through the Depression, many local property owners continued to demand the subsidies they had received in the booming 1920s, forcing even opponents of those subsidies to buckle under pressure. The "flipping" of Raymond Ingersoll on local assessments is instructive in this regard. Elected borough president of Brooklyn in 1933, Ingersoll had criticized citywide assessments for local improvements on grounds that would have pleased any Georgist: "There would be too many unearned increments. Real estate speculators with their local pressure groups would bankrupt the city."[16] By the end of the decade, however, Ingersoll had succumbed to such "pressure groups" and boasted in campaign literature of taking 40 percent of the cost of a sewer assessment off his constituents while placing it upon the broader city—just as his machine-backed predecessors had done.[17]

The CPC's efforts to use land-use regulation for growth control met with similar defeat. The commission's 1939 annual report complained that any proposals for land platting or subdivision disapproved by the City Planning Commission could be reinstated by the Board of Estimate. "Under this," the CPC grumbled in its 1939 annual report, "developers may build on land where streets have been legally laid out regardless of other considerations, and quite without reference to any directive agency."[18]

The commission's campaign to pass tighter use and height restrictions in the city's older districts met similar resistance. As Tugwell recounted, most of these voices hailed from "owners of property, each of whom hoped that intensified uses would enhance the value of his particular holding."[19] Opponents, however, argued that Tugwell's proposals would harm the city's finances: as one critic stated, such restrictive provisions would ensure that "many property owners won't be able to pay their realty taxes, and that won't help the city."[20] Ultimately, the commission's efforts were defeated by a Board of Estimate veto.

The City Planning Commission's largest failure, however, was the defeat of its first master plan in December of 1940—a plan that had emphasized stabilization rather than growth as its guiding principle. Such a principle was unwelcome not only to borough boosters but to organizations representing the broader city, including the RPNY and the New York Chamber of Commerce. A commentary from the realty-laden Citizens Budget Commission argued that the new city plan was "based on an anticipated decentralization of business and industry, with a population approaching stability, both of which platforms are debatable."[21] One Brooklyn resident complained that CPC was "afflicted with the same type of pessimistic or defeatist attitude in regard to our city as . . . their confreres have regarding the country as a whole."[22] Even the RPNY, having predicted in 1941 that New York's population would reach nearly eight and a half million by 1970 (the actual number would be less than seven million), gave it little public defense.[23] Ultimately, the plan was unanimously vetoed by the city's Board of Estimate, with both City Wide representatives (Mayor, Comptroller) and Borough Presidents aligning against it.

This defeat reflected the broad political currents raging against Tugwell's CPC on the part of property owners—a rage that caught up to La Guardia as well. Shortly before the gubernatorial elections of 1941, the City Planning Commission argued that new public facilities should be located in "established neighborhoods" rather than outer-borough subdivisions.[24] Queens homeowners did not take kindly to this statement, and this precise report was referenced by the *Queens Evening News* as contributing to the defeat of La Guardia's Fusion ticket in the outer boroughs.[25] A member of the City Planning Commission later admitted the justice of this interpretation, stating that small homeowners "voted against Fusion" during this election because they feared that the commission—and, by extension, La Guardia—would cease to fund their improvements.[26] Quick to recognize a political liability when he saw one, La Guardia put pressure on Rexford Tugwell to resign following the election—which Tugwell gladly accepted. His replacement was Robert Moses, who swiftly turned the CPC away from any radicalism it once possessed. The war over subsidizing the city's periphery had been definitively won by the periphery.

Subsidizing the Center

Even as outer-borough property owners fought to retain their fiscal privileges, their central-city counterparts fought to retain theirs. Such subsidies, however, would take a slightly different form and rationale than those that guided aid toward the urban periphery. Rather than reduced tax assessments and infrastructure on behalf of existing property owners, central-city landlords looked to new forms of property ownership on behalf of large-scale housing as a means of rescuing their investments. The policies they developed toward this end—urban redevelopment—would magnify all the inequities and speculation that had accompanied the central city's growth prior to the Depression.

By the mid-1930s, many landlords had recognized that a demand for high-income offices or residences—particularly in central-city districts—was at least temporarily saturated. And on these grounds, some property owners were willing to wait for public housing authorities to "buy out" their land at a hefty price.[27] Indeed, this was part of the rationale for public housing: none other than Langdon Post argued that public housing projects could help rescue the "tottering mortgages which cover half the wealth of our cities."[28] Banks also benefited from housing authorities "buying out" their money-losing mortgages. "Nearly half the properties to be taken" for new housing projects, one newspaper noted, "are owned by the banks. This seems a salvage project as much as it is one of slum clearance. It will end in better housing, but it begins by helping out the banks."[29]

The NYCHA's ability to act as the savior of landlords and banks, however, was limited. Central-city land was priced at speculatively high rates, and the NYCHA lacked the money to purchase such land en masse. And even if those values were allowed to deflate sufficiently enough to let the NYCHA purchase land, many landlords believed this cure might be worse than the disease.[30] As one critic wrote to the president of the Institutional Securities Corporation in 1935, "Unless somebody is given the necessary power to do things in a big way, we might just as well sit back and wait until our investments have dwindled to practically nothing, at which time the Municipal Government or Federal Government could then afford to buy the land and provide plenty of accommodations at a low rental."[31]

By the mid-1930s, however, many realty owners and lenders saw hope in another form of realty development—moderate-income housing. While not as profitable as housing for wealthier groups, there was nonetheless an existing demand for it. And middle-income housing was more remunerative than lower-income housing, which could encourage developers to pay higher prices for land than the NYCHA was willing to. Realtors and bankers thus embraced the cause of moderate-income housing not "because the people were interested in providing more housing for moderate-income people," in the cynical words of one housing reformer, "but mainly to relieve themselves of the cost of carrying the vacant land which they had been holding for a number of years."[32]

During the late 1930s, a special committee of the New York Chamber of Commerce and Merchants Association met and considered different methods of enticing capital to the moderate-income housing field. While theoretically the public sector could enter this field, private developers were generally not interested in giving up a potentially lucrative middle-income market to the public sector—indeed, they had already lobbied mightily to ensure that the non-poor wouldn't be eligible for Federal public housing.[33] Nor were they interested in seeing the city's existing central-city landlords collaborate among themselves to rehabilitate central-city districts: as Robert Moses stated, "big money was necessary" for redevelopment rather than cooperation by individual "little fellows."[34] Rather than the public sector or cooperative enterprises, the committee looked to large, "outside" private insurance companies and savings banks as the most appropriate owners and operators of urban redevelopment projects. Used to operating at an economy of scale and receiving slow but steady dividends, public officials like state housing commissioner Louis Pink believed that such institutions would be more willing to use their resources to finance such projects more than the traditional booster interested only in short-term profits.[35]

The result of the special committee's negotiations was the Redevelopment Corporations Law of 1940: the legislative template for urban renewal in New York State and the United States at large. The law created the framework for state-charted private corporations tasked with both slum clearance and constructing middle-income housing. And to encourage such development, the state extended fiscal privileges. For example, rent in so-called redevelopment corporations could be used not merely to cover maintenance costs, maintain low rents, and repay debts—as in public housing authorities—but for dividends and profits as well. The laws also provided tax exemptions for the redevelopment corporations, as well as the powers of eminent domain needed to purchase and assemble land. And subsequent versions of the Redevelopment Laws submitted between 1941 and 1943 further liberalized these privileges.

Left-leaning housing and labor groups quickly mobilized against the terms of the Redevelopment Laws. Exempting such projects from taxation, some public housing advocates charged, was an unwarranted subsidy for the wealthy and a fiscal burden on the municipality. Charles Abrams argued that "if the tax exemption that must necessarily be given on low-rent housing will now be given on higher-rental housing as well, municipal bankruptcy is inevitable."[36] Others argued that the bills would lead to an undue escalation of speculative land values. The Citizens Housing Council complained that the bill would lead to "the deeper concentration of slum families in remaining slum areas" and that it would increase "already impractical land values."[37] And opponents also feared that empowering corporate franchises with carrying out public purposes was fundamentally undemocratic, invoking Gilded Age struggles over utilities as they did so. New York's acting state commissioner of housing, for example, complained that "the dangers involved in special franchises granted in the past to railroads and other utilities before the era of public utility regulation might reappear" in the Redevelopment Laws.[38]

But these voices of opposition were outmatched by those of supporters, who saw these bills as perfectly in keeping with New York's tradition of allowing private actors to (profitably) accomplish public purposes under regulatory supervision. The *New York Times* hailed the Redevelopment Laws as promoting "long-term investment with the prospect of operating profits and equity appreciation as incentives rather than the expectation of quick speculative profits."[39] Commercial associations, which routinely railed against tax exemptions for public housing, found virtue in such subsidies for private redevelopment. Similarly, the Bronx Chamber of Commerce stated in 1941 that "while we look upon the tax exemption features of the ordinary slum clearance projects as highly adverse to adjacent taxpaying properties," such reservations were "overshadowed by the beneficial effects of having these areas cleaned up by private capital."[40]

New York's Redevelopment Law was passed in 1943. Initially it accomplished little: few institutional investors were interested in central-city redevelopment in the midst of World War II, and even the subsidies proffered by the law were seen by them as insufficient. Those few redevelopment projects that were constructed, however, demolished entire neighborhoods while reinforcing segregation within the city—most notoriously in the case of Stuyvesant Town in the Lower East Side, which explicitly barred Black tenants. And a 1945 plan by the banker-rife Manhattan Development Committee warned against efforts to pass anti–housing discrimination laws that might undue this segregation, arguing that "it is at present the opinion of many large institutional investors that [anti-discrimination laws] will make it very difficult to create private capital redevelopment projects."[41] Not until 1951 would New York pass such a law—by which point New York's "redevelopment" was even further advanced.

Nonetheless, the Redevelopment Laws were important less as bills than as signals: that the more radical elements of New Deal statecraft, with its suspicion of the for-profit sector's motivations and capacities, were no longer in the saddle. This reflected, in part, broader political mobilization against the New Deal's more radical components such as the CPC and the Works Progress Administration (WPA).[42] But it also represented a tendency within the New Deal itself, long strong but dominant by the early 1940s: that private growth needed to be accelerated through public spending. While New York's New Deal welfare state would greatly expand in the postwar period, expenditures on its behalf would no longer be portrayed as economic "investments" compared with, say, public spending on behalf of private real estate. And if local governments were unable to provide this spending, then many public officials and property owners were eager to let the federal government take up the slack. As they would, with gusto.

The Federal Bulldozer

In addition to their domestic opponents, CPC and NYCHA officials faced another obstacle: the federal government, and specifically federal aid on behalf of urban realty. Such aid partially reflected newer economic theories ranging from "pump priming" to Keynesian demand management.[43] Partially it reflected older beliefs, shared by local officials and realty groups alike, that only restored property values could restore urban finances. For critics like Tugwell and Cornick, however, federal aid rewarded and accelerated the same kind of realty speculation that had led to urban fiscal crisis in the first place. But now such wreckers were assisted not merely by local subsidies but by the mighty coffers of the federal government. And attempts to place local finances on more resilient footing in the face of this "aid" would be akin, as Tugwell put it, to attempting "a skyscraper excavation with a spoon."[44]

As much as some federal officials believed that the American economy had reached a period of "maturity," many more believed that the federal government had the power and duty to revive its expansion. Even believers in "secular stagnation"—such as Alvin Hansen, who argued that the private sector suffered from chronic overproduction—nonetheless thought that federal spending could help create new markets and stimulate private investments.[45] Just as local public works spending could smooth boom-and-bust cycles of employment, so the federally funded projects could help create the infrastructure necessary to boost private sector markets. Such counter-cyclical spending was a rationale that many cities had informally embarked on during previous periods of crisis—and mayors eagerly looked to similar remedies during the early Depression.

As early as 1932, the United States Conference of Mayors (USCM) organized to demand federal public works programs.[46] While some in the USCM doubted that the private sector would regain prior growth rates any time soon, this was framed less as a critique of growth than as a spur for the federal government to take up the slack. "The recommendations of the United States Conference of Mayors for a future Federal Relief and Public Works program," declared the vice president of the USCM, "are based upon one fundamental economic condition: namely, that we are reaching a *new normal level*." And "[T]he best method of absorbing a large number of the unemployed," he asserted, was "a Major Public Works Program[.]"[47]

Many in Roosevelt's administration were partial to these calls. Early in his administration, Roosevelt had looked to local governments and civic bodies to help inform and direct his broader policy program. Near the beginning of his tenure, Roosevelt asked Hugh Johnson, head of the National Recovery Administration, to send telegraphs to local chambers of commerce assuring them of his administration's support.[48] Many of his officials, moreover, had backgrounds in local economic development: the chair of the Reconstruction Finance Corporation (RFC), for example, was a prominent real estate developer in Houston prior to his appointment. Such synergies ensured that aid on behalf of local governments would often take the same form they did before the crash: aid on behalf of real estate. "Real estate is the basis of all wealth," the RFC chair assured the Real Estate Board of New York in 1935, echoing the beliefs of early-twentieth century fiscal officers like Lawson Purdy. "It supports our schools, pays for our fire and police protection, and to a very large extent supports state, county, city, and town governments."[49] Those who valued these public services and offices, no less than those involved more directly in real estate, now had a "stake" in realty's recovery, as Frederick Ackerman had noted earlier.[50]

Moreover, most federal officials—believing time was of the essence if their nation's economy was to be restored—were relatively indisposed to deeply question or rethink the role of real estate in bringing on the Depression. As FHA economist Ernest Fisher later wrote, "The Government absorbed most of the men interested in the field [of urban economics] and loaded them down with problems of an administrative character requiring ad hoc rather than basic research."[51] Rather than seek out new solutions, particularly in the Depression's early years, many of these officials attempted to supplement older approaches with new financing, standing ready to pick up the municipal slack for assisting realty along the same lines local governments had—now not only in the name of local property values but in the name of work relief and national economic recovery.[52]

Agencies such as the WPA and the Public Works Administration, for example, helped finance the very improvements that REBNY and others had demanded since the 1920s. These ranged from large projects like the Triborough Bridge and the Queens–Midtown Tunnel to smaller improvements such as street repairs and the construction of local sewer lines (see figure 6.2). As Harry Hopkins noted in 1935, 37 percent of all the money spent by the WPA—the single largest category of spending by the agency—was spent on repaving and opening new streets.[53]

The experience of "suburban" Queens embodied how federal programs picked up where local subsidies left off. Just as the borough benefited from

FIGURE 6.2. *35th Av. W. at Murray Street*, October 6, 1938. Queens Borough President Collection, New York City Department of Records and Information Services. Courtesy Municipal Archives, City of New York. Note the WPA sign on the right: the power of the federal government is being used here to provide a service—street repair—that many homeowners had originally paid from their own tax dollars through special assessments.

city-financed improvements during the 1920s, so it benefited from nationally financed projects in the 1930s. For example, more than half of the city's new WPA-paved roads and more than half of the city's four hundred additional WPA playgrounds were built in Queens despite possessing far less than half the city's population.[54] The vice president of a Queens civic association attested to the WPA's munificence toward his borough: "No matter what the political or personal viewpoint of a taxpayer toward WPA may be . . . the taxpayer will prefer non-assessable WPA improvements to such improvements which, due to the necessity to pay assessments above his ability to pay, may ultimately drive him from his home."[55] Or as one political scientist wrote, "To Queens, more than to any other borough, the W.P.A. was a God-send."[56]

Tugwell's City Planning Commission, however, believed these federal programs were undermining the city's ultimate fiscal health. First, the new peripheral developments made possible by federal infrastructure would have to be serviced through local budgets. Tugwell lashed out at the fiscal

implications of federal aid in the pages of the *New Republic*—whether federally backed projects forced the city to "duplicat[e] *existing* school and other
facilities and maintain unnecessary streets" in new districts, he wrote, "may
be a choice which seems simple in Washington" but was not so simple in
New York, which had "high debt-service costs and no power to make investments with unbalanced budgets."[57] Second, federal aid freed fiscally unreconstructed local governments to continue their old habits—that is, to incur even
more local debt for public improvements.[58] And finally, federal infrastructure
itself—even ones funneled through nominally self-financing public authorities such as Robert Moses's Triborough Bridge Authority—still needed to be
maintained through local budgets. Upon his inauguration in 1934, La Guardia's comptroller, Joseph McGoldrick, was warned by his predecessor that "if
you don't watch [Moses], he's going to bankrupt the city."[59]

Federal support for suburban homeownership similarly worked against
efforts to restrict peripheral growth. Ironically, such programs were initially
framed as a fiscal prop for cities. Protecting homeowners from foreclosure,
after all, would enable them to better pay their property taxes. In 1933, Democratic senator Robert F. Wagner declared that "the conversion of every dis-
tressed mortgage means the clearing up of tax and assessment arrears," which
would enable "many an embarrassed municipality or township throughout
the country to pay its public servants and to safeguard properly the welfare
of its people."[60] Federal agencies such as the FHA, Home Loan Banks, and the
Home Owners Loan Corporation (HOLC), well staffed by former real estate
appraisers and builders, were soon providing mortgage relief and insurance
to white homeowners on generous terms.[61]

For critics like Tugwell, however, the FHA and HOLC were simply reproducing the same wasteful land uses that had wrecked New York's finances
earlier. New York housing commissioner Langdon Post argued in 1939 that
"except for an insistence on higher standards for planning and construction . . . the United States Government is doing just exactly what the real
estate speculator and the small-time home developer did for years."[62] Tugwell
concurred, complaining that the FHA was "guaranteeing loans and thus encouraging banks to furnish the funds with which cities were often involved
in serious trouble. Speculative builders, with this backing, were scattering a
population which would demand the extension far and wide of city facilities."[63] And just like in the 1920s, it would be central-city tenants who would
pay the costs of subsidized peripheral development, except now this development was guaranteed and accelerated by federal aid.[64]

And such federal aid on behalf of peripheral development would soon
be made available for central-city developers. Between 1941 and 1943, four

proposals for federally subsidized urban redevelopment corporations were developed by the Federal Housing Authority, the Urban Land Institute, the National Association of Real Estate Brokers, and the National Planning Association.[65] Each of the plans advocated for a version of New York's urban redevelopment corporations that would each have the power to buy, lease, rent, condemn, and sell land in "blighted" areas. But now these corporations would have federal financing behind them—giving these corporations the funding needed to both purchase land at the inflated prices landlords demanded and sell them at a loss to developers hoping to build upon that land.

This so-called markdown was, for Georgist critics, a particularly egregious example of how the public sector was not only subsidizing private sector growth—it was subsidizing private sector losses.[66] It was realty investors who had made central-district areas "blighted" in the first place, both by acting as absentee landlords and by promoting peripheral development outside the urban core. It was realty owners who refused to sell this land except at the most exorbitant prices, preventing either private buyers or public housing authorities from purchasing the land. And now the public sector was not only purchasing that land, thus rewarding realty speculators for the expensive social costs their "blight" had placed on cities: they were subsidizing *new* speculative developments with the proceeds of those sales, developments that would wreak similar social and fiscal havoc on cities.

It was all too much for some critics. "How can we assume," Philip Cornick complained in response to one redevelopment proposal, "that they [the real estate industry] will now become omniscient enough to eradicate their own past mistakes, merely because they will have at their disposal billions in federal loans and grants? Isn't there at least a possibility that they will repeat their old mistakes on a much grander scale[?]"[67] Public housing advocate and RPAA member Catherine Bauer assailed the terms of the redevelopment bills along similar lines. "It is proposed," she wrote, "to bail out with Federal subsidy the owners of slum and blighted property—not in order to rehouse their present tenants properly, but to stimulate another wave of speculative overbuilding for well-to-do and thus, it is naively hoped, to turn the tide of decentralization and preserve downtown property values based on high densities and even higher hopes."[68]

But Cornick and Bauer were writing against the tide. For as much as regional planners and public housing officials had sought to limit local subsidies on behalf of real estate growth, they lacked the power to stop state and federal statutes supplementing such aid—and such mistakes. By the late 1940s, twenty-five states possessed urban redevelopment laws, and the varied mayors, businessmen, bankers, and developers of America's cities would not be denied a federal equivalent.[69] Joining them were prominent economists like Alvin Hansen and soon-to-be Council of Economic Advisors chair Leon Keyserling, each of whom looked at urban redevelopment as a means of overcoming the "secular stagnation" of America's central cities. And in 1949, following years of advocacy and a severe postwar housing shortage, the Housing Act was passed enabling the federal government to purchase swaths of "blighted" land with federal backing and turn that land over to private developers for "higher and better" uses. The Depression-era revolt against realty speculation was definitely over.

Subsidizing Mistakes

The local and federal subsidies claimed by private realty during the Depression and accelerated during the 1940s entrenched older paradigms of municipal financing and land development. Once again, the city grew its debt on behalf of realty-boosting capital infrastructure. Once again, small homes were assessed at low rates at the expense of low-income neighborhoods. The local costs of such policies, however, were now more thoroughly hidden and less politicized than ever—in no small part by federal aid and the "modern" economic frameworks that rationalized them.

As early as 1936, municipal finance researcher Frederick Bird, while railing against the debt cities had expended on behalf of realty in the 1920s, warned that federal aid could only exacerbate such city-wrecking subsidies. Such aid, he warned, could "become a menace to the future financial stability of many municipalities by offering tempting inducements for the incurring of more municipal debt when there was neither real need nor adequate capacity to pay."[70] His fears would prove prescient. Beginning in 1945, New York increased its capital spending per capita to $20.73, a growth of 485 percent from its wartime low. Between 1950 and 1953 under Mayor Vincent R. Impellitteri, the city further increased its capital budget 176 percent, while the city's gross debt expanded by 23 percent and short-term debt by 172 percent—the greatest such increase for any single mayoral term between the late 1920s and the late 1980s.[71] And yet, such public spending on behalf of conventional growth strategies occurred even though New York's intergovernmental revenue had shot from 5.8 percent to nearly 20 percent of its revenue sources.[72] Increased extralocal assistance, it seemed, had done little to wean New York off its compulsion to promote realty growth via local public improvements.

Such spending would finance the cities' great postwar highways and bridges, built upon neighborhoods sacrificed for the white homeowners then filling up New York's remaining meadows with sprawling subdivisions. And just as in the 1920s, the sunk costs of these projects and the debts on their behalf would weigh heavily on New York's future finances. But power brokers like Robert Moses, Tugwell's successor at the City Planning Commission, dismissed any fiscal criticism of his projects.[73] "Drastic and hysterical postponement of public work," he warned, "will result in paralysis of all local enterprise and substantial loss to private as well as public interests."[74] "The trouble with the pay-as-you-go system," he quipped, "is that usually you don't pay, and you don't go."[75]

And just as in the 1920s, New York's homeowners were spared from paying the full cost of the "improvements" perpetrated in their name. Partly this was reflected by citywide subsidies on behalf of local projects: as Robert Haig noted in the early 1950s, "One of the most striking developments of the last twenty-five years in the finances of the city of New York is the reduction . . . almost to the vanishing point of the use of special assessments."[76] Favorable tax assessment policies further privileged New York homeowners: the economist Robert Haig noted in 1953 that small homes in the city were assessed "at well below market value . . . roughly 67% of the value." Haig went on to notice that this practice had official approval, stating that "the municipal authorities have openly acquiesced in, and have in fact been responsible for, the policy of underassessment."[77] In the postwar era, as before, white homeowners had vested interests in maintaining New York's fiscal regime.

But if these debt and assessment policies reproduced earlier paradigms of local development policy, the prospect of federal aid helped depoliticize their costs—particularly among the kind of left-liberals who had led previous campaigns for land-value taxation and municipal ownership. This is not to say that American policymakers no longer viewed the local state as a crucial vector for implementing policy or that cities did not pursue economic development on their own volition during the postwar era (as we shall see). But the early twentieth-century ideal of an urban "cooperative commonwealth," a city capable of flourishing through public and democratic ownership, was largely eclipsed in progressive political thought by the 1940s. As Thomas Bender has written of this time, "The address of citizenship in modern, industrial society, whether one refers to the disciplinary agenda of political scientists or the location of political action, had shifted from the city to the nation."[78] Such a transfer of political fealty, together with the broader eclipse of radical New Deal tendencies toward economic planning in the early 1940s, would severely weaken the constituency for heterodox local development strategies in postwar America.[79]

And a similar shift from the cities was taking place in economic thought. Neo-Keynesians in such influential bodies as the Council of Economic Advisors (established in 1946), for example, generally treated the nation "as an economic unit" through macroeconomic techniques and national statistics such as the GDP.[80] Such frameworks, however, generally "assumed the local economies," in the words of political scientist Norton E. Long, "to be mere by-products of a national economy hung in the sky above them, independently controlling them without being controlled by them."[81] And many liberals looked to broader economic developments—from the development of continent-spanning corporations to the increasing decentralization of jobs and populations beyond city boundaries themselves—as further proof that cities were no longer privileged economic actors.[82] In both politics and economics, then, a significant strain of the postwar liberal imagination turned beyond the city to the nation-state as the ideal loci of policy intervention.[83]

There was, of course, an opportunistic dimension to what Long called this "dogma of (local) powerlessness," particularly among policymakers—for one thing, it helped deflect blame for misguided local growth strategies.[84] An excellent example of this was in the person of Charles White Berry, New York City's comptroller from 1926 to 1933. Through the late 1920s, Berry had encouraged citywide assessments and debt on behalf of realty-boosting public improvements, all while writing pamphlets with such titles as *Why New York City Can Never Become Bankrupt*.[85] Three years later, however, the comptroller released another pamphlet—more soberly titled *Financial Problems of the City of New York*—and argued that New York's financial problems stemmed exclusively from "the prolonged economic depression and the necessity of providing relief for the needy and unemployed."[86] Hubris was apparently not among the contributing factors. The problem, rather, had to do with the national economy alone—local growth was unproblematic. Such excuses, as we shall see, would be repeated during the urban fiscal crises of the 1970s.

And when local economic problems *were* considered as both distinctive and important, the kind of solutions posited by property owners and their allies framed them as "technical" or "technological" in nature—certainly not political (see figure 6.3). A proposal for urban redevelopment authored by the Urban Land Institute (ULI)—a prominent real estate industry think tank that was called by one housing official the "Fabian society of the real estate boards"—insisted that the fiscal problems of cities rested primarily "upon technological changes which permit an ever-lengthening urban radius, plus defective city patterns of land use, which make escape from old areas desirable."[87] This is not to say that realty groups did not admit that high land values had contributed to "blight," as we shall see in the next chapter, but they generally did so in an exceptionally nonpolitical manner. The ULI, in an extraordinary use of the passive voice, delicately admitted in 1940 that "excessively

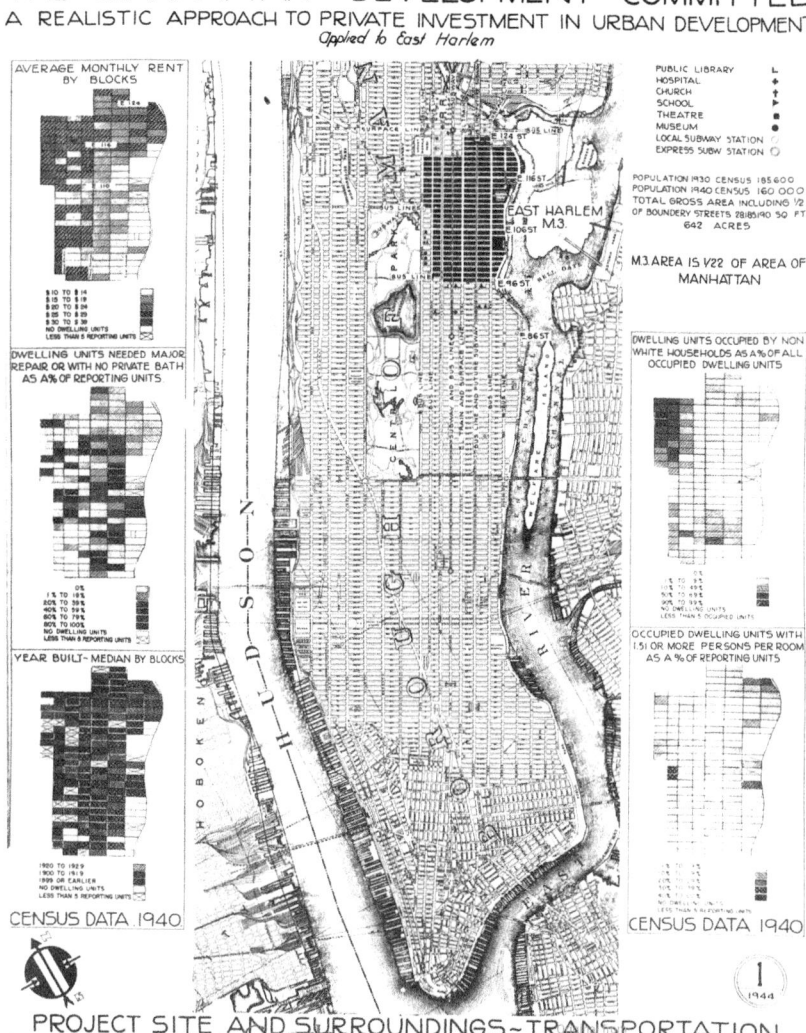

THE MANHATTAN DEVELOPMENT COMMITTEE
A REALISTIC APPROACH TO PRIVATE INVESTMENT IN URBAN DEVELOPMENT
Applied to East Harlem

PROJECT SITE AND SURROUNDINGS~TRANSPORTATION
-77-   HAROLD R SLEEPER A A BRUNNER FUND SCHOLAR UN S HARMON GURNEY AIA

FIGURE 6.3. Harold Sleeper, *A Realistic Approach to Private Investment in Urban Redevelopment Applied to East Harlem as a Blighted Area* (New York: Architectural Forum, 1945). In 1945, the Manhattan Development Committee—whose members included officials in the Bowery Savings Bank, the Bank for Savings, and the Mutual Life Insurance Company—developed a plan for taking advantage of New York's new redevelopment legislation as a way to "protect institutional investments" in East Harlem. Their "realistic approach" stressed the age and disrepair of buildings as causing "blight" while underplaying the role of private land speculation in bringing about these conditions. By framing the problems of cities as largely technical in nature, these and similar studies helped depoliticize developmental issues in New York during the early postwar period.

high land values are cited as a cause of blight in central districts."[88] A similar redevelopment proposal coauthored by Keynesian economist Alvin Hansen argued that technological developments in "society as a whole can be held mainly to blame" for blight, rather than "a[n] individual, group of individuals, or even a group of institutions such as the life insurance companies and savings bank."[89] Thus while Hansen and groups like the ULI could admit that high land values or even speculation could cause urban ills, they rarely critiqued the broader hopes for growth and profit—hopes shared and pursued for decades by public and private actors with "stakes in congestion"—that helped establish such "blight" to begin with.

For fiscal radicals like Philip Cornick, of course, all this was criminal evasion. Responding to a redevelopment proposal by the National Association of Real Estate Brokers, Philip Cornick complained that the "undue emphasis" that this bill placed on "technological change" or "societal mistakes" as the source of urban fiscal crises obscured the *political* origins of these crises: realty speculators and their enablers.[90] Similarly, defining "blight" in terms of technical "obsolescence" obscured how speculative landlords drove central-city disinvestment and decay—which was how housing reformers like Mabel Walker had defined "blight" to begin with.[91]

But it was perhaps Charles Abrams who identified the most troubling implication of the federal government's urban interventions during the 1940s. Writing at the end of the decade, Abrams reflected on how, all through the Depression, local business interests had pressured local governments into providing them with subsidies. In acquiescing to these demands, cities had rendered local budgets, employment, and welfare services dependent on those interests and their growth. And now the federal government, rather than wean the nation's fiscal and social well-being off this destructive dependency, had immeasurably deepened it by devoting the tax dollars of the public at large toward guaranteeing the profits and subsidizing the losses of local business interests (while paying for their social costs via an expanded welfare state). Of course, such subsidies and welfare services were necessary because of businesses' failures in the first place—but rather than address this root cause, the federal government preferred to follow the lead of these business interests, "as short sighted as they [were] powerful." Seen from this perspective, the postwar growth of federal spending was not a sign of progress but of the nation "stumbling blindly" toward a "subsidies to business economy"—or what he elsewhere termed a "business welfare state."[92]

But Abrams's criticisms were out of step with the times. While discussions of economic "maturity" and the need for restrictions upon "irresponsible growth" might have accompanied the early Depression, by the mid-1940s, such pessimistic voices had largely been banished from the public sphere. Despite fears of a postwar recession, World War II seemed to indicate that whatever "secular stagnation" private enterprise was experiencing could be reversed through robust public spending. And while the economic challenges of America's cities still appeared grievous, the general tone among the American realty industry and its allies was of confidence and technical mastery. As Guy Greer stated toward the conclusion of one redevelopment proposal, "We are learning at last how to make our financial mechanisms, not the masters but the servants of our society—how to make them fit the facts of our power to produce what we want when we want it."[93]

And so, insulated by subsidies and laden with the "sunk costs" of confidence, New York surged into the postwar era, ready for growth once more.

Conclusion

Those who had benefited from local subsidies on behalf of real estate in the 1920s—landlords, developers, realty investors, and the city's growing ranks of small homeowners—campaigned to demand these subsidies in the midst of the Depression. They were joined by many public officials who believed any curtailment of realty subsidies threatened their city's property values and hence budget. And these groups were generally successful. Through ceaseless mobilizations in local government, by the early 1940s, these groups had succeeded in maintaining high capital spending on behalf of infrastructure, passing urban redevelopment legislation on behalf of central-city realty investors, continuing citywide subsidies for local improvements, and defeating "restrictive" zoning and planning initiatives from the CPC. And these local victories were accompanied by federal assistance in the form FHA mortgages, WPA infrastructure projects, and urban renewal legislation.

While these subsidies helped realty recover its strength, more insidious was the depoliticization of local economic development that accompanied it. On the one hand, bodies like the Urban Land Institute framed the fiscal problem of cities as largely matters of technique and technology. On the other hand, the kind of liberal policymakers and economists who had previously joined campaigns for local economic reconstruction now largely looked to the national state for deliverance. In either case, both the need and possibility for radical fiscal reform in American cities was increasingly questioned by the 1940s—further narrowing the fiscal imaginary of American cities.

Nonetheless, the shock wrought by the realty crash of the early Depression had not entirely dissipated. Federal aid might be useful as a stopgap, those concerned with the future of urban realty believed, but a broader rethinking of urban economics was necessary if the value of cities—and the value of their investments—was to be preserved. And by the 1940s, this rethinking was indeed producing such a paradigm shift, one oriented around income-producing enterprises as the economic "base" of cities. But however different in form, the way cities translated this imaginary into policy in the postwar era would ultimately reproduce fiscal inequity and instability in ways that continue to harm American communities.

PART III

No Alternative, 1945–1981

7

"Front Office to the World"

When municipal bond dealers J. A. White & Company wrote a guide for bond purchasers in 1942, they included a warning. "From the creditor's standpoint," they advised, ". . . it is important to know, not so much how much foreign element there is in a community, but rather, from where does this foreign element come."[1] Their reasoning was simple. The collapse of real estate values during the Depression, they believed, indicated that property values alone were an insufficient surety for municipal loans. Only the future income stream of a borrower could provide lenders with security. And insofar as the "character-traits" of an applicant were relevant for their future income—including their "racial" or "ethnic" traits—these were factors that responsible lenders needed to take into account before making a loan to a city. Thus J. A. White & Company proceeded to discuss the relative credit risks of lending to cities with a large northern European population (whose "characteristics" included "being thrifty, for being slow to spend money, for thinking of the winter that is to come") versus those with a large southern European population (whose "characteristics" included "gaiety, for spending money freely, for thinking of the summer that is here").[2]

But discriminating among income holders was not sufficient when appraising local economies, J. A. White & Company cautioned. Attention also needed to be paid to a city's *sources* of income—that is, its occupational sectors. Cultivating such sectors, building up what economists were beginning to call an "economic base," was becoming a critical test of local fiscal health in the eyes of both loan officers and municipal officials alike in the wake of the Depression. And insofar as industries that provided greater incomes represented greater surety for both realty and municipal loans, developers and public officials turned to large corporations and white-collar industries for economic salvation. As one New York developer later exclaimed, "As we have lost industrial workers from the population, we have gained higher-paid, higher-educated administrative personnel." The decline of New York manufacturing, he asserted, was a "magnificent thing."[3] But just as the assumptions held by loan officers around the "natural" work habits of different nationalities could be faulty, so assumptions by local boosters around the stability of a white-collar economic base could also be faulty—as they would soon prove to be.

This chapter explores how shifts in urban economic thought during the 1940s, prompted in part by the collapse of realty values during the Depression, promoted both white supremacy and white-collar enterprise in the postwar era. The value of real estate parcels and cities alike, a growing number of realty investors and municipal bondholders argued, could not be gauged by the location and condition of its structures alone.[4] Rather, it was the *income* earned by individuals and generated by industry that constituted the fiscal health of a city. And during the 1940s, prominent New York realty groups and commercial organizations looked specifically to white-collar enterprises, with their high profits and highly paid employees, as their city's most "natural" economic base. Aligning with local policymakers, these organizations pushed to reshape New York to meet the needs of these enterprises and their workers through tools like urban renewal, expelling manufacturing jobs and altering the economic makeup of the metropolis as they did so. And most policymakers, even those supportive of New York's burgeoning "social-democratic" welfare state, assured themselves that cultivating large corporations and wealthy financial industries would help finance generous social services and prevent a repeat of their city's earlier fiscal crisis. But even when the fiscal crisis of the 1970s put a lie to such assumptions, few had the imagination to re-think the city's dominant growth strategies—or the strength to overturn them.

By tracing the transformation of urban economic thought after the Great Depression, we can better understand why many local actors seized upon white-collar work as the fiscal salvation of American cities during the postwar era.[5] Chastened by the boom-and-bust cycle of real estate speculation, by the late 1930s, urban economists and realty bodies increasing believed that attracting income-generating enterprises represented a more secure revenue source than earlier theories of urban growth based around land and location. And if we understand this postwar development strategy as a *response* to the speculative excesses of the Depression, we can better understand why such a wide range of interests—financial service organizations, public planners, and developers—accepted and promoted this cultivation.

From Land to Income

The mechanics of urban economic development remained only hazily theorized before the 1930s.[6] The RPNY's chief economist, Robert Haig, confessed in 1926 that developing "a clear conception of the city as an economic phenomenon" was a "broad and virgin field which the economist is called upon to cultivate in connection with modern city planning."[7] And as late as 1937, the National Resources Committee lamented that "planning agencies and planners have been slow to recognize or to give proper emphasis to the . . . economic objectives and aspects of planning and zoning."[8] That it remained uncultivated was partly due to a complacency engendered by the general realty "boom" of the 1920s. But it was also due to the era's prevailing theories of urban economies themselves, which stressed growing land values rather than enterprises as the key to local fiscal health. This began to change during the early 1930s, however, as those concerned with the broader future of urban economies—larger realty investors, planners, and developers—grappled with the rapid and seemingly permanent collapse of urban land values. Attention shifted to attracting and retaining income-generating industries as the key problematic of urban economics—a shift embodied by the prominence of new concepts like the "economic base." And many prominent commercial organizations, who had long valorized white-collar work, wasted little time in promoting their industry as the best such base for cities.

Before the 1930s, urban realty investors and municipal finance officers generally stressed the location of structures as the source of property values and, via the medium of property taxation, urban finances as a whole. While theorists like Richard Hurd and Lawson Purdy had identified the *use* of land as an important factor in valuation, they generally gave little attention to what the most productive uses of land actually were—or how such uses might shape broader patterns of urban growth. Rather, they assumed that growing land values would eventually sort out "higher and better" land uses on their own accord (with some occasional nudging from zoning authorities). And real estate speculators, municipal assessors, and left-leaning Georgists agreed that urban land values were on a perennial upward trajectory—growing populations and the "monopoly value" of central-city locations would ensure that the most intensive and hence "highest" uses would invariably occur there and radiate outward. The only question was who would appropriate these increased values. As one realty appraiser noted in 1935, "Past ideas of value held by owners have tended to uphold Henry George's theory of the value of land. . . . All one had to do was to buy land and wait for the profits which were sure to come, and recurrent booms imparted a semblance of truth to the theory."[9]

The early 1930s collapse of realty values and local finances, however, shattered these assumptions—and prompted a broader rethinking of what made for a healthy urban economy. True, many realty bodies and their political allies, as we have seen, remained unreconstructed realty "boosters" who sought federal aid based on the assumption that growing land values alone would be sufficient to restore the private realty market. But other urban economists and larger realty organizations—concerned (they liked to believe) with the broader future of their cities and less desperate for immediate aid than smaller "curbstoners"—believed something fundamental had changed in urban economies.[10] In titles like *Revolution in Land* (by housing reformer Charles Abrams) and "The Land-Tax Illusion" (by Emigrant Savings Bank president Robert Hoguet), prominent voices argued that new transportation and communication technologies had permanently lessened urban land's monopoly value.[11] And there was some grounds for this: by 1922, most of New York's taxes were being derived from improvements upon the land rather than land values themselves.[12] And Manhattan's land values would continue to fall until 1950 and would not reach their pre-crash heights until 1977.[13] But if high land values alone could not ensure financial stability for individual realty parcels or entire cities, what could?

By the early 1930s, a new generation of appraisal theorists and realty practitioners were arriving at an answer: *income*. It was capitalized net income, drawn either from the wealth of individuals or the profits generated by enterprise, that was the ultimate surety for real estate—and, by extension, urban finances. As early as 1926, the economist Robert Haig argued that whereas previous realty theorists like Richard Hurd had earlier called buildings "servants of land," in fact it was "the uses which determine the land values rather than vice versa."[14] And as older ideas of land valuation were discredited in the wake of the 1930s crash, this alternative approach toward valuation was increasingly taken up in appraisal journals and textbooks: one such article in the *Journal of the American Institute of Real Estate Appraisal* insisted that "there never has been any value in land other than that arising from its income or use."[15]

By the later 1930s, this argument was taken up by a broad range of realty investors and municipal finance bodies, for whom a focus on "income" seemed a more reliable basis for appraising the value of a parcel or city than older approaches. It was proselytized by realty groups like the National Association of Real Estate Brokers and the Urban Land Institute, with the latter arguing that "modern valuation theory tends more and more to the viewpoint that all property values are dependent upon productivity and income."[16]

It was taken up by municipal bond purchasers as well: loan officers, a 1938 article on municipal credit in *Banker's Magazine* argued, needed to know "the sources of income and other base elements upon which . . . the income of the population of a community is derived" in order to determine whether to buy bonds or not.[17]

And where municipal bond purchasers went, public officials were sure to follow, including fiscal radicals in the CPC for whom "income" represented a less speculative source of urban finances than land values alone. "The assumption that taxes are produced by land is no more than a fiction," Rexford Tugwell growled in 1942. Rather, "taxes come out of incomes—the total annual income—of the city's population which is yielded by productive activities."[18] And a year later, his fellow City Planning Commission member Roger Cleveland concurred, writing that the only way to restore New York's finances was to "raise the total of incomes" in Gotham.[19] And if raising "income" was becoming a priority for local finance officials, an additional theory—the "economic base"—was providing a framework explaining precisely which activities were most important for growing that income.[20]

Base Building

The need for such a new framework for understanding urban economies became a cause of planners during the 1930s, many of whom lamented that earlier land economists had focused more on zoning and transportation than on the mechanics of urban prosperity itself. As the National Resources Committee complained in 1937, studies of "the economic base of the community, its soundness, deficiencies and its prospects, and the need for a selective program of industrial development have been almost wholly overlooked."[21] By the early 1940s, however, economists like Homer Hoyt—a former real estate broker and realty economist (as well as a firm believer in the "income-stream" theory of appraisal)—were filling in this gap. After working as chief economist for the FHA and performing research for the Urban Land Institute, Hoyt served as director of economic studies at the RPNY. There, in 1944, he authored the influential report *The Economic Status of the New York Region*— what one scholar called the first "complete statement of the theory of the economic base."[22]

In this and other papers written in the early 1940s, Hoyt argued that a city's fiscal health was determined not by the value of its land but by the income of its residents and enterprises. And this income was determined by a city's economic "base"—its main sources of employment, particularly exports (see figure 7.1). The domestic market for city enterprises, Hoyt argued,

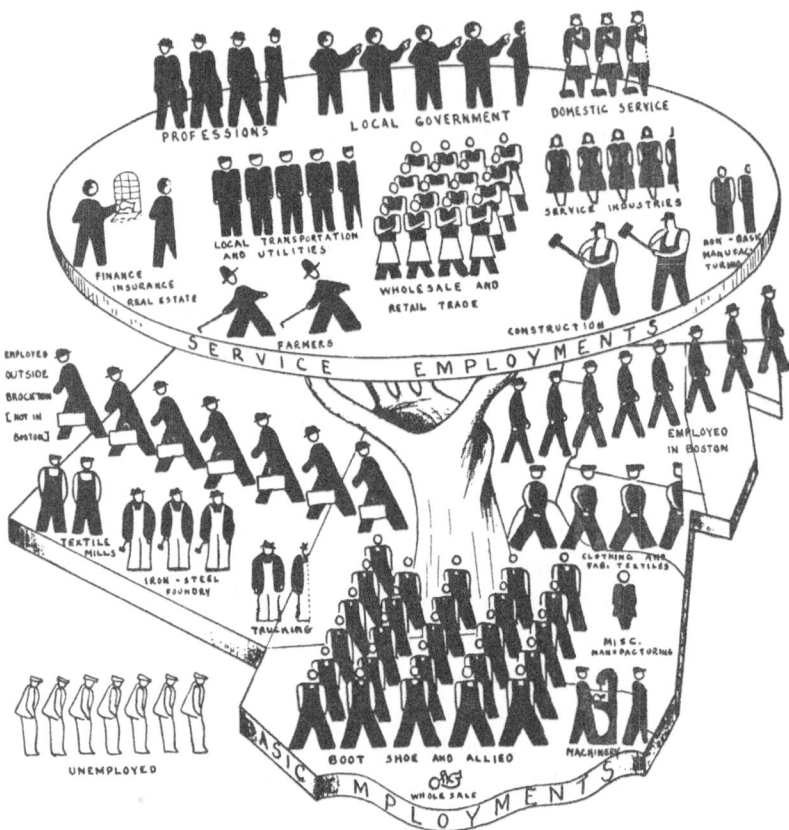

BASIC & SERVICE EMPLOYMENTS

BROCKTON ECONOMIC AREA - 1946

EACH FIGURE REPRESENTS 500 PERSONS

PROFESSIONS

LOCAL GOVERNMENT

DOMESTIC SERVICE

FINANCE INSURANCE REAL ESTATE

LOCAL TRANSPORTATION AND UTILITIES

SERVICE INDUSTRIES

NON-BASIC MANUFACTURING

FARMERS

WHOLESALE AND RETAIL TRADE

CONSTRUCTION

SERVICE EMPLOYMENTS

EMPLOYED OUTSIDE BROCKTON [NOT IN BOSTON]

EMPLOYED IN BOSTON

TEXTILE MILLS

IRON-STEEL FOUNDRY

CLOTHING AND FAB. TEXTILES

TRUCKING

MISC. MANUFACTURING

UNEMPLOYED

BOOT SHOE AND ALLIED

MACHINERY

WHOLESALE

BASIC EMPLOYMENTS

EACH 1.225 BASIC JOBS SUPPORT 1.0 SERVICE JOB

HOMER HOYT ASSOCIATES - MAY 1948

FIGURE 7.1. Homer Hoyt, *According to Hoyt: 53 Years of Homer Hoyt, 1916 to 1969* (Washington, DC: Homer Hoyt, 1970), 713. Permission rights granted by Michael Hoyt. A visual depiction of Homer Hoyt's economic base theory from 1949, emphasizing how a city's exports—in the case of Brockton, the boot shoe industry—provided the basis for the city's domestic, service, professions, and government work. Later urban economists like Raymond Vernon would build on this work while stressing white-collar work as the ideal economic "base" for cities.

was simply too small to handle the fiscal needs of a modern metropolis. Locally oriented industries were, at best, spin-offs from the more fundamental
and "basic" component of the urban economy: exports. While producing for
outside markets was, of course, not a novel development strategy for cities,
Hoyt elevated it to *the* organizing principle for urban economies. "A city,"
he argued, "cannot live on itself."[23] It was therefore imperative to Hoyt that
cities use whatever means they had to attract and retain income-generating,
export-oriented employers. High land values alone could not replace such
employers: as Hoyt complained, "If the assessed value of New York City's real
estate would be made to conform to values that exist at the present time as
evidenced by income . . . New York City would be legally bankrupt." But to
attract such employers, New York and other cities needed to address all that
might alienate them, which ranged from "racketeering labor practices," "high
taxes," and "traffic difficulties" to local governments "unfriendly to business"
and "poorly laid out and planned areas in which business may be conducted."
All these factors, Hoyt warned, could alienate future employers from a city–
employers who now, aided by technologically induced mobility, were quite
free to take their business elsewhere unless cities responded promptly.[24]

There was one final component of Hoyt's theory: growth was no longer
optional for cities. This was not, he admitted, because growth was necessarily *better* for its citizens' well-being. "A city," he admitted, "may have been
just as well off, and a better place in which to live, if it had never received the
influx of new industries which caused it to expand its residential areas and to
increase its utility and school plant." But once that expansion had taken place,
once investments had been laid and expectations set, there was no turning
back. It was "of fundamental importance," Hoyt declared, "for a city that has
attained a certain size to maintain that size by strengthening its economic
base so that it can continue to employ the same or a greater number of people." The options were clear: grow or die.[25]

Hoyt's theory of the economic base was immediately hailed as path breaking and by 1950 had become, as one historian has described, both one of the
"the primary tools of regional planning" and "accepted, uncritically, as an
explanation of local-area growth and economic development."[26] Part of the
reason for the popularity of the "economic base" can be explained by its post-
Depression context: after a decade of fiscal crisis and realty collapse, the idea
of forging local economies around productive income seemed a more reliable, less speculative approach toward local growth than antediluvian strategies stressing land values alone. Economist Richard U. Ratcliff, a fellow veteran of the FHA, declared that Hoyt's analysis "might easily be employed with
great benefit by local and state planning boards the country over."[27] National

Housing Agency president Charles S. Ascher asserted that Hoyt's base analysis "should be applied to cities of various sizes and types."[28] And this was certainly the case in New York, where postwar policy documents addressing concepts as varied as rezoning, urban renewal, and statewide development policy all explicitly employed the phrase "economic base."[29]

But while these new theories of urban economics might appear to be "scientific" improvements over earlier approaches, their implementation would nonetheless reflect—and entrench—older assumptions and inequities. Insofar as Black and other nonwhite citizens were perceived as "less employable" or generated less income than white citizens, for example, loan officers adopting the "income-stream" theory would be less likely to provide them with credit or a mortgage. The FHA's first underwriting director, Frederick Babcock, for example, boasted that his organization's underwriting manual had popularized "the long-range probabilities of satisfactory future income" as a component of mortgage loan evaluation—and the manual used this criteria as a basis for arguing that districts with "incompatible racial elements" should be denied such loans.[30] Similarly, the *Banker's Magazine* article on municipal finance warned that bond purchasers needed to appraise the racial constituency of cities before a purchase—as "the economic capacity or the earning power is not equal for all races."[31] And Homer Hoyt himself, who worked with Babcock to produce the FHA's first underwriting manual, warned that the "infiltration of diverse racial groups" could lower property values and ultimately erode a city's economic base.[32] Such assumptions would help block nonwhite neighborhoods from both public and private sources of financing, thus weakening the economic health of cities more broadly as urban nonwhite populations proportionately grew in the postwar period.[33] In attempting to use the tools of discrimination to establish economic resilience, Hoyt and other advocates of the "income stream" would ultimately defeat their own purposes.

But if practitioners of the "new" urban economics were reproducing older assumptions regarding which citizens were most economically "reliable," they were doing something similar regarding which *industries* were most reliable for cities. For white-collar industries, like white-people, had long been seen by prominent realty groups as the greatest surety for property values. And now, in the wake of the Great Depression, these older assumptions would be updated, entrenched, and translated into public policy as never before.

White Collar

If developing an "economic base" was a relatively new priority for postwar economists and planners, seeing white-collar work as the pinnacle of urban economies was not. From urban "boosters" like RPNY in the 1920s to agrarian critics of urbanism in the 1930s, all saw what have come to be known as "advanced service" professions—those related to finance, insurance, corporate management, law, communications, and information processing—as the quintessential "urban" occupations. Such perceptions, however exaggerated and distorted, were reinforced by a host of postwar planning, realty, and commercial associations. Their white-collar fiscal imaginary, once translated into policy, would render the corporate office as the supreme means and ends of postwar urban economic development.

The belief that financial operations on a national scale represented the "culmination" of urban economies predated the 1950s, of course. Public expenditures on behalf of New York's linkages to the broader nation, exemplified through its port, canals, railroads, and new communication devices like the telegraph, had garnered public support through the nineteenth century. And many boosters of the "Empire City" hailed their city's financial services for the wealth it drew and dispensed across the nation, with some framing the relationship in an unabashedly colonial fashion: as one declared in 1865, "Every new mine opened, every town built up, comes into relations with New York; and every railroad, no matter how short, has one terminus here."[34] Nonetheless, most planning on behalf of the city's extralocal linkages were through projects like roads or docks—they did not necessarily address questions of land use and land valuation themselves, particularly in central-city districts.[35]

By the early 1920s, however, the growing disciplines of land economics and the profession of urban planning began to concern themselves with the "highest and best" use of urban land itself—a question that would become of growing concern as the trajectory of land values plummeted during the early Depression. And the Regional Plan Association of New York, whose members included a mixture of realty investors, urban planners, and the city's more influential corporate and financial figures, had begun to develop a corpus of works expressing white-collar work as *the* highest and best use of urban space.

The chief developer and exponent of this theory, expressed in books like *Major Economic Factors in Metropolitan Growth and Arrangement* and articles in the *Quarterly Journal of Economics*, was RPNY's chief economist, Robert Haig. Haig argued that the best use of land was one that made the most profitable use of the "physical proximity"—and white-collar work was that use.[36] "Managerial functions," Haig asserted, required frequent person-to-person contact in order to share complex information and coordinate activities. Urban space facilitated such contact by giving "the greatest possible ease of contact among men whose presence is desired in arriving at decisions."[37] On the grounds of efficiency and income, therefore, the central portions of a metropolis should be reserved for managerial work—or, as Haig argued elsewhere, "It would be a tragic waste to turn Times Square into a potato patch."[38] And all things being equal, large and internationally oriented firms should be cultivated within the central city more than smaller and more locally oriented firms—again, on the grounds of income. Haig used the example of an international bank processing a $25 million loan to Norway versus a branch bank deciding whether a haberdasher should be granted a loan of $250. "One transaction may require no more physical space than the other and about the same amount of time," he wrote, "but the Norway decision will be made by a man whose time may be worth more per hour than the branch bank manager earns in a month."[39] The former could take greater advantage of urban space to generate far greater income than the latter and thus should be given precedence.

Haig's valorization of international finance was mirrored, ironically, by those who criticized large cities in the 1930s. The city, in the mind of agrarians like Herbert Agar, was "rooted in high finance—the most abstract and inhuman of man's devices."[40] For these critics, urban economies were synonymous with the kind of cosmopolitan and parasitic bankers who had ruined the economy—with "monopoly capitalism," "credit finance," "realty speculation," and more besides. Even Lewis Mumford, who saw some value in metropolitan life, asserted that "any effort to reconstitute the metropolis" along nonfinancial and nonspeculative lines "must go against the basic pattern of the metropolitan economy."[41] In saying this, of course, Mumford was suggesting that speculation and finance constituted the "basic pattern" of the metropolis. The notion that metropolitan economies could be reconstituted along different lines was not entertained by him or many others.

But if financial activities were disparaged by planners like Mumford, other elements of the urban economy—such as manufacturing—were given even less credence by many fiscal radicals. Rexford Tugwell's master plan of 1940, for example, anticipated that while New York's financial district would remain in place over the coming decades, many of its industrial areas were diminishing in importance and "will eventually be abandoned" for more "appropriate purposes."[42] Even left-wing housing reformer Catherine Bauer made a similar assertion when speaking of decentralizing manufacturing plants. "There's no use trying to 'bring back' the industries that have moved out or the workers in those industries," she declared. Rather, New York needed to attract "offices for business and government" and "professional services," which were among "those truly metropolitan functions that remain centralized and are now its prime reason for existence."[43] There is some irony here, of course, as financial

and corporate actors had been heavy investors in the kind of speculative realty development that had helped wreck local economies in the Depression.
Most radical urban planners and housing advocates, however, saved their ire
for their most immediate opponents—the urban realty industry. The broader
corporate sector was, for these groups, not generally an object of opprobrium.

And if radicals like Catherine Bauer were willing to celebrate "offices for
business," New York's financial and corporate firms were even more eager to
proclaim their industry's indispensability. A 1946 Bankers Trust report, *New
York and the Future*, for example, stated that New York represented, above
all, a "great reservoir of private credit and investment capital." "The nation
needs," it boldly declared, "this concentration of fluid wealth and the machinery required to administer it."[44] Twelve years later, this rhetoric was echoed
by the Downtown–Lower Manhattan Association (DLMA), a powerful association of corporate and financial entities with deep ties to (and investments
in) the blocks surrounding Wall Street. "Banks and trust companies, stock
exchanges and brokers, investment banking houses and insurance firms," its
inaugural report asserted, "made the narrow tip of Manhattan the center of
international finance. This is the very heart-pump of America's free economy,
circulating creative capital to the furthest reaches of the Union." It was thus
"international finance" that made New York the "front office to the world," in
the DLMA's words.[45]

The city's realty industry similarly welcomed white-collar deliverance,
seeing corporate income (and the rents drawn from their well-compensated
managers) as a more reliable source of revenue than rising land values alone.
One developer, for example, hailed white-collar offices as being "ten times
more valuable than industrial space" because they "draw the profits from . . .
all over the country and abroad."[46] Indeed, New York's larger realty developers
and investors saw their relation with the city's corporate sector as largely sym-
biotic, with the president of REBNY declaring that "the real estate industry is
keeping New York City 'The Front Office of the Nation.' "[47]

And these assumptions around white-collar work's urban centrality were
further refined in the late 1950s by massive studies prompted by, yet again,
the Regional Plan Association of New York. Conducted in partnership with
Harvard University and financed by some of the nation's largest private foundations (Rockefeller, Ford, Twentieth Century Fund), the New York Metropolitan Region Study (NYMRS) was a large-scale effort to quantify and pre-
dict the future of as many aspects of the region's economic base as possible
in preparation for the RPA's Second Regional Plan. The study was directed
by Raymond Vernon, who had both worked on the Securities and Exchange
Commission and helped develop the International Monetary Fund, among

other accomplishments.[48] Through the NYMRS Vernon brought his international financial experience—and bias—to bear on the urban economy.

In many ways, Vernon's work was a more theoretically complex version of Haig's arguments—which was unsurprising as, by 1961, "Haig's analytical framework and conclusions have been accepted by virtually all land economists," in the words of one economist.[49] The economic value of urban density for enterprises, Vernon argued, was twofold. On the one hand, density enabled firms to take advantage of shared capital infrastructure.[50] On the other hand, density could allow firms, suppliers, and customers to speedily communicate complex information between individuals. On these grounds, large manufacturing concerns had less of a functional need for a dense urban location—their products were largely standardized, and their capital requirements were largely handled internally.[51]

White-collar firms, however, had to process such complex topics as "the credit of an individual, the affairs of an enterprise, the condition of a trade, the politics of a nation," and other weighty issues.[52] And urban proximity, Vernon asserted, was required for adequately dealing with this information.[53] It was on these grounds that white-collar work was the "natural" heir to the dense city center, regardless of the decentralization of other industries. Vernon's overall summary of the NYMRS in 1961 unsurprisingly confirmed his belief that New York would, in the words of one reviewer, become a "center for the financial and industrial 'elite'" who would "make the top-level decisions concerning the workings of the nation's economy."[54]

There was somewhat of a self-serving nature to these assumptions that white-collar work was the "heir" to the city center, of course. Groups who held or invested in downtown property, as we have seen, were wary of writing off or even writing down their losses during the Depression—and feared that even more losses could be to come in the wake of postwar decentralization. But by asserting that their property's central locations were permanent assets for the nation's largest and wealthiest corporations, realty developers could ensure there was a steady demand for said property. As developer David Tishman asserted in 1958, "With our economy still being accelerated because of the wider use of automation" and "the rise of new technologies and business services, the demand for new office space [in the central city] should continue as strong as ever."[55]

Nonetheless, bodies like REBNY and the RPNY cautioned against complacency. As Hoyt had warned and others had seconded during the early 1940s, transportation and communication advances had robbed cities of any "automatic" locational advantages they might have enjoyed in the past.[56] In order to survive, they argued, New York needed to make its environment more

NEW YORK CITY DEPARTMENT OF

COMMERCE AND PUBLIC EVENTS

HIGHLIGHTS

Published by New York City Department of Commerce and Public Events · Richard C. Patterson, Jr., Commissioner
Margot Gayle, Editor · Mary Gorman, Managing Editor
Edward L. Bernays, Public Relations Counsel

JANUARY, 1961 129 VOL. V, No. 1

NAMED CHAIRMAN

Robert Watt, left, Acting First Deputy Commissioner of the Department of Commerce and Public Events, on the event of his appointment as chairman of the Advisory Committee of the U.S. World Trade Fair Corp. He is shown above with Z. B. Hyde, general manager, and Charles Snitow, president of the corporation. They are examining the official poster for the 1961 U.S. World Trade Fair to be held in the Coliseum May 3 to May 14.

Mayor Gets Fed. Grant For Two Renewal Jobs

Two of Mayor Wagner's proposals for removing eyesores and cleaning up Lower Manhattan were activated recently when the Federal Housing and Home Finance Agency allocated New York City $681,000 for their survey and planning.

The advances, according to the Mayor, are against grants totaling $20.8 million which have been earmarked by the

(Continued on Page 6)

Realtor Claims City Gains New Industries

"Industry beginning to move back to cities," is the headline of an article by C. Armel Nutter, Camden, New Jersey, president of the National Association of Real Estate Boards, which appeared in a recent issue of The United States Municipal News published by the U.S. Conference of Mayors. New York City's regional economists have long attested this.

(Continued on Page 3)

Business, Finance Look At 1961 City, Industrial, Real Estate

Led by Mayor Robert F. Wagner and subscribed to by business men ranging from the apparel trades to the sedate board rooms of Wall Street, there is optimism for the business outlook in 1961. Although sometimes guarded, according to a Department of Commerce and Public Events survey just completed, the forecasts are bright.

The guarded optimistic predictions came from transportation and apparel for the most part. Almost nobody expects a sharp upturn during the first part of the year. However, a staunch belief in the soundness of the city's economy, based in many instances on confidence in the change of Federal Government Administration, pervaded all statements from leaders in finance, commerce and industry in New York City.

Mayor Robert F. Wagner's comment on New York City's economic climate is:

"Based on the optimism expressed by leaders of commerce and industry in New York City for the outlook in 1961, and on my own observances of local economic conditions, I feel that this year for New Yorkers

(Continued on Page 2)

NEW VEEPS

Bankers Trust Company has named three new vice presidents—John W. Fiske Jr., Arthur B. Griffin Jr., and James F. O'Donnell. All formerly were assistant vice presidents.

Surplus Dealers To Display $100,000,000 Worth Of Goods

Between February 12th and 14th dealers from all over the United States and buyers for foreign countries will see samples of $100,000,000 worth of surplus merchandise at the 15th Trade Show, sponsored by the Institute of Surplus Dealers at the New York Trade Show Bldg., Eighth Ave. and 35th St. Wares on display will include government surplus material and excess stocks of industrial goods and it is estimated that about 4,000 dealers from all parts of the country, including

exporters and representatives of foreign governments and business firms, will attend, according to Fred D. Reder, executive director of the Institute.

Those attending will include retailers, jobbers, purchasing agents for discount houses, chain drug and variety stores, bargain basements of department stores and non-food departments in supermarkets.

Among items in the display will be plumbing supplies, electronics, hardware and tools,

(Continued on Page 4)

FIGURE 7.2. New York Department of Commerce and Public Events, *Highlights* 5, no. 1 (1961). Courtesy General Society of Mechanics and Tradesmen. Whereas before World War II, most of New York City's public-led developmental strategies had revolved around transportation, real estate, and port development, its postwar approach (as indicated by this 1961 brochure by the city's Department of Commerce and Public Events) stressed income-generating firms as the city's economic "base."

friendly to businesses—more specifically, white-collar enterprises whose national purview gave them both the ability and inclination to move once better business conditions beckoned elsewhere. And policymakers, heeding the advice of influential bodies like REBNY and the DLMA, were receptive to their urgency (see figure 7.2). As New York's Mayor Wagner declared in a speech

on "New York as the World's Financial Center," "We are competing with every other community—small and large, north, south and west—for business
to come here and add to our growth."[57] But only certain kinds of businesses,
many of New York's citizens found out, would be welcome.

Renewing

During the 1940s and 1950s, large commercial bodies like the DLMA, professional planning groups like the RPNY, and influential journals like the *New
York Times* pressed for policymakers to promote a particular fiscal imaginary:
that of a white-collar metropolis. Policymakers like Mayor Wagner generally obliged, declaring in 1961 that "augmented by the vigorous and imagina-
tive programs generated by business interests themselves," his administration
would promote "commercial construction in mid-Manhattan," a "huge redevelopment program in Downtown Manhattan," "a new heliport," and other
amenities on behalf of white-collardom.[58] And postwar economic paradigms
like the "economic base" and "central business districts" helped further rationalize these policies. For example, the City Planning Commission argued
that efforts to improve the city's port should be based on "strengthening or
maintaining the City's economic base"—a base they generally saw as coexten-
sive with "the Central Business District as the nation's business and financial
headquarters."[59] In this way, the revolution in urban economics prompted by
the Depression was translated into policies that rendered New York more
dependent than ever upon its wealthiest "business interests."

That white-collar work should have been the focus of municipal aid in the
postwar era was not entirely self-evident. Blue-collar workers, after all, comprised 60 percent of the metropolitan region's workforce in 1944 and close to
half of New York City's workers.[60] And there were some efforts to promote
and retain these industries; an industrial survey released to the city's comptroller in 1937 asserted that "we cannot take our continued industrial power
for granted" and argued that the city should have a central agency dedicated
to "keeping worthwhile industry here and getting new and acceptable manufacturers to locate here."[61] This report led to the formation of a Department of
Commerce in 1940, which was instrumental in procuring industrial contracts
for New York during World War II.[62] As late as 1956, a report by the New York
Area Research Council declared that "manufacturing has been the economic
base of the city" and "every effort must be expended to preserve it."[63]

Most of New York's political leaders, however, were, in labor historian
Joshua Freeman's words, "sanguine" about the flight of industrial jobs.[64] The
same 1956 report by the New York Area Research Council found that public

agencies in the city had "not been sufficiently sympathetic to and conscious of the manufacturing industry as a vital force" in the region.[65] Such lack of concern was reflected in a later statement from Frank Connaughton, the deputy commissioner of the city's Department of Commerce. While "other communities are offering all kinds of inducements to industry to locate there, including tax exemptions, outright gifts of land and other concessions," he declared in 1956, "New York City won't do business that way. We offer the City of New York."[66]

But New York would be quite willing to offer such "gifts" to white-collar enterprise and their employees. As a 1960 report from the New York State Commission on Governmental Operations noted, "There is no doubt that the city government of New York can play a determining role in the retention and expansion of office work jobs. It must, because the future pattern of office employment in New York City will influence its economic future heavily."[67] There was a degree of self-fulfilling prophecy to this statement, of course, given how inhospitable the city had made itself to manufacturing over the previous decades (thanks in no small part to its mono-focus pursuit of high land values).[68] But that aside, New York policymakers in the postwar period—accepting their city's growing dependence on white-collar work and its ancillary industries—sought to make their city further acceptable to corporate industries and their employees.

The notion that cities should cultivate wealthy individuals and globally oriented corporations was not, of course, new to the postwar era. Merchants and urbanists like Frederick Law Olmsted had long stressed international trade as a pillar of New York's economy, and during the early 1930s, the director of the RPNY had stressed "the importance, from the point of view of landowners and taxing authorities, of emphasizing or improving those qualities and aspects of a place which make it attractive to well-to-do people."[69] But with some prominent exceptions like waterfront development, most early city planning policies in New York were generally on behalf of promoting *real estate values* rather than any specific economic enterprise or sectors. By contrast, many post-Depression planners saw a need to drastically remodel the city in order to cultivate particular kinds of businesses, rather than simply land values alone.[70] Such calls for replanning New York for business were echoed through the 1950s from venerable agencies such as the RPNY and the City Club, liberal outlets like the *New York Times*, and more recent bodies like the Rockefeller-formed Downtown–Lower Manhattan Association. These bodies were already committed to a white-collar fiscal imaginary. Now they pressed the city to realize this imaginary through public policy.

Partly these shifts took place through that venerable tool of city planning, zoning reform. Such reforms need not have led to the displacement of industry. No less than Homer Hoyt argued, as a special advisor for a 1950 citywide rezoning plan, that "facilitating the growth of manufacturing employment in New York by zoning more well-located potential industrial sites for factory use" was of "tremendous importance for the future growth and welfare of the city."[71] But it was not to be. During the later 1950s, a private Committee for Modern Zoning, headed by City Investing Company chair Bob Dowling and featuring developers William Zeckendorf and David Tishman, successfully lobbied for drastically restricting zoning for manufacturing enterprises in Manhattan—leading to what one historian has called "the largest elimination of blue-collar jobs in the city's history."[72]

Lowered tax assessments similarly aided white-collar office construction. This is ironic: as we saw before, Tax Department president Lawson Purdy had placed high levies on land in order to *promote* new construction during the early 1900s. But the shift in appraisal theory prompted by the Depression led both realty groups and tax assessors to reevaluate this policy. High taxes on land, they argued, were increasing the price of land to the point where, rather than spur its "higher and better use," it was preventing new income-generating uses from being erected upon them. Indeed, Purdy's successor as president of the Tax Department complained to La Guardia that "assessed valuations on land (had) reached a point where the owners could not develop the property successfully, and builders would not buy the land because of their inability to produce a revenue from the intended improvements on such high-priced land."[73]

Rather than provoking higher and better uses through what Charles Abrams called "the bludgeon of the tax levy," realty groups argued that New York needed to reduce assessments in order to spur development. And this was gradually accomplished—partly on purpose, partly because growing realty values in the postwar era outpaced the city's own reassessments. As early as 1948, a report by the Municipal Department of Lazard Frères wrote approvingly that New York was successfully "eliminating the over-assessment of central area property."[74] By 1960, Manhattan property was generally assessed at less than 90 percent of its market value.[75] And just as before, this assessment was unequal: older and less "high-earning" structures continued to be over-assessed compared to their new skyscraper neighbors.

New York's most conspicuous postwar policy on behalf of white-collar work, however, was urban renewal. The rationale for redesigning cities on behalf of upper-income firms and residents predated the 1950s, of course: the RPNY had forthrightly argued in the 1920s that "where land has a value based on a more profitable use than low-cost housing, such as businesses or expensive residences it should not be used for such housing."[76] But such rationales were given additional credence during the 1940s, as Depression-chastened public officials and business associations sought to avoid further rounds of realty collapse and fiscal crisis. A 1943 article in *Business Week* asserted that only by redesigning New York would "income-earning, rent and tax-paying people" return to the city; the article's headline, "BANKS PUSH WHITE-COLLAR HOUSING," identified which type of people they were talking about.[77] New York's comptroller agreed, arguing the following year that New York's "obsolete" street pattern system and "inadequate" system of small land parcels was a "complete deterrent" to economic development in the metropolis.[78] By 1960, New York's special adviser on housing and urban renewal could declare that "to urban economists, city business leaders, and the responsible heads of municipal governments, urban renewal is the *vital* and *indispensable* condition of sound economic growth and of municipal solvency."[79]

And by this time, billions of dollars were available for urban redevelopment, authorized through local, state, and federal legislation such as Title 1 of the 1949 Housing Act (see figure 7.3). Such aid was often used explicitly on behalf of a white-collar workforce in New York City and elsewhere. A study prepared for New York's Urban Renewal Board in 1960, for example, noted that Manhattan's "manufacturing, retailing, and wholesaling" industries were being replaced by "finance, commerce, and tourism as underlying economic base factors." Title 1 urban renewal, they asserted, could help "attract the broad, quality group" who would help direct this economy. Pointing to plans already in motion, it asserted that "the Coliseum convention hall [and] office building and apartments at Columbus Circle are other illustrations of the literal wonders which Title 1 may achieve, and with substantial tax revenue increases for the city."[80]

Such "literal wonders" were built on the rubble of some of New York's most deprived neighborhoods. Urban renewal projects displaced 170,000 New Yorkers between January 1946 and March 1953 in New York City alone.[81] And this was just a portion of the broader costs of urban renewal, which would displace 609,000 people across the country by 1963, two-thirds of whom were racial minorities. A full 2,500 neighborhoods in 993 cities, filled with citizens and small businesses and factories, were annihilated, replaced by housing towers, university and hospital buildings, large commercial spaces, and convention centers.[82] But such was the cost of progress for many of the city's advocates of urban renewal. White-collar employees, Raymond Vernon argued, could hardly be expected to "wade through the filth and insecurity" of "rundown, obsolete" neighborhoods in order to reach their workplaces. Only by placing "luxury housing close by the central district" on behalf of the "vice-president for finance, who demands a city location," could white-collar

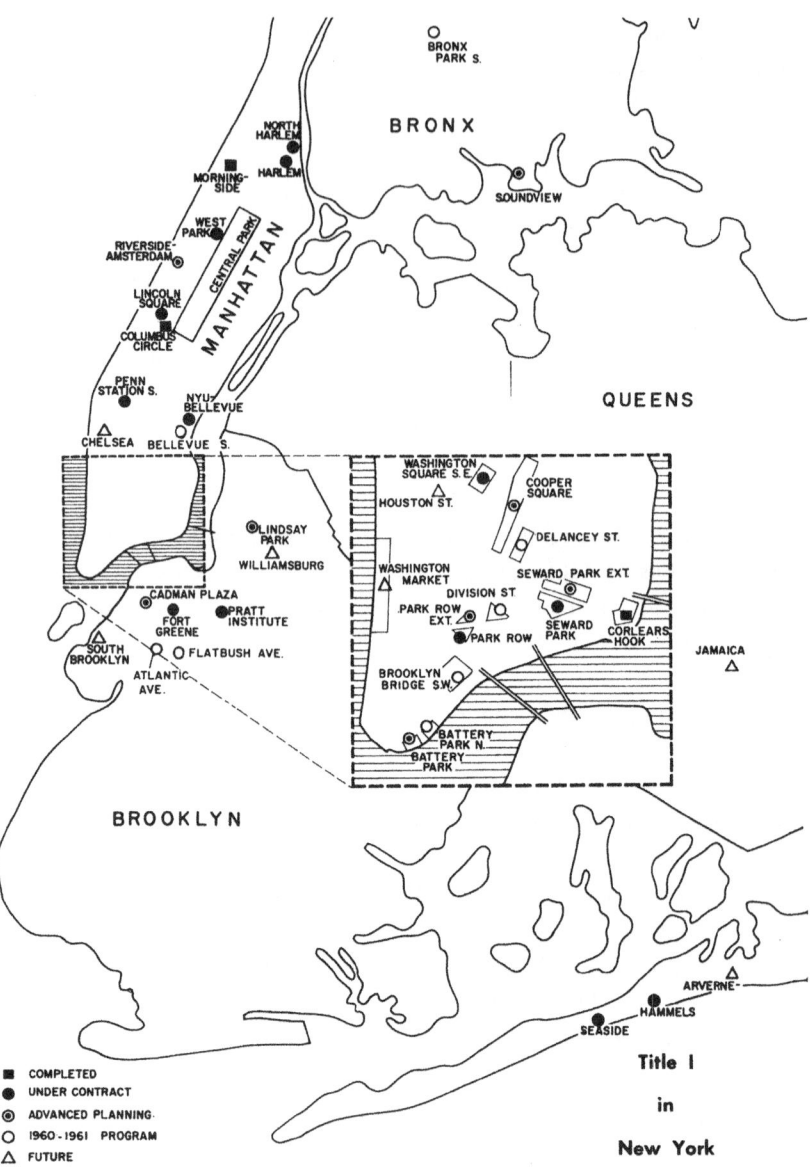

BRONX
PARK S.

BRONX

NORTH
HARLEM

MORNING-
SIDE HARLEM

SOUNDVIEW

WEST
PARK

RIVERSIDE-
AMSTERDAM

CENTRAL PARK

MANHATTAN

LINCOLN
SQUARE

COLUMBUS
CIRCLE

PENN
STATION S.

NYU-
BELLEVUE

QUEENS

CHELSEA BELLEVUE S.

WASHINGTON
SQUARE S.E.

COOPER
SQUARE

HOUSTON ST.

LINDSAY
PARK

DELANCEY ST.

WILLIAMSBURG

WASHINGTON
MARKET

SEWARD PARK EXT.

CADMAN PLAZA

DIVISION ST

PARK ROW
EXT.

FORT
GREENE

PRATT
INSTITUTE

PARK ROW

SEWARD
PARK

CORLEARS
HOOK

SOUTH
BROOKLYN

FLATBUSH AVE.

JAMAICA

ATLANTIC
AVE.

BROOKLYN
BRIDGE S.W.

BATTERY
PARK N.

BROOKLYN

BATTERY
PARK

ARVERNE-

HAMMELS

SEASIDE

Title 1

in

New York

■ COMPLETED
● UNDER CONTRACT
◉ ADVANCED PLANNING
○ 1960-1961 PROGRAM
△ FUTURE

FIGURE 7.3. Image from Anthony J. Panuch, *Building a Better New York: Final Report to the Mayor Robert F. Wagner* (New York: n.p., 1960), 55. Courtesy Municipal Archives, City of New York. Many of these Title 1 projects, such as the Coliseum convention center at Columbus Circle, were on behalf of the city's white-collar industries and employees. Tellingly, many of them were located at areas of the city whose moderate-to-high land values had largely repelled new private construction in the interwar period (see figure 4.5). By purchasing land for redevelopment at inflated prices, Title 1 helped rid landlords and investors of unwanted property at public expense.

workers be anchored close to their employment.[83] And their demands would largely be met.

Altogether, developers built 45.6 million square feet of office space in New York between 1947 and 1959, more than was built even during the boom years of the 1920s. Similar residential construction growth was pursued on behalf of the employees of these offices—during these same years, $6 million was invested in high-rental apartment houses in the city.[84] New York's established office districts in Midtown and (to a lesser extent) downtown were made over in glass, while new modernist slabs remade Fifth and Park Avenues. Running up and down the island's western and eastern avenues were the new apartment blocks where their employees lived. Over a quarter of all jobs in New York were, by 1960, white-collar positions for corporate, fashion, finance, and media firms.[85] And this growth would continue: positions in finance, insurance, and real estate grew by 36 percent in New York between 1955 and 1970, largely at the expense of its manufacturing enterprises.[86] The "highest and best" use of New York was, at least for some, being realized. As the city's Department of Commerce exclaimed, "In the changes that it has wrought on the face of the city and in the revolution it has sparked in the work and filing rooms of thousands of New Yorkers, the commercial-building boom of the post-war era in our city is utopia come true."[87]

"Literal Wonders"

New York's white-collar transformation in the postwar era was, in part, a product of political mobilizations by New York's established commercial and real estate actors. But it was also due to broader postwar assumptions around the politics of growth: a politics oriented around the redistribution of capitalist growth's fruits rather than critiquing or finding alternatives to it. Such a narrowed politics, reinforced by New York's racialized and technocratic fiscal structure, helped obscure the costs of urban America's white-collar transformation during the early postwar period.

"Economic growth" as accomplished through private ownership and large-scale enterprise, of course, enjoyed a deep and wide range of support in the postwar United States.[88] From Keynesian economists like Leon Keyserling, to government agencies like the Congress of Economic Advisors, to large business associations and established labor groups—all converged on growing the "economic pie" as the means and ends of public life. True, local revolts against growth, whether in the form of questioning the costs of suburban sprawl or skirmishes over preservation, were beginning to increase. So too were the concerns of "qualitative liberals" over the psychic ills and "materialism" that accompanied this growth, together with the growing poverty of those whom growth seemed not to reach.[89] But posing alternative frameworks of economic development built around sufficiency rather than expansion, or suggesting that poverty could increase with "progress"—these were not dominant themes of the 1950s and the broader Cold War political culture that enveloped it.[90] And if the era's broader culture of consumption helped marginalize such perspectives, the ideological ice age wrought by the early Cold War and the "second red-scare" confirmed it.[91]

Many New York's local left-liberals, for their part, similarly believed that the economic future of their city tended toward the kind of large-scale enterprises that chose New York as their capital. This was not necessarily a new interpretation. Even before the ideological chill of the Cold War, many progressives and socialists believed that the general tendency of business enterprises was to grow in size and scale—the task of the left was to deliver them into public ownership, thus unleashing and directing their productivity on the public's behalf.[92] In his 1932 treatise *What's the Matter with New York*, for example, socialist leader Norman Thomas declared that "a policy for the New York of the future" could be reduced to (1) organiz[ing] the city governmental machine so far as possible without waste, favoritism, or inefficiency; (2) let[ting] the people through their government own and operate the great natural economic monopolies without private profit or special privilege; (3) let[ting] the workers of hand and brain share in the control of those monopolies."[93] This was, to be sure, a strategy to change ownership in the city's economy—but not necessarily to *change* it in the sense of altering what was produced, at what rate, for what purposes. And it was certainly not an "industrial strategy" for empowering small or worker-owned firms as a complement to the traditional municipal socialist goal of housing and public utility ownership.[94]

This tendency continued into the postwar period. As we have seen, both agrarian critics and radicals like Catherine Bauer had associated New York with white-collar enterprises in the past. And such beliefs were reinforced by postwar "modernization" narratives stressing increasing "economies of scale," embodied by the national corporation or state-capitalist governments, as the historical *telos* of modern economies.[95] In *Dissent*, for example, Daniel Bell, called New York's small manufacturers "non-rationalized enterprises" doomed to extinction at the hands of the "white-collar dominance of the large corporation and its advertising-media satellites."[96] Bell thought this an unfortunate inevitability, while researchers for the Urban Redevelopment Board thought it the result of a "logical and desirable evolutionary process."[97] But neither thought it could or even should be changed. Indeed, the white-collar transformation of New York City—or, conversely, its deindustrialization—was relatively uncontested by New York's organized left more broadly, who concentrated instead on civil rights, public-sector union drives, and welfare-state expansion. "The Left," complained radical journalist Jack Newfield during New York's 1970s fiscal crisis, as the legacies of this quiescence became clear, "has totally ignored the [economic] issues of New York over the last twenty years."[98] And if some radicals were at least ambivalent over their city's corporate transformation, most of the city's liberal press and policymakers were positively boosterish. The *New York Times*, for example, exulted in the construction of the World Trade Center and how, in the Lower East Side, the "empty lot has been transformed into a gleaming skyscraper, the slum-dwelling into a majestic apartment."[99]

This is not to say that postwar urban economic development was entirely uncontested on economic grounds before the mid-1960s. Economist Max R. Bloom noted, for example, that the funding criteria for urban renewal projects typically made no note of whether projects would contribute to the greater city's revenue or even whether there was demand for the project's uses.[100] MIT research fellow Martin Anderson claimed that urban renewal had generally "caused a decrease in cities' tax revenue."[101] Similarly, at least some critics worried that New York was experiencing a return to the overheated realty speculation of the past. A reporter for the *International Herald Tribune* worried in 1961 that the city was witnessing "a repetition of the overbuilding of the 1920s in which, like fabled Midas whose touch turned everything to gold, the city will throttle itself."[102]

But such critiques generally failed to address the broader economic assumption underlying New York's white-collar transformation—that cities could only prosper by attracting wealthy individuals and corporations. Friedenberg's concern around overbuilding, for example, assailed real estate *developers* rather than the corporate firms within their developments. And buoyed by an expanding economy and secured by "reliable" new theories of urban growth, relatively few of New York's professional planners saw danger in New York's corporate transformation. The RPNY's studies proclaimed that the future New York would have 7.8 million people and 4.4 million jobs by 1985—and this number was considered pessimistic at the time (the actual figures would be 7 million and 3.6 million).[103] "The worries of a Riesman, the strivings of a Mumford, are inarticulate, scarcely incomprehensible murmurings," declared Raymond Vernon in 1965. "Let the sociologists fume; except for such intractable problems as death, war, and taxes, things are getting slightly better all the time."[104]

Conclusion

The expansion of New York's white-collar sector was propelled and justified by new understandings of the urban economy accelerated by the Great

Depression. Reeling from the collapse of land values during the 1930s, plan-ning bodies like the RPNY and realty groups like the ULI identified *income* as a superior guarantor of local finances. This theory helped rationalize calls by these and other commercial bodies—many with vested interests in keeping up demand for central-city property—to position high-profit financial and corporate firms as the "natural" base of the urban center. And local policy-makers like Mayor Robert Wagner, seeking additional tax revenue and taking advantage of federal funding, translated the demands of these groups into policies ranging from urban renewal legislation to rezoning. The result was a metropolis committed to—and increasingly dependent on—large corpo-rations and financial services for revenue. And few policymakers, liberal or leftists alike, seemed willing to challenge this transformation.

But not entirely. Even in the wilderness of postwar boosterism, scattered movements and rogue texts critiqued prevailing canons of urban economic policy. Critical intellectuals like Jane Jacobs wondered whether urban rede-velopment was causing more economic harm than good. Harlem activists argued that "outside" firms, no matter how wealthy, would and could never deliver prosperity to their community. In subtle and explicit ways, these figures articulated another paradigm of urban economics built around the needs of its neighborhoods rather than its downtown, of residents rather than external markets. Whether this vision would have a constituency willing and able to displace the city's white-collar development strategy, however, was another matter.

"Communitas"

"Cities need not 'bring back' a middle class, and carefully protect it like an artificial growth. Cities grow the middle class. But to keep it as it grows, to keep it as a stabilizing force in the form of a self-diversified population, means considering the city's people valuable and worth retaining, right where they are, before they become middle-class."[1] These words, written in 1961 by Jane Jacobs, challenged many of the economic canons underlying postwar America's urban development. The prosperity of New York, Jacobs argued, did not depend on remaking itself for the sake of international corporations and their employees. Rather, it depended on the well-being of its existing residents amid its existing "inefficient" streets.

This chapter examines how a small but significant strata of New York activists critiqued their city's economic development strategies during the early postwar decades. Critics ranging from Jane Jacobs to Black Power advocates argued that the economic well-being of their city depended not on the prosperity of corporate firms but on the well-being of its ordinary people and existing neighborhoods. Elements of this fiscal rationale lay behind grassroots campaigns for historic preservation, participatory planning, and community control over land and housing during the late 1960s and 1970s. Nonetheless, these activists, whom I call "fiscal communitarians," generally lacked the power—and often the inclination—to directly supplant their city's white-collar transformation. Rather, figures like liberal New York mayor John Lindsay adopted their communitarian language and localist stratagems while accelerating the city's commitment to private and large-scale corporate enterprises.

While historians have studied many alternative strains of postwar urbanism, the radical implications of these theories on urban *economics* deserve further exploration. Jane Jacobs's insights in identifying the economic costs of what she called "cataclysmic money" are generally unrecognized by her contemporary allies and detractors.[2] Similarly, scholars have yet to trace how the Black struggle to gain community economic control informed postwar theories of urban economies more generally.[3] By restoring the economic thought of these and other postwar activists, this chapter provides a deeper context for postwar conflicts over the use, ownership, and preservation of urban space.

Nonetheless, this chapter argues that the vision and constituency for postwar radical urban economics was narrower in the postwar period than in previous decades. The radical coalitions of white workers, professional economists, and urban planners who had shaken New York's fiscal imaginaries in the past were, by the postwar period, largely reconciled to the city's white-collar transformation. And while many activists were willing to criticize downtown firms over their refusal to distribute wealth to the city's neighborhoods, far fewer were willing to posit *alternatives* to those firms as the economic base of the metropolis.[4] As a result, when that corporate base began to falter in the early 1970s, New Yorkers had few strategies to replace it with—or coalitions to do the replacing.

Localism

Small, locally oriented enterprises have long been hailed for their political and civic benefits, of course.[5] But the idea that an economy built around such enterprises can be *economically* superior to one built around nationally scaled corporations—this was relatively rare in American economic thought before the Great Depression. And even when such a "localist" or "decentralist" vision was proffered, such arguments were rarely applied to small businesses within cities rather than small towns. Rather, cities were associated with the kind of financial gigantism that defenders of small enterprises typically feared. Only in the postwar era would the neighborhood, and the small businesses that constituted it, be looked at by some as a model for urban economic development more generally.

During the Depression, a group of loosely connected social critics argued that smaller and locally oriented firms could provide a more secure basis for economic prosperity than large-scale and nationally oriented ones.[6] These critics shared no single banner: they ranged from "country life" advocates like Liberty Hyde Bailey, cosmopolitan social critics at the Regional Planning Association of America, the Catholic rural life movement, and the agrarian editors of the political journal *Free America*. Many of their writings evinced a broader critique of the centralization and professionalization that they

associated with modern politics and culture. But the writings of these "decentralists" often contained an incisive *economic* critique as well: that large-scale
corporations producing for a national market invariably produced enormous
wastage and fragility.

The economist Ralph Borsodi, for example, found that while the costs of
production had fallen by a fifth between 1870 and 1920, the costs of marketing and distribution had nearly tripled.[7] Such inefficiencies, Borsodi argued,
would be unnecessary in an economy geared for local production. Along
similar lines, Lewis Mumford asserted that the only way to create what he
called a "balanced economy" was by decentralizing economic activity across
the nation's regions rather than by extending the market of a few unstable
metropoles (see figure 8.1).[8] The "advantages of the modern industry will be
spread," Mumford declared, "not chiefly by transport—as in the nineteenth
century—but by local development."[9]

The kinds of enterprises promoted by these critics, however, remained de-
fiantly un-urban. Rural hamlets or "new towns" were generally looked to for
economic deliverance—cities, in contrast, were associated with the gigantism
and growth of their largest enterprises. Rather than revitalize the city, many
decentralists happily waited for it to die.[10] And even when a new generation
of communitarian and anarchist-inflected critics such as Leopold Kohr and
Herbert Marcuse criticized postwar economic growth along similar lines
as the decentralists, they continued to offer little in the way of an economic
countervision—particularly as regards to the urban economy.[11]

One of the few works to attempt such a vision was Paul and Percival Goodman's *Communitas*, published in 1947 and republished to a more receptive
public in 1960. An anarchist by temperament and program, Paul Goodman
harshly criticized both welfare capitalism and what he called Soviet "state-
socialism" throughout the 1940s. Collaborating with his architect brother, he
produced a series of articles and eventually a book sketching out what he
believed to be a more cooperative and humane form of urban economics.
In certain respects, the Goodmans' diagnoses matched those of earlier critics like Henry George: their book complained that "real estate" and "great
financiers," along with their allies in city hall, had a vested interest in raising
the value of urban land to unreasonably high levels. They echoed Tugwell in
calling for "large-scale zoning" as a means of "nullifying" such speculation in
land values. They critiqued what they not-so-subtly called a "powerful Park
Commissioner" for constructing "escape highways" at the city's periphery,
which encouraged "blight" in the city's center.[12]

As an alternative, the Goodmans called for another economic paradigm—
what they called an "economy of things rather than money." Workers, they held,

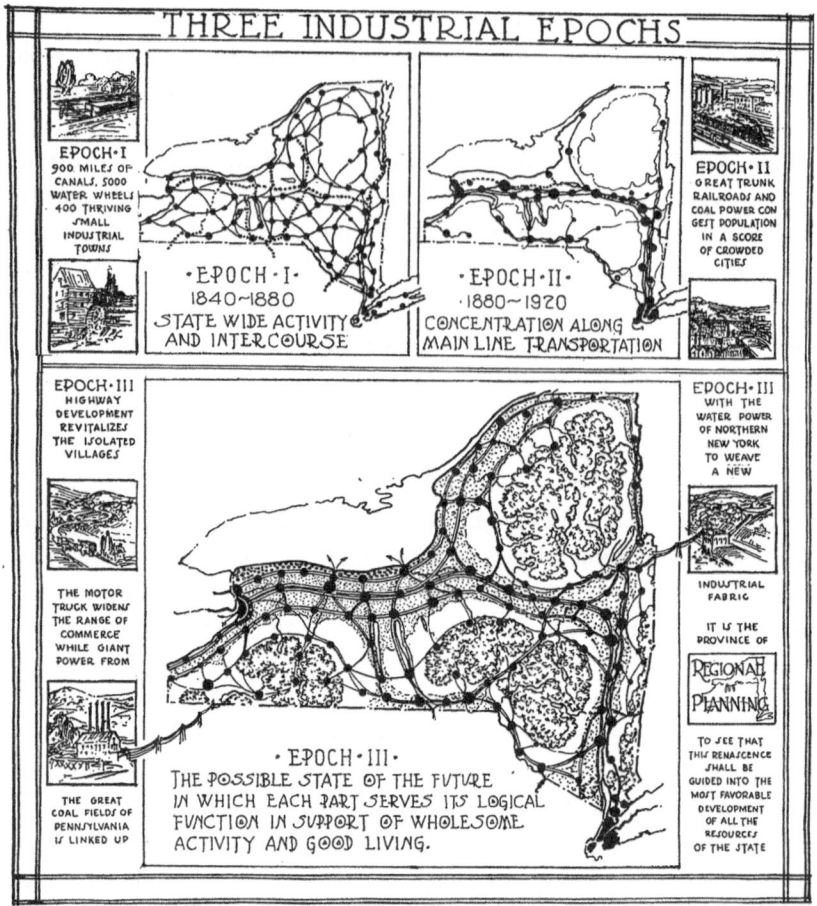

Maps and charts prepared by Henry Wright for New York Commission of Housing and Regional Planning

FIGURE 8.1. "Three Industrial Epochs." Commission on Housing and Regional Planning, *Survey Graphic* 54 (May 1, 1925), 159. During the 1920s and 1930s, members of the RPAA and other "decentralists" asserted that an efficient and balanced economy could only be developed by encouraging locally oriented development across a larger area (Epoch III), rather than by allowing a few extractive cities to siphon economic activity from their hinterlands (Epoch II). Theorists like Jane Jacobs would later extend this insight to cities themselves, arguing that urban economies depended on the vitality of their individual neighborhoods and not necessarily their "central business district."

should only engage in enterprises that were useful and necessary and not for the sake of "expansion" alone. Hailing Israeli kibbutzim and Lewis Mumford's plans for regional decentralization as models, the Goodmans argued that self-contained rural communities could easily produce subsistence goods for their own use through the "use of the skills and resources [they] happen ... to have."[13]

While undeniably humanistic, the Goodmans' platform of "community anarchism" provided little guidance for how urban economies should actually be reconstructed. Their stress on "production for use," while marking a departure from the profit orientation that ran through even the Georgist and municipal ownership remedies of the early 1900s, was more impressionistic than concrete. And what few counsels they did offer were surprisingly congruent with mainstream prescriptions. The Goodmans' 1944 plan for New York, for example, celebrated the fact that although the city's manufacturing was decentralizing, the metropolis still promised to be the "cultural, business, style and entertainment capital of the World."[14] Their 1946 plan for the "Rejuvenation of a Blighted Industrial Area in New York City," corresponding roughly to Long Island City in Queens, complained that the area was a "liability" to the metropolis due to "delinquent taxes" and "low values."[15] Ultimately, the Goodmans were more concerned with creating a humane than a prosperous city. Their plan for New York focused less on reconstructing the city's economy than on pedestrianizing the city's streets and placing "leisurely and comfortable residences and parks along the city's waterfront."[16]

And if the Goodmans proffered at least some hopes for urban revival, such hopes were not shared by the other great postwar urban humanist, Lewis Mumford. Deepening his critiques from the 1930s, Mumford assailed the modern metropolis as the outward form of monopoly and bureaucracy, enthralled by "purposeless expansion" and "sprawling gigantism." Ironically, Mumford agreed with local boosters that the metropolis was the natural center for finance: "The more constant the need for credit capital, the more important for the borrower to be closer to the big banks that advance it."[17] But where boosters saw finance as the city's base, Mumford saw it as the last stage of cancer. Such beliefs, articulated in Mumford's 1961 work *The City in History*, would only become more morbid in his subsequent volumes.

Nonetheless, by the 1950s, a growing number of social scientists, planners, and upper-income urban residents were identifying the "local" in specifically urban terms—and as something worth preserving.[18] Sociologists like Herbert Gans brought academic attention to the vibrant communities that survived in supposedly "blighted" districts. A new generation of urbanites, many of them employed by white-collar industries, saw in local urban neighborhoods a "quality of life" denied them in the suburbs.[19] And neighborhood organizations like the Cooper Square Committee, made up of many longtime veterans of leftist politics in the city like Frances Goldin, increasingly insisted that established communities could and should be improved without displacing their original residents. "Physical improvements which will attract a higher-income group," their "alternative plan" for Cooper Square declared, "must—first of all—benefit those affected by the program, not cause them to suffer from it."[20]

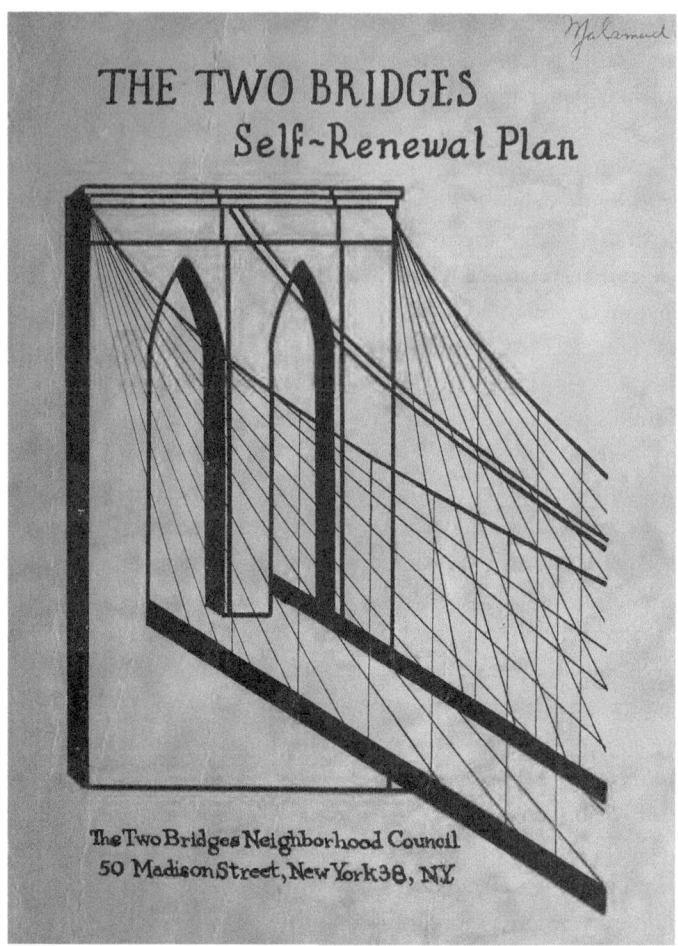

FIGURE 8.2. Two Bridges Neighborhood Council, *The Two Bridges Self-Renewal Plan* (New York: Two Bridges Neighborhood Council, 1959), cover. During the late 1950s, neighborhood associations like the Two Bridges Neighborhood Council asserted that their communities could become "renewed" not through wholesale transformation but by carefully leveraging their existing assets and industries on behalf of their existing residents.

And if most of these groups sought to preserve the aesthetic or (more radically) social qualities of these urban neighborhoods, at least some made cases for preserving their occupations and trades. A prominent example here was the Two Bridges Neighborhood Council's 1959 "self-renewal" plan—one of the first "counterplans" produced by a New York neighborhood, in this case, a working-class neighborhood located between the Manhattan and Brooklyn Bridges in southern Manhattan (see figure 8.2). The plan insisted that "jobbers," "wholesale houses," and "light industry" in their districts not only maintained their communities' "character" but helped meet the "economic needs of the heterogeneous population living in the area." While the plan admitted that some of the district was "obsolete and inefficient," it nonetheless argued that creating new facilities for commercial tenants that would "serve the needs of the people in the community" should be studied in detail. Planned carefully, the council concluded, the Two Bridges neighborhood could "revitalize itself to meet its own housing and community needs."[21]

That preserving and supplementing a community's existing economy, that business should be prioritized which best served the needs of local residents—all this ran against the dominant trends in postwar urban development theory, which stressed white-collar "modernization" and producing for external markets as the ends and means of local growth. These challenges, however, were rarely made explicit in the pages of counterplans like those of the Two Bridges Council or in sympathetic academic treatments of urban neighborhoods by Herbert Gans. Rather, most defenses of neighborhood economies did so strictly on the grounds of their community benefits, not of their benefit to the city as a whole.

But this would soon change.

Death and Life

Jane Jacobs was one of the first critics to refute and provide a comprehensive alternative to postwar urban economic theory on specifically economic grounds. Like earlier critics of realty speculation such as Tugwell and Mumford, Jacobs critiqued the effects of what she called "cataclysmic money" on the economy of cities. Unlike many of these critics, however, Jacobs did not look to the self-contained town as the ultimate model for local economies. Rather, she saw preserving the *existing* city's diversity, in terms of both demographics and land use, as the basis for its own revitalization. And her words would soon resonate for thousands of readers—not least of whom were middle-class professionals rediscovering the value(s) of older central-city property.

While Jacobs was initially sympathetic to urban redevelopment's economic rationale as a reporter for *Architectural Forum*, this changed after she visited ten redevelopment projects in East Harlem in 1956. These projects not only uprooted structures and residents, Jacobs noted, but eradicated 1,569 small businesses employing more than 4,500 people.[22] These kinds of businesses, Jane Jacobs suspected, were not simply obsolete victims of "progress." Rather, she believed they represented a form of flexible, innovative work that was *vital* to the modern city's economic health. And in *The Death and Life of Great American Cities* (1964) and later in *The Economy of Cities* (1969), Jacobs built on this insight to develop a new model for how urban economies functioned and flourished.

A healthy urban economy for Jacobs was marked not by its enterprises' individual wealth but by their collective innovation. As Jacobs later summarized, "Cities, individually, must generate their own economic bases; and cities, taken collectively, must generate the innovations that make developing economies possible."[23] While acquiring external markets or capital could help a city develop the wealth needed for such innovation, external income would be self-destructive if a single sector—whether manufacturing or white-collar work—dominated a city's economic activity. Without the spur of competition or the presence of diverse entrepreneurs, cities would be too brittle and uncreative to survive. Only a diverse mixture of small and midsize firms could provide a stable base for a flourishing urban economy.

In some ways, Jacobs's critiques of mainstream urban economics were surprisingly aligned with those of previous fiscal radicals. Like advocates of Henry George, she argued that urban "slums" could not be fully addressed unless the "profit is taken out of slums by taxation."[24] Her emphasis on the source of land's value also mirrored that of Robert Haig; the "value of land does not derive from anything inherent in the land," she stated, "but from the concentrations of work upon city land."[25] Jacobs also echoed Hoyt's "economic base" theories by stressing the need for cities to export goods and services, even as she insisted that cities replace their imports with domestic substitutes as quickly as possible to speed up the overall cycle of innovation. Even Jacobs's stress on proximity, communication, and interaction as features of urban economies mirrored the theories of Haig and Vernon.

Nonetheless, Jacobs's original insight—that *diversity* was the heartbeat of local economies—led her to quite original conclusions about how to best cultivate those economies. For example, both economic development officers and scale-enraptured intellectuals like Daniel Bell assumed that large corporations were the inevitable successor to parochial small businesses."[26] But Jacobs identified how the collective flexibility and interdependence of small enterprises made them far more capable of innovation and "flexible specialization" than market-dominating corporations.[27] Only by cultivating networks of small enterprises, Jacobs argued, could urban economies flourish. Economies of scale *within* firms, Jacobs argued, were less important than economies of competition and collaboration *between* firms.

Along similar lines, Jane Jacobs's economic defense of the existing city's diverse land uses ran counter to planners ranging from Robert Moses to Rexford Tugwell. All through the interwar period, such planners had looked to large-scale construction and functionally segregated zoning as a means of insulating different economic sectors from "inefficient" actors and uses. The proximity of skyscrapers with tenements, of office work with slaughter-houses, of chain stores and elite restaurants—all this, Haig wrote of New York's existing cityscape in 1926, "outrages one's sense of order."[28] Jacobs, how-ever, believed such diversity was already quite "efficient." By bringing together a variety of different land uses, mixed cityscapes brought together a variety of different land users and, hence, opportunities for economic innovation. To homogenize this cityscape was to stifle innovation and, ultimately, urban prosperity.

Perhaps most importantly, Jacobs's stress on diversity led her to consider *income* diversity as a prerequisite for urban economic health. The goal of planners and municipal finance officials, she argued, should not be to attain a uniformly high level of rent and land values, as this would exclude the lower-equity firms and lower-income residents that were essential for a truly diverse economy. "Premium land and building prices" and policies toward those ends, she stated, are "associated with the self-destruction of diversity"—a dy-namic she termed "Cataclysmic Money."[29]

Mixtures of high and low land prices, however, would ensure that a wider range of actors could take part in the metropolitan economy and thus spur collective innovation. "The way to raise the tax base of a city," she contin-ued, "is not at all to exploit to the limit the short-term tax potential of every site." Rather, a "certain amount of close-grained, deliberate, calculated varia-tion in localized tax yields" could help "anchor diversity and forestall its self-destruction."[30] If there was to be wealth growing in the city, it should not be through the "replacement of the old slum population by a new and different middle-class population," she argued, but "the old population moving into the middle class."[31]

At its best, the work of Jane Jacobs represented one of the boldest counters to postwar theories of urban economic development. An appreciative 1969 review of *The Economy of Cities* by public housing veteran Charles Abrams revealed the depth of her heterodoxy. Jacobs's book, he stated, was "a chal-lenge to the common assumption that economic growth is hinged mainly to the large corporate complex." Rather, "she argues that the men making machine parts in their little shops have been and will be more responsible for city growth in the long run than the tycoons and conglomerates."[32]

White-Collar Community

But if Jacobs's theories provided a rationale for preserving such "little shops," she and her followers failed to achieve or even pursue this in practice. Partly this was because Jacobs herself, with her celebration of urban "spontaneity" and general hostility toward public planning, rarely called for public campaigns on behalf of promoting (or curbing) specific economic sectors. But it was also because the groups who most eagerly took up the "Jacobsean" banner in the 1960s—largely white households who were themselves often part of the city's white-collar economy—ignored the potentially radical economic prescriptions of Jacobs's book in favor of those that would render the city more "aesthetically" or "culturally" desirable for themselves.[33] And being that both white households and white-collar industries were politically (and fiscally) desirable for policymakers, figures like Mayor Lindsay were quick to translate the "brownstoners'" selective readings of Jacobs into policy.

"Mrs. Jacobs is the urban Milton Friedman and creates just as much controversy."[34] While somewhat of an exaggeration, this statement—made by a disaffected urban economist in 1970—captures at once the strength and weakness of Jacobs's work.[35] While the targets of her polemics were often public agencies promoting "cataclysmic growth" on behalf of well-connected developers, the voluntarism underlying her agenda would be largely insufficient for preserving the economic diversity she cherished.

Nowhere was this clearer than in her understanding of Black poverty. Jacobs saw discrimination as a profound threat to local finances, as it prevented the kind of competition and innovation that enabled a flourishing economy. As Jacobs stated, "People the world over understand (and the more downtrodden, the better they understand) that juggling social hierarchies and economic improvement go hand in hand."[36] Nonetheless, Jacobs was equally skeptical of the possibility of positive state action to provide assistance to Black communities.[37] Her attitude was summarized by a Black neurosurgeon she approvingly quoted in response to a well-meaning white official: "Get out of our way, and let us try something."[38] She was also suspicious of income-targeted public housing, which might help sustain diversity in terms of race and class. "It is wrong to set one part of the population, segregated by income, apart in its own neighborhoods with its own different scheme of community," she stated primly in *Death and Life*.[39]

But if Jacobs's policies for preserving diversity could be somewhat underdeveloped, those of her followers were even more so. Many of these followers were what historian Suleiman Osman called "a new postindustrial wing of young white-collar professionals and college students" who had moved to the brownstones of western Brooklyn and the rowhouses of Greenwich Village.[40] Employed by the city's universities, public bureaucracies, and corporations, these residents opposed urban renewal projects less for fear of losing their jobs (which were generally not located in the neighborhoods in any case) than for fear of losing their neighborhoods and the "unique" built environment that they believed constituted it.

And these groups were well poised to achieve their goals. Many of those who purchased copies of *Death and Life* were also members of "independent" political organizations such as the East Side Lexington Club. Combining electoral work with street-level protests, these "brownstoners" were able to win policy victories such as defeating street widening proposals in Greenwich Village and creating a Landmarks Preservation Commission by the early 1960s. Their mobilizations also encouraged urban renewal officials to place a greater focus on "rehabilitation" as a means of combating blight, as evidenced by new projects in Chicago's Lincoln Park, Seattle's Pioneer Square, and Baltimore's Mount Royal–Bolton Hill.[41] The physical structures of such neighborhoods would be legally protected from displacement—but not the people and businesses who inhabited them.

Perhaps the brownstoners' earliest and greatest policy ally was Mayor John Lindsay, whose administration (1966–1973) embodied how the fiscal communitarian cause could not only be reconciled with New York's white-collar transformation—it could accelerate it. Elected by a coalition of young professionals, students, and leaders of the city's banking and real estate industry (the Rockefeller family alone produced nearly half the funds for his first mayoral campaign), Lindsay promoted pathbreaking initiatives in historical preservation and "human-scaled" planning during the 1960s—while *simultaneously* promoting the city as a center of international finance and tourism.[42] This is not to say there were no conflicts between his administration and fiscal communitarians, of course. But while conflicts over preservation and urban planning were framed as fundamental clashes between "grassroots" and "top-down" forces, the clashes rarely addressed or questioned the broader goals of that development. The city's white-collar transformation, and the costs of its "cataclysmic growth," were off the political agenda.[43]

Even before Lindsay's administration, New York policymakers had adopted more "sensitive" approaches toward land-use planning and preservation as a means of attracting and satisfying a white-collar workforce. New York's Landmark's Law of 1965, for example, asserted in its opening paragraph that the city's standing as a "world capital of business" could not be "maintained or enhanced" by allowing the destruction of its "cultural assets."[44] And Mayor Lindsay entrusted the City Planning Commission to apply this rationale toward broader preservation and planning efforts. The Commission's 1969 plan, for example, specified that their goal in preserving the city's brownstone

districts was partly to attract the "elite workforce that takes up important positions in the business and professions of the national center" and who sought
to live in these neighborhoods.[45] A documentary on the plan similarly hailed
the return of "young white middle-class executives and their families" to the
city's brownstone neighborhoods, emphasizing the role of good urban design
as magnets for these desirable residents.[46] Even a CPC plan for the Lower
East Side, while stressing the importance of "well-paying jobs in stable industries committed to the community," nonetheless insisted that the district's
"accessible location between Manhattan's office centers" would make it wise
to attract data processing, technical, and business services to the area—"half
of which" would be filled by the neighborhood's existing residents.[47] This appeal to outside industries and residents as the district's salvation was a far
cry from the "self-renewing" vision of the Two Bridges Council from ten
years earlier.

Perhaps the most obvious appropriation of "Jacobsean" economic motifs
in service of white-collar planning was the CPC's Lower Manhattan Plan of
1966. The plan generally followed the DLMA's strategy for redeveloping New
York below Canal Street in the interest of its financial service "core." It did
so, however, using the language of diversity. "The Plan," it read, "must provide diversity to the Core which will give its business owners, managers and
workers that quality of life and richness of environment which is necessary
for modern working conditions." Nonetheless, such diversity was strictly on
behalf of the financial core—as the plan stated, "the continued strength and
growth of the Core depends on diversifying its base and mix, what the business community and the Administration decide to do about the evident need
for broadening downtown's economic base, enriching its mix of activities,
and improving its environment." Unsurprisingly, then, the types of diversity
it stated were of the consumer variety—"more recreation, more restaurants,
more entertainment, more parks, better shopping, new urban services and
new urban excitement are needed." "Industry or wholesaling-with-stock," by
contrast, "rank[ed] low" in their list of priorities.[48]

New York's government thus promoted the city's white-collar transformation together with more human-scaled urban design and planning: indeed, it
portrayed them as linked. Even the way the City Planning Commission described New York's appeal to white-collar enterprise—the presence of diverse
services, its "vitality" and "excitement," and above all the opportunities for
"face-to-face contact" that complex and information-rich trades apparently
required—seemed to echo the prescriptions of Jane Jacobs herself (see figure 8.3).[49] CPC proposals for "greening" the city's waterfront while preserving

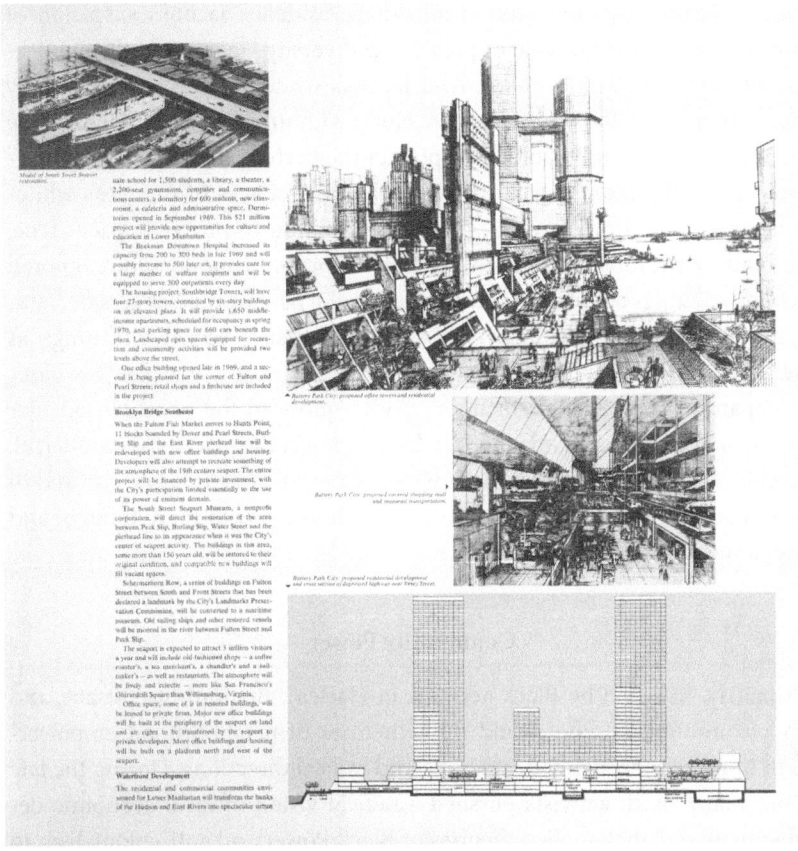

FIGURE 8.3. Page from City Planning Commission, *Plan for New York City 1969: A Proposal*, vol. 4, *Manhattan* (New York: City Planning Commission, 1969), 21. Image courtesy Lionel Pincus and Princess Firyal Map Division, New York Public Library. During the late 1960s, New York's City Planning Commission embraced Jacobsean themes such as historic preservation (as in the case of the South Street Seaport on the top left), mixed-use developments like Battery Park City, and pedestrian-friendly design features into their proposals. But where Jacobs at her most ambitious proposed to transform the entire economy of cities, most urban planners saw her ideas as a means to further accelerate the city's white-collar transformation.

the South Street Seaport, RPNY and Urban Design Group proposals for pedestrianizing Times Square, and other enlightened planning acts similarly indicated that a "fun city" and a "headquarters city" (two contemporary sobriquets of New York) need not conflict.

In the end, neither Jacobs nor her followers built on the radical implications of Jacobs's economic thought. While potentially opening a route to an urban economy built around *all* urban residents, Jacobs's suspicion of planning—even for the sake of preserving diversity—narrowed the application of her insights into policy. And Jacobs's white acolytes were generally happy to preserve the corporate state along with urban brownstones. By the late 1960s, their efforts had helped protect themselves and "their" neighborhoods from the more disruptive *physical* consequences of the city's white-collar transformation, allowing the transformation to proceed apace. True, the Lindsay administration's cultivation of a corporate monoculture ignored Jacobs's warnings about a too-narrow economic base or the dangers of "cataclysmic growth." But Jacobs herself was guilty of such selective readings: as she stated in an earlier article for *Fortune*, while fiscal issues like "tax bases in jeopardy" were "serious matters," it was "more to the point to consider what makes a city center magnetic, what can inject the gaiety, the wonderful, the cheerful hurly-burly that make people want to come into the city and to linger there."[50] And few cities considered such issues with more thought and care in the 1960s than New York.

Community Power

Ultimately, it would be Black activists in Harlem, Bedford-Stuyvesant, and other communities who would push theories of neighborhood empowerment in more thoroughly democratic and radical directions. During the late 1960s, many Black activists pursued a radical vision of local economic development: one that applied theories of Black Power and anti-colonialism to urban neighborhoods. White institutions, they argued, siphoned money and jobs away from Black communities while blocking them from outside investment. Only neighborhood control over land and productive enterprises, they argued, could ensure the vitality of Black neighborhoods. And flourishing neighborhoods, by extension, could help invigorate urban economies more generally.

New York's Black citizens had contributed to—and suffered from—the growth of New York since the colonial era, and this exploitation continued as the city's Black population increased in the postwar era. High property taxes drawn from Black neighborhoods fueled the growth of New York while burdening Black tenants with high rents and poorly maintained housing. Services denied Black neighborhoods were spent instead on behalf of white communities. Black neighborhoods were razed in order to spur private development and "protect institutional investments": seven out of the sixteen Title 1 projects built in New York by 1957 targeted nonwhite neighborhoods.[51]

And neither the jobs provided by the city's white-collar enterprises nor the welfare state their taxes helped finance seemed to make up for such plunder: 11 percent of Harlem's housing was dilapidated in the early 1960s, while the average family income in Harlem was $2,000 *less* than the official poverty line.[52]

Faced with the failures of both the welfare state and the developmental state, by the mid-1960s, many Black activists saw a common issue behind their disadvantage: a lack of local economic control. Four-fifths of Harlem's commercial and residential properties were owned by nonlocals or companies by the early 1960s. Four-fifths of the Harlem workforce was employed outside the community.[53] The majority of Harlem savings were invested in banks owned by those outside the community. This dependence reduced the economic function of Harlem and other "ghettoes" to providing revenue and low-skilled labor on behalf of outsiders. There was an analogy for this process: colonization. As Black psychologist Kenneth Clark argued, "The dark ghettos are social, political, educational, and, above all, economic colonies."[54]

But activists and radical economists pushed further, enlisting the framework of both urban and developmental economics to argue that this economic colonialism was "underdeveloping" ghettoes as *places*. Because Harlem wages and savings went to outsiders, their income could not multiply through local purchases and investments. Instead, money passed through "the ghetto," sieving out to those who exploited it and depriving their inhabitants of the chance to accumulate additional income and savings.[55] As Black activists Stokely Carmichael and Charles Hamilton summarized, "Exploiters come into the ghetto from outside, bleed it dry, and leave it economically dependent on the larger society."[56]

Based on this framework, economic "growth" in the outside community could only lead to the *under*development of Harlem. On the one hand, the growth of this economy was increasingly taking a capital rather than labor-intensive turn: its expansion promised only growing "technological unemployment" for the Harlem workforce.[57] On the other hand, any money transferred to the "ghetto" through this economy's growth—either in the form of wages or tax-financed welfare transfers—would swiftly flow out of the neighborhood and back to its exploiters. As radical economist Daniel Fusfield wrote in the *Review of Black Political Economy*, "The outward flow of income also helps to explain why increased welfare payments may help the individuals or families who receive them, but have little or no impact on the ghetto economy as a whole."[58] Or as he put it later and more bluntly, "larger incomes for the ghetto population mean an enlarged flow through the ghetto. The chief beneficiaries would not be ghetto residents, but those in strategic positions to benefit from the flow through of income and resources."[59]

There was an alternative, however: self-directed economic development. While drawing partly from older traditions of "buying Black," many Black activists were also inspired by how "decolonized" countries like Cuba, India, and Egypt had taken on the task of economic development on their own terms. As two economists wrote of Harlem's economy in 1970, "developing countries use a planned effort to build up their national income within the world [economy]" through methods such as "import substitution, the generation of new exports, and broad productive enterprises." Through such techniques, these countries were able to establish a surplus of income within their borders that—at least in theory—could be invested on behalf of *their own* consumption and investment needs. And this would, in turn, strengthen and diversify their economy even further, leading to further rounds of economic development. "Urban ghettos can, and must," they argued, "follow a similar planned development strategy."[60]

As the economists' reference to "import substitution" reveals, by the mid-1960s Black calls for neighborhood empowerment were given increasingly sophisticated economic rationales. Partly this was taken up by activists themselves: promoting community rather than outside ownership of enterprises, the Harlem Commonwealth Council declared, would "vastly improve the basic economic structure of our community by creating more financial multipliers, more jobs and better services."[61] But a broader cohort of white and Black academics, inspired by the Black Freedom Movement, also applied their research to the economics of urban racism, ghetto formation, and liberation during this time. Among their innovations was to measure a community's fiscal health not by the profitability or number of firms within it but by the flows of income—earned wages, investments, transfer payments, rents, taxes—within and without it.[62] And such studies were published in both older and newer journals, with the *Review of Black Political Economy* being a particularly vibrant site for these analyses.

Within these calls for neighborhood empowerment was, at least tacitly, a theory of broader urban economic development: one centered on neighborhoods rather than central business districts. While some Black activists argued for purely autarkic approaches toward neighborhood empowerment, this was not a mainstream position. Rather, many theorists looked not so much to reduce imports but to develop a sufficient level of ownership, economic diversity, and investable capital necessary to "substitute" locally produced goods for outside-produced ones as frequently as possible.[63] And by developing enterprises in this dynamic fashion, communities like Harlem could contribute to the economic flourishing of the city in a way they could not when "underdeveloped." As Kenneth Clark noted, "The ghetto feeds upon itself; it does not produce goods or contribute to the prosperity of the city."[64] He was not entirely right: white plunder of Black communities was allowing at least some to prosper at the ghetto's expense. But a self-directed export strategy could ensure that Black goods *and* Black dollars would remain within Black control, even as the goods and services they provided helped the city more broadly prosper. Indeed, the 1969 plan of New York's City Planning Commission encouraged the city to directly purchase goods and services from lower-income communities not so much to "create an independent ghetto economy" but to "create more skilled workers who can participate effectively in the City's whole economy."[65]

Nonetheless, the City Planning Commission's definition of what "skilled work" meant—and on behalf of what kind of "citywide" economy—was quite different than what many Black activists had in mind. But these activists not only faced opposition from "outside" agencies from the CPC—they faced it from within as well.

Home Rulers

The movement for Black community autonomy was riven with a fundamental tension: which elements of the Black community should be responsible for guaranteeing that autonomy. Many Black radicals promoted worker- or community-owned enterprises as a nonhierarchical and nonexploitative means of promoting local economies. But most Black businesspeople believed that conventional private ownership was sufficient for this purpose. And through their political strength—and the support of white policymakers and funders—conventional Black businesses were able to gain the legitimacy and resources needed to direct "neighborhood empowerment" in ways quite amenable to the city's broader white-collar transformation.

More radical advocates of "ghetto" economic development believed that such development could not take place through uncoordinated privately owned businesses. Scattered small-scale enterprises would be unable to accumulate the capital necessary for large-scale investments: as one critic wrote, "independent private black capitalism is doomed to corner store capitalism; inefficient, non-competitive, low-wage, and low profit. There is slim chance that such a beginning can produce the savings for reinvestment and development."[66] But neither could development take place through large white-owned enterprises, who would simply siphon money away from the "ghetto."

The solution, they argued, was collective ownership and planning: as Black radical Robert Allen declared, "If the community as a whole is to benefit, then the community as a whole must be organized to manage collectively its internal economy and its business relations with white America."[67] Through either owning or purchasing majority shares in local businesses, ghetto residents could pool the profits of these enterprises together. These pooled profits could then be used to develop additional enterprises that could complement rather than compete with the area's existing firms—"Supermarkets, department Stores, banks, and intermediate-size factories," rather than simply more "corner drugstores," in the words of radical economist William K. Tabb.[68] By creating a "vertically integrated" suite of local enterprises encompassing all stages of manufacturing, wholesaling, and retailing in this way, "ghetto" residents could produce an increasingly elaborate array of products and services for local consumption. And the profits generated by these sales would be recycled back into local firms, thus repeating the cycle of local economic development. Here was "planned diversity" of a type well beyond what Jane Jacobs could envision.

Put perhaps the most distinguishing feature of radical neighborhood empowerment was not their approach toward ownership but their approach toward conflict. Few of these radicals envisioned that growing the economic autonomy of "ghettoes" would do away with the systemic forces exploiting and oppressing them. Only collective power and mobilization could counter such forces. Nonetheless, campaigns for building up local economic power could *help establish* the cohesion and power necessary for that broader struggle. As one radical economist stated, while "a black economy in the ghetto may not lead inexorably to a viable economic base," the "act of striving toward an inner city economy yield a powerful tool for organizing the black community into a coherent political force capable of extracting concessions on jobs, housing, income, and dignity from the government and from the corporate establishment."[69] And while the profits and services rendered by a "black economy" could help build up this political force, it was ultimately the organization and empowerment of the "ghetto's" *people*—all of them—that would make this force prevail. It was for this reason, as Robert Allen asserted in 1969, that the "capital must be accumulated to make possible the economic development of the black community, but this must be done in a way that precludes the enrichment of one class at the expense of those below it."[70]

The most impressive attempt to translate this radical fiscal imaginary into concrete proposal was *The Economic Development of Harlem*: what a Howard University economist called "perhaps the most important and detailed treatise which has looked at the black ghetto from a development perspective."[71]

The book was based on a study conducted in 1967–1968 by two white economists in collaboration with CORE leader Roy Innis, the Radical Architects Renewal Committee of Harlem, and the Harlem Commonwealth Council (see figure 8.4). Later published as a book, the report—entitled *The Economic Development of Harlem*—combined a study of Harlem's existing economy, a market analysis of the broader city, and a detailed financial strategy for how to develop Harlem's economy. Harlem's salvation, the authors declared, required "community-owned or sponsored manufacturing, commercial, and service enterprises whose main function is the upgrading of the area's labor force and economic base."[72] But the elements of this base, the book asserted, was already there. "The slum communities, individually and considered as a loosely knit network," it declared, "contain a sufficient number of consumers with enough purchasing power to make ghetto industries producing and distributing for local consumption a viable proposition."[73]

Their strategy was detailed and comprehensive. Because investing in productive enterprises in the ghetto was unprofitable for market actors, the authors argued, it was necessary for a nonprofit corporation—the Harlem Commonwealth Council (HCC)—to own, sponsor, and control business development within the district. New industry associations linking the community's business, such as drugstores and job printing, would allow enterprises to pool purchases at economies of scale. The HCC would spearhead contracts with public procurers to ensure a steady market: Harlem schools alone purchased over $100 million in goods and services each year.[74] It would also use its pooled funds to establish loans with lenders, further expediting profitable developments. A portion of all these profits would return to the HCC, allowing it to invest in further enterprises. And all of this, the authors asserted, would be not only for the sake of economic empowerment but for the sake of political victory. Summarizing their position, a reviewer of *The Economic Development of Harlem* stated that "these economic techniques provide a basis for community organization, the only means through which economic success will lead to political power."[75]

By the early 1970s, community development corporations (CDCs) modeled on the HCC, funded by a mixture of private and federal funding, were financing community- and worker-owned enterprises ranging from electrical manufacturing plants in Rochester and factories in Los Angeles to collective-owned rubber factories in Cleveland.[76] The Lower East Side Economic Development Association for Cooperatives operated a sewing cooperative, a laundry cooperative, a credit union, several renovated apartments, and a cooperative garment factory.[77] And the HCC itself seemed to demonstrate the feasibility of community-controlled economies: between the late 1960s and

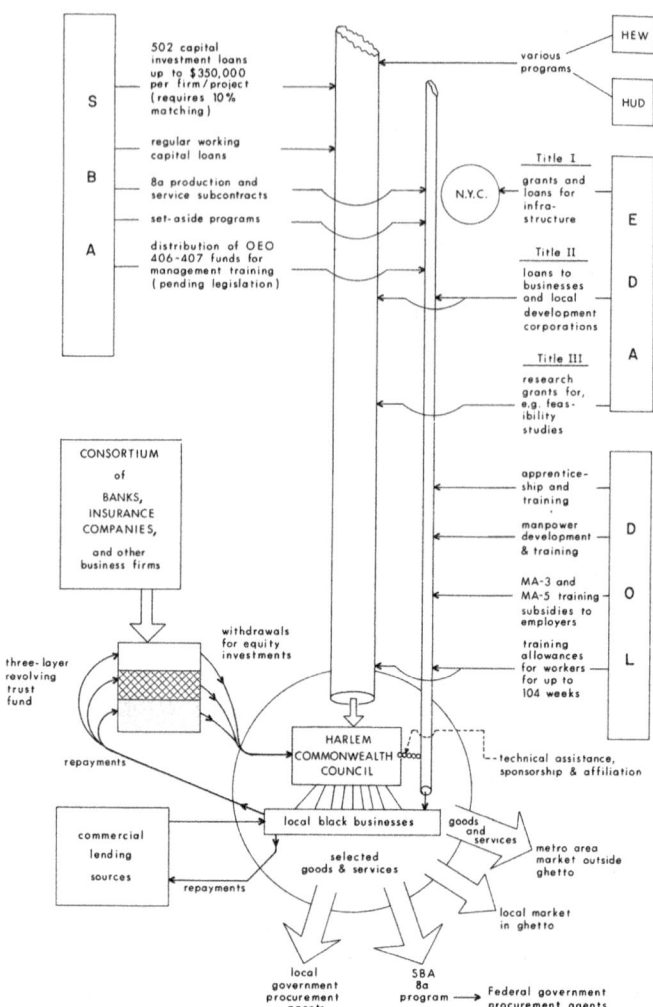

FIGURE 8.4. Chart from Thomas Vietorisz and Bennet Harrison, *The Economic Development of Harlem* (New York: Praeger Publishers, 1970), 74. This chart indicates a sample method of financing the economic development of Harlem and other low-income Black communities. A combination of funds flows to a single nonprofit development agency. The agency uses the funds to both finance existing businesses and seed complementary local businesses. These enterprises then sell to government procurement agents and markets within and outside the community. The pooled revenue from such transactions furnishes profits back to the nonprofit agency, which can then repay its initial loans and finance further enterprises while distributing dividends to local shareholders.

early 1970s, the HCC increased its assets from less than $50,000 to $28 million, became the largest owner of realty on 125th Street, and managed fifteen different businesses. As one historian wrote, "In a faltering national economy, and while American manufacturing in particular declined, HCC's business portfolio helped keep jobs in Harlem that might otherwise have been lost."[78]

And some liberal policymakers were receptive to the demands of activists for community-controlled economies—particularly in the context of the urban uprisings of the late 1960s. The initial funding for the Harlem Commonwealth Council, for example, came from the Federal Office of Economic Opportunity.[79] The Congressional Community Self-Determination Act of 1969 proposed federal funding of businesses whose shares would be sold to members of the community. And the Model Cities program provided for federal aid—nearly $600 million in annual noncategorical funds at the program's height—to be directed toward community-determined economic development initiatives.[80] Black activists were, of course, aware of the dangers of co-optation this financing could engender—but nonetheless hoped that such initial aid would help them acquire the strength needed for self-sufficiency.

But this was generally not to occur. Partly this was because existing Black business and property owners had little interest in seeing their property pooled under collective ownership.[81] As one critic noted in 1974, the *Economic Development of Harlem* plan was roundly "rejected by business interests" in Harlem, while broader plans for CDC-driven economic democracy had generally "fallen on deaf ears among ghetto leadership."[82] And potential donors to CDCs were hesitant to support programs that might alienate both "ghetto" residents and explicitly castigate private property. The result was a diminishment of ambition among CDC heads. As Claire Dunning has detailed, "Eager to extract whatever funding they could from the hodgepodge of government and philanthropic programs available to them, neighborhood nonprofits sought out, participated in, and helped justify governing arrangements that many of the participants would have rejected politically and ideologically."[83]

By the mid-1970s, most CDCs had retreated from broader ambitions of local economic democracy or broader critiques of urban political economies.[84] Rather, the goal of these CDCs was to restore private business and housing markets within their communities through a combination of outside funding and bottom-up entrepreneurship.[85] As early as 1970–1971, a study of thirty-three "Ghetto Economic Corporations" found that only 6 percent pursued goals related to "broad-based economic participation and/or control."[86] By 1977, only 35 percent of CDCs believed providing "opportunities for community-controlled ownership of businesses and property" to be one of their three highest priorities.[87] Even the HCC had, by the early 1970s, largely abandoned the radicalism of its original board members, with the profits from its many community investments failing to reach the community it purportedly served.[88]

For Black business owners, however, supporting enterprises like their own—or, as one critic called them, "ghetto-based versions of conventional economic institutions"—would be sufficient for revitalizing their communities.[89] The financial resources of these business owners, their organization into groups like the Inner City Business Improvement Forum, and the malleability of the "community control" framework itself provided them with many advantages in their struggle for the economic future of Black neighborhoods. And Black businesses were increasingly able to gain outside support: first from white-collar industries, and then from policymakers more generally. As early as 1963, an Interracial Council for Business Opportunity (ICBO) formed by the Urban League of Greater New York worked with Chase Manhattan, Bankers Trust, and Chemical Bank to provide additional loans to conventional Black businesses. Such efforts were accelerated following the urban uprisings of the mid- and late 1960s, when books like *Business Faces the Urban Crisis*, *The War That Business Must Win*, and *Green Power: The Corporation and the Urban Crisis* declared that business could gain prestige—and profits—by investing in the "ghetto."[90] At a 1968 hearing on "Financial Institutions and the Urban Crisis," for example, a representative of the United States Conference of Mayors hailed the ICBO as an example of how the nation's "private financial institutions" were "participating in ventures to bring a new economic vitality to urban inner cores."[91]

And this private support on behalf of "conventional" Black enterprises was further supplemented by local, state, and federal subsidies and support. On the one hand, public officials encouraged white enterprises to locate or invest in "ghettoes" while simultaneously encouraging "business development" initiatives among ghetto residents themselves. On the other hand, policymakers stressed job placement and job training initiatives of a decidedly nonconfrontational sort. First National City Bank's head of "urban affairs" explained this rationale well: "The problem is to get them [Blacks] into the current big mechanism and that's the corporation, to train them to take part in this thing."[92] And later federal agencies like the Office of Minority Business Enterprise further legitimated private ownership as the proper form of "minority" enterprise.

For critics, of course, these efforts at promoting "black capitalism" would be utterly self-defeating. A few individuals and families would benefit, while the income of most "ghetto" residents would continue to filter out of their communities on behalf of those who exploited them. The poor in Harlem and elsewhere would remain vulnerable to what the authors of *The Economic Development of Harlem* called the "social externalities" of exploitation, which would make them less capable of working for the district's further economic development. ("A worker cannot be exiled every day into a rat-infested, over-crowded, personally hazardous environment, while being expected to deliver a high degree of productivity on the job," they noted.)[93] Outside investments in Black communities (secured partly through public subsidies) would at best enrich a few landowners and wealthy whites while leading to the displace-ment of ordinary residents: as the Architect's Renewal Committee in Harlem complained, the "city and state will make costly expenditures in the name of black people while corporations reap the profits."[94] Above all, benefiting a narrow strata of "capitalists," whatever their skin color, would fail to build the kind of economic strength and radical consciousness among the broad mass of people whose struggle was necessary to break the deeper systemic chal-lenges facing the "ghetto." As Richard Cloward and Frances Fox Piven wrote in *The Nation*, "Their economic lot will be improved somewhat, to be sure, but their long-term economic prospects depend on their potential political power, and that will be diminished."[95]

This is not to gainsay the dedication, creativity, and even vision that many Black businesses possessed as they attempted to revitalize their communities. The South Bronx Overall Economic Development Corporation, for example, forthrightly stated in 1975 that "what the experiences of the past ten years or more have taught us is that the city is really no more or less than the sum of all its parts, any of which they neglect at its peril." If New York is to remain the viable, vibrant metropolis it should be," it declared in Jacobsean fashion, "then its most hard-pressed part, the South Bronx, must be revitalized."[96] And through such measures as assisting local factories with loans, provid-ing marketing assistance with local stores, and job training initiatives with ex-offenders, the corporation attempted to arrest the South Bronx's decline. Nonetheless, the corporation's board chair and its entire Business Advisory Council were made up of financial and corporate heads—four from Chase Manhattan Bank alone.[97] Such enterprises generally saw themselves, and not New York's neighborhoods, as the "economic base" of the city, if not the na-tion. And they were quite unlikely to provide any advice to the South Bronx that might threaten their standing—even if it might benefit the South Bronx.

By the early 1970s, then, the movement for Black neighborhood empow-erment had been largely shorn of its more radical elements—like much of the broader Black Freedom Movement itself.[98] Building on their existing advan-tages and the support provided by white America, Black capitalists asserted their control over the economic fate of "their" communities. Such capitalists,

along with white brownstoners and the middle-class "neighborhood preservation" movement discussed earlier, would ultimately offer little in the way
of critique toward the city's broader white-collar developmental strategies—
even as these strategies helped lead their city off the fiscal cliff.

Conclusion

During the 1960s, a countervision of the urban economy, promoted by Black
activists and disaffected urban theorists like Jane Jacobs, began to emerge.
In their vision, the existing and ordinary landscape of cities—their neighborhoods, their mixed-use and mixed-age structures, and their ordinary
citizens—was the grounds for producing thriving and dynamic economies.
At their most ambitious, groups holding this vision claimed that New York's
existing development strategies—recreating the city in the image of its most
powerful and profitable enterprises—was both unjust and uneconomic. And
at their most radical, they argued that the economic health of neighborhoods
could only take place through outright community ownership.

Nonetheless, most of these "fiscal communitarians" lacked the agonistic
edge that earlier fiscal reform movements held. While white brownstoners
were eager to preserve some of the city's existing housing stock, they had
little inclination to displace the white-collar enterprises where many of them
worked. And many in the city's Black neighborhoods were less interested in
empowering their communities than in empowering their own enterprises
within those communities. Ultimately, New York's liberal policymakers were
able to meet these demands while further accelerating the city's white-collar
development.

And if economic heterodoxy had little policy purchase within New York's
"neighborhood defenders" by the mid-1970s, it had even less influence within
New York's government. This was, in some ways, surprising, as New York
City was facing the same kinds of economic dilemmas as the communities
it contained. Both faced the burdens of increasing poverty, disinvestment,
and capital flight. But where at least some neighborhood radicals attempted
to place their local economies on new footing during the period, municipal
officials generally retained their old corporate-retainment strategy. Oblivi-
ous to the costs of private growth and unwilling to imagine alternatives, New
York's liberal establishment would keep their faith in the city's white-collar
economy, even as that economy helped draw them into fiscal crisis.

"Poverty of Ideas"

On Friday January 22, 1971, at a meeting of the Joint Economic Committee of the United States Congress, New York City mayor John Lindsay delivered a prepared speech. The "fundamental fiscal dilemma" of cities, Mayor Lindsay declared, was "the in-migration of the poor to the central city and the out-migration of the well-to-do to the suburbs."[1] Lindsay had striven to provide for these poor as mayor, dramatically expanding the city's social spending over the course of the 1960s. But he had also striven to bring the "well-to-do" back to New York through a suite of policies ranging from tax exemptions for high-income apartments to plans for grand convention centers. This combination of welfare spending and "pro-growth" policies were, for Lindsay and many other New York liberals, not contradictory but complementary: the revenue furnished by taxing the wealthy would help finance both social programs and the city's general budget. Progress would pay for poverty.

A decade later, a decade in which the specter of New York's mid-1970s fiscal crisis haunted local governments across the country, sociologist Robert Friedland came to a very different conclusion as to the sources of fiscal strain in American cities. "Contrary to conventional wisdom," he stated, "local economic growth does not reduce fiscal stress."[2] Faster growth, he found after studying the fiscal profile of 130 large American cities, had no effect on either the total tax burdens or short-term debt of local governments during the 1960s and 1970s—and growth in the office economy actually *increased* those burdens.[3] Public spending meant to address the "externalities" of corporate growth, represented in everything from increased social spending on behalf of underpaid service workers to increased service costs on behalf of new realty developments, further burdened local finances. And if this was true of individual cities, it was also true of entire eras—like the broad wave of economic turmoil that cities like New York had faced the past decade. "The fiscal strains of the 1970s," Friedland asserted, "were not the result of economic decline, but of the nature of economic growth."[4]

Friedman's argument ran counter to the fiscal logic that had underpinned New York's welfare state, and liberal statecraft more generally, since at least the postwar era—with one exception. For in assuming that "economic growth" had a singular "nature"—an assumption shared by both supporters and many critics of New York's white-collar redevelopment—Friedland foreclosed opportunities to place urban growth on an alternative and more egalitarian basis. Still, if Friedland's criticisms were unmatched by an alternative program, liberal policymakers in New York and elsewhere generally lacked one either. And having long promoted corporate growth as a means of financing their city's welfare state even before their city's fiscal crisis, most were prepared to further promote this growth in order to finance their city after the crisis—even if meant jettisoning the welfare state and those who benefited from it (see figures 9.1 and 9.2).

FIGURE 9.1. Developer William Zeckendorf (*center*) presents plans for a new hotel to be built near Radio City before an admiring Mayor Robert Wagner (*right*), 1959. Bettman/Editorial Imagespopu via Getty Images. Even at New York City's postwar height as a "social democratic polity" complete with an expansive welfare state, liberal policymakers like Mayor Wagner supported large-scale real estate developers like Zeckendorf and their vision of a tourist-and-office metropolitan economy. The taxes raised by such an economy, liberals hoped, would help finance social spending on behalf of the broader public.

FIGURE 9.2. Mayor Ed Koch and developer Donald Trump (*on the left*) admire plans for a new hotel to be built near Grand Central Station, 1978. Permission by Associated Press. While New York's fiscal crisis of the early 1970s provoked some retroactive critiques of the corporate-centric development strategies the city had embraced in the postwar era, few policymakers were willing to pursue—or even imagine—alternatives in the wake of the crisis. Rather, postcrisis mayors like Ed Koch continued to ally with large developers like Donald Trump for the same reason Wagner and Lindsay had—to promote tourism and white-collar office expansion in their city. And while some New York liberals critiqued these developments, most sought to tax the city's white-collar economy rather than displace it.

This chapter examines how New York policymakers, rather than replace the city's dominant development strategies in the wake of the fiscal crisis of the 1970s, accelerated them instead. All through the 1960s, New York City liberals had relied on white-collar growth to finance their city and its welfare state. But a "white-collar" economic base, contrary to liberal hopes, would prove to be a poor fiscal and political base for an expansive welfare state. As the costs of Gotham's welfare state increased, the city's office market faltered, and fiscal crisis loomed in the early 1970s, local liberals generally looked to federal aid for assistance without questioning their corporate "economic base." An alternative reading of the crisis was presented by a coterie of New Left critics and writers, who argued that corporate growth and subsidies on its behalf were undermining the city's economy and contributing to its fiscal strains. But these activists generally lacked the power to displace the city's established developmental strategies or detailed alternatives to replace them with. Ultimately, it would be New York's social welfare state and its beneficiaries, and not its corporate welfare state, that would be abandoned in the wake of the city's fiscal crisis.

By recalling the economic debates surrounding New York's 1970s fiscal crisis, this chapter challenges a common claim: that this crisis marked modern New York's obsession with economic growth at the expense of the welfare state. Such a shift, according to this interpretation, was made possible by the inability—or unwillingness—of New York policymakers to tax local wealth or gain intrastate transfers in order to salvage their budget. Deprived of this revenue, New York compensated by encouraging real estate and financial firms at the cost of social programs and social equity more generally.[5] New York's fiscal crisis thus marked a transition from, in Kim Moody's words, a "welfare state to real estate"—a transition that both presaged a similar trajectory in liberal and social-democratic polities across the world.[6]

But the story of New York's 1970s-era fiscal crisis is not why "economic development" triumphed in its wake, but why campaigns to *rethink and reform* urban economic development—so fervent in the wake of prior fiscal crises in the 1870s and 1930s—failed to fully materialize in the wake of this one. To be clear, this chapter does not argue that reconstructing New York's local economy would have been sufficient to salvage its finances in the 1970s. Rather, it focuses on why campaigns for local economic reform as a complement to other fiscal strategies, such as federal aid, did not fully emerge.

The answer, as this chapter argues and previous chapters have suggested, lies in both the "sunk costs" of past developmental decisions and the narrowing of fiscal imagination among postwar reformers. The politics and costs of private growth were more obscure than in the 1870s, channeled away from the kind of liberal professionals and white workers who had led previous fiscal reform campaigns. The sheer inertia of New York's postwar developmental policies, weighing the city down with sunk costs in the form of repair bills and interest charges, made dramatic shifts in economic development policy more difficult than in the past. Most liberal policymakers focused on expanding their city's welfare state rather than questioning the economic development strategies which helped finance it—a gap which echoed what Judith Stein called the broader "poverty of liberal economics" during the 1970s.[7] And while New Left activists and intellectuals would develop cogent critiques of corporate growth strategies, they were less confident than their predecessors that providing an alternative growth strategy for their city was possible or even desirable. For all these reasons, by the late 1970s New York's fiscal crisis—what one radical called "an opportunity, unequaled since the Vietnam war, to organize a broad-based movement for economic change"—had come and gone.[8] And little had changed.

We should not, therefore, interpret New York's fiscal crisis as marking the *rise* of economic growth as an urban policy goal. Rather, we should see it as marking the *bankruptcy* of economic thought and policy in New York and postwar America more broadly: a bankruptcy that rendered its welfare state vulnerable, its finances unstable, and citizens less able to pursue forms of growth that were resilient rather than fragile, regenerative rather than extractive, democratic rather than elitist.[9]

Welfare State

For most New York liberals in the 1960s, the ultimate cause of their city's growing fiscal strains was simple: poverty and the social costs it generated. Growing poverty rates, they believed, were burdening the city's budget with expanded welfare and social spending requirements. And to address these budgetary strains, liberals like Mayor Lindsay (1966–1973) generally looked to tax redistribution from both federal transfers *and* wealthy individuals and corporations in their own city. Earlier critics, of course, had blamed such local "city concentrations of wealth" for generating fiscal strains of their own. But even as New York's finances became increasingly dire in the early 1970s, few New York liberals questioned their city's white-collar transformation as a necessary component of their city's revival.

The idea that attracting "concentrations of wealth" as a necessary supplement to financing New York's welfare state was not new to the 1960s. As we have seen, early twentieth century liberals justified real-estate development partly on the grounds that it could finance more "desirable social services," in the words of E. R. A. Seligman.[10] And while Seligman might not have envisioned an expansive welfare state as part of these services, by the 1940s a growing number of New York liberals did—and believed that promoting white-collar development was necessary in order to finance them.[11] This was revealed in the debates over the redevelopment laws of the early 1940s, when many advocates of public housing—from the Brownsville Neighborhood Council to Mayor La Guardia to the New York City Housing Authority itself—lobbied for the Redevelopment Laws on the assumption that they would bring increased tax revenue to the city and its burgeoning welfare state.[12] Manhattan borough president Stanley Isaacs, for example, promoted urban redevelopment legislation on the grounds that he supported public housing, "provide accommodation for those who are not in the very lowest income groups," and "see business come back to New York." "There seems," he summarized, "to be nothing inconsistent in this attitude."[13]

Such attitudes were maintained into the postwar era.[14] That Mayor Robert Wagner could triple expenditures in schools, hospitals, and welfare on behalf of working-class citizens between 1954 and 1965, even as his redevelopment policies on behalf of corporate firms and staff helped uproot thousands of those same citizens, was generally not seen as "inconsistent" by most New

York liberals.[15] Rather, the funds raised by the private growth would help pay for so-called decommodified services—a fiscal equation that applied both to New York's "social-democratic polity" and the more comprehensive welfare states of Europe to which it has often been compared.[16] Not everyone approved of this arrangement: anarchist Paul Goodman, for example, complained of the "amazing indirectness" by which local states "subsidize[d] the full productivity of the economy" through measures like urban redevelopment, in order to provide tax revenue for welfare measures made necessary by that economy's (faulty) operation in the first place.[17] But Goodman's left-anarchist sentiments were firmly in the minority of accepted political opinion in cold war New York: rather, most progressives hoped to expand this welfare state while taxing—not displacing—the city's wealthy.[18]

And if financing the welfare state was used as a rationale for white-collar development before the 1960s, it only accelerated under Mayor Lindsay. As Lindsay's financial advisor asserted in 1968, "Concentrations of need in the central cities" needed to be "matched" by "city concentrations of wealth and taxpaying capacity."[19] And it was partially on these grounds that Lindsay's administration promoted the further white-collar transformation of their city, as the taxes raised by the central-city "well-to-do" would furnish the revenue needed to service the city's poor. New York's City Planning Commission, for example, argued that "strengthening" New York's "economic base"—which they defined largely in terms of the city's white-collar sector—would help the city "support investment in housing and education."[20] The chair of the CPC concurred, stating in a documentary that "the strength of the city is the vitality of private commercial development which ... makes it possible for us to solve the other problems."[21] He was, tellingly, standing in a west Midtown parking lot when he spoke these words.

Lindsay certainly acted to revive New York's commercial vitality. Even before his administration began, Lindsay had formed an Economic Development Council made up largely of banks and corporate firms as a vehicle for his economic strategy.[22] And he generally followed through—a 1966 report by the First National City Bank commended Mayor Lindsay's "positive attitude towards business" as indicated by strengthened programs to attract corporate firms, "the concern of the City Planning Commission with the future needs and requirements of the business community," and other "very encouraging signs."[23] Such "signs" included progress on initiatives that had long been promoted by groups like the Regional Plan Association of New York and the Downtown–Lower Manhattan Association, such as a new Midtown convention center and the World Trade Center complex. They included newer initiatives on behalf of the city's white-collar workforce, such as tax exemptions for high-income apartments.[24] And they included extensions of earlier policies, such as the underassessments of New York's real estate: between 1960 and 1970, tax assessments in New York fell from 80.2 percent to 57.6 percent of assessed property values.[25]

Nonetheless, Lindsay and his administration insisted that the funds raised by white-collar growth be channeled toward the city's expanding welfare state—and for at least a moment, both welfare spending and white-collar growth seemed to complement each other. Developers added 68 million feet of office to the metropolis in the 1960s—more than double the amount produced in the 1920s and increasing the city's aggregate office space by 33 percent.[26] At the same time, the city increased welfare spending fivefold.[27] Employment in the city's financial, insurance, and real estate firms continued its decades-long growth, expanding by nearly one hundred thousand jobs between 1950 and 1970.[28] At the same time, the city quadrupled its health-care spending.[29] By the mid-1960s, Manhattan was headquarters for more than 138 of the nation's Fortune 500 corporations—a veritable "headquarters city"— even as it doubled its education budget and tripled its service budget over the decade.[30] Progress, it seemed, could pay for poverty.

Some policymakers were aware, of course, that growing welfare costs could also be addressed by providing well-paying *jobs* to New York's poor— particularly in manufacturing.[31] "The growth of financial and service busi- nesses," a 1966 report by a state finance commission declared, "while adding to overall employment, has not provided new blue-collar jobs to counter- balance those lost in manufacturing." The city, it warned, could not afford to have manufacturing flee to the suburbs "only to become responsible for welfare payments to those they formerly employed."[32] Even New York's City Planning Commission noted this and argued that the city should use zoning and urban renewal policies to check manufacturing flight. These industries, it warned, "are the companies that employ the unskilled and the semi-skilled, the workers from the ghetto areas who, without these jobs, must head for the Relief rolls."[33]

But New York's commitment to providing well-paying entry-level jobs was decidedly secondary to attracting corporate firms and their employees. In a 1967 *New York Times* article entitled "Mayor Discounts Loss of Indus- try," Mayor Lindsay dismissed a new report indicating manufacturing flight, pointing to the city's "boom in corporate growth" as a sign of its healthy econ- omy.[34] The same state finance report worrying over manufacturing loss also declared that New York's "special economic genius" was "to be the nation's business and financial headquarters."[35] An unpublished draft report of the same 1969 plan warning of manufacturing flight also argued that the "dis- placement of manufacturing activity is the complement to the expansion of

office construction which results in higher investments . . . than the manufacturing activities they replaced."[36] And the CPC's own commissioner railed
against the finalized plan for "rezoning industrial land for housing, destroying thousands of jobs, in the very areas the Plan desires to preserve for industrial use."[37] But the CPC report was unapologetic: identifying New York's economic function as being the "national center of the United States," the CPC
hailed that economy as the "engine" of the city—"and it is getting stronger."[38]

But the stronger New York's "concentrations of wealth" became, the less
willing they were to provide for its "concentrations of need." To be sure, Lindsay successfully passed a municipal income tax, along with a new stock and
mortgage transfer tax, to redistribute the wealthy's income. But additional
taxes could be risky, one of the mayor's financial advisors warned; it ran "the
risk of inducing the richer residents and business firms to move elsewhere
in the metropolitan area."[39] A year later, the Democratic president of New
York's City Council declared that the city could raise further taxes only at "the
risk of inducing taxpaying residents and business firms to move elsewhere."[40]
Contra Isaacs, relying on "progress" to pay for "poverty" could generate its
own contradictions.

Unwilling to further tax local wealth, but unable to imagine new paradigms of local economic development either, city officials sought a third option: outside aid. Between 1964–1965 and 1970–1971, federal aid grew from
6 percent to 17 percent of the city's budget while state grants rose from 19 percent to 26 percent of the city's budget. By 1969, 43 percent of the city's total revenues came from outside its borders.[41] But while Jane Jacobs argued that such
federal aid should be paired with a "positive strategy" to rethink the economy
of cities, no such strategy was forthcoming from city hall.[42] Rather, as an economist wrote of this period looking back from the late 1970s, local liberals—like
many of their Great Society counterparts at the Federal level—continued to
rely on "white-collar jobs, federal revenue sharing and continued general economic progress" to "overcome the problems" of poverty and public financing.[43]

But "white-collar jobs" were not as reliable as local finance officers might
have hoped. By the early 1970s, companies that planners assumed were anchored to the city's core by virtue of its "vibrancy" and "face-to-face contact"
began to leave the city en masse: 37.5 percent of all finance, insurance, and
real estate sectors jobs in New York left between 1970 and 1975.[44] By 1975,
12 percent of all city offices and nearly all downtown offices were vacant—
nearly more than all the occupied offices of Boston, Philadelphia, and Houston combined.[45] Annual office space construction fell from 17.4 million in
1972 to 1.6 million in 1975.[46] Once again, half-constructed and half-vacant office towers haunted New York's skyline. And at a time when the office industry

produced over 30 percent of the city's tax revenue, this white-collar implosion exacerbated the city's revenue woes.[47]

But in the face of this collapse and their city's deepening fiscal crisis, New York's "liberal democrats" were "immobilized," in radical journalist Jack Newfield's words, by their "poverty of ideas."[48] Rather than rethink their city's antediluvian strategy of relying upon white-collar work and federal transfers to restore local finances, New York's policymakers and policy advisors redoubled their efforts. A 1975 *New York Times* article on the city's fiscal crisis revealed the general spread of opinion among liberal bien-pensants. For Columbia professor Eli Ginzburg, the solution was additional white-collar jobs. For economist John Kenneth Galbraith, the solution was federal aid.[49] Nowhere to be seen in the article, however, were discussions of alternative *local* fiscal policies or *local* development strategies that could complement these strategies. Largely absent were discussions of how the city's flawed developmental strategies could have exacerbated the city's fiscal crisis. Tax-financed redistribution remained, for the most part, the furthest horizon of liberal political thought.

But if local liberals held to older diagnoses of fiscal crisis as rooted in poverty and solved by progress, other voices were presenting a radically different interpretation: one that placed the blame for the city's crisis on the forces of "progress" itself.

Radical Diagnoses

Beginning in the late 1960s and peaking in the mid-1970s, a cohort of critics and activists accused New York's economic strategies of economic disaster.[50] Corporate growth and subsidies on its behalf, they argued, were eroding the city's budget. Real estate speculation, accelerated by public capital spending, was destabilizing the city's finances. And the social costs of this growth were leading to higher welfare costs for the metropolis, further compounding its crisis. But where these critics were strong on diagnosing the city's crisis, their solutions for it were less assured.

Many critics of New York's development policies during the city's crisis at this time were informed by the politics of the New Left. Assassinations, urban uprisings around the world, and the escalating Vietnam War convinced many late 1960s activists that so-called corporate liberalism was not only failing to secure justice—it was weakening. And nowhere were such failures experienced on such a daily level than in America's cities, where imperious skyscrapers and impoverishment coexisted and where tightening housing markets threatened the "student-bohemians" who made up the era's activist rank and file.[51] Moving beyond the canons of consensus-based political theory, a new generation of students, professors, and journalists drew from broader currents of radical political economy—Marxism, Black theories of internal colonialism, new strains of political ecology—to explain the urban crises of their era.[52] And while the New Left had generally condemned corporate power on political or social grounds during the more "prosperous" 1960s, New York's fiscal crisis prompted these critics to identify the specifically *economic* costs that corporations and their enablers were foisting on America's cities.

These critiques took many forms. Some leftist critics argued that New York's white-collar growth came at the expense of manufacturing enterprises and small businesses, thus raising unemployment rates and welfare costs for the city: an argument that some liberals made but these critics pursued with a vengeance. Journalist Robert Fitch lamented in 1976 that "once you have granted the city's real estate and financial entrepreneurs the freedom to build and rebuild ever greater concentrations of office buildings . . . a budget many times the size of the existing one would be inadequate to cope with the resulting congestion, industrial location unemployment, pauperism, etc."[53] Jason Epstein, editor of the *New York Review of Books*, later wrote that "New York's combined leadership conspired in broad daylight to hack to pieces as if they were not simply worthless but a menace, thousands of businesses and block after block of stable, tax-paying households." He continued, "Had a team of Khmers Rouges come to New York with a similar scheme, they would soon enough be thrown out of town or shot."[54] Others pointed out that the city's policy of underassessing realty, particularly of the more expensive variety, was costing the city billions that could otherwise be used to resolve its crisis: as labor researcher Joseph Harris complained, "If Mayor Beame and Governor Carey enforced the laws they have sworn to uphold, New York City's financial crisis would disappear."[55]

Where these critics went further than liberals, however, was in accusing the city's reliance on the white-collar sector *itself* as an economic failure. For example, the commitments of corporate firms to profit rather than place, together with their orientation toward national rather than local markets, made them liable to move from the city at the slightest opportunity. The early 1970s exodus of large corporations—almost a quarter of all New York's Fortune 500 companies left between 1967 and 1975—put a lie to the RPA's theory that "telecommunications will have, on balance, a concentrating impact on location of administrative activity."[56] As a postcrisis study of corporation flight from Manhattan noted, while "central city proponents tend to speak of the center's linkage advantages as being constant over time, this does not appear to be realistic."[57]

And those corporations that *did* stay were vulnerable to recession by virtue of their involvement and exposure to global financial fluctuations—and this, by extension, made city finances more vulnerable as well (figure 9.3).[58] Tellingly, the much-heralded World Trade Center lost 130 brokerage firms to mergers, bankruptcies, or relocations in the early 1970s.[59] Indeed, the largest single category of job losses for New York City between 1972 and 1976 was in financial services, more even than in manufacturing.[60] As Jane Jacobs complained in 1975, "A city can't let its skills, manufacturing plants and suppliers plants wither away and then not suffer the consequences. . . . The notion that the city could live on financial and white-collar services was nonsense."[61] Or as Epstein wrote a year later, city officials and "obtuse bankers" had "back[ed] the wrong horse."[62] And at least one official admitted the city's culpability: looking back at his tenure as New York's assistant budget director in the early 1970s, Charles Morris admitted that New York's postwar white-collar boom "was built on a peculiarly fragile base."[63]

But New York's financial sector was not the only source of New York's economic collapse: so was public spending on its behalf. New York's "capital budget debt," economist William K. Tabb complained, "owes far more to the banker-real estate developer agencies—the Housing Finance Administration, the Urban Development Corporation—than it does to helping the poor, more to subsidizing commuters than to helping the unemployed get jobs."[64] And by June of 1975, New York had incurred $9.4 billion in long-term debt on behalf of capital projects alone—much of it for new construction rather than maintenance, and far more than the $5.3 billion of short-term notes upon which so many critics harped.[65] Even capital construction on behalf of public hospitals and housing was partially paid for via bonds sold to investment firms and banks, further enriching the city's financial class: as Harlem activist William W. Sales Jr. declared, "Municipal deficit financing by making the capitalist investor a creditor of the city, repaid out of tax revenues exacted from working people, converts unprofitable social responsibility into profitable, private investment."[66] And when these projects failed, the banking actors who had promoted and financed them sought repayment—with high interest rates— for their troubles.[67] As journalist Jack Newfield later stated, "The true story [is that] New York didn't jump [into fiscal crisis]: it was pushed."[68]

And if the city was burdened by debt explicitly earmarked for corporate growth, it was also burdened by the equally costly "social costs" of the private sector. This argument, reflective of both Marxist political economy and older strains of municipal ownership, was best expressed in James O'Connor's 1973 masterwork, *The Fiscal Crisis of the State*.[69] Barred from generating revenue on its own terms, local governments were forced to rely on taxes drawn from

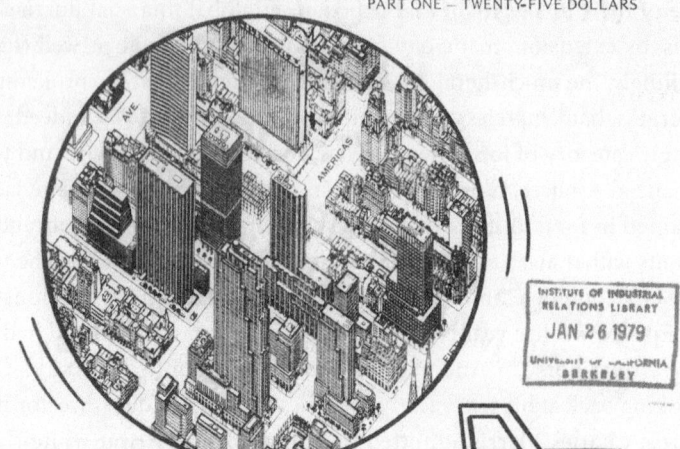

EXODUS FROM NEW YORK CITY,
PART 1

An Investigation And Analysis Of The Relocation Of Corporate Headquarters Out Of New York City

by: Robert N. Barratt, Vice President

SCHLESINGER _{a firm}
INDUSTRIAL REALTORS SINCE 1890
1373 Broad Street, Clifton, New Jersey 07013 • N.J. (201) 473-3400/Out of State (800) 631-8584
June 1977

FIGURE 9.3. Cover of Robert N Barratt, *Exodus from New York City, Part 1: An Investigation and Analysis of the Relocation of Corporate Headquarters Out of New York City* (Clifton, NJ: Schlesinger, 1977), 1. During the early 1970s, as New York slipped into fiscal crisis, the metropolis' much-vaunted realty and office economy suffered a crisis of its own as news of corporate relocations and vacant office towers grabbed local headlines. Few policymakers, however, were willing to question—much less reimagine—the corporate-retainment development strategies that had so manifestly failed the city.

private actors for revenue. Such fiscal leverage allowed those actors to foist the costs of their externalities—poor wages, poor housing, pollution—upon the local state with impunity. As Sales summarized, "The state's job under capitalism is not to appropriate profits" but to "socialize losses."[70] Between 1966 and 1979, for example, New York spent 3.5 billion dollars on sanitation and pollution-control plants—plants made necessary by private actors unwilling to "internalize" their externalities.[71] Similarly, the city's costly welfare services were themselves not so much a *driver* of the city's fiscal crisis as a downstream *product* of the private sector's irresponsibility and power—their power to pay low wages, charge high rents, and deny investment to needy communities.[72] The simultaneous expansion of New York's white-collar economy and its welfare spending was thus neither complementary (as liberals understood it) or coincidence, but cause and effect.

And if New York was suffering from growth, so too were other cities. Higher public service costs, higher costs to alleviate traffic, higher costs to alleviate environmental damage, and growing debts all seemed to accompany mainstream growth strategies. A 1985 study of fiscal strains in 130 central cities between 1972 and 1977 found that "investment expenditures" in economic growth by local governments were "no more 'productive' than social expenditures."[73] "From a budgetary perspective," a later study conducted of the decade's fiscal crises concluded, "a concentration on developmental expenditures is no strategy for fiscal health; it might even exacerbate fiscal stress."[74] Or as political scientist John Mollenkopf stated more pungently in 1976, "Growth, to put it mildly, failed to provide the fiscal bonanza for which its original patrons hoped."[75]

In summary, New York's fiscal crisis prompted a resurgence of economic critiques directed at New York's postwar growth strategies. Springing from a narrow but prolific stratum of left-leaning professionals and activists, these critiques broke from liberal diagnoses in blaming New York's crisis not on overgenerous welfare expenditures on behalf of the city's poor but on misguided economic development decisions promoted by the city's wealthy. As Robert Fitch argued, the "financial collapse" of New York was a consequence of its "national-center strategy," which "pushes out industry, requires an enormous infrastructure and generates very heavy debt."[76] And as reporter Pete Hamill stated with typical pith to the New York Labor Forum, "The people who caused the illness should not really be allowed to prescribe its solution."[77]

No Alternative

But if New York's fiscal radicals were unwilling to accept liberal strategies for local economic growth, they were unable—at times even unwilling—to replace them. Partly this was because the constituency for fiscal radicalism was far narrower than in the past. Partly it was because the "sunk costs" of previous fiscal arrangements both reproduced and obscured the social costs of New York's white-collar economy to a greater extent than before. But it was also because many fiscal radicals did not believe that alternative local growth strategies were possible—or even desirable. In doing so, however, New Left critics left the policy terrain open as to how cities *should* revive their economies. As one critic wrote in 1976, even in the wake of liberal incapacity, "the left, for its part, did not step in to fill the void."[78] Their opportunity would not come again.

We should not underestimate, of course, the extent to which activists *did* attempt to reimagine and democratize local economies in the early 1970s. Drawing from a revived interest in Socialist political economy, Black initiatives around community control, and the broader framework of participatory democracy, advocates of what was called the "new localism" argued that the surest path to local fiscal health was to wrest local economic operations away from "nonresident corporate managers and private stockholders" and put them into the hands of local residents through cooperative or public ownership.[79] This belief, strongest among the more policy-oriented ranks of the New Left, was promulgated across the country through magazines like *Alternatives* and *Working Papers for a New Society*, associations like the Institute of Local Self Reliance and the Community Ownership Organizing Project, and affiliations of progressive legislators like the National Conference on Alternative State and Local Policies.[80]

A sense of the "path not taken" for American cities during this time can be found in perhaps the most detailed proposal to emerge from the "new localist" movement: *The Cities' Wealth: Programs for Community Economic Control in Berkeley, California* (figure 9.4).[81] Authored in 1976 by a slate of veteran activists, in many ways the plan offered for a municipality what *The Economic Development of Harlem* offered for a neighborhood: a path toward economic development using the tools of collective ownership and local investments. The plan called for the city of Oakland to deposit its funds and pensions in local municipal banks, rather than extortionate Wall Street firms. These funds would be invested in local cooperatives and municipal enterprises, rather than extractive and nonproductive enterprises outside the city. Public land would be leased to these local firms, rather than to unproductive speculators. And the profits of these community enterprises would flow into local governments and local pocketbooks, sparking another round of investment and local wealth building. The plan cautioned that local economic reconstruction would not be an end to itself, of course—but by demonstrating that workers

$2.50

The CITIES'
WEALTH

PROGRAMS FOR COMMUNITY ECONOMIC
CONTROL IN BERKELEY, CALIFORNIA

PUBLIC
OWNERSHIP
OF
P.G.&E.

Written by the Community
Ownership
a publication of the
CONFERENCE/Alternative State and   Organizing
Institute for Policy Studies
Washington D.C., 20009   Local Public Policies   Project

FIGURE 9.4. Community Ownership Organizing Project, *The Cities' Wealth: Programs for Community Economic Control in Berkeley, California* (Washington, DC: National Conference on Alternative State and Local Public Policies, 1976), cover. One of the most ambitious and detailed New Left plans for transforming local economies, *The Cities' Wealth* proposed that Berkeley's local government use municipal ownership and cooperatives as tools of local economic development.

could earn livelihoods and material benefits under conditions of economic democracy, cities like Oakland could help build a constituency for expanding such policies while breaking the power that private employers had over local economies—and hence, local politics. Local economic reforms, in short, could "help meet the needs of poor and working people, and at the same time point the way to still better ways of distributing wealth and power."[82]

New York, too, witnessed some campaigns for economic reconstruction in the wake of its fiscal crisis. Arthur Holden, a veteran critic of booster policies since the 1920s, wrote to New York's comptroller in 1975 that what New York needed was not "more towering office buildings" but to "make better productive use of the facilities it already possessed, by the people who already lived there."[83] A 1978 candidate for City Council proposed that the city's funds be deposited in neighborhood and municipal banks to be invested in reformed community development corporations.[84] That same year, the Energy and Economics Appropriate Technology Action Coalition (their name referring to a key idea by localist hero E. F. Schumacher) proposed a citywide network of fuel purchasing and distribution cooperatives.[85] And scattered experiments in alternative forms of provisioning, ranging from formal cooperatives to "sweat equity" rehabilitations to squatting, represented some seeds of heterodox economic thought that under the right conditions might have further blossomed.[86]

Nonetheless, the "new localists" of the early 1970s arguably achieved less political and policy success than earlier fiscal radicals like Henry George, acting in the wake of the city's earlier fiscal crisis, had achieved. Changes in the city's fiscal structure since the 1870s, together with the narrowed "fiscal imagination" of the very groups who had previously joined the cause of Georgism and similar movements, made the task of fiscal reconstruction far more politically and economically difficult than in the past.

The disciplines of urban economics and urban planning, for example— which in the past had furnished some of the most prominent advocates of radical fiscal reform, like Benjamin Marsh or Richard T. Ely in the 1880s— were now more closed to heterodox thinking. As we have seen, by the early 1900s, urban economic and municipal finance texts generally discounted the kinds of social costs brought about by the monopoly and land speculation that Henry George had attended to earlier. This intellectual narrowing continued through the postwar period, by which time urban economics texts generally portrayed the city as a neoclassical landscape where the collective land bid of "rational" voter-consumers led to aggregate efficiency.[87] "Externalities are, or should be, central to any theory of locational arrangement," complained English geographer Doreen Massey in a 1973 *Antipode* article.

But such externalities were, she lamented, "not a main thread" of "neoclassical" urban economics.[88]

The politics of economic development policies was also more obscure than in the 1870s—and thus harder to challenge. Efforts by reformers to bring "businesslike" expertise and efficiency into local financing decisions, begun in earnest during the Progressive Era, helped conceal and depoliticize such decisions. Where welfare spending was decided in the scrum of the City Council, for example, economic development decisions were often made in closed-off public authorities and visible only in the city's arcane capital budget.[89] To be sure, the costs of New York's growth were less visible on this budget than in the past: whereas, in 1929, capital spending comprised 22 percent of the city's budget and interest on that debt comprised 16 percent of city spending, these numbers stood at only 11 percent and 5.2 percent in 1975.[90] Rather, such costs were expressed in the broader economic fragility and underdevelopment of the metropolis—costs only truly evident once the politics and operations of local economic policy were open to critical inspection.

But it was this precise openness that was denied to most New Yorkers: as Frances Fox Piven wrote in 1977, "Agencies that control the conditions of economic growth are structured in a way which render[s] them relatively autonomous from popularly elected officials and relatively invisible to the urban population at large."[91] Indeed, many of these agencies were not even within the city's jurisdiction: between 1976 and 1980, roughly 80 percent of local economic development aid in New York—and hence, local economic policy—was made by well-insulated federal and state bureaucracies.[92] A 1977 article in the Review of Radical Political Economics described how identifying an "attackable source" that was "blocking urban improvement," one "comparable to that of the transit monopolies in the 1880's," was essential for forming radical unity and cohesion in the 1970s.[93] But the operations and sources of urban fiscal crises were far more obscure in the 1970s than in the days of Gilded Age traction companies, whose fiscal (and often physical abuse) of the public was far harder to conceal.

The kind of white workers who had joined Hearst and Henry George in calling for radical fiscal reform were also, by the postwar period, far less compelled by the cause of fiscal radicalism. Since the 1920s, such homeowners had been assessed at low values and provided generous public services. Now in the 1970s, they continued to receive such benefits, even as they assailed the city's poor using the "producerist" language of their republican antecedents. One Brooklyn neighborhood group, for example, exclaimed that "for years, we have witnessed the appeasement of nonproductive and counterproductive 'leeches' at the expense of New York's middle-class workforce."[94]

Such critiques stemmed partly from the city's divided fiscal structure, as discussed previously, which highlighted the politics and costs of welfare spending rather than economic development decisions. But it also stemmed from the racist assumptions that had accompanied much of populist thought since the late nineteenth century and had only calcified since. In the eyes of white "taxpayers," the editor of the *Black Scholar* wrote in 1975, Blacks were "lazy, unproductive, and a rapidly procreating mass representing an ever-increasing drain on the city's treasury."[95] Such beliefs, in the editor's words, served to "obfuscate" the role of white property owners themselves in bringing about their city's crisis.[96]

The "sunk costs" of previous planning and public finance decisions similarly prevented the city from rapidly changing economic course. The roads and other infrastructure that had been built at great expense and now required maintenance, the new neighborhoods that had been built on the city's outskirts and now required public services, the debts that had been accrued for the sake of this growth and now required repayment plus interest: all these costs of growth now weighed down the city's budget in a way that seemed impossible to extricate except through more growth. Similarly, whereas many urbanites positively insisted that municipalities default as a response to insistent creditors during the fiscal crises of the 1870s, the comparative reliance of postwar urbanites on an extensive array of municipal services made the prospect of default far more fraught by the 1970s.[97]

And just as the city's finances appeared dependent on growth in general to repay its debts, so the city's decisions to promote white-collar work had made it disproportionately dependent on that sector's growth in particular. In 1970–1971, for example, offices contributed 15 percent of the city's real estate taxes, 25 percent of the city's income taxes, and 80 percent of its commercial occupancy taxes. Thirty percent of the city's total tax revenue now came from offices and office workers alone.[98] It would be difficult to replace this economic "base" with an equally lucrative one on short notice. Of course, it was the social costs of New York's growth that had helped generate the *need* for copious tax revenue to begin with, but this argument was not prevalent among most witnesses to New York's fiscal crisis.

But if these legacies of past fiscal decisions made the task of radical fiscal reform more difficult, it was also because many fiscal radicals themselves did not proffer alternatives. Partly this was due to the sheer brutality and speed with which the city's creditors attacked New York's welfare state in the wake of the city's crisis. Under such conditions, pursuing alternative economic strategies could appear less of a priority for city residents than defending the public services many already relied upon (even if such alternatives might have made some public services, such as welfare spending, arguably less necessary). As the inaugural article in *Working Papers for a New Society* noted in 1973, "For most of us, the pressing question is how to keep conditions in America from deteriorating even further."[99] It was this motivation, reasonable but defensive, that led groups like the New America Coalition and the Citywide Community Coalition to engage in mass meetings, protest marches, and strikes in order to prevent the firing of public employees and restore the city's welfare services.[100]

But many fiscal radicals were also convinced that reconstructing local economies was a misguided if not impossible task in the modern era. Partly this was because both the Marxist and Keynesian canons that many New Left activists drew from stressed the "structural dependence" of urban economies on macro-level economic shifts, or at least on factors of capital mobility and economies of scale that cities could not arrest. William Tabb, a Marxist scholar who titled an essay on New York's fiscal crisis "Blaming the Victim," believed that there was no heterodox economic platform that could salvage city finances. "Unfortunately," he wrote in a previous article, "a rational central city government will probably act to subsidize the rich at the expense of the poor."[101] And Jason Epstein, who called the destruction of New York's small businesses akin to the work of the murderous Khmer Rouge, also described the pre–white collar New York as an "anachronism," a "living museum of pre-monopoly capitalism" unable to be revived.[102] "The prevailing wisdom," he stated, "is that New York and other old eastern cities are finished anyway."[103] The less fatalistic argued that only federal aid could salvage local finances. But neither optimistic Keynesians nor dour Marxists generally believed that cities were capable of acting as "cooperative commonwealths" on behalf of their own people. The notion that the struggle for local economic democracy could *itself* produce and reinforce political strength, so vital in the thought of Black radicals of the late 1960s and early 1970s, was largely absent here—replaced by what political scientist Norton E. Long called a "dogma of powerlessness" that helped foreclose creative progressive responses to New York's fiscal crisis.[104]

And if some critics believed that placing urban economic growth on new foundations was impossible, others believed it was undesirable. By the early 1970s, an increasingly influential body of white professionals was challenging expressions of economic growth across the country: preservationists in New York City, conservationists in California, and think tanks concerned with "limits to growth" on a planetary basis.[105] By framing their campaigns in stark terms of "growth" versus "anti-growth"—or, put differently, by conflating a narrow example of economic "growth" with economic "development" more generally—this coalition restricted efforts to place America's economic development on more equitable footing. Of course, this was not necessarily the intention of white homeowners seeking merely to preserve their property values from the costs of sprawl or "upzoning"—but if this lacuna existed even among well-intentioned liberal professionals, it was also true among some of the radical theorists who were most adept at identifying the failures of mainstream growth strategies.

In his influential 1976 article, "The City as a Growth Machine," for example, sociologist Harvey Molotch blamed the fiscal crisis of American cities partly on unremunerative local growth strategies. Rather than suggest alternative models of growth along the lines of Oakland's *The Cities' Wealth*, however, Molotch saved his praise for efforts to *limit* growth via intensive land-use controls by residents in Santa Barbara and Beverly Hills. Molotch admitted that many of these movements consisted of "a leisured and sophisticated middle class," but he hoped that they would eventually broaden their base to include "the great majority of the working class in the localities in which they appear."[106] Absent alternative ways of employing people and producing goods, however, this "majority of the working class" was largely uninterested in "de-growing" local economies.[107]

Efforts by radicals to reconstruct urban economies in the 1970s, then, faced different and greater difficulties than their predecessors in the 1870s did. The "sunk costs" of a hundred years' worth of past fiscal decisions made the possibility of economic reconstruction more challenging. The constituency for radical fiscal reform was narrower, and the politics and costs of misguided economic decisions were harder to perceive. Liberals and progressives themselves were divided over the possibility and desirability of local economic reconstruction. And looming over all these factors was the sheer power of established private real estate and white-collar industries. The outcome was that, apart from aborted revolts by figures like Dennis Kucinich in Cleveland and Nicholas Carbone in Hartford, most campaigns to transform and democratize local economies were stillborn during the period of New York's fiscal crisis—as they would be in New York City itself.[108]

A sense of how the fiscal imagination of New York had shrunk since the 1870s was revealed in a 1975 *New York Times* article on the city's fiscal crisis. Robert C. Wood, the former official at President Johnson's Department of Housing and Urban Development, suggested that New York might "go back to Henry George" for solutions to its fiscal crisis. If New York had "leased its land" to developers rather than selling it outright in the nineteenth century, he stated, "most of the cities, including New York, would be better off." But he then averred, stating that such land municipalization was "more theoretical or egghead" than a serious proposal.[109] It was not "theoretical" a hundred years ago, of course, when followers of the Georgist cause had shaken New York's politics for decades. But much had changed since then. Instead, Wood argued for federal aid to the city on the grounds that such transfers could help New York revive the "commercial centers that New York supports between 42nd and 59th street and on Wall Street"—in other words, federal subsidies in order to finance local subsidies to support the private sector. Such was the "liberal imagination" in the early 1970s.

Looking Backward

Where certain New Left critics despaired of cities ever recovering their eco-nomic vitality, those who continued to hold power within New York gener-ally remained boosterish—if unimaginative. Rather than transforming the local economic policies underpinning New York's welfare state, postcrisis policymakers accelerated those policies. Some paired this acceleration with an active hostility to the welfare state; others did so in the hope that it would help raise the taxes needed to finance that welfare state. But in either case, New York's pre-crisis developmental strategy was largely retained, even under the far less hospitable conditions of the 1970s.[110] Matters were not entirely the same, of course: New York's postcrisis policymakers commodified swaths of the city with an relish not seen since the nineteenth century and were more attentive to "demand factors" (i.e., increasing services as well as cut-ting costs on behalf of white-collar quarry) than many postwar policymakers had been. Rather than view these policies as evincing a paradigm-marking shift from "welfare to real estate," however, we should see them as accelerat-ing the destructive—and ultimately self-destructive—dynamics that had long shaped New York's domestic economy.

New York's creditors, like many of New York's liberals, viewed growing wel-fare costs as *the* key local factor behind the city's fiscal crisis. But where precri-sis liberals had hoped to salvage the situation by increasing the welfare state's financing, "conservative" creditors saw the welfare state *itself* as the problem. The "pressing need" in regard to the city's welfare policies, a Salomon Broth-ers investment guide stated in 1975, was not to "finance it" but "to change it."[111] And they would soon have their chance. In June 1975, the state legislature empowered an executive-heavy Municipal Assistance Corporation, or "Big MAC," to lend money to the city in exchange for drastic cuts in the city's budget. By the end of the crisis, New York City had cut its teaching force by 25 percent and forced the historically free City University of New York to charge tuition. The city also closed five public hospitals and twenty-eight city-run drug rehabilitation centers during the decade. By 1977, one-half of the city's Hispanic municipal employees and two-fifths of its Black employees had been fired, and between 1975 and 1980, a *quarter* of the city's entire municipal workforce—sixty-three thousand jobs—was "let go."[112]

But was purging a welfare state enough to ensure New York's economic future? At least some city officials were not sure. This doubt was most famously expressed by Roger Starr, administrator of the city's Housing and Development Administration. In language reminiscent of Tugwell, he complained in 1976 that New York's "rapid-transit system, educational facilities, hospitals and highways—was dedicated to the fulfillment of the dream of constant growth, growth that might last forever." But where Tugwell had poured his ire upon the speculative *drivers* of this growth, Starr targeted the city's poorest. And where figures like Hearst and Frederic C. Howe had sought to transform New York's economy to deliver both prosperity and justice, Starr's ambitions stopped at "planned shrinkage." It was time, he argued, to recognize that the "golden door to full participation in American life and the American economy is no longer to be found in New York."[113]

Those who already enjoyed "full participation" in the American economy, however, remained quite boosterish toward their city—and, seeing little profit in pursuing alternatives, held to New York's precrisis model of economic development as its model going forward. A 1972 profile of New York's economy by First National City Bank argued that New York was a "reasonably healthy, stable economy" in the "advanced stages of postindustrial development."[114] A *New York Times* article on New York's "crumbling economy" nonetheless argued that their city could only recover from its collapsing white-collar economy by *further* bolstering the city's position as the "financial center of the nation, if not the world."[115] And the prominent Twentieth Century Fund argued that the city's economic future lay in becoming a "global marketplace for business, finance, communications," and "the professions."[116] Whereas some well-placed planners and economists evinced at least some skepticism toward antediluvian development strategies during the urban fiscal crises of the 1930s—the Twentieth Century Fund's own executive director (and NYCHA financial advisor) Evans Clark stated in 1936 that the problem of slums could not be addressed through "an excess of higher-priced new dwellings"—this skepticism was largely absent by the 1970s iteration of these crises.[117]

Such recommendations were given formal imprimatur through bodies like the Temporary Commission on New York Finances. Formed in 1975 and made up largely of the city's banking and business elite, the body's reports framed the city's ills as deriving largely from local policies hostile to business—or, as the commission's final report phrased it, behaving "in an economically irrational fashion by attempting to contravene some funda-mental economic forces."[118] And such irrationality could only end, it argued, by reducing taxes, improving management techniques, and restricting un-necessary capital expenditures—with exceptions, of course, made "for proj-ects like the Convention Center where new construction provide a definite stimulus to the city's economic development."[119]

Efforts by the commission to frame their strategies as "bold departures" from the city's purportedly antibusiness past, however, were both self-serving and inaccurate. For as we have seen, attracting and cultivating white-collar enterprises and realty growth more generally had been a long-standing policy of city officials even at the height of their city's welfare state. Departments like the City Planning Commission; agencies like the Department of Commerce, the Economic Development Council, and the Economic Development Ad-ministration; and public-private ventures like the Convention and Visitor's Bureau—all had long promoted New York as a white-collar business center well before the crisis and continued to do so afterward. And the commission's diagnoses ignored the fiscal decay and economic rot that the city's prior de-velopment strategies had saddled upon the metropolis. As one urban planner summarized, "Many of [the Commission's] policy recommendations are not consistent with the problems identified by the time-series analysis of local fis-cal trends. At the same time the recommendations are totally consistent with the business/political interests of the Commission members."[120]

Most New York policymakers, however, had little material or electoral in-centives to counter these developmental recommendations with alternative ones. Figures like Governor Hugh Carey and Mayor Edward Koch, tasked with restoring the city's finances following its fiscal crisis, had few doubts that attracting corporations and tourists would be to the city's benefit: as Koch used to joke, "The taller the building, the more taxes there are." Nonetheless, Koch's rationale for such projects—that the projects would help finance public goods like "parks and schools"—were not so dissimilar from that of pre-crisis liberals.[121] And while defenders of New York's welfare state might critique subsidies on the behalf of realty developments, their political horizon was largely limited to demanding that such enterprises be taxed fairly. Alternative economic models, such as the profitable public ownership of enterprises and land, remained a nonstarter for most postcrisis liberals on both practical and ideological grounds. As Mario Cuomo declared in 1976, "We are not in the business of declaring dividends, we are in the business of improving lives."[122] No—dividends were strictly for the private sector, to their great advantage.

Still, New York's government itself generally lacked a comprehensive *plan* that would coordinate its full repertoire of fiscal, land-use, investments, and other powers to bear on economic development—but this would begin to change in the mid-1970s. A host of new city-initiated plans, from a host of new City Planning Commission surveys to a 1975 "Agenda for Economic Development" to a 1976 five-year "Economic Recovery program." Such plans, architectural critic Ada Louise Huxtable later complained, did "nothing to address the building of a stable economic base beyond the fine art of tax forecasting and financial packaging."[123] But developed they were, providing guidance for what John Mollenkopf later called a "latent, yet highly coherent," economic development agenda on behalf of white-collar development.[124]

To help carry out this agenda, in 1977 New York formed an Office of Economic Development devoted to coordinating and initiating development projects across the city. A task force within this agency devised a new mechanism—an economic development corporation (EDC)—that would "marry public financing tools to private financing and packaging expertise" in order to initiate complex development projects.[125] And to oversee this coordination was a new public position second only to the mayor in authority, the deputy mayor of economic development—one of the first being a former board member of the Lehman Brothers.

Just as before the crisis, New York dispensed subsidies on behalf of upper-income offices and their employees. Tax cuts, for example: in 1980, the Municipal Assistance Corporation demanded a reduction in taxes upon high-income families, corporate headquarters, and other "persons and businesses whose continued presence in New York City is peculiarly significant to its survival as a great community."[126] The following year, New York State passed a law establishing that certain property categories, such as larger residential buildings and single-family homes, were to be assessed at only a fraction of their market value.[127] Where New York properties were generally assessed at 34 percent of market value in 1983, that ratio dropped to 18 percent by 1989—even while the property tax rates themselves fell from 3 percent to 1.7 percent.[128] And this was in addition to the millions of dollars' worth of tax abatements provided to individual developments by agencies like the Public Development Corporation, the Urban Development Corporation, Battery Park City Authority, and others.[129]

Subsidies on behalf of grand capital projects to attract white-collar enterprise and tourism also continued apace. The much-longed-for Jacob Javits Convention Center (appropriately named after the senator sponsor of the Community Self-Determination Act of 1968), the South Street Seaport, Hunters Point, the redevelopment of Times Square and Columbus Circle— all these projects contributed to the city's expanding postcrisis capital budget. Even as the city's expense budget declined by almost 16 percent in real terms between 1976 and 1981, its capital budget rose by 18 percent.[130] Not all realty-benefiting capital projects went through, of course, most notably the defeat of Westway—a $4 billion "real-estate development project masquerading as a highway."[131] Nonetheless, what was built helped return the city's finances to old form. As historian Ester Fuchs noted, "After the 1975 crisis was resolved, trends in New York's capital budget and debt burden looked remarkably like those in the pre-fiscal crisis period."[132]

It would be wrong, of course, to argue that all of New York City's postcrisis development policies were oriented around white-collar work. As before, many city planners recognized the economic threat of manufacturing flight.[133] A slew of new programs, such as the Industrial Development Agency (IDA), the In-Place Industrial Park Program, and the Industrial Security Program, were empowered to acquire property, finance construction, sell property, and otherwise assist manufacturing in the city.[134]

But such programs, as John Mollenkopf stated, were more "symbolic than substantive."[135] To wit: between 1977 and 1980, the IDA negotiated $130 million worth of bond sales, less than 20 percent of which was for manufacturing projects.[136] Meanwhile, specialized tax-exemption programs for upper-income residences and offices between 1976 and 1981 cost the city $2.5 billion.[137] "The dollar amounts and administrative priority devoted" to industrial retention, Mollenkopf summarized, "have been minuscule compared to those lavished on enhancing the central business district."[138] Similar discrimination was practiced on behalf of the city's lower-income neighborhoods: in 1978, for example, the Board of Estimate approved $9 million for nine neighborhood commercial revitalization programs, while a single company—AT&T—was granted a tax exemption worth $20 million in the early 1980s.[139]

And such formal aid was in addition to the "soft" branding of New York during this time nearly exclusively as a global, white-collar metropolis, as when the Business Marketing Corporation produced a brochure hailing it as a center of corporate enterprise and high finance (see figures 9.5 and 9.6).[140] Yes, these promotions placed a greater emphasis on New York as an "information" or "global" capital, rather than being a mere "national center," as in the city's 1960s-era promotions. But their rationales remained the same: New York's future relied on providing services and financing on behalf of an outside market. Producing goods, much less for an internal market, was generally out of the question. A writer for the *New York Times* captured this rationale well in 1979. Living "only on their ideas," he exclaimed, a new generation of "professional upper class, an achievement-oriented gentry," was turning New York's central business district into a machine for "producing, processing, and trading specialized intelligence." These workers and the corporations

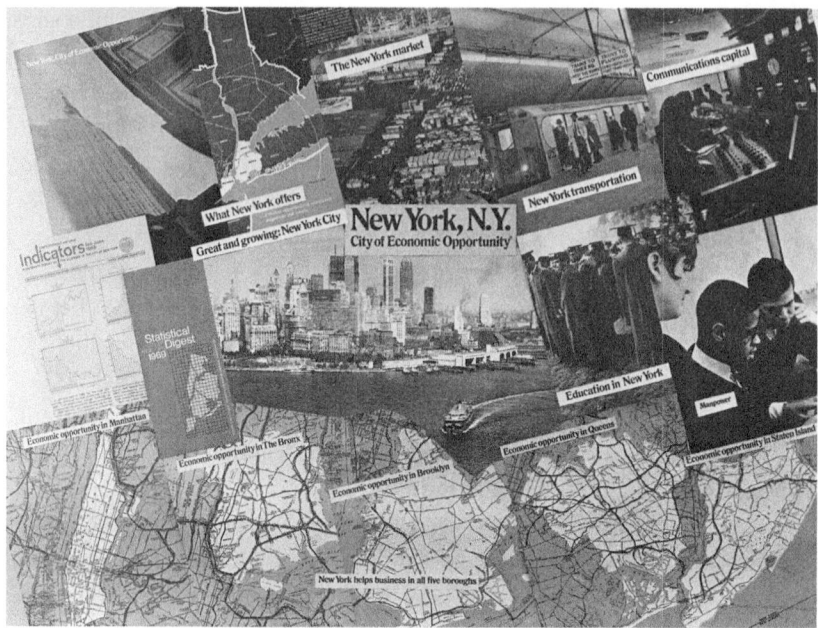

FIGURE 9.5. *Economic Development, Collage*, March 30, 1970. Courtesy Municipal Archives, City of New York. A promotional brochure produced by the New York Mayor's Office in 1970. While this promotional poster appeared before New York's fiscal crisis, it reflected themes that were already well established among postwar metropolitan "boosters": key among them the city's white-collar workforce and status as a global "capital" of trade and communications.

they worked for were (as always) the future of the city. And while New York might have once been a factory town full of "workers and immigrants," the author wrote, it would "be folly to try to recreate that bustling younger city." No, "the survival and recovery of New York City," the author concluded, "depends on an educated, integrated urban elite."[141]

New York would indeed survive—but in important ways, it did not recover.

Consequences

The policies carried out by and on behalf of New York's "urban elite" further accelerated the city's transformation into a white-collar metropolis during the 1980s. Just as in the 1960s, office towers rose alongside poverty rates—the progress of some accompanying and driving the poverty of others, now unmitigated by a generous welfare state. And while New York's self-styled "economic base" might have enriched some private actors, it would prove just as unreliable and costly to the metropolis as a whole. But those who would fight

The New York City Advantage

THE BRONX
QUEENS
MANHATTAN
BROOKLYN
STATEN ISLAND

Business Marketing Corporation for New York City

FIGURE 9.6. "The New York City Advantage," 1978, p. 36, Folder 16, Box 80, Departmental Correspondence Series, Edward I. Koch Documents Collection, La Guardia and Wagner Archives, New York. Courtesy Municipal Archives, City of New York. This table of contents, culled from a promotional brochure produced for New York by a private firm following the city's fiscal crisis, indicates how the city's postcrisis fiscal imagination remained bound to the corporate-and-tourism motifs established in the postwar period (while placing a somewhat greater emphasis on the city's "lifestyle" amenities).

for an alternative model of local economic developmental—or even imagine such a model—seemed to be in short supply.

Signs of "growth"—narrowly defined—could be found everywhere in New York during the 1980s. Between 1981 and 1990, 53 million square feet of new offices were constructed in New York.[142] The market value of New York's property rose by 174 percent during the same period.[143] After bottoming out in the late 1970s, Manhattan's land values grew from roughly $48 to $644 dollars per square foot by 1988—an increase of roughly 24 percent per year.[144] Financial service positions in New York City increased by 15.9 percent between 1977 and 1989 and corporate service positions by 42.6 percent. Fifty-three thousand banking jobs,[145] thirty-seven thousand legal service jobs, eleven thousand management consultant jobs, and ten thousand accounting jobs were added in New York City.[146]

And then, as was traditional, came the crash. By the early 1990s, office building vacancy rates in New York were twice those of the fiscal crisis era. Altogether, nearly 65 million square feet—more than was built even during the whole of the 1980s boom—was vacant. And broader indicators of social immiseration, which had grown all through that boom, spiked at this crash. The number of residents in New York living in poverty rose from 1.1 million in 1975 to 1.7 million in 1984 until, by 1990, more than a quarter of all New Yorkers lived in poverty. And these numbers were awful even by comparison with other cities experiencing the broader early 1990s recession. The global capital of finance, insurance, real estate (FIRE) was also the nation's capital in terms of unemployment, inequality, *and* office vacancies. For journalist Robert Fitch, this was not a coincidence but a consequence. "The downturn of the nineties—New York's 'second slump,'" he wrote, "could only be identified as the product of its FIRE structure. Here is an industrial structure more skewed towards FIRE than any other city and it had produced what was demonstrably the nation's worst urban downturn."[147]

But if New York's FIRE economy was failing the city, few could imagine an alternative to this economy—much less implement it. Not all cities were so hopeless: during the early 1980s, the Greater London Council (GLC) attempted to restructure their city's economy on terms favorable to labor. To accomplish this, the GLC used its procurement powers to purchase from worker cooperatives, provided loans to industrial companies in exchange for worker-developed "industrial plans," and developed a Popular Planning Unit to help communities develop alternative proposals for economic development in their communities. Such initiatives were promoted not just on the grounds of justice or even nostalgia for the industrial era but on the grounds of economic viability: as one economist at the GLC wrote, their proposals were "as technically 'efficient' as capital's version of restructuring. What all of them imply is a quite different product, technology, and conditions for labor return." And the journalist Robert Fitch proposed a suite of similar policies in his magisterial book *The Assassination of New York*.[148]

But there would be no economic restructuring for labor in New York City—or restructuring for its citizens. As one critic lamented in 1989, although "there was probably nothing New York could have done to avert the crash of 1975," it might have made "some difference" if we were "blessed with political leaders honest enough to explain to the people the shape and weight of the forces we are up against." Then, he argued, "we might at least begin to develop a new civic consciousness, appropriate to an age of deindustrialization and dematerialized capital."[149] But New York's leaders were generally uninterested in developing such a new civic consciousness—or the new economic base that could support it. And what few activists were able to imagine reconstructing New York's economy lacked the broad constituency needed to do so.

And if this was true in New York, so it was true of "probusiness administrations" across the country. Some, like Pittsburgh and Chicago, experienced modest fiscal recoveries during the 1980s—whether alternative development strategies would have delivered such outcomes with greater justice to its people, we will never know. Others, like Detroit and Baltimore, continued to wither. And Sun Belt cities like Phoenix, Denver, and Houston continued to grow apace.[150] But all generally used the same policy repertoire—largely zoning, subsidies, and combinations of enhanced police budgets and variations on the festival marketplace—to lure the same wealthy and corporate quarry. All had "learned," as Blake Fleetwood in the *New York Times* observed in 1979, that "only the middle and upper classes—not the poor—can rebuild the cities."[151] And all enforced the same economic division of labor that had first been entrenched in the nineteenth century: that "the path to well-being lies exclusively through the private sector," and more specifically the largest and most profitable components of that sector. As one policymaker stated in 1984, "Government's proper role is to enhance resources, promote a healthy and fair climate for business, and assist business in doing what business does best."[152]

What that precisely is, only history can judge.

Conclusion

Through the late 1960s and early 1970s, liberal policymakers in New York promoted white-collar expansion as a means of financing their city's expanding welfare state and avoiding fiscal crisis. They did not succeed. And for several years, a body of heterodox social scientists and journalists, grounded in various strands of radical political economy, suggested why. Corporate-centric growth, they argued, generated extensive externalities, required enormous subsidies, and proved to be both flighty and fragile fiscal partners. Courting corporations was not a strategy for urban development—it was a strategy for urban crisis. Moreover, such a reliance on elite-driven growth meant that postwar liberalism's social ambitions—such as they were—were built on an unstable and unsustainable foundation.

Nonetheless, critics were unable to replace New York's regnant growth strategies with alternatives. Partly this was due to the "sunk costs" of past developmental decisions, which had narrowed both the options and constituency for radical fiscal reform by the 1970s. Partly it was from the inherited power that the city's dominant realty and commercial forces enjoyed. But it was also because many critical urbanists themselves no longer believed that cities could, or even should, place growth on alternative footing.

The result was that, where the city's fiscal crisis of the 1870s was met with popular mobilizations for municipal ownership and land-value taxation, where the city's fiscal crisis of the 1930s was met with bold if incomplete re-imaginings of urban economics, the city's fiscal crisis of the 1970s was met with—more of the same. New York's pre-crash economic logic survived the 1970s, while its welfare state stumbled into the twenty-first century fiscally dependent on the same wealthy actors who displaced and despised its constituency. A similar fate was meeting liberal and social-democratic welfare states across the world. And for the first time in more than a century, it seemed, there was no alternative.

Conclusion

Economism ... does not consist in giving too much importance to the economy, but in giving it too narrow a scope.

MAX HORKHEIMER[1]

In 2019, James Patchett, president and CEO of the New York City Economic Development Corporation, asked New York's City Council to approve $2.6 billion worth of subsidies on behalf of Amazon. In making his case, he invoked New York's 1970s-era fiscal crisis. "We still feel the effects of the 1970s fiscal crisis, the aftermath of which devastated our public hospitals and schools," he stated.[2] "The billions in tax revenue" that Amazon would generate for the city as the result of municipal subsidies, he proclaimed, would enable the city to construct 289,000 units of affordable housing, hire 5,600 new public school teachers, and improve social services like medical care and disability assistance across the city. "With this additional revenue," he asserted, "some of our boldest, most progressive ideals can become policies and our greatest needs are more likely to be met."[3] He then presented Amazon's plan for a second headquarters in New York, which included a helipad.

Here, once again, was the old argument. Public subsidies would bring public solvency. Wealth would pay for welfare. Progress would pay for poverty. Nowhere in Patchett's speech was the fact that wealth-driven growth can immiserate as well as enrich. And nowhere in Patchett's capsule history of Gotham's 1970s-era fiscal crisis did he mention the subsidies and speculation that helped *bring* New York to that crisis—or to the crises of the 1930s or 1870s, for that matter.

Other New Yorkers, however, held different understandings of how New York's economic development should proceed. Even as Patchett spoke, there were forty-seven worker-owned cooperatives in the city—a number that would reach triple figures by 2021.[4] These businesses were provided, for the first time, with economic development subsidies from New York in the form of a Worker Cooperative Business Development Initiative (see figure C.1).

FIGURE C.1. Community land trust (CLT) activists rally at New York City Hall in June 2023. Photo via the New Economy Project. CLTs, of which there are 19 in NYC alone, provide a tool for managing land-use for the long term benefit of residents rather than outside shareholders. As such they can provide an alternate means of urban economic development, delivering both fiscal resilience and social equity to New York and other cities.

Eleven community land trusts, working to provide affordable housing and economic activity on community-controlled land, were provided similar public funding that year.[5] Across the ocean in England, the city of Preston was embracing municipal enterprise and cooperatives as a means of economic development.[6] And across the world, a new generation of activists was developing new economic strategies for meeting human needs within planetary boundaries.[7]

These cooperators are the inheritors of a proud tradition. As this book has shown, many activists between the 1870s and 1960s sought to place their cities on firmer fiscal ground by restricting public aid on behalf of the wealthy. Their campaigns helped shape new strategies and policies of economic development, underwriting the broader transformation of American cities during the twentieth century. And at their most farsighted, they sought to ground the prosperity and resilience of American cities not in the largesse of the powerful but in the well-being and participation of ordinary citizens.

Nonetheless, these reformers' definitions of what constituted economic development often reflected and deepened social inequities and fiscal contradictions. Reacting to the underassessment of speculative real estate values in the early 1900s, municipal finance officers committed local governments to raise such values through debt-financed improvements for tax purposes. Postwar reactions against realty speculation contributed to theories stressing the importance of developing a corporate and financial "base." In this way, revolts against mainstream growth paradigms have themselves both augmented and undermined the economic health of cities. The story this book tells is thus a warning as well as an inspiration.

But this book also contains a broader directive: we cannot frame the fiscal dilemmas of local governments in simple terms of economic development versus economic decline. Too often, this framing contains unvoiced and narrow assumptions as to what constitutes "development" and how best to achieve it. Rather, practitioners, historians, and ordinary citizens need to ask a different question: what *kind* of development, with what *kind* of consequences, do American towns and cities need to cultivate today?

Practitioners

Economic development and planning practitioners must not conflate the wealth of the local private sector with the health of the local public sector. Throughout the twentieth century, urban planners have assumed that retaining wealthy individuals and firms is necessary for local fiscal health. This assumption is wrong. These individuals and firms can place greater direct and indirect costs upon the public sector than those with smaller yields. And an agglomeration of smaller, locally oriented firms with alternative ownership structures—cooperative, public, or private—can provide more public revenue, with less public costs, than seemingly "wealthier" firms.[8]

For this reason, public officials must develop a comprehensive means of measuring how different developmental decisions lead to different public benefits or burdens. Developing a "public balance sheet" in this way can reveal how many seemingly "cost-neutral" private investment decisions can, in fact, pass on substantial and unsustainable burdens to the public sector. It can reveal how developmental decisions that go beyond mainstream corporate-retainment strategies can lead to greater public fiscal benefits than those based purely on firm size and wealth. Finally, it can suggest how public policy spending typically not associated with economic development at all—such as public housing and public education—can yield greater economic benefits than conventional forms of development spending.[9]

But if one aspect of this book stresses the public costs of private growth, another lies in how relations of power and privilege can obscure these costs and stigmatize those who bear them. Black tenants, in particular, have consistently borne the fiscal costs of developmental decisions made on behalf of white developers and homeowners—costs that ultimately undermine the finances of local governments more broadly. It is therefore essential that the least privileged members of a community participate in and direct economic development decisions for their own benefit.

Historians

If this book's lesson for practitioners is to understand the public costs of different development paradigms, its call for historians is to help enrich the work of these practitioners. We can do this by researching how the costs of different economic development paradigms have been perceived, obscured, and contested through time.[10] By examining how and why different forms of economic development were adopted in different cities and with what effects, historians can contribute to developing better development strategies in the present.

Such analysis can also provide insights and enrich crucial debates within the scholarly community. It shows how the distribution of fiscal activity and losses across space—what I call "fiscal geography"—shapes the economic health and political alignments of different groups. It shows how the consequences of and struggles over "social costs"—the harm any business activity imposes upon third persons or the community at large—are a basic element of political life. And it shows how different groups, with different fiscal imaginaries, have navigated fundamental tensions in their quest to build a more just economic system. These tensions—between accumulation and egalitarianism, efficiency and equity, sustainability and profit—are perhaps irreconcilable, but they are ones that our dominant growth paradigms barely pretend to resolve. By learning from how past actors have attempted to navigate them, we can cultivate better habits in our struggles to build a better economy today.

Finally, understanding how economic costs and alternatives were understood by past actors can help us rethink our broader political narratives. As this book has shown, the crises of New York's welfare state had much to do with the social costs of past growth strategies, the way those costs were channeled and politicized, and the narrowness of fiscal imagination with which liberals addressed them. Were similar dynamics behind the crises of social-democratic and Keynesian welfare states during the 1970s? And more controversially: does framing these crises in terms of "economic" versus "social" priorities, as some scholars do today, prevent us from seeing the just and viable economic alternatives that were and are available to us?[11]

Citizens

The final lesson of this story is simple: we cannot afford to finance progressive policies through taxes on a regressive economy. For progressives to be fiscally dependent upon the same economic enterprises whose existence displaces their constituency, whose owners contest their policy agenda, and whose operations consistently undermine both private and public finances is profoundly self-defeating. Neither, however, can local progressives rely entirely upon federal transfers for their deliverance. As this book has shown, outside aid delivered to unreconstructed local political economies can often exacerbate rather than eradicate existing inequalities and fiscal fragility.

Rather, citizens must develop methods of promoting economic development without reproducing hierarchy. The most reasonable method of accomplishing this is by lodging the ownership and operation of economic enterprises within its most marginalized communities. The growth generated by such firms can then provide these communities with much-needed resources while expanding their political capacity. Such capacity can, in turn, provide a launching pad for further efforts to democratize our economy more broadly. Who will carry out this agenda, through what means, remains unknown—but there are worse things on which to speculate.

Acknowledgments

Like New York itself, this book has developed largely without a plan and through the collaborative effort of many people. And like the metropolitan radius, my gratitude exceeds all reasonable boundaries.

I am grateful for the archival staff I consulted with during my research—I never could have assembled the sources for this project without your assistance. I am particularly thankful to Matt Knutzen at the New York Public Library, Shannon O'Neil at the Tamiment Library and Robert F. Wagner Labor Archives, Eisha Neely at the Cornell University Library Division of Rare and Manuscript Collections, Cecily Dyer at the Brooklyn Historical Society, Douglas DiCarlo at the La Guardia and Wagner Archives, James D. Folts of the New York State Archives, and both Ken Cobb and Dwight Johnson at the New York City Hall of Records. Special thanks go out to the staff of the Hagley Museum who helped me complete this project in the fall of 2019 and spring of 2020—Roger Horowitz, Carol Lockman, Lucas Clawson, and Linda Gross (no more interlibrary loans, I promise!).

This project has received financial support from several institutions, without which it could never have been completed. These institutions include Cornell University's School of Architecture Art and Planning, the New York State Archives, the Hagley Museum and Library, and the New York University History Department. I would like to give particular thanks to the Jefferson National Scholars Foundation, especially the hardworking Linda Winecoff and the mighty Brian Balogh, for their support. Postdoctoral fellowships from New York University's Urban Democracy Lab and NYU Shanghai provided me with further assistance.

I have been able to refine my arguments in several publications, including *Tribune*, *Jacobin*, the *Washington Post's Made by History*, *Dissent*, and *Metropole*;

I am thankful to the editors of these publications. Portions of chapter 4 have been published in *Urban Infrastructure: Historical and Social Dimensions of an Interconnected World*, published by the University of Pittsburgh Press and edited by Joseph Heathcott, Jonathan Soffer, and Rae Zimmerman. I thank you all, as well as Boyd Cothran, with whom I collaborated on a very special issue of the *Journal of the Gilded Age and Progressive Era*.

I also thank the faculty members who have inspired my own career and passions, beginning with Stephen P. Rice and Carter Jones Meyer at Ramapo College: you are my first professor-heroes. At the CUNY Graduate Center, I benefited from the guidance of Thomas Kessner, David Harvey, and Joshua Freeman and was similarly inspired by the hundreds of students I helped teach throughout the "CUNY-verse." And at NYU, I was privileged to learn from Guy Ortolano, Thomas Augst, and Thomas Bender. I would especially like to thank N.D.B. Connolly, whose course on Race and the Archives awakened and expanded my political consciousness at a crucial moment. Thank you so much.

At NYU, I benefited from the greatest dissertation committee ever assembled: Andrew Needham, Thomas Sugrue, and Kim Phillips-Fein. Your scholarly inspiration and personal support have and will always be treasured by me. Together with my "outside readers," Mason Williams and Owen Gutfreund, you helped guide and ground what would otherwise have been an unmanageable research agenda.

I am deeply grateful for my colleagues at Bard for the warmth, generosity, and spirit of intellectual adventure I have found there. I am particularly grateful for my conversations with Robert Culp, Nate Aschenbrenner, Dror Abend-David, Christian Crouche, Emmanuele Citera, Michael Martell, Gautam Sethi, Pavlina Tcherneva, and Chrys Margaritidis.

Working with the University of Chicago Press in preparing this book has been one of the great experiences of my life. Tim Mennel, I can never thank you enough. Your faith in this project, your patience with me, your words of encouragement and constructive criticism: they inspired me to identify and hone my arguments into their best possible form. Amanda Seligman, your care and detailed reading, your confidence that my argument had merit— you helped me persevere in this project amid deeply difficult circumstances. Andrea Blatz, your tolerance for my intolerable last-minute queries and image suggestions is the stuff of saints. And Beth Ina, Anne T. Strother, and Pete Feely, I could not imagine this book being produced without your painstaking assistance. Thank you so much.

I also thank the faculty of other colleges and universities with whom I have had the pleasure of speaking and learning from over the course of my research. Special thanks go out to David Imbroscio, Terrence J. McDonald, Stephen Petrus, Noam Maggor, Harvey Molotch, Nicholas Bloom, Louis Galambos, Alison Isenberg, Andrew Kahrl, Richard Schragger, Jonathan Zimmerman, Timothy Weaver, Louis Hyman, Brent Cebul, Jason Spicer, Jeffrey Broxmeyer, Becky Nicolaides, Richardson Dilworth, Ira Katznelson, John Mollenkopf, James Siodla, Tim Keogh, Sun Kyoung Lee, Joshua Mound, and Gianpaolo Baiocchi. Your insights helped create the work you see here.

I would like to thank my professional colleagues who have greatly helped my thinking around the themes addressed in this project. I am grateful for my former colleagues at the Museum of the City of New York, particularly Steve Jaffe, Jessica Lautlin, Liz McEnaney, Stephen Petrus, Sarah Henry, and Brian Murphy. I am thankful for all my comrades at the Wellbeing Economy Alliance, particularly Amanda Janoo and Simon Ticehurst. My experiences working with Brian Czech and Gary Gardner at the Center for the Advancement of the Steady State Economy were particularly helpful in grounding my ideas around "uneconomic growth." I also honor the memory of Benjamin Barber, whose efforts to establish a Global Parliament of Mayors I assisted before entering New York University.

I would also like to thank the broader cohort of colleagues and comrades I have met and discussed this project with through its course. I would like to thank fellow history of capitalism "campers" Amy Zanoni, Jacqueline Brandon, and Michael Glass, as well as my fellow Jefferson National Fellows Dylan Gottlieb, Brianna Nofil, Charles Peterson, Gili Vidan, Mary Bridges, and my "dream mentor," Robin Einhorn. I also thank my fellow researchers, Isabelle Held, Kyle Van Hemert, Greg Hargreaves, and Li Cornfield, at the Hagley Museum. I am also grateful for the advocates pursuing ecological and social justice whom I have gotten to know through this project, including Erich Sahn, Helena Norbert-Hodge, Sarah Horowitz, Michel Bauwens, Elias Crim, Michael H. Shuman, Kohei Saito, Kate Aranoff, Zen Trenholm, Neil McInroy, Gar Alperovitz, Pete C. Davis, Evan Caspar-Futterman, Sarah McKinley, Rigo Melgar-Melgar, Joshua C. Farley, Peter Victor, Sam Pizzagati, Maiko Mathiesen, and Neal Gorenflo. I would also like to thank Annie Levin and other comrades in the North Brooklyn chapter of the Democratic Socialists of America: organizing and working with you helped inspire and sustain this project.

And then there are my closest friends, old and new. Stephanie Schwartz, Misha Leptic, Paige Gottheim, Yitzchak and Galit Schwartz, John Raimo, Jacqueline Brandon, Catherine Baldwin, Christopher Aigner, Alan Welner, Jordan and Jeremy Brown, Sara Martucci, and Kevin Andrus: I am so lucky to have you in my life. I would like to extend a particular thanks to Peter Aigner and Joseph Gibbons: you are indeed my best men, and I never could have made it this far without you.

My mother, Diana Schuman: you have nurtured the spark inside me from the beginning and protected it when circumstances or my own doubts threatened to snuff it out. You have the strongest love and sweetest soul I have ever known, and I have learned more of importance from them than from any other source. You are a gift to the world, and I treasure you forever. Thank you, thank you, thank you.

I am also grateful to be the brother of Annie Rose, who has taught me to embrace the unpredictable juiciness of life in a way no one else possibly can. To my beautiful family-in-love, Jackie, Bobby, Meghan, Codie, and Bob of blessed memory: your strength and joy have lifted me up and taken me in, and I cannot thank you enough for it. I am also grateful to my large family of aunts and uncles and to the memory of my beautiful grandparents: Gladys and Jack, Harry and Jean.

To my father of blessed memory, Ross D. London. I can see and feel you in every part of me that receives and appreciates the blessing of being alive. You have shown me what a life lived with purpose and passion looks like. And though you are gone, I will never stop working to ensure your work and story live on, until we cross Brooklyn ferry again together.

My children, Samuel and Eva: you *zisskeits* have opened me to new horizons of feeling and responsibility from the moment you entered this world and well before. You have taught me how to be a better man, and I will continue caring for, loving, and learning from you all through my life.

Above all, Stephanie Wortel-London: to know you, to love you, to care for you, to laugh and cry and build a family with you, is the deepest and most sustaining source of joy in my life. And although I have learned much while writing this book, I have learned far more from your strength, kindness, and love. A lifetime is too short to spend with you. Never, in all time and space, has there been such a love as ours. I will never stop working to make myself worthy of it.

Notes

Introduction

1. Stanley Elkin, *City and Regime in the American Republic* (Chicago: University of Chicago Press, 1987), 98–99.

2. Chris Smith, "In Conversation: Michael Bloomberg," *New York Magazine*, September 6, 2013, https://nymag.com/news/politics/bloomberg/in-conversation-2013-9/.

3. Joseph Parilla and Sifan Liu, *Examining the Local Value of Economic Development Incentives: Evidence from Four US Cities*, Metropolitan Policy Program at Brookings, March 2018, https://www.Brookings.Edu/Wp-Content/Uploads/2018/02/Report_Examining-The-Local -Value-Of-Economic-Development-Incentives_Brookings-Metro_March-2018.Pdf.

4. See Andrew J. Diamond and Thomas J. Sugrue, *The Neoliberal City: The Remaking of Postwar Urban America* (New York: New York University Press, 2020); Timothy Weaver, *Blazing the Neoliberal Trail: Urban Political Development in the United States and the United Kingdom* (Philadelphia: University of Pennsylvania Press, 2016).

5. Ibid.

6. Richard T. Ely, *Taxation in American States and Cities* (New York: Thomas Y. Crowell, 1888), 248.

7. Henry H. Klein, *Bankrupting a Great City (the Story of New York)* (New York: Henry H. Klein, 1916), 167.

8. A. M. Hillhouse, *Municipal Bonds; A Century of Experience* (New York: Prentice-Hall, 1936), 10.

9. See Sebastian Berger, *The Social Costs of Neoliberalism: Essays on the Economics of K. William Kapp* (Nottingham, UK: Spokesman, 2017).

10. The concept of "social costs" derives from a broad tradition of incorporating economic "externalities," broadly defined, as a central component of economic and political analysis, such as Marxist economist James O'Connor, ecological economist Herman Daly, and feminist economist J. K. Gibson-Graham. The term "social costs" itself is derived from the work of postwar economist K. William Kapp. See Berger, *The Social Costs of Neoliberalism*; Herman Daly, *From Uneconomic Growth to a Steady-State Economy* (Cheltenham, UK: Edward Elgar Publishing, 2014); J. K. Gibson-Graham, *The End of Capitalism (As We Knew It): A Feminist Critique of Political Economy* (Minneapolis: University of Minnesota Press, 2006); James O'Connor, *Natural Causes: Essays in Ecological Marxism* (New York: Guilford Press, 1998).

11. See Richard Jacques, *Radical Ecological Economics and Accounting to Save the Planet: The Failure of Mainstream Economists* (New York: Routledge, 2023); Gibson-Graham, *The End of Capitalism (As We Knew It)*.

12. See Daly, *From Uneconomic Growth to a Steady-State Economy*.

13. See the concept of "failure demand" in Katherine Trebeck and Jeremy Williams, *The Economics of Arrival: Ideas for a Grown-Up Economy* (Bristol, UK: Policy Press, 2019), 66–67.

14. For efforts to apply the notion of social costs to local budgets, see David L. Imbroscio, "The Local Public Balance Sheet: An Alternative Evaluation Methodology for Local Economic Development," in *Critical Evaluations of Economic Development Policies*, ed. David Fasenfest and Laura Reese (Detroit: Wayne State University Press, 2004), 87.

15. The idea of how social programs can be dependent on capitalist growth, originally developed by Neo-Marxists like James O'Connor, has been taken up today by ecological economists aware of how the modern welfare state is reliant for financing on environmentally harmful forms of economic growth. See Christine Corlet Walker, Angela Druckman, and Tim Jackson, "Growth Dependency in the Welfare State: An Analysis of Drivers in the UK's Adult Social Care Sector and Proposals for Change," *Ecological Economics* 220 (June 2024), https://www.sci encedirect.com/science/article/pii/S0921800924000569#ab0005 (accessed June 4, 2024); James O'Connor, *The Fiscal Crisis of the State* (New York: St. Martin's Press, 1973).

16. J. Ron. Stanfield, *The Economic Thought of Karl Polanyi: Lives and Livelihood* (New York: St. Martin's Press, 1986), 56. Polanyi's open-ended understanding of economics had been anticipated by the economists of the German Historical School of the early twentieth century. Polanyi would elaborate on this definition of economics in his 1977 work, where he distinguished between a "formal" definition of economics built around the "logical character of the means-ends relationship" and a "substantive definition" built around how people meet their material needs more broadly. See Jamie Peck, *Variegated Economies* (Oxford: Oxford University Press, 2023), 165.

17. The work of feminist geographers such as J. K. Gibson-Graham, who have drawn on anti-essentialist Marxian political economy and feminist poststructuralist thinking to theorize the existence of plural economies, is a source of inspiration for this book. For an overview of their thought, see J. K. Gibson-Graham, *The End of Capitalism (As We Knew It): A Feminist Critique of Political Economy* (Minneapolis: University of Minnesota Press, 2006); J. K. Gibson-Graham and Kelly Dombroski, eds., *The Handbook of Diverse Economies* (Cheltenham UK: Edward Elgar Publishing).

18. This is not, of course, to suggest that the economy is a purely cultural product. According to Polanyi's "substantive" definition, which is worth quoting at length, "The substantive meaning stems, in brief, from man's patent dependence for his livelihood upon nature and his fellows. He survives by virtue of an institutionalized interaction between himself and his natural surroundings. That process is the economy, which supplies him the means of satisfying his material wants. This phrase should not be taken to signify that the wants to be satisfied are exclusively bodily needs, such as food and shelter, however essential these may be for his survival, for such a restriction would absurdly restrict the realm of the economy. The means, not the wants, are material. Whether the useful objects are required to avert starvation or are needed for educational, military or religious purposes is irrelevant. So long as the wants depend for their fulfilment on material objects, the reference is economic." Stanfield, *The Economic Thought of Karl Polanyi: Lives and Livelihood*, 34. This implies that although wants can be social in their origin, they are unavoidably material in their realization—a fact that implies that there can be

physical limits to certain kinds of economic activity. A major project of ecological economics has been to stress this point. William J. Sewell's sophisticated approach to understanding
how "schemas" and "resources" interact to form social structures is useful here. See William H.
Sewell Jr., *Logics of History: Social Theory and Social Transformation* (Chicago: University of
Chicago Press, 2005), 133.

19. I use the term "fiscal imagination" rather than "economic imagination" to stress the economic options meant to address the revenue needs of the public sector, and not just the "private"
needs of private individuals and firms. For an article which productively uses the term "economic imagination," see Hannah Appel, "Occupy Wall Street and the Economic Imagination,"
Cultural Anthropology 29, no. 4 (2014), 602–25.

20. For more on how historical research can uncover alternative models of economic
thought and development, see John Lodewijks, "Research in the History of Economic Thought
as a Vehicle for the Defense and Criticism of Orthodox Economics," in Warren J. Samuels, Jeff E.
Biddle, and John B. Davis, eds., *A Companion to the History of Economic Thought* (Oxford, UK:
Blackwell Publishing, 2003), 655–68.

21. Morris Pearl and Erica Payne, *Tax the Rich! How Lies, Loopholes, and Lobbyists Make
the Rich Even Richer* (New York: The New Press, 2021); Emmanuel Saez and Gabriel Zucman,
The Triumph of Injustice: How the Rich Dodge Taxes and How to Make Them Pay (New York:
W.W. Norton, 2019) .For a broader history of "fiscal fairness" as a political cause, see Kenneth F.
Scheve, *Taxing the Rich: A History of Fiscal Fairness in the United States and Europe* (Princeton,
NJ: Princeton University Press, 2016) and Ajay K. Mehrorta, *Making the Modern American Fis-
cal State: Law, Politics, and the Rise of Progressive Taxation, 1877–1929* (Cambridge: Cambridge
University Press, 2013).

22. For an excellent overview of the historiography on neoliberalism, see Kim Phillips-Fein,
"The History of Neoliberalism," in Brent Cebul, Lily Geismer, and Mason Williams, eds., *Shaped
by the State: Toward a New Political History of the Twentieth Century* (Chicago: University of
Chicago Press, 2019), 347–62. For a classic work that stresses the political origins of neoliberalism, see David Harvey, *A Brief History of Neoliberalism* (Oxford: Oxford University Press, 2007).
For a work stressing the improvised nature of this outcome, see Greta R. Krippner, *Capitalizing
on Crisis: The Political Origins of the Rise of Finance* (Cambridge, MA: Harvard University Press,
2012). For a work that stresses our era's inequities as the result of bi-partisan politics preceding
the 1970s, see Brent Cebul, *Illusions of Progress: Business, Poverty, and Liberalism in the American
Century* (Philadelphia: University of Pennsylvania Press, 2023). While I do not use the phrase often in this work, I define "neoliberalism" as a suite of policies designed to increase the economic,
political, and social influence of large-scaled corporate firms. As such, it has nothing inherently
to do with deregulation or expanding the market or even commodification per se. See Ian Bruff,
"Detaching 'Neoliberalism' from 'Free Markets': Monopolistic Corporations as Neoliberalism's
Ideal Market Form." *Review of Social Economy*, July 2024 1–28, and Terry Hathaway, "Neoliberalism as Corporate Power," *Competition & Change* 24(3–4) (2020): 315–37.

23. Until recently, most historians argued that the immediate postwar period marked the
(partial) triumph of the "redistributive" state, as exemplified by the New Deal and European
social democracy, only to be eclipsed in the 1970s by a more developmentalist state. Recent
scholars have challenged this interpretation by demonstrating that "pro-growth" statecraft has
been a long-standing and bipartisan practice in American life dating back well before the 1970s.
While I agree that developmental statecraft has generally been ubiquitous in American history,
I believe conceptions of what constitutes development have been less uniform than heretofore

understood. See Brent Cebul, Lily Geismer, and Mason B. Williams, eds., *Shaped by the State: Toward a New Political History of the Twentieth Century* (Chicago: University of Chicago Press, 2019); Kim Phillips-Fein and Richard R. John, eds., *Capital Gains: Business and Politics in Twentieth Century America* (Philadelphia: University of Pennsylvania Press, 2017); Brian Balogh, *The Associational State: American Governance in the Twentieth Century* (Philadelphia: University of Pennsylvania Press, 2017); Stefan Link and Noam Maggor, "The United States as a Developing Nation: Revisiting the Peculiarities of American History," *Past and Present* 246, no. 1 (2020): 269–306; Bruce J. Schulman, "Post-1968 U.S. History: Neo-Consensus History for the Age of Polarization," *Reviews in American History* 47, no. 3 (2019): 479–499.

24. For works that emphasize external pressures on urban budgets due to capital mobility and jurisdictional competition for resources under a federal system, see Paul E. Peterson, *City Limits* (Chicago: University of Chicago Press, 2012); Neil Brenner, *New State Spaces: Urban Governance and the Rescaling of Statehood* (Oxford, England: Oxford University Press, 2004). For works that stress internal political pressures as the cause of fiscal strains, see Ester Fuchs, *Mayors and Money: Fiscal Policy in New York and Chicago* (Chicago: University of Chicago, 2010); Steven P. Erie, Vladimir Kogan, and Scott A. Mackenzie, *Paradise Plundered: Fiscal Crisis and Governance Failures in San Diego* (Stanford, CA: Stanford University Press, 2011). For works that stress a longer history of bipartisan probusiness policies in American politics, see Cebul, Geismer, and Williams, *Shaped by the State*; Schulman, "Post-1968 U.S. History."

25. Indeed, there is a strong vein of current scholarship that frames "economic" activities themselves as being necessarily opposed to social well-being, at least when unaccompanied by robust taxation. For example, we are told that the "Ideological Dynamics" of our era can be reduced to "The Primacy of Economics versus the Primacy of Politics." We are also told of how our era is dominated by a "neoliberal" form of reasoning which "configures all aspects of existence in economic terms." And no less than Tony Judt, before his untimely passing, declared that "The new master narrative—the way we think of our world—has abandoned the social for the economic." Such narratives, however, only entrench modern capitalism as the only conceivable model of what "the economy" can be. See Sheri Berman, "The Primacy of Economics versus the Primacy of Politics: Understanding the Ideological Dynamics of the Twentieth Century," *Perspectives on Politics* 7, no. 3, 2009: 561–78; Wendy Brown, *Undoing the Demos: Neoliberalism's Stealth Revolution* (New York: Zone Books, 2017), 17; Tony Judt, "The Wrecking Ball of Innovation," *New York Review of Books*, December 6, 2007, https://www.nybooks.com/articles/2007/12/06/the-wrecking-ball-of-innovation/. See also Elizabeth Popp Berman, *Thinking Like an Economist: How Efficiency Replaced Equality in U.S. Public Policy* (Princeton, NJ: Princeton University Press, 2022); Stephen A. Marglin, *The Dismal Science: How Thinking Like an Economist Undermines Community* (Cambridge, MA: Harvard University Press, 2008).

26. See Daniel Wortel-London, "The Tax Trap," *Dissent* 68, no. 1 (2021): 125–134; Claudia Chwalisz and Patrick Diamond, eds., *The Predistribution Agenda: Tackling Inequality and Supporting Sustainable Growth* (New York: I. B. Tauris, 2015); Joe Guinan and Martin O'Neil, "The Instituitoanl Turn: Labour's New Political Economy," *Renewal* 26, no. 2, 2018, 5–16. For a classic work on the limits of the liberal redistributive state, see James O'Connor, *The Fiscal Crisis of the State*. Recent work on degrowth and "limits to growth" reflect a similar insight. See Matthias Schmelzer, Andrea Vetter, and Aaron Vansintjan, *The Future Is Degrowth: A Guide to a World beyond Capitalism* (London: Verso, 2022).

27. Gibson-Graham, *The End of Capitalism (As We Knew It)*, 35. Gibson-Graham calls this tendency of conflating all forms of the economy and economic thought with capitalism

"capitalocentrism." By defining the economy narrowly and capitalism broadly, "capitalocentric" scholars assume that capitalism penetrates every economic practice, and that every economic practice—wage labor, commodity production, private enterprise and property, etc.—is irredeemably capitalist. Unfortunately, elements of this tendency occasionally occur in the historical subfield known as the "history of capitalism." Paul V. Kershaw has noted how in the work of some of these historians "capitalism effectively becomes totalizing, which is precisely the conclusion that they want to avoid." See Paul V. Kershaw, "Hamlet without the Prince of Denmark: Bringing Capitalism Back into the 'New' History of Capitalism." *Journal of Historical Sociology* 33, no. 1, 2020, 67. For more criticisms along these lines, see Kenneth Lipartito, "Reassembling the Economic: New Departures in Historical Materialism," *The American Historical Review* 121, no. 1, February 2016, 127; Angela P. Harris, "Forward: Racial Capitalism and Law" in Destin Jenkins and Justin Leroy, eds. *Histories of Racial Capitalism* (New York: Columbia University Press, 2021), xvii. For my part, I follow Gibson-Graham's broad-but-manageable definition of Capitalism as "a system of generalized commodity production structured by (industrial) forces of production and exploitative production relations between capital and labor." See Gibson-Graham, *The End of Capitalism (As We Knew It)*, 3. For more on the inescapably economic dimension of "social" policies, see Jimi Adésínà, "Return to a Wider Vision of Social Policy: Re-reading Theory and History," *South African Review of Sociology* 46, no. 3, 2015, 99–119.

28. This is not to say that taxing the rich is a regressive goal, of course—for example, it can and should be used to help finance alternative economic strategies. I maintain, however, that relying on the wealthy, and conventional growth strategies more broadly, as a long-term strategy for financing progressive policies is neither politically, environmentally, nor financially sustainable.

29. Tony Judt, "The Wrecking Ball of Innovation." I recognize, of course, that there are dangers in reducing all social questions to those of economy. Nonetheless, I view the economy—defined broadly as how humans produce and provide for one another—as being an essential element of human existence. What matters are the consequences of how one goes about doing this. As Quinn Slobodian has stated, "economistic thinking can serve a range of political projects, and a range of political and social outcomes." See Kate Raworth, *Seven Ways to Think like a 21st Century Economist* (White River Junction, VT: Chelsea Green Publishing, 2017), 207; see Spiro Liat, "Global Histories of Neoliberalism: An Interview with Quinn Slobodian," Toynbee Prize Foundation, March 21, 2018, https://toynbeeprize.org/posts/quinn-slobodian.

30. This is not to say that "redistributive" programs *cannot* conceivably contribute to economic development. As long as we view such policies purely as "social expenditures," however, their role and capacity to act as *alternatives* to mainstream growth models, and the implications for this on our historical narratives and present political possibilities, will remain largely unknown. See James Midgley, *Social Development: The Developmental Perspective in Social Welfare* (Thousand Oaks, CA: Sage Publications, 1995).

31. For works on populism, see Charles Postel, *The Populist Vision* (Oxford: Oxford University Press, 2009); Noam Maggor, *Brahmin Capitalism: Frontiers of Wealth and Populism in America's First Gilded Age* (Cambridge, MA: Harvard University Press, 2017). For work on alternative local development strategies, see Nishani Frazier, *Harambee City: The Congress of Racial Equality in Cleveland and the Rise of Black Power Populism* (Fayetteville: University of Arkansas Press, 2017); Julia Rabig, *The Fixers: Devolution, Development, and Civil Society in Newark, 1960–1990* (Chicago: University of Chicago Press 2017); Brian D. Goldstein, *The Roots of Urban Renaissance: Gentrification and the Struggle over Harlem* (Princeton, NJ: Princeton University

Press, 2017); Guian A. McKee, *The Problem of Jobs: Liberalism, Race, and Deindustrialization in Philadelphia* (Chicago: University of Chicago Press, 2019).

32. For work on the production of economic knowledge, see Stephen J. Macekura, *The Mismeasure of Progress: Economic Growth and Its Critics* (Chicago: University of Chicago Press, 2022); Keith Tribe, *Constructing Economic Science: The Invention of a Discipline 1850–1950* (New York: Oxford University Press, 2022); Matthias Schmelzer, *The Hegemony of Growth: The OECD and the Making of the Economic Growth Paradigm* (Cambridge: Cambridge University Press, 2016).

33. See David L. Imbroscio, *Reconstructing City Politics: Alternative Economic Development and Urban Regimes* (London: Sage Publications, 1997); Kioupkiolis Alexandros, *Common Hegemony Populism and the New Municipalism: Democratic Alter-Politics and Transformative Strategies* (New York: Routledge, 2022); David Harvey, *Rebel Cities: From the Right to the City to the Urban Revolution* (London: Verso, 2013). The growth of progressive industrial policy at the national level also indicates this tendency: see Josh Bivens, *The Industrial Policy Revolution Has Begun, but Another Is Still Needed,* Economic Policy Institute, May 18, 2023, https://www.epi.org/publication/industrial-policy/.

34. See L. Owen Kirkpatrick and Michael Peter Smith, "The Infrastructural Limits to Growth: Rethinking the Urban Growth Machine in Times of Fiscal Crisis," *International Journal of Urban and Regional Research* 35, no. 3 (2011): 477–503; Mark Schneider, "Undermining the Growth Machine: The Missing Link between Local Economic Development and Fiscal Payoffs," *Journal of Politics* 54, no. 1 (1992): 214–230; Timothy J. Bartik, *Making Sense of Incentives: Taming Business Incentives to Promote Prosperity* (Kalamazoo, MI: W. E. Upjohn Institute for Employment Research, 2019); Richard C. Schragger, "Rethinking the Theory and Practice of Local Economic Development," *University of Chicago Law Review* 77, no. 1 (2010): 311–339.

35. See Victoria Mawtree and Majid Rahnema, eds., *The Post-Development Reader* (London: Bloomsbury Publishing, 1997); Arturo Escobar, *Encountering Development: The Making and Unmaking of the Third World* (Princeton, NJ: Princeton University Press, 2012).

36. Michael Brocker and Christopher Hanes, "The 1920s American Real Estate Boom and the Downturn of the Great Depression: Evidence from City Cross-Sections," in *Housing and Mortgage Markets in Historical Perspectives,* ed. Eugene N. White, Kenneth Snowden, and Price Fishback (Chicago: University of Chicago Press, 2014); Alexander J. Field, "Uncontrolled Land Development and the Duration of the Depression in the United States," *Journal of Economic History* 52 (December 1992): 785–805; Douglas E. Booth, "Transportation, City Building, and Financial Crisis: Milwaukee, 1852–1868," *Journal of Urban History* 9, no. 3 (1983): 335–363; Samara Gunter and James Siodla, "Local Origins and Implications of the 1930s Urban Debt Crisis" (unpublished conference paper, Annual Conference on Taxation and Minutes of the Annual Meeting of the National Tax Association, September 2, 2019); Eric H. Monkkonen, *The Local State: Public Money and American Cities* (Stanford, CA: Stanford University Press, 1996), 118; see also Eric H. Monkkonen, "What Urban Crisis? A Historian's Point of View," *Urban Affairs Quarterly* 20, no. 4 (1985): 429–447.

37. During such crises, actors are "unable to rely on materialistic rationales to order their preferences," in the words of Mark Blyth, thus providing openings for new fiscal imaginaries to emerge. See Mark Blyth, *Great Transformations: Economic Ideas and Institutional Change in the Twentieth Century* (New York: Cambridge University Press, 2002), 30–37.

38. A strong element of my argument is that prevalent patterns of growth in New York since the 1870s, particularly those related to real estate growth, incentivized New York officials to pursue further growth not just to accomplish goals but to avoid negative consequences. Expanded physical infrastructure, for example, required further growth to finance repairs and debts expended on that infrastructure's behalf—and failure to do so would cause cascading cycles of fiscal

and physical disaster. Such negative feedback loops are not insoluble, of course, and different growth strategies can resolve them with varying degrees of success. But the "growth dependencies" established in one period nonetheless increases the stakes, and often the difficulty, of identifying alternative growth strategies in the future. For a fuller treatment on "growth dependencies" and their political significance, see Christine Corlet Walker, Angela Druckman, and Tim Jackson, "Growth Dependency in the Welfare State: An Analysis of Drivers in the UK's Adult Social Care Sector and Proposals for Change," *Ecological Economics* 220 (June 2024), https://www.sciencedirect.com/science/article/pii/S0921800924000569#ab0005 (accessed June 4, 2024).

39. Kim Moody, *From Welfare State to Real Estate: Regime Change in New York City to the Present* (New York: New Press, 2007); for a paradigmatic overview of these shifts, see David Harvey, *A Brief History of Neoliberalism*.

40. See Kim Phillips-Fein, *Fear City: New York's Fiscal Crisis and the Rise of Austerity Politics* (New York: Metropolitan Books, 2017); Joshua Benjamin Freeman, *Working-Class New York: Life and Labor since World War II* (New York: New Press, 2001); Benjamin Holtzman, *The Long Crisis: New York City and the Path to Neoliberalism* (New York: Oxford University Press, 2021).

41. My approach toward historical explanation, with its stress on the power-laden intercurrence and layering of ideas, institutions, material resources, and policies, borrows heavily from the work of William H. Sewell Jr. and the broader field of historical institutionalism. See William H. Sewell Jr., *Logics of History*; Richardson Dilworth and Timothy P. R. Weaver, *How Ideas Shape Urban Political Development* (Philadelphia: University of Pennsylvania Press, 2020); Andre Sorenson, "Taking Path Dependence Seriously: An Historical Institutionalist Research Agenda in Planning History," *Planning Perspectives* 30, no. 1 (2015): 17–38.

42. Importantly, local revenue policies are intimately connected to local urban planning strategies. On the one hand, public officials often promote transit and land-use policies based on what they are empowered to make money off of—as Alan E. Land stated in 1967, "Fiscal policy is often a moving force behind planning decisions, and taxation often determines the pattern, time, character and planning of land development." Conversely, urban planning and economic development decisions can have effects on the bottom lines of a city—in the words of planner Jack R. Huddleston, "The things planners do on a daily basis—land use planning, transportation planning, environmental planning, social services planning and so forth—directly affect local government budgets." See Alan E. Land, "Toward Optimal Land Use: Property Tax Policy and Land Use Planning," *California Law Review* 55, no. 3 (1967): 1856–1897; Jack R. Huddleston, *The Intersection between Planning and the Municipal Budget* (Cambridge, MA: Lincoln Institute of Land Policy, 2007).

43. See Lorenzo Fioramonti, *Gross Domestic Problem: The Politics behind the World's Most Powerful Number* (London: Zed Books, 2013); Joseph Stigltiz, Amartya Sen, and Jean-Paul Fitoussi, *Mismeasuring Our Lives: Why GDP Doesn't Add Up* (New York: New Press, 2010).

44. By "conventional" enterprises I mean enterprises that are privately owned (as opposed to worker-or community owned), whose purpose is maximum return on investment through their operations (as opposed to pursuing social and ecological well-being through their operations), and whose priority is to transfer profits to owners or shareholders (as opposed to recycling profits back into operational costs and wages). For more on alternative frameworks of business design, see Laura Niessen and Nancy M.P. Bocken, "How Can Business Drive Sufficiency? The Business for Sufficiency Framework." *Sustainable Production and Consumption* 28 (October 2021), 1090–1103. For works which examine the division between "public" expenditures and "private" revenue-generation as a core component of liberal statecraft, see Heather Whiteside, "Beyond Death and Taxes: Fiscal Studies and the Fiscal State," *Environment and Planning*

A: *Economy and Space* 55, no. 7, 1744–1761. For a broader discussion of how liberalism distinguishes between the "public" and "private" spheres, see Michael Walzer, "Liberalism and the Art of Separation." *Political Theory* 12, no. 3 (1984), 315–30. For an excellent overview of liberalism's core concepts and historical development, see Michael Freeden, *Liberalism: A Very Short Introduction* (Oxford: Oxford University Press, 2015).

45. Herman Daly, *Steady-State Economics* (Washington, DC: Island Press, 1991); Donella H. Meadows, Jorgen Randers, and Dennis L. Meadows, *Limits to Growth: The 30-Year Update* (London: Earchscan, 2004).

46. Jason Hickel, *Less Is More: How Degrowth Will Save the World* (London: William Heinemann, 2020); Matthias Schmelzer, Andrea Vetter, and Aaron Vansintjan, *The Future Is Degrowth: A Guide to a World beyond Capitalism* (London: Verso, 2022).

47. For one prominent exception, see Matthias Schmelzer and Iris Borowy, eds., *History of the Future of Economic Growth: Historical Roots of Current Debates on Sustainable Degrowth* (London: Routledge, 2018).

Chapter 1

1. L. K. Stein, review of *The History of Municipal Ownership of Land on Manhattan Island*, by George Ashton Black, *Annals of the American Academy of Political and Social Science* 2 (1892), 100.

2. George Ashton Black, *The History of Municipal Ownership of Land on Manhattan Island* (New York: Columbia University Press, 1891), 76.

3. See Robin L. Einhorn, *Property Rules: Political Economy in Chicago, 1833–1872* (Chicago: University of Chicago Press, 1991).

4. For a classic account establishing "privatism" as a theme of American urban historiography, see Sam Bass Warner, *Streetcar Suburbs: The Process of Growth in Boston, 1870–1900* (Cambridge, MA: Harvard University Press, 1962). For more recent iterations on this theme, see Balogh, *The Associational State*; Domenic Vitiello, "Monopolizing the Metropolis: Gilded Age Growth Machines and Power in American Urbanization," *Planning Perspectives* 28, no. 1 (2013): 71–90; Monkkonen, *The Local State*, 118.

5. Elizabeth Blackmar, *Manhattan for Rent, 1785–1850* (Ithaca, NY: Cornell University Press, 1989), 161.

6. Blackmar, 28.

7. Blackmar, 28, 269.

8. For more on how voting rights in the early republic were conditioned by property ownership, see Katherine Levine Einstein and Maxwell Palmer, "Land of the Freeholder: How Property Rights Make Local Voting Rights," *Journal of Historical Political Economy* 1, no. 4 (2021): 499–530.

9. Edward Dana Durand, *The Finances of New York City* (New York: Macmillan, 1898), 138; Hendrik Hartog, *Public Property and Private Property: The Corporation of the City of New York in American Law, 173–1870* (Ithaca, NY: Cornell University Press, 1983).

10. Hartog, *Public Property and Private Property*, 48, 165, 262.

11. For the classic treatise on the rise of "market thought" during this era, see Charles Sellers, *The Market Revolution: Jacksonian America, 1815–1846* (New York: Oxford University Press, 1991).

12. Hartog, *Public Property and Private Property*, 9.

13. Citizens' Association, *Report of the Citizens' Association; How Our Taxes May Be Reduced, Our Resources Developed, and the Local Government Improved* (New York: Citizens' Association, 1868), 16–17.

14. See Joyce W. Warren, *Women, Money, and the Law: Nineteenth-Century Fiction, Gender, and the Courts* (Iowa City: University of Iowa Press, 2005), 51; Jane E. Dabel, *A Respectable Woman: The Public Roles of African American Women in Nineteenth Century New York* (New York: New York University Press, 2008), 69–70.

15. Rexford Tugwell, "The Sources of New Deal Reformism," *Ethics* 64, no. 4 (1954), 255.

16. David Scobey, *Empire City: The Making and Meaning of the New York City Landscape* (Philadelphia, PA: Temple University Press, 2002), 127.

17. John W. Reps, *The Making of Urban America: A History of City Planning in the United States* (Princeton, NJ: Princeton University Press, 1965), 45.

18. Blackmar, *Manhattan for Rent*, 97, 159. See also Eugene P. Moehring, *Public Works and the Pattern of Urban Real Estate Growth* (New York: Arno Press, 1981)

19. Blackmar, *Manhattan for Rent*, 161.

20. Frederick L. Olmsted, "Report on Damage by Crowds," 1877, in *Forty Years of Landscape Architecture*, ed. Theodora Kimball Hubbard (Cambridge, MA: MIT Press, 1971), 436.

21. For an overview of this system, see Einhorn, *Property Rules*.

22. *Report to the New York Legislature of the Commission to Select and Locate Lands for Public Parks in the Twenty-Third and Twenty-Fourth Wards of the City of New York, and in the Vicinity Thereof* (New York: Marin B. Brown, 1884), 80.

23. Board of Commissioners, *First Annual Report on the Improvement of the Central Park, New York* (New York: Chas W. Baker, 1857), 22.

24. Hillhouse, *Municipal Bonds*, 34; Monkkonen, *The Local State*, 56.

25. Durand, *The Finances of New York City*, 138.

26. Durand, 146.

27. Durand, 148.

28. "The Tammany Ring," *Real Estate Record and Builders' Guide*, no. 403 (December 4, 1875), 1368. This is not to say that local property owners were entirely pleased with their elected representatives: one such owner complained in 1858 that whereas "in Brooklyn, the [local government] have [*sic*] graded streets and avenues, and covered them with railroads in every direction," New York remained a laggard. "All the rise in real estate [in New York] has been in *spite* of the city government—not by their *help*." Such grievances, however, were generally paired with encomiums, as in the *Real Estate Record*'s statement cited prior. Clinton, *The Value of Real Estate in the City of New York, Past, Present, and Prospective: As Illustrated in a Series of Articles from the Evening Post, in 1858, 1859, and 1860 by a Retired Merchant* (New York: n.p., 1860?), 5.

29. Scobey, 160.

30. Willis S. Paine, "Savings Banks That Have Failed," *Banker's Magazine* 67 (July–December 1903), 32.

31. Durand, *The Finances of New York City*, 149; Scobey, 259.

32. See David M. Scobey, *Empire City: The Making and Meaning of the New York City Landscape* (Philadelphia, PA: Temple University Press, 2002).

33. Correspondence, August 10, 1876, Subject Roll 33, Office of the Mayor Collections: William H. Wickham, City Hall Library, New York.

34. "How to Keep Down the City Debt," *New York Times*, March 23, 1875, 1.

35. "What Will Be the Effect of the Fall of the Ring on the Value of Real Estate?," *New York Times*, October 14, 1871, 4.

36. Hillhouse, *Municipal Bonds*, 17.

37. Pennsylvania Commission, *Report of the Commission to Devise a Plan for the Government of Cities* (Harrisburg, PA: Lane S. Hart, 1878), 6.

38. Monkkonen, *The Local State*, 25.

39. Pennsylvania Commission, *Report of the Commission to Devise a Plan for the Government of Cities* (Harrisburg, PA: Lane S. Hart, 1878), 6.

40. LaDale C. Winling and Todd M. Michney, "The Roots of Redlining: Academic, Governmental, and Professional Networks in the Making of the New Deal Lending Regime," *Journal of American History* 108, no. 1 (2021), 47; Walter Isard, *Location and Space-Economy* (Cambridge, MA: MIT Press, 1956), 25.

41. David A. Wells, Edwin Dodge, and George W. Cuyler, *Second Report of the Commissioners to Revise the Laws for the Assessment and Collection of Taxes in the State of New York, with a Code of Laws Relative to Assessment and Taxation* (Albany, NY: Argus, 1872), 32; William Cronon, *Nature's Metropolis: Chicago and the Great West* (New York: W. W. Norton, 1991); Carl Abbott, *Boosters and Businessmen: Popular Economic Thought and Urban Growth in the Antebellum Middle West* (Westport, CT: Greenwood Press, 1981); Scobey, 127. See Frederick Law Olmsted, "The Future of New York," *New York Daily Tribune*, December 28, 1879, 5; Frederick Law Olmsted, *Observations on the Progress of Improvements in Street Plans with Special Reference to the Parkway Proposed to Be Laid Out in Brooklyn* (Brooklyn, NY: I. Van Anden's Print, 1868), 19; Frederick Law Olmsted et al., "Report to the Staten Island Improvement Commission of a Preliminary Scheme of Improvements (1871)," in *Landscape into City Scape: Frederick Law Olmsted's Plans for a Greater New York*, ed. Albert Fein (New York: Van Nostrand Reinhold, 1981), 352.

42. Lewis Lattin Bower, "An Examination of the Emergence, Development and Current State of Urban Land Use Theory" (PhD diss., Syracuse University, 1964), 4. Such a lack of definition reflected the broader, indeterminate state of American economic thought before the Civil War. See Dorothy Ross, *The Origins of American Social Science* (Cambridge: Cambridge University Press, 1991); Nancy L. Cohen, *The Reconstruction of American Liberalism 1865–1914* (Chapel Hill: University of North Carolina Press, 2002); Jack High, "Economic Theory and the Rise of Big Business in America, 1870–1910," *Business History Review* 85, no. 1 (2011): 85–112; Stephen Leccese, "Economic Inequality and the New School of American Economics," *Religions* 8, no. 6 (2017), 99, https://doi.org/10.3390/re18060099.

43. Real Estate Record and Builders' Guide , *A History of Real Estate, Building and Architecture in New York City during the Last Quarter of a Century* (New York: Real Estate Record and Builders' Guide, 1898), 61.

44. For more on the history of municipal finance officers during this time, see Terry K. Patton and Paul D. Hutchison, "Historical Development of the Financial Reporting Model for State and Local Governments in the United States from Late 1800s to 1999," *Accounting Historians Journal* 40, no. 2 (2013): 21–53; Daniel W. Williams, "Measuring Government in the Early Twentieth Century," *Public Administration Review* 63, no. 6 (2003): 643–659.

45. John L. Crompton, "A Review of the Economic Data Emanating from the Development of Central Park and Its Influence on the Construction of Early Urban Parks in the United States," *Journal of Planning History* 20, no. 2 (2020), 143.

46. See Cohen, *The Reconstruction of American Liberalism*; Rosanne Currarino, *The Labor Question in America: Economic Democracy in the Gilded Age* (Urbana: University of Illinois Press, 2011).

47. Herbert Adams, *Public Debts* (New York: D. Appleton, 1893), 855.

48. Adams, 358.

49. Ely, *Taxation in American States and Cities*, 196, 248.

50. Correspondence, October 9, 1875, Subject Roll 33, Office of the Mayor Collections: William H. Wickham, City Hall Library, New York.

51. Correspondence, August 10, 1876, Subject Roll 33, Office of the Mayor Collections: William H. Wickham, City Hall Library, New York.

52. Scobey, 259.

53. Durand, *The Finances of New York City*, 324.

54. See Terrence J. McDonald, *The Parameters of Urban Fiscal Policy: Socioeconomic Change and Political Culture in San Francisco, 1860–1906* (Berkeley: University of California Press, 1986); Alberta M. Sbragia, *Debt Wish: Entrepreneurial Cities, U.S. Federalism, and Economic Development* (Pittsburgh, PA: University of Pittsburgh Press, 1996),

55. Eric H. Monkkonen, *American Becomes Urban: The Development of U.S. Cities and Towns, 1780–1980* (Berkeley: University of California Press, 1988), 144.

56. Monkkonen, *The Local State*, 21, 25.

57. Sanders Shanks Jr., "The Extent of Municipal Defaults," *National Municipal Review* 24, no. 32 (1935): 32–34.

58. Terrence J. McDonald, "Building the Impossible State: Toward an Institutional Analysis of Statebuilding in America, 1820–1930," in *Institutions in American Society: Essays in Market, Political, and Social Organizations*, ed. John Edgar Jackson (Ann Arbor: University of Michigan Press, 1990), 229.

59. Scobey, 261.

60. Durand, *The Finances of New York City*, 297.

61. See Mark David Spence, *Dispossessing the Wilderness: Indian Removal and the Making of the National Parks* (New York: Oxford University Press, 1999).

62. Currarino, *The Labor Question in America*, 26.

63. Charles Abrams, *Revolution in Land* (New York: Harpers, 1939), 297.

Chapter 2

1. Editorial, *New York Evening World*, September 6, 1897, 1; Edward M. Grout, *Municipal Ownership: Its Necessity Demonstrated: From Writings and Speeches of Edward M. Grout* (New York: Commonwealth, 1897).

2. "The New York Tax Reform Association," *Financial and Mining Record*, November 7, 1891, 327.

3. See Gail Radford, *The Rise of the Public Authority: Statebuilding and Economic Development in Twentieth Century America* (Chicago: University of Chicago Press, 2013); Georg Leidenberger, *Chicago's Progressive Alliance: Labor and the Bid for Public Streetcars* (Dekalb: Northern Illinois University Press, 2006); John D. Fairfield, *The Public and Its Possibilities: Cities and Civic Life in American History* (Philadelphia, PA: Temple University Press, 2010); Ted Rutland, "The City Is an Apartment House: Property, Improvement, and Dispossession in Early Twentieth-Century Halifax, Nova Scotia," *Urban Geography* 36, no. 3 (2015): 359–384; Robert D. Johnston, *The Radical Middle Class: Populist Democracy and the Question of Capitalism in Progressive Era Portland, Oregon* (Princeton, NJ: Princeton University Press, 2006)

4. In recalling this history, this chapter contributes to a burgeoning literature on heterodox urban development strategies, particularly those revolving around public ownership. See Imbroscio, *Reconstructing City Politics*; Joe Guinan and Martin O'Neill, *The Case for Community Wealth Building* (Medford, MA: Polity Press, 2020); Harvey, *Rebel Cities*.

5. For studies of the "urban" dimension of progressivism, see James Connolly, *The Triumph of Ethnic Progressivism: Urban Political Culture in Boston, 1900-1925* (Cambridge, MA: Harvard University Press, 1998); Fairfield, *The Public and Its Possibilities*. For the relation between the Progressive and New Deal eras, and particularly in its "urban" dimensions, see J. Joseph Hutchmacher, *Senator Robert F. Wagner and the Rise of Urban Liberalism* (New York: Atheneum, 1971); Daniel T. Rodgers, *Atlantic Crossing: Social Politics in a Progressive Age* (Cambridge, MA, Harvard University Press, 1998); Kenneth E. Miller, *From Progressive to New Dealer: Frederic C. Howe and American Liberalism* (University Park, PA: Penn State University Press, 2014).

6. For more work that emphasizes the "developmental" aspects of American populism, see Postel, *The Populist Vision*; Maggor, *Brahmin Capitalism*; Currarino, *The Labor Question in America*; Anton Jager, "State and Corporation in American Populist Political Philosophy, 1877–1902," *Historical Journal* 64, no. 2 (2021): 1035–1059.

7. See Barcelona En Comu, eds., *Fearless Cities: A Guide to the Global Municipalist Movement* (Oxford: New Internationalist Publications, 2019); see Imbroscio, *Reconstructing City Politics*; Guinan and O'Neill, *The Case for Community Wealth Building*; Harvey, *Rebel Cities*.

8. See Currarino, *The Labor Question in America*.

9. David Hammack, *Power and Society* (New York: Russell Sage Foundation, 1982), 90.

10. See Joanna Reitano, *The Restless City: A Short History of New York City from Colonial Times to the Present* (New York: Taylor & Francis, 2010), 96.

11. Rowena Gray, "Inequality in Nineteenth Century Manhattan: Evidence from the Housing Market," *Social Science History* 44, no. 3 (2020), 573. For a work comparing movements against inequality over time, see Steve Fraser, *The Age of Acquiescence: The Life and Death of American Resistance to Organized Wealth and Power* (New York: Basic Books: 2016).

12. See Alexander Gourevitch, *From Slavery to the Cooperative Commonwealth: Labor and the Republican Liberty in the Nineteenth Century* (New York: Cambridge University Press, 2015).

13. John Curl, *For All the People: Uncovering the Hidden History of Cooperation, Cooperative Movements, and Communalism in America* (Oakland, CA: PM Press, 2009), 11.

14. Postel, *The Populist Vision*, 18.

15. Curl, *For All the People*, 11.

16. Jessica Gordon Nembhard, *Collective Courage: A History of African American Cooperative Economic Thought and Practice* (University Park, PA: Penn State University Press, 2015), 21.

17. Leon Fink, *In Search of the Working Class: Essays in American Labor History and Political Culture* (Urbana: University of Illinois Press, 1994), 41.

18. Fink, 22.

19. Curl, *For All the People*, 94.

20. Richard T. Ely, *Problems of To-Day: A Discussion of Protective Tariffs, Taxation, and Monopolies* (New York: Thomas Y. Crowell, 1888), 113.

21. Henry George, *Progress and Poverty* (originally published 1879; New York: Schalkenbach Foundation, 1935), 48.

22. George, 6.

23. Lawson Purdy, "Reminiscences of Lawson Purdy," 1948, 176, Oral History Archives, Columbia University,; John H. MacCracken, "Taxation of City Real Estate and Improvements on Real Estate as Illustrated in New York City," in *State and Local Taxation First National Conference under the Auspices of the National Tax Association*, ed. National Tax Association (New York: Macmillan, 1908), 379.

24. Purdy, "Reminiscences of Lawson Purdy," 176; MacCracken, "Taxation of City Real Estate and Improvements on Real Estate As Illustrated in New York City," 379.

25. Ely, *Problems of To-Day*, 165.

26. Purdy, "Reminiscences of Lawson Purdy," 18.

27. David Scobey, "Boycotting the Politics Factory: Labor Radicalism and the New York City Mayoral Election of 1884," *Radical History Review* 28 (1984): 280–325; Edward T. O'Donnell, *Henry George and the Crisis of Inequality: Progress and Poverty in the Gilded Age* (New York: Columbia University Press, 2015).

28. "Pleads for Land Tax Bill: Sullivan Says His Measure Will Help the Poor People," *New York Times*, March 22, 1912, 10; *Real Estate Record and Builders' Guide* 93 (June 27, 1914), 214.

29. "Congestion of Population in New York," *The Public* 14 (September 15, 1951).

30. *The Public* 11 (July 24, 1908), 404.

31. Benjamin C. Marsh, "Taxation versus Congestion," *Single Tax Review* 14 (January–February 1914), 19.

32. Purdy, "Reminiscences of Lawson Purdy," 18.

33. See *Report of the National Tax Relief Convention* (Chicago: Manufacturers and Merchants Federal Tax League, 1923).

34. Benjamin C. Marsh, *Taxation of Land Values in American Cities: The Next Step in Exterminating Poverty* (New York: Benjamin C. Marsh, 1911), xiii. For more on the fluctuating politics of "professionalism" during this period, see Thomas L. Haskell, ed., *The Authority of Experts: Studies in History and Theory* (Bloomington: Indiana University Press, 1984).

35. Marsh, 39.

36. George, *Social Problems*, 323. See also Lawrence M. Lipin, "Nature, the City, and the Family Circle: Domesticity and the Urban Home in Henry George's Thought," *Journal of the Gilded Age and Progressive Era* 13, no. 3 (2014): 305–335.

37. *Report of the New York City Commission on Congestion of Population* (New York: Lecouver Press, 1911), 15–16.

38. Rev. Mr. Pentecost, "The New York of the Future," *The Standard*, August 20, 1887, 1.

39. Felix Adler, "The Vision of New York as the Ideal Metropolis of the Future," January 12, 1917, Box 66, Folder 22, Columbia University Rare Book and Manuscript Library, New York.

40. Frederic C. Howe, *The City: The Hope of Democracy* (New York: Charles Scribner's Sons, 1906), 241.

41. Committee on Taxation, *Final Report of the Committee on Taxation of the City of New York* (New York: O'Connell Press, 1916), 228.

42. Lawson Purdy, "Condemnation, Assessments and Taxation in Relation to City Planning," in *Proceedings of the Third National Conference on City Planning* (Boston: Harvard University Press, 1911), 125.

43. Howe, *The City*, 251, 253, 259.

44. C. W. Tooke, "Uniformity in Municipal Finance," *Municipal Affairs* 2 (June 1898), 196; Purdy, "Reminiscences of Lawson Purdy," 176; MacCracken, "Taxation of City Real Estate and Improvements on Real Estate As Illustrated in New York City," 379.

45. Purdy, "Condemnation, Assessments and Taxation in Relation to City Planning," 125.

46. Commission on New Sources of City Revenue, *Report Submitted to the Mayor, Chairman of the Board of Estimate and Apportionment*, January 11, 1913, 1; Marsh, "Taxation versus Congestion," 16–20.

47. See Edwin G. Burrows and Mike Wallace, *Gotham: A History of New York City to 1898* (New York: Oxford University Press, 1999), 1069.

48. Citizens' Association, *Report of the Citizens' Association*, 5.

49. Durand, *The Finances of New York City*, 236.

50. Durand, 222.

51. Max West, "Municipal Franchises in New York," in *Municipal Monopolies: A Collection of Papers by American Economists and Specialists*, ed. Edward W. Bemis (New York: Thomas Y. Crowell, 1899), 396.

52. John Christopher Schwab, "History of the New York Property Tax," *Publications of the American Economic Association* 5 (September 1890), 442.

53. "Franchises and Taxes," *New York Times*, August 24, 1883, 4; Editorial, *New York Tribune*, March 18, 1886, 14.

54. *Real Estate Record and Builders' Guide* 59, no. 1523 (1897), 873; *Real Estate Record and Builders' Guide* 44, no. 1112 (1889), 941.

55. Durand, *The Finances of New York City*, 44.

56. Durand, 242.

57. West, "Municipal Franchises in New York," 388.

58. Samuel Seabury, *Municipal Ownership and Operation of Public Utilities* (New York: Municipal Ownership Publishing, 1905), 133.

59. See Rodgers, *Atlantic Crossings*.

60. Richard T. Ely, *Natural Monopolies and Local Taxation* (Boston, MA: Robinson & Stephenson, 1889), 15.

61. Ely, *Problems of To-Day*, 183.

62. Howe, *The City*, 63–35.

63. Frederic C. Howe, *European Cities at Work* (New York: Charles Scribner's Sons, 1917), 208.

64. L. G. Powers, "Increasing Municipal Indebtedness," *National Municipal Review* 3, no. 1 (1914): 102–106.

65. Delos F. Wilcox, "Fundamental Planks in a Public Utility Program," *Proceedings of the Conference of American Mayors on Public Policies as to Municipal Utilities* 57 (January 1915), 18.

66. Klein, *Bankrupting a Great City*, 167.

67. Klein, *Bankrupting a Great City*, 167.

68. Correspondence, Theodore Roosevelt to Platt, May 8, 1899. *Letters of Theodore Roosevelt*, Elting E. Morison and John Blum, eds., 8 vols. (Cambridge, MA: Harvard University Press, 1951–1954), Volume 2, 1005.

69. Seabury, *Municipal Ownership and Operation of Public Utilities*, 45.

70. Edward M. Grout, *Speech Delivered before the Franchise Tax and Municipal Ownership League, New York City, January 30, 1903, on the Franchise Tax Law* (New York: Mail and Express, 1903).

71. John Ford, "Municipal Government in the United States," *North American Review* 172, no. 534 (1901), 751.

72. Editorial, *Brooklyn Daily Eagle*, May 18, 1899, 1; Editorial, *New York Tribune*, May 11, 1899, 1.

73. State Board of Tax Commissioners, *Annual Report of the State Board of Tax Commissioners of the State of New York* (New York: J. B. Lyon, 1901), 17.

74. "Taxation of Franchises: Methods Discussed at Municipal Ownership . . . ," *New York Times*, February 28, 1903, 3.

75. "Franchise Taxation Valid," *New York Tribune*, May 30, 1905, 6; Grout, *Speech Delivered before the Franchise Tax and Municipal Ownership League*, 5.

76. Howe, *The City*, 35–63.

77. Seabury, *Municipal Ownership and Operation of Public Utilities*, 133.

78. Oliver Carlson and Ernest Sutherland Bates, *Hearst: Lord of Simeon* (New York: Viking Press, 1936), 137.

79. "Hearst Ticket Through: Indorsed with Great Enthusiasm at M. O.," *New York Tribune*, October 13, 1905, 2.

80. Editorial, *Evening Journal*, October 14, 1905, 1.

81. George B. McClellan, *The Gentleman and the Tiger: The Autobiography of George B. McClellan, Jr.* (New York: Lippincott, 1956), 226; "Hearst Boom Grows," *Washington Post*, October 24, 1905, 3.

82. Lincoln Steffens, "Hearst, The Man of Mystery," *American Magazine* 63, no. 1 (1906), 22.

83. Gerald Kurland, *Seth Low: The Reformer in an Urban Industrial Age* (New York: Arden Media, 1971), 164.

84. "Assess Fully, Says Citizens Union," *New York Herald*, October 20, 1902, 6.

85. Kurland, *Seth Low*, 165.

86. "Pleads for Land Tax Bill," *New York Times*, 10; Christopher William England, "Land and Liberty: Henry George, the Single Tax Movement, and the Origins of Twentieth Century Liberalism" (PhD diss., Georgetown University, 2005), 297.

87. Robert Murray Haig, "New Sources of City Revenue," *National Municipal Review* 4 (October 1915), 599; "Guiding Principles in Selecting New Sources," *American City* 16 (January 1917), 33.

88. "About New Sources of Revenue," *Real Estate Record and Builders' Guide* 91 (January 18, 1913), 124.

89. Frederic C. Howe, "Municipal Ownership in America," in *Selected Articles on Municipal Ownership*, ed. Julia E. Johnsen (New York: H. W. Wilson, 1918), 176.

90. See Arthur Nichols Young, *The Single Tax Movement in the United States* (Princeton, NJ: Princeton University Press, 1916).

91. "Front Matter," *Real Estate Record and Builders' Guide* 85 (May 7, 1910), 979.

92. "The Election in New York City," *The Public* 8 (November 11, 1905), 508.

93. Currarino, *The Labor Question in America*, 36, 41, 56.

94. Bird Sim Coler, *Municipal Government: As Illustrated by the Charter, Finances and Public Charities of New York* (New York: D. Appleton, 1901), 166.

95. For a broader history of populism's political shifts over time, see Michael Kazin, *The Populist Persuasion: An American History* (Ithaca, NY: Cornell University Press, 2017).

96. Pittsburgh Committee on Taxation Study, *Report of the Committee on Taxation Study to Council of the City of Pittsburgh, Pennsylvania* (Pittsburgh, PA: n.p., 1916), 20.

Chapter 3

1. Albert W. Noonan, "Lawson Purdy's Influence on Assessment Practice," *American Journal of Economics and Sociology* 9, no. 1 (1949), 25.

2. Lawson Purdy, "The Best Taxed City in the World: Address before the Real Estate Board of Brokers of the City of New York," Henry George School of Social Science, New York, February 24, 1906, https://hgarchives.org/historical-collections-2/new-york-tax-reform-association -1891-1924/series-one/.

3. Purdy.

4. The term "fiscal corporatism" is of course indebted to the concept of "corporate liberalism," understood both as an ideology that reconciled classical liberal commitments (e.g., sanctity of property and contract) with the organizational and economic requirements of large corporations, and as a political project to enable the political and economic dominance of these corporations, through the co-optation of reforms if necessary. My definition of "fiscal corporatist" here is slightly broader—it includes both groups who supported and questioned corporate benevolence but who were united in believing that corporations and large property owners more generally should be the fiscal "base" of a given polity. For an excellent overview of the term, see Gerald Berk, "Corporate Liberalism Reconsidered: A Review Essay," *Journal of Policy History* 3, no. 1, 1991, 70–84.

5. For a historical overview of American liberalism up to this point, see Gary Gerstle, "The Protean Character of American Liberalism"; Nancy L. Cohen, *The Reconstruction of American Liberalism, 1865-1914* (Chapel Hill: University of North Carolina Press, 2002); Marc Stears, *Progressives, Pluralists, and the Problems of the State :Ideologies of Reform in the United States and Britain, 1909-1926* (Oxford: Oxford University Press, 2002). For a work stressing the interplay of fiscal theories with the advent of modern liberalism, see Ajay K. Mehrotra, *Making the Modern American Fiscal State.*

6. For a historical work examining how state taxes on corporations inadvertently provided fiscal—and hence political—leverage to these interests, see R. Rudy Higgens-Evenson, *The Price of Progress: Public Services Taxation and the American Corporate State 1877 to 1929* (Baltimore, MD: Johns Hopkins University Press, 2003). For a contemporary study of the effects of "fiscal zoning," see J. M. Pogodzinski, "The Effects of Fiscal and Exclusionary Zoning on Household Location: A Critical Review," *Journal of Housing Research* 2, no. 2 (1991): 145–160. See also Wortel-London, "The Tax Trap."

7. For more on the associational life and civic involvement of local businesses during this time, see Jeffrey Haydu, *Citizen Employers: Business Communities and Labor in Cincinnati and San Francisco, 1870-1916* (Ithaca, NY: Cornell University Press, 2008).

8. See Mike Wallace, *Greater Gotham: A History of New York City from 1898 to 1919* (Oxford: Oxford University Press, 2018), esp. chap. 16. While historians have recovered more radical strains of middle-class reform during the early twentieth century, the dominant currents remained concerned with preserving rather than questioning the dominant form of property ownership. See Rodgers, *Atlantic Crossing*, esp. chaps. 1–4.

9. Paine, "Savings Banks That Have Failed," 32.

10. Keith D. Revell, *Building Gotham: Civic Culture and Public Policy in New York City, 1898–1938* (Baltimore: Johns Hopkins University Press, 2005), 151; Jason M. Barr, *Building the Skyline: The Birth and Growth of Manhattan's Skyscrapers* (New York: Oxford University Press), 312.

11. Philip H. Cornick, "The Real Estate Tax," *American Journal of Economics and Sociology* 26 (1967): 251–262; Lawson Purdy, *City Real Estate Assessment* (Columbus, OH: International Tax Association, 1908), 40.

12. C. G. Fecil, *New York City's Land: The Safest and Most Profitable Investment in the World* (Wilkes-Barre, PA: Reader Press, 1908), 9; George A. Hurd, "Real-Estate Bonds as an Investment Security," *Annals of the American Academy of Political and Social Science* 30 (September 1907), 160.

13. "Taxpaying Bodies Combine," *New York Times*, March 29, 1914, XX1.

14. Bower, "An Examination of the Emergence, Development and Current State of Urban Land Use Theory," 4.

15. Francis H. Sisson, "New York Real Estate as a Field for Investment," *Banker's Magazine* 75 (1907), 96.

16. Richard M. Hurd, *Principles of City Land Values* (New York: Real Estate Record and Builders' Guide, 1903), i.

17. Hurd, 17.

18. Hurd, 13.

19. Hurd was not entirely alone in his effort to place theories of urban economics on more "scientific" footing. In 1901, W. A. Somers, a Georgist tax appraiser, released a report on the "valuation of real estate for taxation." Nonetheless, Somers emphasized that the significance of these conditions on local values was almost entirely a matter of local opinion. William A. Somers, *The Valuation of Real Estate for Purposes of Taxation* (St. Paul, MN: William Somers, 1901), 6.

20. Hurd's theories on how changes in land values "sorted" the spatial arrangement of cities was in many ways a precursor to the influential "urban ecology" theories of the Chicago School of Sociology. For more work on the relation between Hurd's theories and urban ecology, see Fred P. Bosselman, "The Commodification of 'Nature's Metropolis': The Historical Context of Illinois' Unique Zoning Standards," *Northern Illinois University Law Review* 12, no. 3 (July 1992), 560; Robert Beauregard, *Voices of Decline: The Postwar Fate of US Cities* (Cambridge, MA: Blackwell Publishers, 1993), 69.

21. "Bibliography of Historically Significant Valuation and Mortgage Risk Documents," AEI Housing Center, October 13, 2015, https://www.aei.org/wp-content/uploads/2015/10/Housing Conference_10.28.15_Appraisal-History-Bibliography.pdf.

22. Hurd, *Principles of City Land Values*, 78, 115; Winling and Michney, "The Roots of Redlining," 47.

23. Ryan P. McDonough, Paul J. Miranti, and Michael P. Schoderbek. "The Search for Order in Municipal Administration: Herman A. Metz and the New York City Experience, 1898–1909," *Accounting Historians Journal* 47, no. 1 (2020): 55–74; Patton and Hutchison, "Historical Development of the Financial Reporting Model for State and Local Governments"; Williams, "Measuring Government in the Early Twentieth Century."

24. Noonan, "Lawson Purdy's Influence on Assessment Practice," 25.

25. Lawson Purdy, "The Influence of Taxation on the Prosperity of Cities," *The Public* 11, no. 444, October 6, 1906, 639.

26. Purdy, "Condemnation, Assessments and Taxation in Relation to City Planning," 124.

27. Benjamin C. Marsh, *An Introduction to City Planning: Democracy's Challenge to the American City* (New York: Benjamin C. Marsh, 1909), 11; Edward Polak, "Reduction of Tax on Buildings in the City of New York," *Annals of the American Academy of Political and Social Science* 59, no. 1 (1915), 186; Louis F. Post, "The Taxing Power and the Housing Problem," *Municipal Affairs* 6, no. 418 (1902), 428.

28. Howe, *The City*, 295, italics added.

29. Polak, "Reduction of Tax on Buildings in the City of New York," 186, italics added.

30. Purdy, "The Best Taxed City in the World."

31. "The New York Tax Reform Association," *Financial and Mining Record*, 327.

32. See Ajay K. Mehrorta, *Making the Modern American Fiscal State: Law, Politics, and the Rise of Progressive Taxation, 1877–1929* (Cambridge: Cambridge University Press, 2013).

33. E. R. A. Seligman, "Discussion," in *The Government of the City of New York*, ed. New York State Constitutional Convention Commission (New York: Academy of Political Science, 1915), 168.

34. George, *Social Problems*, 200.

35. "Tenement-House Reform: A Mass-Meeting Held at Cooper Union To Promote . . ," *New York Tribune*, Jan 31, 1895, 4. A week after saying these words, George Guston, President of the School of Social Economy in New York's Union Square, critiqued them. "Henry George says that if the East side were made into a park the wealthy would promptly take possession of that section of the city and the poor would move away to less attractive parts of the city. Where would the poor go? To Fifth Avenue? Well, that would be good enough for them." At this point, reported the *Times*, a single taxer interrupted the speaker and said the poor would be driven to dirty streets—to which Gunton optimistically responded that those streets would all be cleaned by that point, serenely missing his interlocutors' point entirely. "Called Him a Quack: George Gunton's Severe Criticism on Henry George." *New York Times*, Feb 7, 1895, 6.

36. "Busy Man: Pioneer in Tax and Housing Reforms Proud of Record in Long City Career," *New York Times*, September 13, 1953, 83.

37. Revell, 160–61.

38. R. Rudy Higgens-Evenson, *The Price of Progress: Public Services Taxation and the American Corporate State 1877 to 1929* (Baltimore, MD: Johns Hopkins University Press, 2003), 1.

39. Coler, *Municipal Government*, 32.

40. See Jonathan Kahn, *Budgeting Democracy: State Building and Citizenship in America, 1890–1928* (Ithaca, NY: Cornell University Press, 1997).

41. H. W. Batt, "Land Value Maps Are Not New, but Their Utility Needs to Be Rediscovered," *International Journal of Transdisciplinary Research* 4, no. 1 (2009): 108–158; see Lawson Purdy, *The Assessment of Real Estate* (Philadelphia, PA: National Municipal League, 1923), 15.

42. Henry H. Klein, *My Last Fifty Years: An Autobiographical History of 'Inside' New York* (New York: Isaac Goldman, 1935), 60.

43. Marsh, *Taxation of Land Values in American Cities*, 69.

44. Coler, *Municipal Government*, vi.

45. Purdy, "Condemnation, Assessments and Taxation in Relation to City Planning," 124.

46. Committee on Taxation, *Final Report of the Committee on Taxation of the City of New York*, 368.

47. Lawson Purdy, "Districting and Zoning of Cities," in *Proceedings of the Ninth National Conference on City Planning* (Cambridge, MA: Harvard University Press, 1917), 171.

48. Purdy, "Reminiscences of Lawson Purdy," 26.

49. "Sees Little Gain in High Buildings," *New-York Tribune*, January 21, 1915, 9.

50. Purdy, "Reminiscences of Lawson Purdy," 8; New York Tax Reform Association, "Platform," *Financial and Mining Record*, November 7, 1891, 39.

51. Lawson Purdy, *Zoning as Related to City Planning* (n.p., 1919), 5.

52. Delos F. Wilcox, "The New York Subway Contracts," *National Municipal Review* 2, no. 3 (1913), 388.

53. Hammack, *Power and Society*, 234; Clifton Hood, *722 Miles: The Building of the Subways and How They Transformed New York* (Baltimore: Johns Hopkins University Press, 2004), 66.

54. Lewis Mumford, *The City in History: Its Origins, Its Transformation, Its Prospects* (New York: Harcourt, Brace & World, 1961), 425.

55. Francis H. Sisson, "New York Real Estate as a Field for Investment," *Banker's Magazine* 75 (1907), 95.

56. "Homes for the Poor and Rapid Transit," *New York Times*, March 7, 1896, 4.

57. Letter from Mayor, December 13, 1910, Roll 10, Mayor Gaynor Subject Files, City Hall Library, New York; "Urge Transit for Suburbs: Housing of Poor Discussed," *New-York Tribune*, February 6, 1911, 3.

58. Calvin Tomkins, July 29, 1910, Roll 10, Mayor Gaynor Subject Files, City Hall Library, New York; "Letter to Governor Hughes," May 6, 1908, Roll 10, Mayor Gaynor Subject Files, City Hall Library, New York.

59. "Front Matter," *Real Estate Record and Builders' Guide* 71, no. 1826 (1903), 693.

60. Felix Adler, "The Homes and Rookeries of New York," 1895, p. 18, Box 63, Folder 8, Felix Adler Papers, Columbia Rare Books and Manuscript Collection, Columbia University Libraries, New York.

61. Marsh, *An Introduction to City Planning*, 40; Adler, "The Homes and Rookeries of New York," 18; George, *Social Problems*, 200.

62. Marsh, *Taxation of Land Values in American Cities*, 69.

63. Marsh, 42.

64. Wilcox, "The New York Subway Contracts," 388.

65. For more work examining homeownership as a means of capital accumulation for many working-class Americans during this time, see Elaine Lewinnek, *The Working Man's Reward: Chicago's Early Suburbs and the Roots of American Sprawl* (New York: Oxford University Press, 2014).

66. Reform Club, *Subway Policy of New York* (New York: Reform Club, 1908), 40.

67. "The Real Estate Field: Some Phases of the Plan for Full Value," *New York Times*, August 31, 1902, 20; "The Readjustment of the Sinking Fund and Its Consequences," *Real Estate Record and Builders' Guide*, March 14, 1903, 284.

68. From Committee of the Tax Board to Mayor Gaynor, July 28, 1910, Roll 28, Subject Files, Mayor Gaynor Collection, New York Hall of Records, New York.

69. "To Extend City Debt: For Docks and Subways Metz Drafts Proposed Amendment," *New York Tribune*, January 26, 1908, 7; "Public Service Commission: Relation of Constitutional Debt Limit to . . . ," *Wall Street Journal*, March 31, 1908, 2.

70. New York Advisory Commission on Taxation and Finance, *Final Report: October 1908* (New York: M. B. Brown, 1908), 95.

71. Calvin Tomkins, "Brief Submitted by the New York City Transit Conference Favoring the Repassage of the Constitutional Amendment Providing for the Extension of the City Debt Limit by Excluding Them from Self-Sustaining Dock and Subway Bonds" [publisher not identified, place of publication not identified], 1909, 3. https://archive.org/details/briefsubmittedby00tomk (accessed March 12, 2023).

72. "Bankers Urge City to be Economical: Committee Reports against . . . ," *New York Times*, February 4, 1909, 5.

73. For Debt Amendment: Its Passage Probable City in State of Siege by . . . ," *New York Tribune*, March 18, 1909, 2.

74. "Higher Debt Limit Wins by 113 Votes: Assembly Passes Act Calling for . . . ," *New York Times*, April 28, 1909, 1.

75. Letter from Gaynor, December 13, 1910, Roll 10, Mayor Gaynor Subject Files, City Hall Library, New York; "Urge Transit for Suburbs," *New-York Tribune*, 3; *Real Estate Record and Builders' Guide* 81, no. 2083 (1908), 284.

76. Letter from Mayor, December 13, 1910, Roll 10, Mayor Gaynor Subject Files, City Hall Library, New York; "Urge Transit for Suburbs," *New-York Tribune*, 3.

77. "618 Miles of Track in the Dual System; City Will Have Invested $226,000,000 When Rapid Transit Project Is Completed," *New York Times*, August 3, 1913, 4.

78. Wallace, *Greater Gotham*, 238.

79. "Wagner Bill Signed; Sent Back to Dix: Mayor Accepts Transit Act . . . ," *New York Times*, April 9, 1912, 13.

80. Wilcox, "The New York Subway Contracts," 388.

81. Andrew Wright Crawford, "Certain Aspects of City Financing and City Planning," *National Municipal Review* 3, no. 3 (1914), 480.

82. "Homes for the Poor and Rapid Transit," *New York Times*, 4; "The Socialist Party Algernon Lee's Letter of Acceptance to the Campaign Committee and the Members of the Socialist Party of New York City," Box 6, Folder "New York (N.Y.): 1905," Printed Ephemera Collection on the Socialist Party (U.S.) Pe.032, Tamiment Library and Robert F. Wagner Labor Archives, New York; "Correspondence," July 15, 1911, Socialist Party New York Ny Letter Books, 1907–1914—Reel 6, Socialist Party (U.S.) New York (N.Y.) Letter Books Tam.056.005, Tamiment Library and Robert F. Wagner Labor Archives, New York; Calvin Tomkins, July 29, 1910, "Letter to Governor Hughes," May 6, 1908, Roll 10, Mayor Gaynor Subject Files, City Hall Library, New York; "The Franchise Tangle," *New York Times*, May 14, 1909, 8.

83. Allen Ripley Foote, *Low Fares for Public Service vs. Franchise Taxation* (Norfolk, VA: n.p., 1907), 4.

84. "The People and the Subways," *New York Times*, March 1, 1912, 10.

85. Wilcox, "The New York Subway Contracts," 387.

86. "Letter from Gaynor to Abraham Abraham Esq," February 7, 1911, Roll 28, Subject Files, Mayor Gaynor Collection, New York Hall of Records, New York. Ultimately the New York subway would become publicly operated in the 1940s, and a municipally owned subway line would be planned by the 1920s. By this time, however, most of New York City's subway lines had been financed and planned in a way that was decidedly not profitable—even for the lines' owners. New York's assumption of public subway ownership was thus more a matter of absorbing the cost of an unprofitable utility rather than acquiring a revenue-generating asset, as it largely was in the early 1910s. See Kyle M. Kirschling, "An Economic Analysis of Rapid Transit in New York, 1870–2010" (master's thesis, Columbia University, 2012).

87. Herbert H. Lehman, *The Finances and Financial Administration of New York City Recommendations and Report of the Sub-committee on Budget, Finance, and Revenue, of the City Committee on Plan and Survey* (New York: Columbia University Press, 1928), 47.

88. Hillhouse, *Municipal Bonds*, 35.

89. See Kara Murphy Schlichting, *New York Recentered: Building the Metropolis from the Shore* (Chicago: University of Chicago Press, 2019).

90. See Richard T. Ely, "Land Speculation," *Journal of Farm Economics* 2, no. 3 (1920), 121; Marc A. Weiss, "Richard T. Ely and the Contribution of Economic Research to National Housing Policy, 1920–1940," *Urban Studies* 26 (1988): 115–126.

91. See Geoffrey R. Stone, *Perilous Times: Free Speech in Wartime from the Sedition Act of 1798 to the War on Terrorism* (New York: W. W. Norton, 2004).

92. See Radford, *The Rise of the Public Authority*.

93. Revell, *Building Gotham*, 157. Indeed, in some ways the binary established between profit-seeking corporations and nonprofit governmental enterprises at this time mirrors the broader conceptual binary between "altruistic" nonprofit corporations and more conventional corporations. In either case, "profit-seeking" was confined to the private sector. See Jonathan

Levy, "Altruism and the Origins of Nonprofit Philanthropy" in Rob Reich, Lucy Bernholz, and Chiara Cordelli, eds., *Philanthropy in Democratic Societies: History, Institutions, Values* (Chicago: University of Chicago Press, 2016), 19–43.

Chapter 4

1. "The Campaign Ends," *Long Island Daily Press*, November 5, 1928, 1.

2. "Cross Bay Boulevard Decision Great Victory for Queens Borough and President Connolly," *Long Island Daily Press*, October 3, 1921, 6; "Queens Reaps Many New Improvements: Board of Estimate Bows to . . . ," *New York Times*, August 14, 1921, 86.

3. John F. Hylan, *Staten Island's Future*, in Staten Island Chamber of Commerce, *Annual Yearbook* [publisher not identified, place of publication not identified], 1924, 9–11. Subject Files Roll 2, Mayor Hylan Collection, City Hall Library, New York City.

4. "Memorial Dedication," *Long Island Daily Press*, April 9, 1946, 1.

5. For a historical treatment of discriminatory assessments, see Andrew W. Kahrl, "The Short End of Both Sticks: Property Assessments and Black Taxpayer Disadvantage in Urban America," in *Shaped by the State: Towards a New Political History of the Twentieth Century*, ed. Brent Cebul, and Lily Geismer, and Mason B. Williams (Chicago: University of Chicago Press, 2019).

6. See Lewinnek, *The Working Man's Reward*; Becky Nicolaides, *My Blue Heaven: Life and Politics in the Working-Class Suburbs of Los Angeles, 1920–1965* (Chicago: University of Chicago Press, 2002); David M. P. Freund, *Colored Property: State Policy and White Racial Politics in Suburban America* (Chicago: University of Chicago Press, 2010).

7. There were, to be sure, small but significant experiments in alternative residential ownership forms in New York during time, particularly in the form of union-owned cooperative housing. Such experiments, however, had little broader effect on the physical and fiscal transformation of New York during the 1920s. See Robert Fogelson, *Working-Class Utopias: A History of Cooperative Housing in New York City* (Princeton, NJ: Princeton University Press, 2022); Sarah Horowitz, *Mutualism: Building the Next Economy from the Ground Up* (New York: Random House, 2021).

8. United States Department of Labor, *Family Income and Expenditure in New York City, 1935–36* (Washington, DC: US Government Printing Office, 1941), 1:62.

9. US Census Bureau, *Families by Tenure*, 1930. https://www.socialexplorer.com/ (accessed July 10, 2019).

10. For more on the postwar suppression of progressive and left-wing actors following World War I, see Stone, *Perilous Times*.

11. Cornelius Donovan, "The Sullivan-Brooks Bill," *New-York Tribune*, February 19, 1912, 6.

12. Board of Estimate, "Minutes of the Meeting of the Board of Estimate and Apportionment," September 15, 1922, Board of Estimate Minutes and Proceedings from 1911 to 1962, City Hall Library, New York.

13. Abraham Cahan, *The Rise of David Levinsky: A Novel* (New York: Harper & Brothers, 1917), 464. See also Leon Wexelstein, *Building Up Greater Brooklyn: With Sketches of Men Instrumental in Brooklyn's Amazing Development* (Brooklyn, NY: Brooklyn Biographical Society, 1925), xvii, 33.

14. US Census Bureau, *Families by Tenure*.

15. The builder's reference to "racial groups" spoke to the liminal racial status of the city's new immigrants. National Industrial Conference Board, "The Cost of Living in the United States, 1914–1926" (New York: National Industrial Conference Board, 1926), 22.

16. National Industrial Conference Board, *The Cost of Living in the United States, 1914–1926* (New York: National Industrial Conference Board, 1926), 22.

17. "New Plan to Aid Small Home Builder," *New York Times*, December 4, 1927, RE2.

18. For more information on the physical form of Brooklyn's expansion during this time, see Thomas J. Campanella, *Brooklyn: The Once and Future City* (Princeton, NJ: Princeton University Press, 2019).

19. See Schlichting, *New York Recentered*.

20. Eugene N. White, *Lessons from the Great American Real Estate Boom of the 1920s* (Cambridge, MA: National Bureau of Economic Research, 2009), 24, https://www.nber.org/papers/w15573.pdf.

21. Regional Plan Association of New York, *Population, Land Values, and Government: Studies in the Growth and Distribution of Population and Land Values, and Problems of Government* (New York: Arno Press, 1929), 174.

22. See Nicolaides, *My Blue Heaven*.

23. William O'Dwyer, "William O'Dwyer Interview," 1962, Oral History Archives, Columbia University, 292.

24. Roy Peel, *The Political Clubs of New York* (New York: Putnam, 1935), 334.

25. Joseph Daniel McGoldrick, "The New Tammany," *American Mercury* 15, no. 27 (1928), 4.

26. Edward J. Flynn, *You're the Boss* (New York: Viking Press, 1947), 53. For more on how the subway altered New York's politics, see Daniel Wortel-London, "All's Fare: Subways and the Transformation of Metropolitan Politics in New York City, 1904–1934," in *Urban Infrastructure: Historical and Social Dimensions of an Interconnected World*, ed. Joseph Heathcott, Jonathan Soffer, and Rae Zimmerman (Pittsburgh, PA: University of Pittsburgh Press, 2022).

27. "Cambria Heights Civic Association of St. Albans," 1933, Queens County, Civic, 1926–1939 Vertical Files, Archives at Queens Public Library, Queens Public Library, New York.

28. Joseph Daniel McGoldrick, *The Board of Estimate and Apportionment of New York City* (New York: National Municipal League, 1932), 19.

29. McGoldrick, 215; "100% Valuation of Realty Urged on Mayor-Elect: P. S. Institute Tells," *New York Herald, New York Tribune*, December 14, 1925, 7.

30. Lewis Mumford, "Botched Cities," *American Mercury* 27, no. 70 (1929), 146; Arthur Curt Holden, *Has the City Betrayed the Homeseeker?* Unpublished, 1930, p. 10. Box 28, Folder 1, Articles by Arthur Cort Holden, Arthur Cort Holden Papers, Princeton University Library, Princeton NJ.

31. Letter from Stanley Miller to Fiorello La Guardia, April 4, 1938, Box 3219, Folder 7, Departmental Correspondence, Mayor Fiorello La Guardia Collection, New York Hall of Records, New York.

32. Al Smith, "Report on Charter Recommendations," May 28, 1935, New York City Charter Revision Commission Collection, New York Public Library Milstein Division, New York.

33. Lehman, *The Finances and Financial Administration of New York City*, 37; "Delegations Ask Subways in Queens: Many Organizations Submit Pleas," *New York Times*, August 9, 1924, 6.

34. Holden, *Has the City Betrayed the Homeseeker?*, 10.

35. "Berry's Promise of Sewer Relief Hailed in Queens," *Brooklyn Daily Eagle*, October 19, 1929, 1; "Predicts 2,000,000 Queens Population: Mark Will Be Reached at End of . . ." *New York Times*, Oct. 13, 1929, RE1; "Queens Has Record in School Building," *New York Times*, June 24, 1928, W18; New York Office of the Comptroller, *New York City's Parks, Playgrounds and Parkways and Their Proposed Extension* (New York: n.p., 1930), 41.

36. Edwin Harold Spengler, *Land Values in New York in Relation to Transit Facilities* (New York: Columbia University, 1930), 17, italics in original.

37. See Einhorn, *Property Rules*; Lehman, *The Finances and Financial Administration of New York City*, 55.

38. Lehman, *The Finances and Financial Administration of New York City*, LV.

39. Charles W. Berry, *Why New York City Can Never Become Bankrupt* (New York: n.p., 1930), 14.

40. "Hylan's Fate Before the Big Five Today," *New York Times*, July 28, 1925, 23.

41. "For Higher Debt Limit: Community Councils Want It to Be $300,000,000 as Transit Solution," *New York Times*, March 2, 1927, 3; "Eightieth Meeting," *Economic Club of New York*, March 28, 1927, 47.

42. "Asks Fare Increase to Lower Tax Rate," *New York Times*, October 29, 1925, 27.

43. Regional Plan Association of New York, *Population, Land Values and Government* (New York: Arno Press, 1929), 175.

44. Milo R. Maltbie, "Transportation and City Planning," *American City* 8, no. 5 (1913), 589.

45. Purdy, "Reminiscences of Lawson Purdy," 32–33.

46. Robert Fitch, *The Assassination of New York* (New York: Verso, 1993), 79.

47. Samuel Untermyer, *Land and Freedom*, 28 no. 2, March–April 1928, 58.

48. Holden, *Has the City Betrayed the Homeseeker?*, 10.

49. Robert Murray Haig, *Major Economic Factors in Metropolitan Growth and Arrangement: A Study of Trends and Tendencies in the Economic Activities within the Region of New York and Its Environs* (New York: Arno Press, 1928), 43.

50. Robert Fitch, "Planning New York," in *The Fiscal Crisis of American Cities*, ed. Roger E. Alcaly and David Mermelstein (New York: Vintage Original, 1976), 282; Citizens Budget Commission, *Report on the Master Plan of Land Use Proposed by the City Planning Commission* (New York: Citizens Budget Commission, 1941), 14.

51. George McAneny, "Planning the Future City," May 1928, p. 3, Box 2, "Miscellaneous Speeches," George McAneny Papers, Mudd Manuscript Library, Princeton, New Jersey.

52. "Realty Men Take Optimistic View of the 1928 Real Estate Market," *New York Times*, January 8, 1928, 187; "New York Ranks as World Metropolis," *New York Times*, December 19, 1926, RE6.

53. Lehman, *The Finances and Financial Administration of New York City*, 244; Fuchs, *Mayors and Money*, 129.

54. Sbragia, *Debt Wish*, 5, 103; Hillhouse, *Municipal Bonds*, 11.

55. Citizens Budget Commission, *Report on the Master Plan of Land Use*, 10.

56. Stephen Smith, "Methods of Improving the Homes of the Laboring and Tenement House Classes of New York," paper read before the N.Y. Public Health and Dwelling Reform Association [publisher not identified, place of publication not identified], April 1875, 5; "Accepted by Mr. George: Cooper Union Crowded with His Friends. A Speech in Which the Labor Candidate Gave Out His Ideas of True Government," *New York Times*, October 6, 1886, 1. For a more general treatment of homeownership and race during the late nineteenth century, see Lewinnek, *The Working Man's Reward*.

57. Robert M. Fogelson, *The Great Rent Wars: New York 1917–1929* (New Haven, CT: Yale University Press, 2013), 173.

58. LeeAnn Lands, *The Culture of Property: Race, Class, and Housing Landscapes in Atlanta, 1880–1950* (Athens: University of Georgia Press, 2011), 112; Simone Knewitz, *The Politics*

of Private Property: Contested Claims to Ownership in U.S. Cultural Discourse (Lanham, MD: Lexington Books, 2021), 141.

59. "Lay Tax Rate Rise to Method of Levy," *New York Times*, April 4, 1920, E8.

60. "Small Home Owners Hard Hit by Ruling against Tax Exemption," *New York Times*, April 8, 1923, X12.

61. David H. Richards, *Your Taxes: An Explanation and a Program* (New York: New York State Committee, Communist Party, 1938), 24; "Housing Public Hearing," April 6, 1935, Box 408, Folder 7, Fiorello La Guardia Subject Files, New York Hall of Records, New York; Abrams, *Revolution in Land*, 74.

62. Holden, *Has the City Betrayed the Homeseeker?*, 10.

63. John E. Burton and Dorothy C. Burton, "New York Real Estate: Its Taxation and Assessment," *Journal of Land & Public Utility Economics* 13, no. 3 (1937), 253; Joint Legislative Committee on Assessing and Reviewing of the State of New York, *Final Report* (New York: Fort Orange Press, 1941), 103.

64. Richards, *Your Taxes*, 24; Housing Hearing, New York Hall of Records.

65. Abrams, *Revolution in Land*, 74.

66. Holden, *Has The City Betrayed The Homeseeker?*, 11.

67. M. J. Mcauley Letter, February 4, 1918, Box 38, Folder 2, Departmental Correspondence Sent, John F. Hylan Collection, New York Hall of Records, New York.

68. "Tax Rate Increase Hurts Landlords in Harlem Accounting to Uptown Realtors," *New York Amsterdam News*, October 15, 1930, 5.

69. "Housing Public Hearing," April 6, 1935, Box 408, Folder 7, Fiorello La Guardia Subject Files, New York Hall of Records, New York.

70. William Bosler, "Why Harvey Will Win"; "Queens Borough President on the Side of the Taxpayers," *New York Herald Tribune*, September 17, 1929, 1.

71. U.S. Census Bureau, *Families by Tenure*.

Chapter 5

1. Baruch Charney Vladeck, "Speech," May 13, 1934, Box 14, Folder 7, Baruch Charney Vladeck Papers and Photographs, Tamiment Library and Robert F. Wagner Labor Archives, New York.

2. Baruch Charney Vladeck, "The Housing Movement Today," 1937, Box 14, Folder 7, Baruch Charney Vladeck Papers and Photographs, Tamiment Library and Robert F. Wagner Labor Archives, New York.

3. In recalling this history, this chapter provides context for contemporary efforts to place local finances on more stable footing by restricting real estate speculation and unnecessary capital expenditures. See Charles Marohn, *Strong Towns: A Bottom-Up Revolution to Rebuild American Prosperity* (Hoboken, NJ: John Wiley & Sons, 2020).

4. Nicholas Dagen Bloom, *Public Housing That Worked: New York in the Twentieth Century* (Philadelphia: University of Pennsylvania Press, 2008); Lawrence Vale, *From the Puritans to the Projects: Public Housing and Public Neighbors* (Cambridge, MA: Harvard University Press, 2007); Gail Radford, *Modern Housing for America: Policy Struggles in the New Deal Era* (Chicago: University of Chicago Press, 1996).

5. For more on the importance of "productiveist" arguments in spurring the growth of universalistic welfare programs in the interwar period, see Jimi Adésínà, "Return to a Wider Vision

of Social Policy: Re-reading Theory and History," *South African Review of Sociology* 46, no. 3, 2015, 99–119; Jenny Andersson, *Between Growth and Security: Swedish Social Democracy from a Strong Society to a Third Way*. Manchester: Manchester University Press, 2006.

6. Lewis Mumford, *The Culture of Cities* (New York: Harcourt, Brace & Company, 1938), 281.

7. For a rival interpretation of the RPAA members, see Steven Conn, *Americans against the City: Anti-Urbanism in the Twentieth Century* (New York: Oxford University Press, 2014).

8. Stanley Buder, *Visionaries and Planners: The Garden City Movement and the Modern Community* (New York: Oxford University Press, 1990), 165.

9. Herbert S. Swan, "Land Values and City Growth," *Journal of Land and Public Utility Economics* 10, no. 2 (1934): 188–201.

10. Charles Abrams, "New Social Trends in Land Utilization," *American Institute of Real Estate Appraisers Journal* 9, no. 4 (1941), 344.

11. Donald H. Davenport, *Report of Commission of Housing and Regional Planning to Governor Alfred E. Smith . . . on Cost of Government, Land Value and Population* (Albany, NY: J. B. Lyon, 1923).

12. Mumford, *The Culture of Cities*, 281.

13. Mumford.

14. Frederick Ackerman, "Our Stake in Congestion," *Survey Graphic* 54, no. 1 (1925), 142.

15. Mumford, "Botched Cities," 146.

16. Clarence Stein, "Dinosaur Cities," *Survey Graphic* 54, no. 1 (1925), 136.

17. Abrams, "New Social Trends in Land Utilization," 344.

18. Ackerman, "Our Stake in Congestion," 142.

19. Catherine Bauer, "Cities in Flux: A Challenge to the Postwar Planners," *American Scholar* 13, no. 1 (1943–1944), 82.

20. Mumford, *The Culture of Cities*, 339.

21. Paul Betters, "Federal Aid for Municipalities," *National Municipal Review* 22, no. 4 (1933), 176.

22. Tom Nicholas and Anna D. Scherbina, "Real Estate Prices during the Roaring Twenties and the Great Depression," *Journal of Real Estate Economics* 4 (2013), 297.

23. Edith Elmer Wood, *Slums and Blighted Areas in the United States* (Washington, DC: US Government Printing Office, 1936), 20. See also White, *Lessons from the Great American Real Estate Boom and Bust of the 1920s*; Fitch, 57.

24. James Agee, *Brooklyn Is: Southeast of the Island: Travel Notes* (New York: Fordham University Press, 2005), 40.

25. Hillhouse, *Municipal Bonds*, 244. See also Field, "Uncontrolled Land Development and the Duration of the Depression in the United States"; Brocker and Hanes, "The 1920s American Real Estate Boom and the Downturn of the Great Depression"; Gunter and Siodla, "Local Origins and Implications of the 1930s Urban Debt Crisis."

26. Joel Schwartz, "Tenement Renewal in New York City in the 1930s: The District-Improvement Ideas of Arthur C. Holden," *Journal of Planning History* 1, no. 4 (2002), 295.

27. David L. Wickens, *Residential Real Estate: Its Economic Position as Shown by Values, Rents, Family Incomes, Financing, and Construction, Together with Estimates for All Real Estate* (Washington, DC: National Bureau of Economic Research, 1941), 292; William H. Wheelock, "The Effects of the Present Financial Situation upon Real Estate," *Harvard Business Review* 9 (April 1931), 318.

28. Herbert Simpson, "Real Estate Speculation and the Depression," *American Economic Review* 23, no. 1 (1933), 163.

29. James Siodla, "Debt and Taxes: Fiscal Strain and US City Budgets during the Great Depression," *Explorations in Economic History* 76 (April 2020), 6, https://www.sciencedirect.com/science/article/abs/pii/S0014498320300140?via%3Dihub (accessed April 4, 2020).

30. Hillhouse, *Municipal Bonds*, 166.

31. Hillhouse, 23.

32. Hillhouse, 10.

33. Terrence J. McDonald, "The Burdens of Urban History: The Theory of the State in Recent American Social History," *Studies in American Political Development* 3 (Spring 1989), 28.

34. Hillhouse, *Municipal Bonds*, 10.

35. See Rodgers, *Atlantic Crossing*, esp. chap. 10.

36. Clarence Stein, "Our Cities Are Obsolete," *Washington Post*, July 30, 1933, 6.

37. Alan Brinkley, *Liberalism and Its Discontents* (Cambridge, MA: Harvard University Press, 2000), 37; Carol Sussman, *Planning the Fourth Migration: The Neglected Vision of the Regional Planning Association of America* (Cambridge, MA: MIT Press, 1977), 43.

38. Robert M. Collins, *More: The Politics of Economic Growth in Postwar America* (New York: Oxford University Press, 2002), 5.

39. See Sarah T. Phillips, *This Land, This Nation: Conservation, Rural America, and the New Deal* (Cambridge, UK: Cambridge University Press, 2007); Neil M. Maher, *Nature's New Deal: The Civilian Conservation Corps and the Roots of the American Environmental Movement* (New York: Oxford University Press, 2005).

40. See Lin Zhang and Yingli Xu, "The Influence of Institutionalists on the New Deal," *World Review of Political Economy* 2, no. 1 (2011). https://www.scienceopen.com/hosted-document?doi=10.2307/41931920.

41. Richard P. Adelstein, "'The Nation as an Economic Unit': Keynes, Roosevelt, and the Managerial Ideal," *Journal of American History* 78, no. 1 (1991): 160–187.

42. National Resources Committee, *Our Cities: Their Role in the National Economy* (Washington, DC: US Government Printing Office, 1937), 74.

43. Stuart Chase, *The Tragedy of Waste* (New York: Macmillan, 1937); Paul Sears, *Deserts on the March* (Washington, DC: Island Press, 1988)

44. "Tax Troubles Laid to Land Gambling," *New York Times*, July 23, 1933, N13; Hillhouse, *Municipal Bonds*, 12.

45. New York Chamber of Commerce Committee on Public Planning, "Report," March 3, 1937, Box 249, Folder 12, New York Chamber of Commerce Collection, Columbia Rare Books and Manuscripts, New York; Citizens Budget Commission, *Killing the Goose* (New York: Citizens Budget Commission, 1935), 9.

46. Hillhouse, *Municipal Bonds*, 12. See also Conference of Mayors and Other City Officials of the State of New York, *No Wonder the Taxpayers Howl!* (New York: Government Publication, 1936), 6.

47. "Real Estate Bonds Held Speculative," *New York Times*, August 24, 1939, 33.

48. "Era of Stability for Realty Seen: Speculative Booms Probably Never . . . ," *New York Times*, December 9, 1934, 8.

49. Wheelock, "The Effects of the Present Financial Situation upon Real Estate," 318, italics in original.

50. Citizens Budget Commission, *Killing the Goose*, 9; New York Chamber of Commerce Committee on Public Planning, "Report."

51. Revell, *Building Gotham*, 178.

52. Frederick Bird, "Cities and Their Debt Burdens," *National Municipal Review* 25, no. 12 (1936), 14.

53. *The Finances of New York City* (New York: Dun & Bradstreet, 1934), 63; "Real Estate Bonds Held Speculative," *New York Times.*

54. City Planning Commission, *Annual Report of the City Planning Commission and the Department of City Planning* (New York: Julien Printing, 1938), 36.

55. Fuchs, *Mayors and Money*, 83.

56. Mason Williams, *City of Ambition: Franklin Roosevelt, Fiorello La Guardia, and the Making of New Deal New York* (New York: W. W. Norton, 2013), 128.

57. Daniel O. Prosterman, *Defining Democracy: Electoral Reform and the Struggle for Power in New York City* (New York: Oxford University Press, 2013), 23.

58. Harvey W. Corbett, "Report to Board of Directors," March 3, 1937, Box 249, Folder 11 Columbia University Merchants' Collection, Columbia University Rare Books & Manuscript Collection; Laurence Arnold Tanzer; *The New York City Charter: Adopted November 3, 1936, with Source Notes, a History of the Charter and Analysis and Summary of Its Provisions, Together with Appendices* (New York: Clark Boardman, 1937), 5; David Trosten, *The New Charter for New York City: A Digest of the Proposed Charter for New York City as Filed with the City Clerk on August 17, 1936* (New York: Oxford Books, 1936), 5.

59. David Trosten, *The New Charter for New York City*, 10.

60. "Mayor to Attack Charter Proposal," *New York Times*, April 30, 1936, 2; "Borough Officials Lead Wide Fight on Charter Plan," *New York Times*, April 28, 1936, 1.

61. "New City Charter Adopted by 344,000," *New York Times*, November 4, 1936, 13.

62. See Revell, *Building Gotham*, 261; Mark I. Gelfand, "Rexford G. Tugwell and the Frustration of Planning in New York City," *Journal of the American Planning Association* 51, no. 2 (1985), 155.

63. "Planning the City of Tomorrow," *New York Times Magazine*, June 18, 1939, 8.

64. City Planning Commission, *Annual Report of the City Planning Commission* (New York [publisher not identified], 1940), 30.

65. Rexford Tugwell, "The Real Estate Dilemma," *Public Administration Review* 2 (Winter 1942), 27.

66. Tugwell, 31.

67. City Planning Commission, *Annual Report of the City Planning Commission and the Department of City Planning*, 36.

68. New York City Housing Authority, Frederick L. Ackerman, and William F. R. Ballard, *Work Sheets for a Note on Site and Unit Planning as Previously Published by the Authority* (New York: New York City Housing Authority, 1937), 54.

69. Jason M. Barr, "The Birth and Growth of Modern Zoning [Part II]: The FARsighted Great Depression," *Building the Skyline*, August 9, 2021. https://buildingtheskyline.org/floor-area-ratio-2/ (accessed July 6, 2024).

70. City Planning Commission, *Minutes of Meeting of City Planning Commission*, November 20, 1940, 891. http://cityrecord.engineering.nyu.edu/data/1940/1940-11-30.pdf (accessed September 28, 2024).

71. City Planning Commission, *Annual Report of the City Planning Commission and the Department of City Planning*, 41.

72. Wood, *Slums and Blighted Areas in the United States*, 17.

73. Wickens, *Residential Real Estate*, 292.

74. James Ford, *Slums and Housing: With Special Reference to New York City* (New York: Phelps-Stokes Fund, 1936), 453; Abrams, *Revolution in Land*, 74.

75. Mabel Walker, in her book *Urban Blight and Slums*, gave this definition: "We shall define blighted areas as those sections of a community where, as a result of social, economic, or other conditions, there is a marked discrepancy between the value placed upon the property by the owner and its value for any uses to which it can be put, appropriate to the public welfare, under existing circumstances. This discrepancy prevents or handicaps the improvement of the area." Mabel Walker, *Urban Blight and Slums: Economic and Legal Factors in Their Origin, Reclamation, and Prevention* (New York: Russel & Russell, 1938), 6. For more information on blight's history, see Wendell E. Pritchett, "The 'Public Menace' of Blight: Urban Renewal and the Private Uses of Eminent Domain," *Yale Law and Policy Review* 2, no. 1 (2003): 1–52.

76. Baruch Charney Vladeck, "The Housing Movement Today," 1937, Box 14, Folder 7, Baruch Charney Vladeck Papers and Photographs, Tamiment Library and Robert F. Wagner Labor Archives, New York.

77. Walker, *Urban Blight and Slums*, 125.

78. Stanley Carl Nelson, "Property Valuation in Urban Blighted Areas" (PhD diss., University of California, Berkeley, 1955), 80.

79. Wood, *Slums and Blighted Areas in the United States*, 17; Walker, *Urban Blight and Slums*, 125.

80. Ann L. Buttenwieser, "Shelter for What and for Whom? On the Route towards Vladeck Houses, 1930 to 1940," *Journal of Urban History* 12, no. 4 (1986), 401.

81. Abraham Kazan, "Reminiscences of Abraham Kazan," 1968, p. 284, Oral History Archives, Columbia University.

82. New York State Board of Housing, *Report of the State Board of Housing* (New York: J. B. Lyon, 1933), 11.

83. Catherine Bauer, *Modern Housing* (New York: Houghton Mifflin, 1934), xvi.

84. Vladeck, "The Housing Movement Today."

85. "Smith Cites Work of Port Authority," *New York Times*, March 6, 1926, 24; Norman Thomas and Paul Blanshard, *What's the Matter with New York: A National Problem* (New York: Macmillan, 1932), 260; Clarence Stein, "Housing and Common Sense," *The Nation*, May 11, 1932, 543.

86. A. Scott Henderson, *Housing and the Democratic Ideal: The Life and Thought of Charles Abrams* (New York: Columbia University Press 2000), 71.

87. Abrams, *Revolution in Land*, 293.

88. For more on the early history of the New York City Housing Authority, see Bloom, *Public Housing That Worked*.

89. Housing Authority v. Muller, 270 N.Y. 333, 1 N.E. (2d) 153 (1936).

90. Schwartz, "Tenement Renewal in New York City in the 1930s," 295.

91. Nathan Straus, *Low-Cost Housing Here and Abroad: Report to Mayor La Guardia* (New York: Nathan Straus, 1935), 26.

92. New York City Housing Authority, *Fifth Annual Report*, 1939, 2, Box 98, Folder 2, New York City Housing Authority Collection, La Guardia and Wagner Archives, New York.

93. Straus, *Low-Cost Housing Here and Abroad*, 343.

94. New York City Housing Authority, *Clason Point Gardens, Bronx, New York* (New York: New York City Housing Authority, 1942), 4.

95. See "Realty Board Reports Sharp Increase in Vacancies," *New York Times*, March 17, 1943.

96. Langdon W. Post, *The Challenge of Housing* (New York: Farrar & Rinehart, 1938), 292.

97. "Text of Rheinstein and Straws Letters," *New York Times*, October 9, 1939, 10.

98. "Housing Project for Brownsville Seen Near at Hand," *Brooklyn Daily Eagle*, June 10, 1941, 17.

99. "Housing Public Hearing," April 6, 1935, Box 408, Folder 7, Fiorello La Guardia Subject Files, New York Hall of Records, New York.

100. Post, *The Challenge of Housing*, 38.

101. Cleveland Rodgers, *New York Plans for the Future* (New York: Harper & Brothers, 1943), 225.

102. Editorial, *Brooklyn Daily Eagle*, February 8, 1934, 10.

103. Robert Louis Hoguet, "The Land Tax Illusion: Fiscal Factor in Rise and Fall of Municipal Empires," *Trusts and Estates* 75 (August 1942), 117.

104. Colin Gordon, "Blighting the Way: Urban Renewal, Economic Development, and the Elusive Definition of Blight," *Fordham Urban Law Journal* 31, no. 2 (2004), 305.

105. "Housing Public Hearing," April 6, 1935, Box 408, Folder 7, Fiorello La Guardia Subject Files, New York Hall of Records, New York.

106. "Housing Public Hearing," New York Hall of Records.

107. Clarence Stein, "The Future of New York," Box 5, Folder 52, Clarence Stein Collection, Division of Rare and Manuscript Collections, Cornell University, New York; Bauer, "Cities in Flux," 84.

108. Curl, *For All the People*, 174.

109. Mumford, *The Culture of Cities*, 325.

110. Mumford, 297.

Chapter 6

1. Anne Juppe to Fiorello La Guardia, October 24, 1934, Box 295, Folder 5, Subject Files, Mayor La Guardia Papers, New York Hall of Records, New York.

2. Anne Juppe to Fiorello La Guardia, November 24, 1934, Box 295, Folder 5, Subject Files, Mayor La Guardia Papers, New York Hall of Records, New York.

3. James S. Taylor to Phillip Cornick, January 23, 1941, 2, Box 6, Phillip H. Cornick Papers, Division of Rare and Manuscript Collections, Cornell University Library, Ithaca, New York.

4. City Planning Commission, *Annual Report of the City Planning Commission* (New York, 1939), 23.

5. See Williams, *City of Ambition*, 370; Jason Scott Smith, *Building New Deal Liberalism: The Political Economy of Public Works, 1933–1956* (Cambridge: Cambridge University Press, 2006); John Joseph Wallis, "The Birth of the Old Federalism: Financing the New Deal, 1932–1940," *Journal of Economic History* 44, no. 1 (1984). While other scholars have criticized national New Deal programs for rewarding local private interests, I seek to emphasize the perceived *fiscal* costs of such aid on New York during the 1930s..

6. Maggor, *Brahmin Capitalism*, 370.

7. Rexford Tugwell, "Implementing the General Interest," *Public Administration Review* 1, no. 1 (1940), 36.

8. Ackerman, "Our Stake in Congestion," 142.

9. Harold S. Buttenheim, "If Henry George Were Writing Today," *Journal of Land and Public Utility Economics* 11, no. 1 (1935), 8. This suspicion was confirmed during a 1943 radio program discussing "unearned increments" in land speculation, when New York's comptroller admitted

that "we do not attempt to recapture that increment, but rather to use that increment as a basis for a higher current tax." See "On the Merits of Henry George's Progress and Poverty," Invitation to Learning Radio Program, February 28, 1943, https://cooperative-individualism.org/gideonse -harry_roundtable-on-henry-george-1943-apr-may.pdf.

10. Tugwell, "The Sources of New Deal Reformism," 255.

11. Tugwell, "Implementing the General Interest," 42.

12. "New York in the Long Run," *New York Times*, March 26, 1940, 16.

13. William H. Allen, *Why Tammanies Revive: La Guardias Mis-guard* (New York: Institute for Public Service, 1937), 92.

14. Citizens Budget Commission, *Report on the Master Plan of Land Use*, 14.

15. James Walker, "Speech—Budget," July 22, 1932, 7, Box 50, Folder 613, Subject Files, James Walker Collection, City Hall Library, New York.

16. Raymond Ingersoll, "Speech," October 3, 1935, Box 5, Raymond Ingersoll Papers, Brooklyn Collection, Brooklyn Public Library, 2; "3 Associates Defy Mayor on Economy," *New York Times*, October 13, 1938, 21; Records of Public Hearings and Minutes, p. 3, New York Public Library Milstein Division.

17. Raymond Ingersoll, "Speech," Raymond Ingersoll Papers, Center for Brooklyn History, Brooklyn Public Library; "3 Associates Defy Mayor on Economy," *New York Times*.

18. City Planning Commission, *Annual Report of the City Planning Commission and the Department of City Planning*, 28.

19. Tugwell, "Implementing the General Interest," 45.

20. Gelfand, "Rexford G. Tugwell and the Frustration of Planning in New York City," 155.

21. Citizens Budget Commission, *Report on the Master Plan of Land Use*, 14.

22. Edwin Thatcher, "Meeting of the Citizen's Housing Council," December 19, 1940, Folder 8, Box 7, Master Plan for the City of New York, Brooklyn Collection, Brooklyn College Library, New York.

23. Robert A. M. Stern, David Fishman, and Thomas Mellins, *New York 1960: Architecture and Urbanism between the Second World War and the Bicentennial* (New York: Monacelli Press, 1997), 13.

24. City Planning Commission, *Report Accompanying 1942 Capital Budget and 1943–47 Capital Program* (New York: City Planning Commission, 1941), 10.

25. Editorial, *Queens Evening News*, November 27, 1941, 5.

26. Rodgers, *New York Plans for the Future*, 110, 116.

27. Louis Lyons, "Public Housing: U. S. Brings Private Finance to Building Government as Middleman," *Daily Boston Globe*, November 15, 1939, 5.

28. Post, *The Challenge of Housing*, 292.

29. Lyons, "Public Housing," 5.

30. "Realty Board Reports Sharp Increase in Vacancies," *New York Times*.

31. Letter from Arthur Holden to Institutional Securities Corps., February 16, 1935, Box 20, Folder 6, Arthur Curt Holden Papers, Manuscript Division, Department of Special Collections, Princeton University Library, Princeton, New Jersey.

32. Kazan, "Reminiscences of Abraham Kazan," 1968, 86, Oral History Archives, Columbia University.

33. Williams, *City of Ambition*, 187.

34. Arthur Holden, *The Financial Plight of the City of New York: A Plea for Creative Financial Thinking Respecting the Growing Menace of Overhead Costs* (New York: self-pub., 1976), 54.

35. Commission on Money and Credit, *Life Insurance Companies as Financial Institutions* (Englewood Cliffs, NJ: Prentice-Hall, 1962), 2, 20.

36. Letter from Charles Abram to Governor Dewey, April 3, 1943, Bill Jacket, L. 1943 c. 234, New York State Archives, Albany, New York; Letter from Jackob Mark to Governor Dewey, Bill Jacket, L. 1943 c. 234, New York State Archives, Albany, New York.

37. Letter from Harold Buttenheim to Governor Dewey, March 10, 1943, Bill Jacket, L. 1943 c. 234, New York State Archives, Albany, New York; Letter from Charles Abram to Governor Dewey, New York State Archives.

38. Letter from Ira S. Robbins to Governor Dewey, March 6, 1943, Bill Jacket, L. 1943 c. 234, New York State Archives, Albany, New York; Letter from Harold Buttenheim to Governor Dewey, New York State Archives; Letter from Greater New York Industrial Union Council to Governor Dewey, April 10, 1941, Bill Jacket, L. 1941 c. 89, New York State Archives, Albany, New York; Edward Weinfeld, "New York's Housing Plans: Threat to the Public Interest Seen in Proposed Changes in Law," *New York Times*, April 2, 1943, 20. Perhaps the clearest evidence of continuity between pre- and post-Depression developmental strategies in New York was in the person of George McAneny. For thirty years, McAneny had promoted the "highest and best" use of private land: advocating for the Dual Contracts of 1913 as Manhattan borough president, pressing for the zoning laws of 1916 as president of New York's Board of Aldermen, serving as president of the Regional Plan Association of New York, and supporting the Banker's Agreements as New York's comptroller. And now, in the early 1940s, McAneny wholeheartedly— and revealingly—endorsed the Redevelopment Laws. For, in addition to accruing civic capital, McAneny was also accruing realty capital as both chairman of the Title Guarantee and Trust Company of New York and director of the City Real Estate Company. In a 1942 speech to the New York State Title Association, he admitted that redevelopment policies would give the "business" of urban "replacements"—"which, let us frankly admit, has furnished as an institution and as a practice, a great deal of our current business"—a "new impetus." "Our own part in it," he hoped, "will be, I trust, not only a helpful but a profitable one." Civic virtue, apparently, would have its rewards. Minutes of the New York Title Association, April 10, 1942, Box 2, "Miscellaneous Speeches," George McAneny Papers, Mudd Manuscript Library, Princeton, New Jersey.

39. "Benefits Are Seen in State . . . Merchants Committee Explains," *New York Times*, February 2, 1941; Letter from Bowery Savings Bank and Dry Dock Savings Bank to Governor Lehman, March 7, 1941, Bill Jacket, L. 1941 c. 89, New York State Archives, Albany, New York; Thomas C. Desmond, "Blighted Areas Get a New Chance," *National Municipal Review* 30, no. 11 (1941), 630.

40. Bronx Chamber of Commerce to Governor Dewey, March 26, 1941, Bill Jacket, L. 1941 c. 89, New York State Archives, Albany, New York.

41. Harold R. Sleeper, *A Realistic Approach to Private Investment in Urban Redevelopment Applied to East Harlem as a Blighted Area . . . under the Direction of the Manhattan Development Committee* (New York: Architectural Forum, 1945), 48.

42. For more on political movements against the more radical elements of the New Deal, see Alan Brinkley, *The End of Reform: New Deal Liberalism in Recession and War* (New York: Vintage Books, 1995).

43. See Cebul and Williams, "Revisiting the Question of Federalism"; Timothy Shenk, "Inventing the American Economy," in *Capitalism Contested: The New Deal and Its Legacies*, ed. Romain Huret, Nelson Lichtenstein, and Jean-Christian Vinel (Philadelphia: University of Pennsylvania Press, 2020); Andrew L. Yarrow, *Measuring America: How Economic Growth Came*

to Define American Greatness in the Late Twentieth Century (Amherst: University of Massachusetts Press, 2010).

44. Tugwell, "The Real Estate Dilemma," 32.

45. See Theodore Rosenof, *Economics in the Long Run: New Deal Theorists and Their Legacies, 1933–1993* (Chapel Hill: University of North Carolina Press, 2000).

46. United States Conference of Mayors, *City Problems of 1936* (WI: George Banta, 1936), 12.

47. US Conference of Mayors, "Memorandum for Honorable F.H. La Guardia," December 27, 1934, Box 1, Folder 11, United States Conference of Mayors Series, Fiorello La Guardia Papers, New York Hall of Records, New York, emphasis in original.

48. Cebul, *Illusions of Progress*, 35.

49. Jesse H. Jones, *Real Estate's Importance in Recovery* (Washington, DC: National Capital Press, 1935), 5.

50. Frederick Ackerman, "Our Stake in Congestion," *Survey Graphic* 54, no. 1 (1925), 142.

51. Lloyd Rowdin, "Land Economics in the United States," *Town Planning Review* 21, no. 2 (1950), 172.

52. In this respect, the story of New York's federal assistance both aligns with and revises Daniel Rodgers's approach toward New Deal-era statecraft—rather than pick up policy alternatives in the wake of the Crash, many policymakers insisted that inherited local policies simply be "federalized." See Rodgers, *Atlantic Crossings*, 414.

53. United States Conference of Mayors, *City Problems of 1935* (WI: George Banta, 1935), 23.

54. John D. Millett, *The Works Progress Administration in New York City* (Chicago: Public Administration Service, 1938), 249.

55. Ernest Kerpen to Fiorello La Guardia, June 4, 1936, Box 60, Folder 1, Fiorello La Guardia Departmental Correspondence, New York Hall of Records, New York.

56. Ernest Kerpen to Fiorello La Guardia, 206.

57. Rexford Tugwell, "When the USHA Buys Land," *New Republic*, October 25, 1939, 341–342.

58. City Planning Commission, *Report Accompanying 1942 Capital Budget and 1943–47 Capital Program*, 10; Bird, "Cities and Their Debt Burdens," 16.

59. Robert Caro, *The Power Broker* (New York: Knopf, 1975), 641.

60. "Urged by Wagner: Senator Would Link Sale of Mortgage-Relief Bonds to Campaign of NRA," *New York Times*, August 28, 1933, 27; Home Owners and Taxpayers Association of Staten Island to Fiorello La Guardia, October 10, 1934, Box 295, Folder 5, Fiorello La Guardia Papers, New York Hall of Records, New York; United States Conference of Mayors, *City Problems of 1936* (WI: George Banta, 1936), 14; Letter from Anne Juppe to Fiorello La Guardia, November 24, 1934, Box 295, Folder 5, Mayor La Guardia Papers, New York Hall of Records, New York.

61. "First General Meeting Minutes," March 21, 1934, Box 295, Folder 5, Mayor La Guardia Papers, New York Hall of Records, New York; "Progress Report from the Federal Home Loan Bank of Newark," December 9, 1932, Box 295, Folder 5, Mayor La Guardia Papers, New York Hall of Records, New York.

62. Post, *The Challenge of Housing*, 247.

63. Tugwell, "Implementing the General Interest," 41. At the same time, federal aid did not lessen the necessity of the local state to maintain and raise revenue from its own resources—which in New York City remained the property tax. Housing reformer Charles Abrams noted the potential political consequences of this unstable division of fiscal labor, stating that "the present plan under which federal government advances the subsidies or lends its credit, while the benefits of the credit are neutralized by the local governments in the form of taxation and

restrictions, simply makes no sense." By the late 1930s, his prediction had come true: even as lo-cal taxpayers embraced the New Deal state's transfers and subsidies during the 1930s, they chafed and militated against the local iteration of this state for raising levies during the late 1930s. In this respect, the "decline" of the New Deal coalition after the 1940s can be partially traced to the divi-sion of fiscal labor between federal and local states established in the 1930s—just as the "urban crisis" of the 1960s and 1970s was not only the result of conservative tax revolts or the decline of property values in the postwar era but rather of inequitable and unsustainable patterns of publicly promoted growth established many decades earlier. See Abrams, "New Social Trends in Land Utilization," 344. For classic accounts of the rise and decline of the "New Deal Coalition," see Brinkley, *The End of Reform*, and Jefferson Cowie, *The Great Exception: The New Deal and the Limits of American Politics* (Princeton, NJ: Princeton University Press, 2016), 344.

64. The new construction prompted by the FHA also hiked tax assessments on the city's older districts, further entrenching the "vicious cycle" of urban growth identified by RPAA members earlier. One property owner at a 1940 Tax Commission meeting lamented that "one-family houses financed under the FHA in Queens are being sold on statements by the builders that the assessed valuation of the property will be about 80% of the sales price," whereas "the older house, still a perfectly good and livable house, is being sold, say at $3300, with an assessed valuation of $4,300 (or 130% of sales price)." Such new construction with a lighter tax load, he charged, was "considerably accelerating the decentralization trend in the city." See Joint Legisla-tive Committee on Assessing and Reviewing of the State of New York, *Final Report*, 103.

65. Federal Housing Administration, *A Handbook on Urban Redevelopment for Cities in the United States* (Washington, DC: US Government Printing Office, 1941); Guy Greer and Alvin H. Hansen, *Urban Redevelopment and Housing* (Washington, DC: National Planning Association, 1941).

66. Henderson, *Housing and the Democratic Ideal*, 100.

67. Frederic Delano to Phillip Cornick, July 24, 1941, p. 2, Box 5, Phillip H. Cornick Papers, Division of Rare and Manuscript Collections, Cornell University Library, Ithaca, New York.

68. Robert Fogelson, *Downtown: Its Rise and Fall, 1880–1950* (New Haven, CT: Yale Univer-sity Press, 2008), 373.

69. Alexander Von Hoffman, "The Lost History of Urban Renewal," *Journal of Urbanism: International Research on Placemaking and Urban Sustainability* 1, no. 3 (2008): 281–301.

70. Bird, "Cities and Their Debt Burdens," 16.

71. Fuchs, *Mayors and Money*, 132, 169.

72. Fuchs, 157.

73. Robert Moses, "Report to the Mayor, Board of Estimate, City Planning Commission and City Council by the City Construction Coordinator on Progress and Proposed Revision in the Program of Essential Postwar Public Improvements, New York City," April 15, 1946, 34, City Hall Library, New York.

74. Moses.

75. Moses, 4.

76. Haig, *The Financial Problem of the City of New York: A Report to the Mayor's Committee on Management Survey: General Summary Volume of the Finance Project* (New York: Mayor's Committee on Management Survey of the City of New York, 1952), 308.

77. Robert Murray Haig, *The Financial Problem of the City of New York*, 136–138; Citizens' Housing and Planning Council of New York, *Tax Policies and Urban Renewal in New York City: A Report on a Tax Study with Recommendations* (New York: Citizens' Housing and Planning

Council of New York, 1960), 17; Warren Moscow, *Politics in the Empire State* (New York: Greenwood Books, 1948), 339.

78. Thomas Bender, *The Unfinished City: New York and the Metropolitan Idea* (New York: New York University Press, 2002).

79. See Brinkley, *The End of Reform*.

80. Macekura, *The Mismeasure of Progress*, 40.

81. Norton E. Long, "Have Cities a Future?," *Public Administration Review* 33, no. 6 (1973), 544.

82. See Beauregard, *Voices of Decline*, esp. chaps. 5–8.

83. Bender, *The Unfinished City*, 215.

84. Long, "Have Cities a Future?," 552.

85. Berry, *Why New York City Can Never Become Bankrupt*, 14.

86. Charles White Berry, *Financial Problems of the City of New York* (New York: Office of the Comptroller, 1933), 1.

87. Louis Heaton Pink, "Reminiscences of Louis Heaton Pink," 1949, p. 684, Oral History Archives, Columbia University; Urban Land Institute, *A Proposal for Rebuilding Blighted City Areas* (Washington, DC: Urban Land Institute, 1943), 3.

88. Urban Land Institute, *Decentralization: What Is It Doing to Our Cities?* (Chicago: Urban Land Institute, 1940), 1.

89. Greer and Hansen, *Urban Redevelopment and Housing*, 5.

90. James S. Taylor to Phillip Cornick, Cornell University Library.

91. For more material on the changing meaning of the term *blight*, see Gordon, "Blighting the Way," 30; Daniel M. Abramson, *Obsolescence: An Architectural History* (Chicago: University of Chicago, 2016).

92. Charles Abrams, "Stuyvesant Town's Threat to Our Liberties," *Commentary*, November 1949. https://www.commentary.org/articles/charles-abrams/stuyvesant-towns-threat-to-our-liberties government-waives-the-constitution-for-private-enterprise/.

93. Guy Greer, "Getting Ready for Federal Aid in Urban Redevelopment," *American City* 58 (May 1943), 48.

Chapter 7

1. J. Austin White, *An Analysis of Municipal Bonds* (Cincinnati: J. A. White, 1942), 8.

2. White.

3. Freeman, *Working-Class New York*, 168.

4. Frederick M. Babcock, *The Valuation of Real Estate* (New York: McGraw Hill, 1932), 129; Urban Land Institute, *A Proposal for Rebuilding Blighted City Areas*; Henry E. Reed, "The True Value of Real Estate," *Journal of the American Institute of Real Estate Appraisers* 3, no. 4 (1935), 342; Jones, *Real Estate's Importance in Recovery*, 5; Hoguet, "The Land Tax Illusion," 117; Arthur C. Holden, "The Crisis in Real Estate," *Harper's Magazine*, November 1931, 676; Karl Scholz, "The Valuation of Real Estate," *Annals of the American Academy of Political and Social Science* 169 (September 1933), 219. For a broader history of municipal bonds and credit during this era, see Destin Jenkins, *The Bonds of Inequality: Debt and the Making of the American City* (Chicago: University of Chicago Press, 2021).

5. See Tracy Neumann, *Remaking the Rust Belt: The Postindustrial Transformation of North America* (Philadelphia: University of Pennsylvania Press, 2019); Fitch, *The Assassination of New*

York; Shannan Clark, *The Making of the American Creative Class: New York's Culture Workers and Twentieth Century Consumer Capitalism* (New York: Oxford University Press, 2021).

6. To be sure, scattered economists such as Alfred Marshall and August Losch had considered the growth of cities in terms of agglomeration economics and international trade earlier. But these works were rarely incorporated into the work of American urban economists until the postwar era, when they were incorporated into the work of land economists like Homer Hoyt and regional economists like Walter Isard. See Edwin S. Mills, "A Thematic History of Urban Economic Analysis," *Brookings-Wharton Papers on Urban Affairs*, 2000, 1–38; Harvey S. Perloff, "The Development of Urban Economics in the United States," *Urban Studies* 10 (1973): 289–301.

7. Robert Murray Haig, "Toward an Understanding of the Metropolis," *Quarterly Journal of Economics* 40, no. 2 (1926), 181–182.

8. National Resources Committee, *Our Cities*, 63.

9. Reed, "The True Value of Real Estate," 342.

10. For more on how the Depression shifted thinking among larger realty investors and building owners during this time, see Fogelson, *Downtown*, esp. chap. 5.

11. Hoguet, "The Land-Tax Illusion," 40; Real Estate Analysis, *Real Estate Trends in New York City: With Special Emphasis on the Island of Manhattan* (Saint Louis, MO: Real Estate Analysis, October 1942), 2; Abrams, *Revolution in Land*, 29.

12. Herbert S. Swan, *New York City's Debt and Future Capital Outlays* (New York: Institute of Public Administration, 1943), 78.

13. Barr, *Building the Skyline*, 316–318.

14. See Cornick, "The Real Estate Tax."

15. Reed, "The True Value of Real Estate," 343.

16. Urban Land Institute, *A Proposal for Rebuilding Blighted City Areas*, 6. For more on influence of the Urban Land Institute on urban redevelopment theory and practice, see Sara Stevens, *Developing Expertise: Architecture and Real Estate in Metropolitan America* (New Haven, CT: Yale University Press, 2016).

17. Basil C. Rose, "Appraising Municipal Credit: II. The Economic Background," *Bankers' Magazine* 136 (March 1938), 198; White, *An Analysis of Municipal Bonds*, 7.

18. Tugwell, "The Real Estate Dilemma," 27.

19. Rodgers, *New York Plans for the Future*, 51.

20. Rodgers, 51.

21. National Resources Committee, *Our Cities*, 63. To be sure, scattered economists such as Alfred Marshall and August Losch had considered the growth of cities in terms of agglomeration economics and international trade earlier. But these works were rarely incorporated into the theories of American land economists until the postwar, when they were supplemented by the work of Homer Hoyt and Walter Isard. See Mills, "A Thematic History of Urban Economic Analysis."

22. Robert H. Armstrong and Homer Hoyt, *Decentralization in New York: Preliminary Report to Urban Land Institute* (Chicago: Urban Land Institute, January 1941), 10. While references to an urban "economic base" existed prior to Hoyt's work, his was among the first to develop a formal methodology for studying it. See Richard B. Andrews, "Mechanics of the Urban Economic Base: Historical Development of the Base Concept," *Land Economics* 29, no. 2 (1953), 163.

23. Regional Plan Association of New York, *The Economic Status of the New York Region* (New York: Regional Plan Association, 1944), 16, 3.

24. Armstrong and Hoyt, *Decentralization in New York*, 12–14.

25. Homer Hoyt, "Economic Background of Cities," *Journal of Land and Public Utility Economics* 17, no. 2 (1941), 188.

26. Andrew C. Krikelas, "Why Regions Grow: A Review of Research on the Economic Base Model," *Economic Review* 77, no. 4 (1992), 20.

27. Richard U. Ratcliff, review of *The Economic Status of the New York Region*, by Homer Hoyt, *Journal of Political Economy* 54, no. 3 (1947): 382–333.

28. Charles S. Ascher, review of *The Economic Status of the New York Metropolitan Region in 1944*, by Homer Hoyt, *American Journal of Sociology* 51, no. 4 (1946), 355.

29. Harrison, Ballard & Allen, *Plan for the Rezoning of New York City: Framework for Rezoning: Economic Base* (New York: publisher not identified, 1949); John R. White and Edna L. Herbert, *The Manhattan Housing Market: A Study Prepared for the Urban Renewal Board* (New York: Brown, Harris, Stevens, 1960); New York State Office for Regional Development, *Change, Challenge, Response: A Development Policy for New York State* (Albany, NY: Office for Regional Development, 1964).

30. Frederick M. Babcock, "Influence of the Federal Housing Administration on Mortgage Lending Policy," *Journal of Land and Public Utility Economics* 15 (February 1939), 4.

31. Rose, "Appraising Municipal Credit," 199.

32. Armstrong and Hoyt, *Decentralization in New York*, 12–14.

33. Jenkins, *The Bonds of Inequality*.

34. George W. Wood, *The Growth of New York* (New York: George W. Wood, 1865), 17. See also Frederick L. Olmsted, "The Future of New York," in *Frederick Law Olmsted: Writings on Landscape, Culture and Society Essential Texts*, ed. Charles Beveridge (Washington, DC: Library of America, 2010).

35. For more on the history of debates over New York City's port and its development, see Jameson W. Doig, *Empire on the Hudson: Entrepreneurial Vision and Political Power at the Port of New York Authority* (New York: Columbia University Press, 2001).

36. Haig, *Major Economic Factors in Metropolitan Growth and Arrangement*.

37. Haig, "Toward an Understanding of the Metropolis," 427.

38. Haig, 428, 430.

39. Haig, 428.

40. Herbert Agar, *Land of the Free* (Boston: Houghton Mifflin, 1935), 132.

41. Mumford, *The Culture of Cities*, 296.

42. City Planning Commission, *Minutes of Meeting of City Planning Commission*, 889.

43. Bauer, "Cities in Flux," 84.

44. Bankers Trust, *New York and the Future* (New York: Bankers Trust, 1946), 8.

45. Aaron Shkuda, "Housing the 'Front Office to the World': Urban Planning for the Service Economy in Battery Park City, New York," *Journal of Planning History* 13, no. 3 (2013), 238.

46. Victor Perlo, *The Empire of High Finance* (Ann Arbor: University of Michigan Press, 1957), 33.

47. Suleiman Osman, *The Invention of Brownstone Brooklyn: Gentrification and the Search for Authenticity in Postwar New York* (New York: Oxford University Press, 2011), 65. This linkage between realty growth and financial expansion was not entirely predicted: the Bankers Trust volume *New York and the Future*, for example, predicted that the postwar city would not witness "a renewal of the spectacular building boom of the past," but rather an "adaptation" of its existing physical plant toward the needs of its "financial operations" and their employees. Both, in the end, would occur. Bankers Trust, *New York and the Future*, 8.

48. Steve Lohr, "Raymond Vernon, a Shaper of Global Trade, Dies at 85," *New York Times*, August 28, 1999, B7.

49. Paul F. Wendt, "Influence of Transportation Changes on Urban Land Uses and Values." *HRB Bulletin* 268 (1960), 95–96.

50. Fiorenza Belussi and Katia Caldari, "At the Origin of the Industrial District: Alfred Marshall and the Cambridge School," *Cambridge Journal of Economics* 33, no. 2 (2009): 335–355.

51. Raymond Vernon, *The Changing Economic Function of the Central City* (New York: Area Development Committee of the CED, 1959), 30. See also Raymond Vernon, "Production and Distribution in the Large Metropolis," *Annals of the American Academy of Political and Social Sciences* 314, no. 1 (1957): 15–29.

52. Raymond Vernon, *The Changing Economic Function of the Central City*, 30.

53. Raymond Vernon, *The Myth and Reality of Our Urban Problems* (Cambridge, MA: Harvard University Press, 1966), 37.

54. George H. Deming, review of *Metropolis 1958: An Interpretation of the Findings of the New York Metropolitan Region Study*, by Raymond Vernon, *National Civic Review* 50, no. 2 (1961), 114.

55. Stern, Fishman, and Mellins, *New York 1960*, 63.

56. Armstrong and Hoyt, *Decentralization in New York*, 10; Harland Bartholomew, *The Present and Ultimate Effect of Decentralization upon American Cities* (Chicago: Urban Land Institute, 1940), 3.

57. Robert Wagner, "Speech—New York as the World's Financial Center," February 29, 1956, p. 5, Box 060074W, Folder 37, Speeches Series, Robert F. Wagner Documents Collections, City Hall Library, New York.

58. Robert F. Wagner, "Address by the Hon. Robert F. Wager, Mayor, the City of New York before the Committee for Modern Zoning" (New York: printing privately donated, 1960), 4.

59. City Planning Commission, *Port of New York, Proposals for Development* (New York: City Planning Commission, 1964), 22.

60. Freeman, *Working-Class New York*, 4.

61. Charles E. Murphy, *Report to Hon. Frank J. Taylor Comptroller of the City of New York on Industrial Survey of New York City*, June 30, 1937, 6, City Hall Library, Hall of Records, New York NY.

62. "City Will Set Up a 'Booster' Bureau: Mayor Reveals Plans for New," *New York Times*, November 30, 1939, 1.

63. John I. Griffin, *Industrial Location in the New York Area* (New York: City College Press, 1956), 4.

64. Freeman, *Working-Class New York*, 143.

65. Griffin, *Industrial Location in the New York Area*, 10.

66. Letter from Frank. J. Connaughton, First Deputy Commissioner and Director of Commerce, May 8, 1952, Box 302, "Chamber of Commerce" Folder, Mayor Impellitteri Subject File Collection, New York Hall of Records, New York; "Duggan Tells How to Use Development Funds," *New York City Department of Commerce and Public Events Highlights*, December 1957, 4.

67. New York State Commission on Governmental Operations of the City of New York, *New York City in Transition* (Albany: publisher not identified, 1960), 71.

68. One of the most frequently cited reasons manufacturers provided for leaving New York was the cost of land and lack of space (the latter being one of the consequences of the former). See Fitch, 99–100.

69. Thomas Adams, *The Building of the City: Regional Plan of New York and Its Environs* (New York: Regional Plan Association, 1931), 2:170.

70. Joseph D. McGoldrick, "Blueprints for a Greater New York," *New York Times*, April 30, 1944, SM16.

71. Harrison Ballard, *Plan for Rezoning the City of New York: A Report Submitted to the City Planning Commission* (Ann Arbor: University of Michigan, 1950), 20.

72. Joel Schwartz, *The New York Approach: Robert Moses, Urban Liberals, and Redevelopment of the Inner City* (Columbus: Ohio State University Press, 1993), 238.

73. Letter from Stanley Miller to Fiorello La Guardia, New York Hall of Records.

74. Correspondence from J. S. Satterthwaite, Jr. to William Reid, May 14, 1948, Box 149, Folder 157, Subject Files, Mayor O'Dwyer Mayoral Collection, New York Hall of Records, New York.

75. Citizens' Housing and Planning Council of New York, *Tax Policies and Urban Renewal in New York City*, 17; Moody, *From Welfare State to Real Estate*, 58.

76. Adams, *The Building of the City*, 202.

77. "Banks Push White Collar Housing," *Business Week*, January 20, 1940, 30.

78. McGoldrick, "Blueprints for a Greater New York."

79. Anthony J. Panuch, *Building a Better New York: Final Report to the Mayor Robert F. Wagner* (New York: n.p., 1960), 16, italics in original.

80. White and Hebard, *The Manhattan Housing Market*, 152, 103.

81. Wendell E. Pritchett, *Brownsville, Brooklyn: Blacks, Jews, and the Changing Face of the Ghetto* (Chicago: University of Chicago Press, 2002), 121.

82. See Derek S. Hyra, "Conceptualizing the New Urban Renewal: Comparing the Past to the Present," *Urban Affairs Review* 48, no. 4 (2012), 503.

83. Vernon, *The Myth and Reality of Our Urban Problems*, 72.

84. Daniel Bell, "The Three Faces of New York," *Dissent* 8 (Summer 1961), 223.

85. New York State Commission on Governmental Operations of the City of New York, *New York City in Transition*, 71.

86. New York State Commission on Governmental Operations of the City of New York, 145.

87. "City Claims Title of Office Capital," *New York Times*, November 7, 1956, 39.

88. See Cebul, *Illusions of Progress*; Yarrow, *Measuring America*; Schmelzer, *The Hegemony of Growth*; Lizbeth Cohen, *A Consumer's Republic: The Politics of Mass Consumption in Postwar America* (New York: Knopf, 2008).

89. For more on the conflict between "qualitative liberals" such as John Kenneth Galbraith and Arthur Schleisinger Jr., versus "quantitative liberals" like Leon Keyserling in the postwar era, see Scott Kamen, *From Union Halls to the Suburbs: Americans for Democratic Action and the Transformation of Postwar Liberalism* (Amherst: University of Massachusetts Press, 2023), esp. chapter 1, "The Origins of a Liberal Divide: Debating the Politics of Growth and Qualitative Liberalism in the Affluent Society," 17–58.

90. See Larry Ceplaire, *Anti-Communism in Twentieth-Century America: A Critical History* (New York: Bloomsbury Publishing, 2011).

91. Bell, "The Three Faces of New York," 230.

92. See Marc Stears, *Progressives, Pluralists, and the Problems of the State*, particularly chapter 2, "Building the New Nationalism," 52–87. While scholarly work on the urban economic thought of American socialists and Marxists before the 1940s is not well-developed (except in the case of public utility ownership), Robin Murray's studies can provide an excellent starting point for beginning comparative research. See Robin Murray, "Small Scale Enterprise in the Economic Thought of the British Left," Conference Paper, October 15 and 16, 1990. https://static1.square space.com/static/5bc8924fb9144917ed082349/t/5e1ccc5d35c2516f71b783b0/1578945645932

/SMALL+SCALE+ENTERPRISE+IN+THE+ECONOMIC+THOUGHT+OF+THE+BRITISH +LEFT.pdf (accessed April 4, 2023).

93. Norman Thomas, *What's the Matter with New York: A National Problem*, 318. For a broader history of municipal socialism during this period, see Shelton Stromquist, *Claiming the City: A Global History of Workers' Fight for Municipal Socialism* (London: Verso, 2023).

94. Similarly, New York's labor unions strove mightily to build a "social-democratic" array of social services and even cooperative housing in the interwar era through initiatives like worker-run health care, banking, and housing enterprises. Most unions, however, pursued their activism for securing improved benefits and conditions within their workplaces—and what postwar cooperative business were developed did not appreciably hold back New York's white collar transformation during this time (much like the postwar welfare state, as we shall see). For more on workers' cooperative initiatives before and after World War 2, see Fogelson, *Working-Class Utopias* and Freeman, *Working-Class New York*. For work on ambitious efforts by garment workers to co-manage their trades in the 1900s and 1910s, see Richard Greenwald, *The Triangle Fire, The Protocols of Peace, and Industrial Democracy in Progressive Era New York* (Philadelphia: Temple University Press, 2011).

95. For more on how elements of the postwar left like Michael Harrington embraced elements of "postindustrial" thought, see Howard Brick, *Transcending Capitalism: Visions of a New Society in Modern American Thought* (Ithaca, NY: Cornell University Press, 2016). See also Nils Gilman, *Mandarins of the Future: Modernization Theory in Cold War America* (Baltimore: Johns Hopkins University Press, 2003).

96. Bell, "The Three Faces of New York," 227.

97. White and Hebard, *The Manhattan Housing Market*, 152.

98. Robert Friedman, "Pirates and Politicians: Sinking on the Same Ship," *Working Papers for A New Society* 4, no. 1 (1976), 57.

99. "Topics of the Times," *New York Times*, June 21, 1955, 30.

100. Max R. Bloom, "Fiscal Productivity and the Pure Theory of Urban Renewal," *Land Economics* 38, no. 2 (1962), 135; Robert Moore Fisher, "Public Costs of Urban Renewal," *Journal of Finance* 5, no. 2 (1962), 385.

101. Martin Anderson, *The Federal Bulldozer: A Critical Analysis of Urban Renewal 1949–1962* (Cambridge: MIT Press, 1964), 221.

102. Daniel Friedenberg, "Real Estate Confidential," *Dissent* 8 (1961), 260. And at least some planners evinced a broader discomfort with their profession's growth-orientation: as one satirical volume penned by two planners noted, "Many lay planners are of the opinion that growth and more growth is the solution to our urban problem. The logic behind this idea is obvious, only more growth will supply the tax money needed to solve the problems created by past growth." Richard Hedman and Fred Bair, Jr., *And on the Eighth Day . . . The Last Word on City Planning and Planners by Hedman and Bair* (Philadelphia: Falcon Press, 1967), 8.

103. Peter Ekman, "From Prophecy to Projection: The Metropolitan Region Study and the Rescaling of the Urban Future, 1956–1968," *Planning Perspectives* 36, no. 1 (2021), 19.

104. Vernon, *The Myth and Reality of Our Urban Problems*, 53–54.

Chapter 8

1. Jane Jacobs, *The Death and Life of Great American Cities* (New York: Random House, 2003), 282.

2. See Peter Laurence, *Becoming Jane Jacobs* (Philadelphia: University of Pennsylvania Press, 2016); Dirk Schubert, ed., *Contemporary Perspectives on Jane Jacobs: Reassessing the Impacts of an Urban Visionary* (New York: Routledge, 2014); Roberto Rocco, ed., *Jane Jacobs Is Still Here: Jane Jacobs 100, Her Legacy and Relevance in the 21st Century*, https://issuu.com/robertorocco /docs/jane_jacobs_report.

3. See Frazier, *Harambee City*; Laura Warren Hill and Julia Rabig, eds., *The Business of Black Power: Community Development, Capitalism, and Corporate Responsibility in Postwar America* (Rochester, NY: University of Rochester Press, 2012); Robert O. Self, *American Babylon: Race and the Struggle for Postwar Oakland* (Princeton, NJ: Princeton University Press, 2005); Eric Fure-Slocum, *Contesting the Postwar City: Working Class and Growth Politics in 1940s Milwaukee* (Cambridge: Cambridge University Press, 2015).

4. This chapter also helps provide a historical context for contemporary efforts to "revitalize" marginalized communities via traditional routes of private ownership and capital—a strategy James DeFilippis has called "neoliberal communitarianism." See James DeFilippis, *Unmaking Goliath: Community Control in the Face of Global Capital* (New York: Routledge, 2004).

5. See Jonathan J. Bean, *Federal Policies toward Small Business, 1936–1961* (Chapel Hill: University of North Carolina Press, 1996); Lawrence B. Glickman, *Free Enterprise: An American History* (New Haven, CT: Yale University Press, 2019).

6. See Edward S. Shapiro, "Decentralist Intellectuals and the New Deal," *Journal of American History* 58, no. 4 (1972): 938–957; Allan C. Carlson, *The New Agrarian Mind: The Movement toward Decentralist Thought in Twentieth-Century America* (New York: Routledge, 2000).

7. Ralph Borsodi, *The Distribution Age* (New York: D. Appleton, 1929), v.

8. Petr Kropotkin, *Fields, Factories and Workshops: or, Industry Combined with Agriculture and Brain Work with Manual Work* (New York: G. P. Putnam's Sons, 1904); Howard Ebenezer and Frederic J. Osborn, *Garden Cities of To-Morrow* (Cambridge, MA: MIT Press, 1965).

9. Lewis Mumford, *Technics and Civilization* (New York: Routledge and Kegan Paul, 1934), 388–389.

10. This can be contrasted with the roughly contemporaneous actions of the Spanish Confederación Nacional del Trabajo, which made great efforts to transform the urban economies of Catalonia along cooperative and decentralist lines during the Spanish Civil War. See Gaston Leval, *Collectives in the Spanish Revolution* (Oakland, CA: PM Press, 2018); Sam Dolgoff, ed., *The Anarchist Collectives: Worker's Self-Management in the Spanish Revolution* (Montreal, Canada: Black Rose Books, 1974); Frank Mintz, *Anarchism and Worker's Self-Management in Revolutionary Spain* (Oakland, CA: AK Press, 2013).

11. Daniel Horowitz, *The Anxieties of Affluence: Critiques of American Consumer Culture 1939–1979* (Amherst: University of Massachusetts Press, 2009); Macekura, *The Mismeasure of Progress.*

12. Percival Goodman and Paul Goodman, *Communitas: Means of Livelihood and Ways of Life* (New York: Vintage Books, 1960), 7, 9.

13. Goodman and Goodman, 106.

14. Goodman and Goodman, 183.

15. Goodman and Goodman, 245.

16. Goodman and Goodman, 227.

17. Mumford, *The City in History*, 536.

18. For work on the revival of the local during the 1950s and 1960s, see Jamin Creed Rowan, *The Sociable City: An American Intellectual Tradition* (Philadelphia: University of Pennsylvania

Press, 2017); Benjamin Looker, *A Nation of Neighborhoods: Imagining Cities, Communities, and Democracy in Postwar America* (Chicago: University of Chicago Press, 2015); Daniel Immelwahr, *Thinking Small: The United States and the Lure of Community Development* (Cambridge, MA: Harvard University Press, 2015).

19. See Marci Reaven, "Neighborhood Activism in Planning for New York City, 1945–1975," *Journal of Urban History* 46, no. 6 (2020), 1261–89; Christopher Klemek, *The Transatlantic Collapse of Urban Renewal: Postwar Urbanism from New York to Berlin* (Chicago: University of Chicago Press, 2011); see Dennis E. Gale, *The Misunderstood History of Gentrification: People, Planning, Preservation, and Urban Renewal, 1915–2020* (Philadelphia: Temple University Press, 2021), 161–62.

20. Cooper Square Community Development Committee and Businessmen's Association, *An Alternate Plan for Cooper Square* (New York: Cooper Square Community Development Committee and Businessmen's Association, 1961), 2.

21. Two Bridges Neighborhood Council, *The Two Bridges Self-Renewal Plan* (New York: Two Bridges Neighborhood Council, 1959), 3, 13, 1. For another early example of grassroots planning in New York, see Cooper Square Community Development Committee and Businessmen's Association, *An Alternate Plan for Cooper Square*.

22. Laurence, *Becoming Jane Jacobs*, 183.

23. Jane Jacobs, "Strategies for Helping Cities," *American Economic Review* 49, no. 4 (1969), 654.

24. Jacobs, *Death and Life*, 294.

25. Jacobs, 254.

26. Bell, "The Three Faces of New York," 227.

27. Indeed, Socialist and Communist administrations in northern Italy were planning industrial districts along these principles around the same time Jacobs was writing, demonstrating that restructuring "post-Fordist" economies along progressive lines was not an oxymoron. See Antonio Picciotti et al., "Social Cooperatives in Italy: Economic Antecedents and Regional Distribution," *Annals of Public and Cooperative Economics* 85, no. 2 (2014): 165–325.

28. Haig, "Toward an Understanding of the Metropolis," 403.

29. Jacobs, *Death and Life*, 288.

30. Jacobs, 254.

31. Jacobs, 481.

32. Charles Abrams, review of *The Economy of Cities*, by Jane Jacobs, *New York Times*, June 1, 1969, BR3.

33. Bell, "The Three Faces of New York," 227.

34. Phoebe H. Cottingham, "Review Symposium," *Urban Affairs Quarterly* 5, no. 4 (1970), 481.

35. For efforts to place Jane Jacobs's thought in its political context, see Schubert, *Contemporary Perspectives on Jane Jacobs*; Rocco, *Jane Jacobs Is Still Here*.

36. Jacobs, *The Economies of Cities*, 224.

37. Jacobs, 225.

38. Jacobs.

39. Jacobs, *Death and Life*, 289.

40. Osman, *The Invention of Brownstone Brooklyn*, 131.

41. See Gale, *The Misunderstood History of Gentrification*, 161–162.

42. Fitch, 133.

43. For more on how both "top-down" and "participatory" planning models can abet inequality, see Scott Larson, *Building Like Moses with Jacobs in Mind: Contemporary Planning in New York City* (Philadelphia: Temple University Press, 2013).

44. "New York Landmark Bill," Mayor Wagner Mayoral Papers, Roll 155, MN40155, no. 000097, New York Municipal Archive, New York.

45. City Planning Commission, *Plan for New York 1969*, 48.

46. John Peer Nugent, "What Is the City but the People?," posted August 28, 2021, by Daniel London, YouTube, https://www.youtube.com/watch?v=PGU9dCfp3Ug.

47. Abeles Schwartz and Associates, *Forging a Future for the Lower East Side: A Plan for Action* (New York: City Planning Commission, December 1970), 127–128.

48. City Planning Commission, *The Lower Manhattan Plan* (New York: City Planning Commission, 1966), 60, 21, 59.

49. City Planning Commission, *Plan for New York 1969*, 31.

50. Jane Jacobs, "Downtown Is for People," *Fortune*, April 1958, 133–140.

51. Goldstein, *The Roots of Urban Renaissance*, 20; Sleeper, *A Realistic Approach to Private Investment in Urban Redevelopment Applied to East Harlem as a Blighted Area*, 10.

52. Jonathan Gill, *Harlem: The Four Hundred Year History from Dutch Village to Capital of Black America* (New York: Grove Atlantic, 2011), 408.

53. See Jordan S. Yin, "A Review of Alternative Economic Base Study Methods for Community Economic Development," in *Critical Evaluations of Economic Development Policies*, ed. David Fasenfest and Laura A. Reese (Detroit: Wayne State University Press, 2004), 103; Tom Adam Davies, *Mainstreaming Black Power* (Oakland: University of California Press, 2017), 103.

54. Kenneth B. Clark, *Dark Ghetto: Dilemmas of Social Power* (Middletown, CT: Wesleyan University Press, 1965), 11.

55. Wilfred L. David, "Black America in Developmental Perspective Part II," *Review of Black Political Economy* 3, no. 4 (1973), 84. See also R. Brown, "Cash Flows in a Ghetto Economy: An Introductory Essay," *Review of Black Political Economy* (1971): 28–39; Daniel R. Fusfeld, *The Basic Economics of the Urban Racial Crisis* (New York: Holt, Rinehart and Winston, 1973); Frank G. Davis, *The Economics of Black Community Development: An Analysis and Program for Autonomous Growth and Development* (Chicago: Markham, 1972).

56. Stokely Carmichael and Charles Hamilton, *Black Power: The Politics of Liberation in America* (New York: Vintage Books, 1967), 17.

57. Frank G. Davis, "Problems of Economic Growth in the Black Community: Some Alternative Hypotheses," *Review of Black Political Economy* 1, no. 4 (1971), 86.

58. Daniel R. Fusfeld, "Basic Economics of the Urban and Racial Crisis," *Review of Black Political Economy* 1, no. 1 (1970), 76.

59. Fusfeld, *The Basic Economics of the Urban Racial Crisis*, 108.

60. Thomas Vietorisz and Bennet Harrison, *The Economic Development of Harlem* (New York: Praeger Publishers, 1970), 64.

61. Goldstein, *The Roots of Urban Renaissance*, 121.

62. Thaddeus H. Spratlen, "Ghetto Economic Development: Content and Character of the Literature," *Review of Black Political Economy* 1, no. 4 (1971): 43–71; Bennet Harrison, "Ghetto Economic Development: A Survey," *Journal of Economic Literature* 12, no. 1 (1970): 1–37; James Heilbrun and Stansilaw Wellisz, "An Economic Program for the Ghetto," *Proceedings of the Academy of Political Science* 29, no. 1 (1968): 72–85; William K. Tabb, "Perspectives on Black

Economic Development," *Journal of Economic Issues* 4, no. 4 (1970): 68–81; S. M. Rosen, "Better Mousetraps—Reflections on Economic Development in the Ghetto," *Urban Review* 4 (1970): 14–18.

63. Joel Bergsman, *Alternatives to the Non-Gilded Ghetto: Notes on Different Goals and Strategies* (Washington, DC: Urban Institute, February 1971), 17–18.

64. Clark, *Dark Ghetto*, 27.

65. City Planning Commission, *Plan for New York 1969*, 64.

66. William K. Tabb, *The Political Economy of the Black Ghetto* (New York: Norton, 1970), 51.

67. William K. Tabb, "What Happened to Black Economic Development?," *Review of Black Political Economy* 17, no. 2 (1988), 83.

68. Tabb, *The Political Economy of the Black Ghetto*, 53.

69. Barry Bluestone, "Black Capitalism: The Path to Black Liberation?," *Review of Radical Economics* 1, no. 1 (1969), 53.

70. Robert L. Allen, *Black Awakening in Capitalist America* (New York: Doubleday, 1970), 274.

71. Wilfred L. David, "Black America in Developmental Perspective Part I," *Review of Black Political Economy* 3, no. 2 (1973), 90.

72. Vietorisz and Harrison, *The Economic Development of Harlem*, 67.

73. Vietorisz and Harrison, 206.

74. Vietorisz and Harrison, 3.

75. William W. Goldsmith, "The Ghetto as a Resource for Black America," *Journal of the American Institute of Planners* 40, no. 1 (1974), 25.

76. Gar Alperovitz, "Notes toward a Pluralist Commonwealth," *Review of Radical Political Economics* 4, no. 28 (1972), 47.

77. Schwartz and Associates, *Forging a Future for the Lower East Side*, 119; Paul Hoffman, *Lions in the Street: The Inside Story of the Great Wall Street Law Firms* (New York: New American Library, 1974), 182.

78. Davies, *Mainstreaming Black Power*, 103.

79. Ibid, 122; Michael Woodsworth, *Battle for Bed-Stuy: The Long War on Poverty in New York City* (Cambridge, MA: Harvard University Press, 2016), 277.

80. Charles E. Olken, "Economic Development in the Model Cities Program," *Law and Contemporary Problems* 36, no. 2 (1971), 211.

81. Rosen, "Better Mousetraps," 16.

82. Goldsmith, "The Ghetto as a Resource for Black America," 27.

83. See Claire Dunning, *Nonprofit Neighborhoods: An Urban History of Inequality and the American State* (Chicago: University of Chicago Press, 2022), 17.

84. Kimberley Johnson, "Community Development Corporations, Participation, and Accountability: The Harlem Urban Development Corporation and the Bedford-Stuyvesant Restoration Corporation," *Annals of the American Academy of Political and Social Sciences* 594 (July 2004), 120.

85. For an excellent study of these debates as applied to Black banking, see Mehrsa Baradaran, *The Color of Money: Black Banks and the Racial Wealth Gap* (Cambridge, MA: Harvard University Press, 2019). A similar framework as applied to housing can be found in Keeanga-Yamahtta Taylor, *Race for Profit: How Banks and the Real Estate Industry Undermined Black Homeownership* (Chapel Hill: University of North Carolina Press, 2019).

86. June G. Hopps, "Ghetto Economic Corporation Theory, Reality and Policy Implications," *Review of Black Political Economy* 3, no. 3 (1973), 50.

87. DeFilippis, *Unmaking Goliath*, 51.

88. Goldstein, *The Roots of Urban Renaissance*, 111.

89. Rosen, "Better Mousetraps," 16.

90. John S. Morgan, *Business Faces the Urban Crisis* (Houston, TX: Gulf Publishing, 1969); Philip B. Osborne, *The War That Business Must Win* (New York: McGraw Hill, 1970); George S. Odiorne, *Green Power: The Corporation and the Urban Crisis* (New York: Pitman Publishing, 1969).

91. United States Senate, Subcommittee on Financial Institutions of the Committee on Banking and Currency, *Financial Institutions and the Urban Crisis* (Washington DC: U.S. Government Printing Office, 1968), September 30, 1968, 46.

92. David Leinsdorf and Donald Etra, *Citibank: Ralph Nader's Study Group Report on First National City Bank* (New York: Grossman Publishers, 1973), 87.

93. Vietorisz and Harrison, *The Economic Development of Harlem*, 59.

94. Goldstein, *The Roots of Urban Renaissance*, 109. Ironically, Jane Jacobs could agree with this point.

95. Richard Cloward and Frances Fox Piven, "Corporate Imperialism for the Poor," *The Nation*, October 16, 1967, 367.

96. South Bronx Overall Economic Development Corporation, *Can the South Bronx Save New York?: A Progress Report* (New York: South Bronx Overall Economic Development Corporation, 1975), 22.

97. South Bronx Overall Economic Development Corporation, 23.

98. See Charles E. Jones, "Arm Yourself or Harm Yourself," in *On the Ground: The Black Panther Party in Communities across America*, ed. Judson L. Jeffries (Jackson: University of Mississippi Press, 2010), 19; see also Curlew O. Thomas and Barbara Boston Thomas, "Blacks' Socioeconomic Status and the Civil Rights Movement's Decline, 1970–1979: An Examination of Some Hypotheses," *Phylon* 45, no. 1 (1984): 40–51.

Chapter 9

1. Congress of the United States, Joint Economic Committee, *Economic Prospects and Policies* (Washington, DC: US Government Printing Office, 1971), 28.

2. Roger Friedland, *Power and Crisis in the City: Corporations, Unions and Urban Policy* (London: Macmillan, 1982), 201.

3. Roger Friedland, "Central City Fiscal Strains: The Public Costs of Private Growth," *International Journal of Urban and Regional Research* 5, no. 3 (1981): 356–376.

4. Roger Friedland, *Power and Crisis in the City*, 201.

5. For paradigmatic accounts of New York City's 1970s-era fiscal crisis, see Phillips-Fein, *Fear City*; Fuchs, *Mayor and Money*; Martin Shefter, *Political Crisis/Fiscal Crisis: The Collapse and Revival of New York City* (New York: Columbia University Press, 1992). This reordering of political priorities reflected and encouraged parallel policy shifts on the national and international levels. For studies of fiscal crises in other cities, see Jenkins, *The Bonds of Inequality*; Cebul, *Illusions of Progress*; Neumann, *Remaking the Rust Belt*. For a study of the broader "pivots" of this decade, see Judith Stein, *Pivotal Decade: How the United States Traded Factories for Finance in the Seventies* (New Haven, CT: Yale University Press, 2011);

6. Moody, *From Welfare State to Real Estate*.

7. Judith Stein argues that during the 1970s liberal policymakers held to Keynesian macroeconomic remedies for combatting stagflation and job loss, instead of seeking alternative

strategies such as protecting basic manufacturing. When these remedies failed, liberals felt they had few other options than to embrace austerity politics alongside conservatives. This chapter seeks to extend these insights into the domain of local economic policy as well. See Judith Stein, *Pivotal Decade: How the United States Traded Factories for Finance in the Seventies*, 190. For other works that discuss how "social-democratic" polities embraced pro-finance and pro-corporate policies as a means of evading fiscal crisis during the 1970s, see Greta R. Krippner, *Capitalizing on Crisis: The Political Origins of the Rise of Finance* (Cambridge, MA: Harvard University Press 2012); Wolfgang Streeck, *Buying Time: The Delayed Crisis of Democratic Capitalism*, translated by Patrick Camiller. (London: Verso, 2013). For a broader account of how "social-democratic" welfare states were imbricated with capitalism in the postwar period, and the more general inability (or unwillingness) of left-liberals and socialists to develop economic alternatives to it following the crises of the 1970s, see Adam Przeworski, "Social Democracy as a Historical Phenomenon," *New Left Review* 122 (July–August 1980), 27–58.

8. Friedman, "Pirates and Politicians," 57.

9. It is, of course, my hope that telling this story will provide strategic insights for those seeking to build such an economy today. For an excellent compendium of efforts to build such a new economic system, see James Gustave Speth and Kathleen Courrier, eds., *The New Systems Reader: Alternatives to a Failed Economy* (New York: Routledge, 2021).

10. Revell, 160–61.

11. For more on the development of liberal thought in New York City during this time, see Daniel Soyer, *Left in the Center: The Liberal Party of New York and the Rise and Fall of American Social Democracy* (Ithaca, NY: Cornell University Press, 2022).

12. Joseph McGoldrick to Governor Dewey, April 18, 1941, and April 11, 1941, Bill Jacket, L. 1941 c. 89, New York State Archives, Albany, New York; Brownsville Neighborhood Council to Governor Dewey, April 29, 1942, Bill Jacket, L. 1943 c. 234, New York State Archives, Albany, New York.

13. Letter from Stanley Isaacs to City-Wide Tenants Council, March 13, 1940, Box 4, "City-Wide Tenants Council" Folder, Stanley M. Isaacs Papers, Archives and Manuscripts, New York Public Library, New York.

14. See Goodman and Goodman, *Communitas*, 188.

15. Flanagan, *Robert Wagner and the Rise of New York City's Plebiscitary Mayorality*, 37.

16. Daniel Soyer, *Left in the Center: The Liberal Party of New York and the Rise and Fall of American Social Democracy* (Ithaca, NY: Cornell University Press, 2022). Even where tax systems were not strictly speaking progressive or dramatically redistributive, the broader fiscal linkage between welfare services and conventional development and "growth" held true across different fiscal systems. For more on the imbrication of postwar welfare states with conventional capitalist tendencies, see Adam Przeworski, *Capitalism and Social Democracy*. (New York: Cambridge University Press, 1986).

17. Goodman and Goodman, 189.

18. For more on welfare struggles in New York during the cold war era, see Larry R. Jackson and William Arthur Johnson, *Protest by the Poor: The Welfare Rights Movement in New York City* (New York: Lexington Books, 1974).

19. Luther Gulick and Dick Netzer, "Municipal Income Taxes: An Economic Evaluation," *Proceedings of the Academy of Political Science* 28, no. 4 (1968), 7.

20. City Planning Commission, *Plan for New York 1969*, 31.

21. Nugent, "What Is the City but the People?"

22. Murrah Illson, "Bank-City Team to Aid Business," *New York Times*, February 4, 1966, 1.

23. Barry Gottehrer, "Urban Conditions: New York City," *Annals of the American Academy of Political and Social Science* 371, no. 1 (1967), 153.

24. Holtzman, *The Long Crisis*, 171.

25. Citizens' Housing and Planning Council of New York, *Tax Policies and Urban Renewal in New York City*, 17; Moody, *From Welfare State to Real Estate*, 58.

26. Fitch, *The Assassination of New York*, 145.

27. Phillips-Fein, *Fear City*, 24.

28. Edel, "The New York Crisis as Economic History," 234.

29. Phillips-Fein, *Fear City*, 24.

30. Robert N. Barratt, *Exodus from New York City, Part 1: An Investigation and Analysis of the Relocation of Corporate Headquarters Out of New York City* (Clifton, NJ: Schlesinger, 1977), 3; Phillips-Fein, *Fear City*.

31. Robert Wagner, "Text of Speech—Conference on New York City's Industrial Development and Jobs," May 25, 1965, p. 14, Box 060032W, Folder 25, Robert F. Wagner Documents Collections, City Hall Library, New York.

32. Temporary Commission on City Finances, *Toward Fiscal Strength: Overcoming New York City's Fiscal Dilemma* (New York: publisher not identified, 1965), 91.

33. City Planning Commission, *Plan for New York 1969*, 64.

34. Seth S. King, "Mayor Discounts Loss of Industry," *New York Times*, February 19, 1967, 1.

35. New York State Commission on Governmental Operations of the City of New York, *New York City in Transition*, 71.

36. Fitch, *The Assassination of New York*, 5.

37. City Planning Commission, *Plan for New York 1969*, 175.

38. Fitch, "Planning New York," 248.

39. Fitch, 18.

40. Smith, "New York City's Fiscal Situation," 50.

41. Fuchs, *Mayors and Money*, 30, 156–157, 170.

42. Jacobs, "Strategies for Helping Cities," 654.

43. Raymond D. Horton, "A Diversity Theory of Urban Development: Policy Implications for Business and Government," *Columbia Journal of World Business* 13 (Winter 1978), 74. For more on how the politics of "growth" informed postwar liberal and social democratic parties, see Stephanie Mudge, *Leftism Reinvented: Western Parties from Socialism to Neoliberalism* (Cambridge, MA: Harvard University Press, 2018); Collins, *More*, 5. For more on how "great society" economists and welfare policymakers largely accepted laissez-faire microeconomics, see Judith Stein, *Running Steel, Running America: Race, Economic Policy, and the Decline of Liberalism* (Chapel Hill, NC: University of North Carolina Press, 1998), 21.

44. Holtzman, *The Long Crisis*, 168.

45. William K. Tabb, "Blaming the Victim," in *The Fiscal Crisis of American Cities*, ed. Roger E. Alcaly and David Mermelstein (New York: Vintage Original, 1976), 323–324; City Planning Commission, *Economic Development in New York City* (New York: 1973), 8.

46. Holtzman, *The Long Crisis*, 12.

47. Wolfgang Quante, *The Exodus of Corporate Headquarters from New York City* (New York: Praeger Publishers, 1976), 15.

48. Jack Newfield, "How the Power Brokers Profit," in *The Fiscal Crisis of American Cities*, ed. Roger E. Alcaly and David Mermelstein (New York: Vintage Original, 1976), 337.

49. Israel Shenker, "18 Urban Experts Advise, Castigate and Console the City on Its Problems," *New York Times*, July 30, 1975, 35.

50. For a compilation of these critiques, see Charles Hoch and Joel Friedman, *Radical Urban Political Economy: A Bibliographic Introduction* (Monticello, IL: Vance Bibliographies, 1980).

51. Matthew Edel, "Rent Theory and Working Class Strategy: Marx, George and the Urban Crisis," *Review of Radical Political Economics* 9, no. 4 (1977), 10.

52. For more on the political thought of the New Left, see Max Elbaum, *Revolution in the Air: Sixties Radicals Turn to Lenin, Mao and Che* (New York: Verso, 2002).

53. Fitch, "Planning New York," 283.

54. Jason Epstein, review of "The Cost of Good Intentions: New York City and the Liberal Experiment," by Charles R. Morris, *New Republic* 183 (August 16, 1980), 43.

55. Joseph Harris, "New York City and the Economic Crisis," *Journal of Sociology and Social Welfare* 4, no. 3 (1977), 356.

56. Tabb, "Blaming the Victim," 323–324; Quante, *The Exodus of Corporate Headquarters from New York City*, 134.

57. Quante, *The Exodus of Corporate Headquarters from New York City*, 5.

58. Edel, "The New York Crisis as Economic History," 234.

59. Bruce Freund, review of *The Fiscal Crisis of American Cities*, ed. Roger E. Alcaly and David Mermelstein, *University of Detroit Journal of Urban Law* 55, no. 3 (1978), 849.

60. Fitch, "Planning New York," 271.

61. Shenker, "18 Urban Experts Advise, Castigate and Console the City on Its Problems," 35.

62. Jason Epstein, "The Last Days of New York," in *The Fiscal Crisis of American Cities*, ed. Roger E. Alcaly and David Mermelstein (New York: Vintage Original, 1976), 62.

63. Charles Morris, *The Cost of Good Intentions: New York City and the Liberal Experiment* (New York: W. W. Norton, 1980), 140.

64. Tabb, "Blaming the Victim," 324.

65. Congressional Budget Office, *New York City's Fiscal Problem: Its Origins, Potential Repercussions, and Some Alternative Policy Responses* (Washington, DC: Congressional Budget Office, 1975), 4–5; Dana R. Driskell, "Funding the Capital and Expense Budgets: Report of the Temporary Commission on New York City Finances" (master's thesis, Massachusetts Institute of Technology, 1979), 16.

66. William W. Sales Jr. "New York City: Prototype of the Urban Crisis," *Black Scholar* 7, no. 3 (1975), 23–24.

67. Attiat F. Ott and Jang H. Yoo, *New York City's Financial Crisis: Can the Trend Be Reversed?* (Washington, DC: American Enterprise Institute for Public Policy Research, 1975), 7.

68. Jack Newfield and Paul Du Bruel, *The Abuse of Power: The Permanent Government and the Fall of New York* (New York: Viking Press, 1977), 36.

69. James O'Connor, *The Fiscal Crisis of the State*.

70. Sales, "New York City."

71. David A. G rossman, *The Future of New York City's Capital Plant: A Case Study of Trends and Prospects Affecting the City's Public Infrastructure* (Washington, DC: Urban Institute, 1979), 18–19.

72. Even as the city's white-collar sector expanded, the city's population with income lower than the national median rose by 13 percent between 1960 and 1970, while the number of individuals in the city receiving public assistance more than tripled during roughly the same period. See Matthew Edel, "The New York Crisis as Economic History," in *The Fiscal Crisis of American*

Cities, ed. Roger E. Alcaly and David Mermelstein (New York: Vintage Original, 1976), 234; Phillips-Fein, *Fear City*, 21.

73. Michael B. Kennedy, "The Fiscal Crisis of the City," in *Cities in Transformation: Class, Capital, and the State*, ed. Michael Peter Smith (London: Sage Publications, 1985), 100.

74. W. Muller and R. Rohr-Zanker, "The Fiscal Crisis and the Local State: Examination of the Structuralist Concept," *Environment and Planning A: Economy and Space* 21, no. 12 (1989), 1636. See also Peter K. Eisinger, *The Rise of the Entrepreneurial State: State and Local Economic Development Policy in the United States* (Madison: University of Wisconsin Press, 1988), 45–49. Historian Brent Cebul confirms this finding in his book *Illusions of Progress*, as he finds that the debts of most cities were linked with "maintenance of new capital facilities" and "to subsidize urban renewal and redevelopment agendas"—debts, in other words, "associated with maintaining cities at the highest of midcentury liberalism and in partnership with local business elites- not debts associated with extravagant local social welfare states." See Cebul, *Illusions of Progress*, 215.

75. John H. Mollenkopf, "The Crisis of the Public Sector in America's Cities," in *The Fiscal Crisis of American Cities*, ed. Roger E. Alcaly and David Mermelstein (New York: Vintage Original, 1976), 122.

76. Fitch, "Planning New York," 251.

77. Pete Hamill, "A Vision of What a City Could Be," *Newsletter of the Democratic Left* 5, no. 5 (1977), 1.

78. Friedman, "Pirates and Politicians," 57. This section thus partly bears out a statement of Judith Stein regarding the 1980s: that reform movements of the 1960s "offered more of a moral critique than an economic alternative to . . . supply-side measures. By defining Reaganomics simply as an attack on the poor and seeking welfare solutions to compensate for the decline of industry . . . they yielded the economic terrain and thus offered little to the working class and the poor."

79. Edward M. Kirshner and James Morey, "Controlling a City's Wealth: The Lessons of New Town Development," *Working Papers for a New Society* 1, no. 1 (1973), 10. See Yin, "A Review of Alternative Economic Base Study Methods for Community Economic Development," 103.

80. For an excellent selection of contemporaneous literature on this theme, see Lane deMoll, ed., *Rainbook: Resources for Appropriate Technology* (New York: Schoken Books, 1977), esp. 45–51. There was also a flourishing of feminist economics during this time whose history and political significance has yet to be fully explored. See Louise Toupin, *Wages for Housework: A History of an International Feminist Movement, 1972–77* (New York: Pluto Press, 2018).

81. Community Ownership Organizing Project, *The Cities' Wealth: Programs for Community Economic Control in Berkeley, California* (Washington, DC: National Conference on Alternative State and Local Public Policies, 1976), 2.

82. Community Ownership Organizing Project, 80.

83. Arthur Holden, *Is It Bankruptcy, Part 3: Studies in the Financial Plight of N.Y.* (New York: self-pub., 1975), 5.

84. "New York Economic Development Plan," *Conference on Alternative State and Local Policies*, January 10, 1978, 12. https://ecommons.cornell.edu/server/api/core/bitstreams/9787bf9c -57e5-4231-85ee-d500eacd5541/content (accessed January 14, 2023).

85. "Energy and Economics," May–June 1978, *Ways and Means: Conference on Alternative State and Local Public Policies*, 16, Cornell Rare Books & Manuscripts Collection, Cornell University. https://ecommons.cornell.edu/server/api/core/bitstreams/2680f827-3d99-4b8b-b2ca-4e21 ce967712/content (accessed January 14, 2023).

86. Murray Bookchin, *Toward an Ecological Society* (Quebec, Canada: Black Rose Books,

1980), 184–185. For more on how such "self-help initiatives" could align with broader and less egalitarian trends in "public-private partnerships," see Suleiman Osman, " 'We're Doing It Ourselves': The Unexpected Origins of New York City's Public-Private Parks during the 1970s Fiscal Crisis," *Journal of Planning History* 16, no. 2 (2017): 162–174.

87. Isard, *Location and Space-Economy*. Barclay Gibbs Jones, "The Theory of the Urban Economy: Origins and Development with Emphasis on Intraurban Distribution of Population and Economic Activity" (PhD diss., University of North Carolina, 1961); A. M. Weimer, "A Note on the Early History of Land Economics," *Real Estate Economics* 12, no. 3 (1984): 408–416; Charles M. Tiebout, "A Pure Theory of Local Expenditures," *Journal of Political Economy* 64, no. 5 (1956), 48; Michael Howell-Moroney, "The Tiebout Hypothesis 50 Years Later," *Public Administration Review* 68, no. 1 (2008): 97–109.

88. Doreen Massey, "Towards a Critique of Industrial Location Theory," in *The Doreen Massey Reader*, ed. Brett Christophers, Rebecca Lave, Jamie Peck, and Marion Werner (Newcastle-upon-Tyne, UK: Agenda Publishing, 2018), 56. Nor were these complaints new: As early as 1957, a land economist had complained that the work of Hoyt and Haig was "based upon a highly theoretical and oversimplified application of classical price and rent theory to urban land markets," that "their acceptance requires unrealistic and unstated assumptions," and "they have little or no applicability to present-day." See Paul F. Wendt, "Theory of Urban Land Values," *Land Economics* 33, no. 3 (August 1957), 228.

89. Monkkonen, *The Local State*, 121; Friedland, "Central City Fiscal Strains," 371.

90. Fuchs, *Mayors and Money*, 129.

91. Roger Friedland, Frances Piven, and Robert Alford, "Political Conflict, Urban Structure, and the Fiscal Crisis," *International Journal of Urban and Regional Research* 1, no. 3 (1977), 458.

92. Planning and Development Department, Port Authority of New York and New Jersey, *Economic Development Funding in the New York-New Jersey Metropolitan Region, 1976–1980* (New York: Port Authority of New York and New Jersey, December 1982), 9.

93. Edel, "Rent Theory and Working Class Strategy," 11.

94. Jonathan Reider, *Canarsie: The Jews and Italians of Brooklyn against Liberalism* (Cambridge, MA: Harvard University Press, 1985), 101.

95. Sales, "New York City," 37.

96. Sales.

97. Eric H. Monkkonen, "What Urban Crisis? A Historian's Point of View," *Urban Affairs Quarterly* 20, no. 4 (1985): 437–38.

98. Quante, *The Exodus of Corporate Headquarters from New York City*, 15.

99. Christopher Jencks, "The Perils of Pollyanna," *Working Papers for a New Society* 1, no. 1 (1973), 5.

100. Citywide Community Coalition, *Citywide Community Coalition Statement*, 1976, https://cdha.cuny.edu/items/show/4382 (accessed May 20 2023) ; Ray Market, "Challenge to City Unions: What Strategy to Fight Beame's Layoffs?," *The Militant* 39, no. 20 (1975), 17.

101. Stephen M. Miller and William K. Tabb, "A New Look at a Pure Theory of Local Expenditures," *National Tax Journal* 26, no. 2 (1973), 176.

102. Epstein, "The Last Days of New York," 60.

103. Epstein, 75.

104. Long, "Have Cities a Future?," 552.

105. See Jakob Anbinder, "Cities of Amber: Antigrowth Politics and the Making of Modern Liberalism" (PhD diss., Harvard University, 2023); Thomas Robertson, *The Malthusian Moment:*

Global Population Growth and the Birth of American Environmentalism (New Brunswick, NJ: Rutgers University Press, 2012); Keith Mako, *The Ecocentrists: A History of Radical Environmentalism* (New York: Columbia University Press, 2018); Lily Geismer, *Don't Blame Us: Suburban Liberals and the Transformation of the Democratic Party* (Princeton, NJ: Princeton University Press, 2015).

106. Harvey Molotch, "The City as a Growth Machine: Toward a Political Economy of Place," *American Journal of Sociology* 82, no. 2 (1976), 332.

107. For more on how the shrinkage or stabilization of certain economic sectors can be paired with more general increases in employment and well-being, see Timothy Jackson, *Prosperity without Growth: Foundations for the Economy of Tomorrow* (London: Routledge, 2009).

108. For an overview of these campaigns, see Pierre Clavel, *The Progressive City: Planning and Participation, 1969–1984* (New Brunswick, NJ: Rutgers University Press, 1986). Efforts to democratize economies at the national level through the socialization of investment, industrial planning, or full employment measures were also defeated during this time, of course. See Blyth, *Great Transformations*; Stein, *Pivotal Decade*.

109. Shenker, "18 Urban Experts Advise, Castigate and Console the City on Its Problems," 35.

110. Such a pro-market acceleration characterized liberals on the national scale as well: see Stein, *Pivotal Decade*; Cebul, *Illusions of Progress*; Greta R. Krippner, *Capitalizing on Crisis*.

111. United States Congress, House Committee on Banking Stabilization, Currency and Housing Subcommittee on Economic, *Debt Financing Problems of State and Local Government: The New York City Case: Hearings before the Subcommittee on Economic Stabilization of the Committee on Banking, Currency and Housing, House of Representatives, Ninety-Fourth Congress, First Session* (Washington, DC: US Government Printing Office, 1975), 1882.

112. Freeman, *Working-Class New York*, 259–265.

113. Roger Starr, "Making New York Smaller," *New York Times*, November 14, 1976, 225.

114. First National City Bank, Economics Department, *Profile of a City* (New York: McGraw Hill, 1972), 19.

115. "A Crumbling Economy Underlies the Crisis," *New York Times*, October 19, 1975, 193.

116. Ward Morehouse III, "Banks See New York City Rebounding as Financial Capital," *Christian Science Monitor*, October 5, 1979, 6.

117. Evans Clark, *Dollars and Houses: An Economic Brief on Low Rent Housing in Relation to Government Subsidies and Private Capital* (New York: National Public Housing Conference, 1936), 5.

118. Temporary Commission on City Finances, *The City in Transition: Prospects and Policies for New York: The Final Report of the Temporary Commission on City Finances* (location of publisher not identified, publisher not identified, June 1977), https://www.baruch.cuny.edu/mac/Economic_Reports/Jun-1977.pdf, 2,

119. Temporary Commission on City Finances, app. D-2, 3–4.

120. Driskell, "Funding the Capital and Expense Budgets," 5.

121. Benjamin Holtzman, *The Long Crisis: New York City and the Path to Neoliberalism* (New York: Oxford University Press, 2021), 259.

122. Bernard Bellush, "Letters to the Editor," *New York Times*, July 27, 1976, 28.

123. Ada Louise Huxtable, "Stumbling toward Tomorrow: The Decline and Fall of the New York Vision," in *In Search of New York*, ed. Jim Sleeper (New Brunswick, NJ: Transaction Publishers, 1987), 53,

124. Mollenkopf, "The Crisis of the Public Sector in America's Cities"; Mayor's Policy Committee, *Agenda for Economic Development: A Report of the Mayor's Policy Committee to Mayor*

Abraham D. Beame (New York, 1975), Hathitrust, https://babel.hathitrust.org/cgi/pt?id=nnc2
.ark:/13960/t3qv63z57&seq=3; City Planning Commission, *New York City's Program for 1977–1981* (place of publication not identified: publisher not identified, 1976), https://www.govinfo.gov
/content/pkg/CZIC-hd87-e36-1977/html/CZIC-hd87-e36-1977.htm (accessed August 28, 2023).

125. "New York City's Program for 1977–1981."

126. Phillips-Fein, *Fear City*, 259.

127. NYU Furman Center, *Distribution of the Burden of New York City's Property Tax*, May 2012, https://furmancenter.org/research/publication/distribution-of-the-burden-of-new-york-citys
-property-tax.

128. Moody, *From Welfare State to Real Estate*, 71; Robert Reno, "Economic Boom for Manhattan," *Newsday*, December 6, 1978, 1Q.

129. Fitch, 151.

130. Moody, *From Welfare State to Real Estate*, 67–68.

131. Jim Sleeper, "Boom and Bust with Ed Koch," in *In Search of New York*, ed. Jim Sleeper (New Brunswick, NJ: Transaction Publishers, 1987), 38.

132. Fuchs, *Mayors and Money*, 133.

133. City Planning Commission, *Economic Development Section, Economic Development in New York City: Industrial Redevelopment* (New York: 1973), 7.

134. City Planning Commission, 12; Department of City Planning, *Managing Land Use in New York City* (New York: Department of City Planning, 1977).

135. John Mollenkopf, *A Phoenix in the Ashes: The Rise and Fall of the Koch Coalition in New York City Politics* (Princeton, NJ: Princeton University Press, 1992), 141.

136. Letter from Ken Schuman to Peter Solomon, April 24, 1980, pp. 5–6, Folder 16, Box 81, Departmental Correspondence Series, Edward I. Koch Documents Collection, La Guardia and Wagner Archives, New York.

137. Phillips-Fein, *Fear City*, 259.

138. Mollenkopf, *A Phoenix in the Ashes*, 141.

139. Letter from Ken Schuman to Peter Solomon, p. 3, La Guardia and Wagner Archives; Jonathan Soffer, *Ed Koch and the Rebuilding of New York* (New York: Columbia University Press, 2010), 260.

140. "The New York City Advantage," 1978, p. 36, Folder 16, Box 80, Departmental Correspondence Series, Edward I. Koch Documents Collection, La Guardia and Wagner Archives, New York. See also Miriam Greenberg, *Branding New York: How a City in Crisis was Sold to the World* (New York: Routledge, 2008); Daniel Wortel-London, "Progress and Authenticity: Urban Renewal, Urban Tourism, and the Meanings of Mid-Twentieth Century New York," *Journal of Tourism History* 5, no. 2 (2013): 172–184.

141. Blake Fleetwood, "The New Elite and an Urban Renaissance," *New York Times*, January 14, 1979, SM4.

142. Fitch, 31.

143. Moody, *From Welfare State to Real Estate*, 70.

144. Barr, *Building the Skyline*, 318.

145. Mollenkopf, *A Phoenix in the Ashes*, 55.

146. Freeman, *Working-Class New York*, 293.

147. Fitch, 5, 15.

148. See Daniel Wortel-London, "Building a People's Economy in London," *Tribune*, September 25, 2022, https://www.tribunemag.co.uk/2022/09/glc-gleb-robin-murray-economics
-socialism-london-thatcher; Fitch, *The Assassination of New York*, chap. 9. Similarly, the growth

of "social cooperatives" in 1970s Italy demonstrated that outsourcing social service delivery to nonstate actors did not need to take the form of American "privatization." See Alberto Ianes, "Exploring the History of the First Social Enterprise Type: Social Co-Operation in the Italian Welfare System and Its Replication in Europe, 1970s to 2011," *Journal of Entrepreneurial and Organizaitonal Diversity* 9, no. 1 (September 2020), 1–25.

149. Carlin Meyer, "Whose Windfall?," in *In Search of New York*, ed. Jim Sleeper (New Brunswick, NJ: Transaction Publishers, 1987), 20.

150. See Beauregard, *Voices of Decline*, chaps. 9–10.

151. Fleetwood, "The New Elite and an Urban Renaissance," SM35.

152. Eisinger, *The Rise of the Entrepreneurial State*, 53–54.

Conclusion

1. Max Horkheimer. *Critical Theory: Selected Essays* (New York: Continuum, 1972), 249.

2. "NYCEDC President James Patchett Testimony—NYC Council Finance Committee Hearing," New York Economic Development Corporation, January 30, 2019, https://edc.nyc /press-release/nycedc-president-james-patchett-testimony-nyc-council-finance-committee -hearing.

3. "NYEDC President James Patchett Testimony."

4. Iwan Doherty, "Why Has New York Seen a Boom in New Yorker Cooperatives," *Mutual Interest Media*, September 30, 2021, https://www.mutualinterest.coop/2021/09/why-has-new -york-seen-a-boom-in-new-worker-cooperatives; "Worker Cooperative Business Development Initiative," City of New York, accessed April 31, 2022, https://www1.nyc.gov/nycbusiness/article /worker-cooperatives.

5. Caroline Spivack, "Community Land Trusts Score Crucial Funds in City Budget," Curbed .com, accessed April 3, 2022, https://ny.curbed.com/2019/6/18/18682466/nyc-community-land -trusts-funding-city-budget.

6. "The Preston Model: An Overview," Democracy Collaborative, accessed April 3, 2022, https://democracycollaborative.org/preston-model.

7. See Raworth, *Seven Ways to Think Like a 21st Century Economist*, 207. For a broader overview on cooperative firms and their place in liberatory social movements today, see Daniel Wortel-London, "Worker Co-Ops Have a Role to Play in Socialist Strategy," *Jacobin*, May 5, 2024, https://jacobin.com/2024/05/cooperatives-dsa-left-strategy-solidarity.

8. Imbroscio, "The Local Public Balance Sheet," 87.

9. Midgley, *Social Development*.

10. For an excellent summary of how historical research can inform policy, see Alix R. Green, *History, Policy and Public Purpose: Historians and Historical Thinking in Government* (London: Palgrave Macmillan, 2016).

11. For a study that looks at how the concepts of "nonprofit" and "altruism" were invoked as both contrasts and complements to corporate capitalism by early twentieth-century philanthropists, see Jonathan Levy, "Altruism and the Origins of Nonprofit Philanthropy" in Rob Reich, Lucy Bernholz, and Chiara Cordelli, eds., *Philanthropy in Democratic Societies: History, Institutions, Values* (Chicago: University of Chicago Press, 2016), 19–43.

Selected Bibliography

Archival Sources

Brooklyn College Archives and Special Collections, Brooklyn, New York
    Brooklyn Democratic Party Collection
    Brooklyn History Collection
    Brooklyn Clubs Collection
Brooklyn Historical Society, Brooklyn, New York
    Inapunch Real Estate Collection
    Henry A. Meyer Scrapbooks
    Flatbush Chamber of Commerce publications
    Brooklyn Chamber of Commerce publications
    Brooklyn Real Estate Board magazines and bulletins
    Brooklyn Development Company Records
    Gray-Pyle Real Estate Company Records
    Brooklyn Corporation Counsel Records
    Brooklyn Public Library Brooklyn Collection, Brooklyn, New York.
    Raymond Ingersoll Papers
Citizen's Housing and Planning Council Records, New York
    Organizational Records
Columbia University Rare Book and Manuscript Library, New York
    Citizen Union of the City of New York Record
    Community Service Society Archives
    Edwin Patrick Kilroe Papers
    Edwin Robert Anderson Seligman Papers
    Felix Adler Papers
    Genevieve Earle Papers
    George McAneny Papers
    Herbert H. Lehman Papers
    Lillian D. Wald Papers
    New York Chamber of Commerce and Merchants Association Papers

Robert Haig Papers
Seth Low Papers
Columbia University Center for Oral History Research, New York
Abraham Kazan
Bertram de N. Cruger
Charles Abrams
Charles S. Ascher
Harry James Carman
Henry Bruere
Hobart Stanley Bird
Lawson Purdy
Louis Heaton Pink
Margaret Tanzer Bunzl
Miles Lanier Colean
Robert F. Wagner
Stanley Isaacs
Thomas Edmund Dewey
William O'Dwyer
William Stiles Bennet
Cornell University Division of Rare and Manuscript Collection, New York
Arthur C. Holden Papers
Charles Abrams Papers
Clarence Stein Collection
Coleman Woodbury Papers
Edward M. Bassett Papers
John Nolen Papers
Paul Opperman Papers
Phillip H. Cornick Papers
Warren Jay Vincton Papers
La Guardia Community College La Guardia and Wagner Archive, New York
New York City Housing Authority Papers
Real Estate Board of New York Collection
Edward I. Koch Documents Collection
New York City Mayoral Papers, New York Hall of Records, New York
Fiorello H. La Guardia Papers
James Walker Papers
John Hylan Papers
William Gaynor Papers
William H. Wickham Papers
William O'Dwyer Papers
New York Public Library Manuscripts, Archives, and Rare Books Division, New York
Stanley Isaacs Papers
Robert Moses Papers
New York State Archives, Albany, New York
Bill Jackets
Governor Thomas Dewey Papers

Governor Al Smith Papers
Governor Herbert Lehman Papers
Princeton University Special Collections Manuscript Division, Princeton, New Jersey
Arthur Curt Holden Papers
George B. McClellan Jr. Papers
George McAneny Papers
Princeton University Archives, Princeton, New Jersey
Ivy Lee Papers
Queens Public Library Archives, New York
Vertical Files
Tamiment Library and Robert F. Wagner Labor Archives at New York University, New York
Printed Ephemera Collection on the Socialist Party
Socialist Party (U.S.): Correspondence
Baruch Charney Vladeck Papers and Photographs
Yale University Manuscript and Archives, New Haven, Connecticut
Baldwin Family Papers

Periodicals

American City
Brooklyn Daily Eagle
Chicago Tribune
Christian Science Monitor
Evening Telegram
Fortune
Long Island Daily Press
Long Island Star Journal
New Republic
New York American
New York Amsterdam News
New Yorker
New York Evening Journal
New York Evening World
New York Herald Tribune
New York Sun
New York Times
New York Tribune
North Shore Daily Journal
Queens Evening News
Real Estate Record and Builders' Guide
San Francisco Chronicle
Survey Graphic
Tammany Times
Wall Street Journal
Washington Post

Selected Primary Sources

NONGOVERNMENTAL ORGANIZATIONAL PUBLICATIONS

Academy of Political Sciences. *Municipal Income Taxes: An Economic Evaluation, Problems of Administration, Alternative Sources of Revenue.* New York: Columbia University Press, 1966.

Adams, Thomas. *The Building of the City: Regional Plan of New York and Its Environs.* Vol. 2. New York: Regional Plan Association, 1931.

Bartholomew, Harland. *The Present and Ultimate Effect of Decentralization upon American Cities.* Chicago: Urban Land Institute, 1940.

Betters, Paul, ed. *City Problems: The Annual Proceedings of the United States Conference of Mayors.* Washington, DC: United States Conference of Mayors, 1933–1946.

Borough President's Office. *Borough of Richmond's Solution of Housing Problem.* New York: n.p., 1920.

Citizens' Association. *Report of the Citizens' Association; How Our Taxes May Be Reduced, Our Resources Developed, and the Local Government Improved.* New York: Citizens' Association, 1868.

Citizens Budget Commission. *Killing the Goose.* New York: Citizens Budget Commission, 1935.

Citizens Budget Commission. *Report on the Master Plan of Land Use Proposed by the City Planning Commission.* New York: Citizens Budget Commission, 1941.

Citizens' Housing and Planning Council of New York. *Tax Policies and Urban Renewal in New York City: A Report on a Tax Study with Recommendations.* New York: Citizens' Housing and Planning Council of New York, 1960.

City Club of New York. *Subways or Children?: Which or Both? : A Letter to the Board of Estimate.* New York: City Club of New York, 1927.

Community Ownership Organizing Project. *The Cities' Wealth: Programs for Community Economic Control in Berkeley, California.* Washington, DC: National Conference on Alternative State and Local Public Policies, 1976.

Conference of Mayors and Other City Officials of the State of New York. *No Wonder the Taxpayers Howl!* New York: New York State Conference of Mayors and Other Municipal Officials, 1936.

Cooper Square Community Development Committee and Businessmen's Association. *An Alternate Plan for Cooper Square.* New York: Cooper Square Community Development Committee and Businessmen's Association, 1961.

Drabkin, Murray. "Urban Fiscal Crisis—The New York Experience." *Proceedings of the Annual Conference on Taxation under the Auspices of the National Tax Association,* vol. 59 (1966): 26–32.

Economic Club of New York. "Eightieth Meeting." March 28, 1927. https://www.econclubny.org /documents/10184/109144/1927Mar28Transcript.pdf.

First National City Bank, Economics Department. *Profile of a City.* New York: McGraw Hill, 1972.

Life Insurance Association of America Commission on Money and Credit. *Life Insurance Companies as Financial Institutions.* Englewood Cliffs, NJ: Prentice-Hall, 1962.

National Industrial Conference Board. *The Cost of Living in the United States, 1914–1926.* New York: National Industrial Conference Board, 1926.

New York Tax Reform Association. *Constitution*. New York: New York Tax Reform Association, 1891.

New York Tax Reform Association. *New York Tax Reform Association Platform*. New York: New York Tax Reform Association, 1902.

Real Estate Record and Builders' Guide. *A History of Real Estate, Building and Architecture in New York City during the Last Quarter of a Century*. New York: Real Estate Record and Builders' Guide, 1898.

Regional Plan Association. *The Economic Status of the New York Region*. New York: Regional Plan Association, 1944.

Regional Plan Association. *Population, Land Values, And Government: Studies in the Growth and Distribution of Population and Land Values, and Problems of Government*. 2 vols. New York: Arno Press, 1929.

South Bronx Overall Economic Development Corporation. *Can the South Bronx Save New York? A Progress Report*. New York: South Bronx Overall Economic Development Corporation, 1975.

Two Bridges Neighborhood Council. *The Two Bridges Self-Renewal Plan*. New York: Two Bridges Neighborhood Council, 1959.

Urban Land Institute. *Decentralization: What Is It Doing to Our Cities?* Chicago: Urban Land Institute, 1940.

Urban Land Institute. *A Proposal for Rebuilding Blighted City Areas*. Washington, DC: Urban Land Institute, 1943.

NEW YORK CITY GOVERNMENT PUBLICATIONS

Abeles Schwartz and Associates. *Forging a Future for the Lower East Side: A Plan for Action*. New York: City Planning Commission, December 1970.

Ballard, Harrison. *Plan for Rezoning the City of New York: A Report Submitted to the City Planning Commission*. Ann Arbor: University of Michigan, 1950.

Berry, Charles White. *Financial Problems of the City of New York*. New York: Office of the Comptroller, 1933.

Berry, Charles White. *The Financing of Local Improvements by Local, Borough or City-Wide Assessments*. New York: Office of the Comptroller, 1930.

Board of Commissioners. *First Annual Report on the Improvement of the Central Park, New York*. New York: Chase W. Baker, 1857.

Committee on Taxation. *Final Report of the Committee on Taxation of the City of New York*. New York: The O'Connoll Press, 1916.

City of New York. "Worker Cooperative Business Development Initiative." Accessed April 31, 2022. https://www1.nyc.gov/nycbusiness/article/worker-cooperatives.

City Planning Commission. *Economic Development Section, Economic Development in New York City: Industrial Redevelopment*. New York: City Planning Commission, 1973.

City Planning Commission. *The Lower Manhattan Plan*. New York: City Planning Commission, 1966.

City Planning Commission. *Plan for New York 1969: A Proposal*. Cambridge, MA: MIT Press, 1969.

City Planning Commission. *Port of New York, Proposals for Development*. New York: City Planning Commission, 1964.

City Planning Commission. *Report Accompanying 1942 Capital Budget and 1943–47 Capital Program*. New York: City Planning Commission, 1941.

Commission on New Sources of City Revenue. *Report Submitted to the Mayor, Chairman of the Board of Estimate and Apportionment*. New York: M. B. Browning Printing & Binding Company, January 11, 1913.

Department of City Planning. *Managing Land Use in New York City*. New York: Department of City Planning, 1977.

Haig, Robert Murray. *Some Probable Effects of the Exemption of Improvements from Taxation in the City of New York: A Report Prepared for the Committee on Taxation of the City of New York*. New York: Clarence C. Nathan, 1916.

Lehman, Herbert H. *The Finances and Financial Administration of New York City: Recommendations and Report of the Sub-Committee on Budget, Finance, and Revenue of the City Committee on Plan and Survey*. New York: J. J. Little & Ives, 1928.

Mayor's Policy Committee. *Agenda for Economic Development: A Report of the Mayor's Policy Committee to Mayor Abraham D. Beame*. New York, Mayors' Committee, 1975.

Murphy, Charles E. *Report to Hon. Frank J. Taylor Comptroller of the City of New York on Industrial Survey of New York City*. 1937, New York City Hall of Records.

New York City Commission on Congestion of Population. *Report of the New York City Commission on Congestion of Population*. New York: Lecouver Press, 1911.

New York City Department of Taxes and Assessments. *Questions and Answers about Real Estate Taxation in New York City*. 1937, New York City Municipal Library.

New York City Economic Development Corporation. "NYEDC President James Patchett Testimony—NYC Council Finance Committee Hearing." January 30, 2019. https://edc.nyc /press-release/nycedc-president-james-patchett-testimony-nyc-council-finance-com mittee-hearing.

New York City Housing Authority. *Annual Report*. Various years, La Guardia & Wagner Archives.

New York City Housing Authority. *Clason Point Gardens, Bronx, New York*. 1942, La Guardia & Wagner Archives.

New York City Housing Authority. *Work Sheets for a Note on Site and Unit Planning as Previously Published by the Authority*. 1937, La Guardia & Wagner Archives.

New York City Planning Department. *Annual Report*. Various years, La Guardia & Wagner Archives.

New York Office of the Comptroller. *New York City's Parks, Playgrounds and Parkways and Their Proposed Extension*. 1930, Brooklyn Collection, Brooklyn Public Library.

Temporary Commission on City Finances. *The City in Transition: Prospects and Policies for New York: The Final Report of the Temporary Commission on City Finances*. New York: Arno Press, June 1977.

NEW YORK STATE GOVERNMENT PUBLICATIONS

Commission of Housing and Regional Planning. *Annual Report*. Albany, NY: J. B. Lyon, various years.

Commission of Housing and Regional Planning. *Report of Commission of Housing and Regional Planning to Governor Al Smith and to the Legislature of the State of New York on Tax Exemption of New Housing*. Albany, NY: J. B. Lyon, 1924.

Commission to Select and Locate Lands for Public Parks in the Twenty-Third and Twenty-Fourth Wards of the City of New York, and in the Vicinity Thereof. New York: Marin B. Brown, 1884.

Cornick, Philip H. *A Report to State Planning Council of New York on the Problems Created by the Premature Subdivision of Urban Lands in Selected Metropolitan Districts in the State of New York.* Digital Culture of Metropolitan New York. https://dcmny.org/do/045e96e9 -34c7-403a-9c6c-fba7faf6fccb#page/2/mode/2up (accessed December 3, 2023).

Davenport, Donald H. *Report of Commission of Housing and Regional Planning to Governor Alfred E. Smith . . . on Cost of Government, Land Value and Population.* Albany, NY: J. B. Lyon, 1923.

Joint Committee of the Senate and Assembly of the State of New York Appointed to Investigate the Finances of New York City. *Final Report Transmitted to the Legislature.* Albany, NY: J. B. Lyon, 1909.

Joint Legislative Committee on Assessing and Reviewing of the State of New York. *Assessing for Taxation in New York State.* New York: Fort Orange Press, 1941–1943.

Joint Legislative Committee on Assessing and Reviewing of the State of New York. *Final Report.* New York: Fort Orange Press, 1941.

Joint Legislative Committee on Assessing and Reviewing of the State of New York. *First Report.* New York: Fort Orange Press, 1941.

New York Advisory Commission on Taxation and Finance. *Final Report.* New York: Martin B. Brown Company, October 1908.

New York Board of Education. *Revising Our Tax Structure: A Study of Proposals Affecting New York State and New York City.* Hathitrust, https://babel.hathitrust.org/cgi/pt?id =mdp.39015076053258&seq=7 (accessed December 3, 2023).

New York State Board of Housing. *Report of the State Board of Housing.* Albany, NY: J. B. Lyon, 1933.

New York State Commission on Governmental Operations of the City of New York. *New York City in Transition.* Hathitrust, https://babel.hathitrust.org/cgi/pt?id=coo.31924000595557 &seq=13 (accessed January 4, 2023).

State Board of Tax Commissioners. *Annual Report of the State Board of Tax Commissioners of the State of New York.* Albany, NY: J. B. Lyon, 1901.

OTHER STATE GOVERNMENT PUBLICATIONS

Pittsburgh Committee on Taxation Study. *Report of the Committee on Taxation Study to Council of the City of Pittsburgh, Pennsylvania.* Hathitrust, https://babel.hathitrust.org/cgi/pt?id =mdp.39015036709098&seq=7 (Accessed June 2, 2022).

State Tax Commission of Maryland. *Report of the Maryland Tax Commission to the General Assembly.* Baltimore, MD: King Brothers, 1888.

FEDERAL GOVERNMENT PUBLICATIONS

Congress of the United States, Joint Economic Committee. *Economic Prospects and Policies.* Washington, DC: US Government Printing Office, January 22, 1971.

Congressional Budget Office. *New York City's Fiscal Problem: Its Origins, Potential Repercussions, and Some Alternative Policy Responses.* Washington, DC: US Government Printing Office, 1971.

Federal Housing Administration. *A Handbook on Urban Redevelopment for Cities in the United States,* Washington, DC: US Government Printing Office, 1941.

Hoyt, Homer. *The Structure and Growth of Residential Neighborhoods in American Cities*. Washington, DC: US Government Printing Office, 1939.

Joint Economic Committee. *Hearings before the Joint Economic Committee Congress of the United States, First Session, Invited Comments Part 4*. Washington, DC: US Government Printing Office, 1969.

National Resources Committee. *Our Cities: Their Role in the National Economy*. Washington, DC: US Government Printing Office, 1937.

United States Bureau of Labor Statistics. *Family Income and Expenditure in New York City, 1935–36*. Washington, DC: US Government Printing Office, 1941.

United States Congress House Committee on Banking Stabilization Currency and Housing Subcommittee on Economic. *Debt Financing Problems of State and Local Government: The New York City Case: Hearings before the Subcommittee on Economic Stabilization of the Committee on Banking, Currency and Housing, House of Representatives, Ninety-Fourth Congress, First Session*. Washington, DC: US Government Printing Office, 1975.

United States Senate, Subcommittee on Financial Institutions of the Committee on Banking and Currency. *Financial Institutions and the Urban Crisis*. Washington, DC: US Government Printing Office, September 30, 1968.

Wood, Edith Elmer. *Slums and Blighted Areas in the United States*. Washington, DC: US Government Printing Office, 1936.

LAW CASES

Housing Authority v. Muller, 155 Misc. Rep. 1681, 279 N.Y.S. 299 (1935).

Housing Authority v. Muller, 270 N.Y. 333, 1 N.E. (2d) 153 (1936).

Rindge Co. v. Los Angeles County, 262 U.S. 700 (1923).

SELECTED PRIMARY BOOKS AND ARTICLES

"Average Construction Cost of Dwellings in Large Cities of the United States." *Monthly Labor Review* 27, no. 5 (1928): 27–30.

"A Primer of Slum Clearance." *Fortune* 6, no. 2 (1932): 76.

Abrams, Charles. "New Social Trends in Land Utilization." *American Institute of Real Estate Appraisers Journal* 9, no. 4 (1941): 331–345.

Abrams, Charles. *Revolution in Land*. New York: Harpers, 1939.

Abrams, Charles. "Slum Clearance Boomerangs." *The Nation*, July 29, 1950.

Abrams, Charles. "Stuyvesant Town's Threat to Our Liberties." *Commentary*, November 1949. https://www.commentary.org/articles/charles-abrams/stuyvesant-towns-threat-to-our -libertiesgovernment-waives-the-constitution-for-private-enterprise/.

Abrams, Charles. "The Subsidy and Housing." *Journal of Land and Public Utility Economics* 22, no. 2 (1946): 131–139.

Ackerman, Frederick. "Our Stake in Congestion." *Survey Graphic* 54, no. 1 (1925): 134–138.

Ackerman, Frederick. "Where Goes the City Planning Movement? IV. The Confusion of Viewpoints." *Journal of the American Institute of Architects* 8 (August 1920): 284–287.

Adams, Henry Carter. *Public Debts*. New York: D. Appleton, 1893.

Alcaly, Roger E., and David Mermelstein, eds. *The Fiscal Crisis of American Cities*. New York: Vintage Original, 1976.

Allen, Robert L. *Black Awakening in Capitalist America*. New York: Doubleday, 1970.

Allen, William H. *Why Tammanies Revive: La Guardias Mis-guard*. New York: Institute for Public Service, 1937.

Alperovitz, Gar. "Notes Toward a Pluralist Commonwealth." *Review of Radical Political Economics* 4, no. 28 (1972): 28–48.

Anderson, Martin. *The Federal Bulldozer: A Critical Analysis of Urban Renewal 1949–1962*. Cambridge, MA: MIT Press, 1964.

Andrews, Richard B. "Mechanics of the Urban Economic Base: Historical Development of the Base Concept." *Land Economics* 29, no. 2 (1953): 161–167.

Armstrong, Robert H., and Homer Hoyt. *Decentralization in New York: Preliminary Report to Urban Land Institute*. Chicago: Urban Land Institute, January 1941.

Ascher, Charles S. Review of *The Economic Status of the New York Metropolitan Region in 1944*, by Homer Hoyt. *American Journal of Sociology* 51, no. 4 (1946): 355.

Babcock, Frederick M. "Influence of the Federal Housing Administration on Mortgage Lending Policy." *The Journal of Land and Public Utility Economics* 15, no. 1 (1939): 1–5.

Babcock, Frederick M. *The Valuation of Real Estate*. New York: McGraw Hill, 1932.

Baker Fox, Annette. "The Local Housing Authority and the Municipal Government." *Journal of Land and Public Utility Economics* 7, no. 3 (1941): 280–290.

Bankers Trust. *New York and the Future*. New York: Bankers Trust, 1946.

Barratt, Robert N. *Exodus from New York City, Part 1: An Investigation and Analysis of the Relocation of Corporate Headquarters out of New York City*. Clifton, NJ: Schlesinger, 1977.

Bauer, Catherine. "Cities in Flux: A Challenge to the Postwar Planners." *American Scholar* 13, no. 1 (1943–1944): 70–84.

Bauer, Catherine. *Modern Housing*. New York: Houghton Mifflin, 1934.

Bean, Jonathan J. *Federal Policies toward Small Business, 1936–1961*. Chapel Hill: University of North Carolina Press, 1996.

Bell, Daniel. "The Three Faces of New York." *Dissent* 8 (Summer 1961): 222–232.

Bergsman, Joel. *Alternatives to the Non-Gilded Ghetto: Notes on Different Goals and Strategies*. Washington, DC: Urban Institute, February 1971.

Berry, Charles W. *Why New York City Can Never Become Bankrupt*. New York: n.p., 1930.

Betters, Paul. "Federal Aid for Municipalities." *National Municipal Review* 22, no. 4 (1933): 174–178.

Bird, Frederick. "Cities and Their Debt Burdens." *National Municipal Review* 25, no. 12 (1936): 12–19.

Black, George Ashton. *The History of Municipal Ownership of Land on Manhattan Island*. New York: Columbia University Press, 1891.

Bluestone, Barry. "Black Capitalism: The Path to Black Liberation?" *Review of Radical Economics* 1, no. 1 (1969): 36–55.

Bookchin, Murray. *Toward an Ecological Society*. Quebec, Canada: Black Rose Books, 1980.

Borsodi, Ralph. *The Distribution Age*. New York: D. Appleton, 1929.

Brown, Robert. "Cash Flows in a Ghetto Economy: An Introductory Essay." *Review of Black Political Economy* 1, no.3 (1971): 28–39.

Burnstan, Arthur Rowland. *Special Assessment Procedure; A Critical Study of the Methods and Practices in Improvement Finance in Twenty-One New York Cities*. Albany, NY: J. B. Lyon, 1929.

Burton, John E., and Dorothy C. Burden. "New York Real Estate: Its Taxation and Assessment." *Journal of Land and Public Utility Economics* 13, no. 3 (1937): 253–272.

Buttenheim, Harold S. "If Henry George Were Writing Today." *Journal of Land and Public Utility Economics* 11, no. 1 (1935): 1–11.

Cahan, Abraham. *The Rise of David Levinsky: A Novel.* New York: Harper & Brothers, 1917.

Carlson, Oliver, and Ernest Sutherland Bates. *Hearst: Lord of Simeon.* New York: Viking Press, 1936.

Carmichael, Stokely, and Charles Hamilton. *Black Power: The Politics of Liberation in America.* New York: Vintage Books, 1967.

Chase, Stuart. *The Tragedy of Waste.* New York: Macmillan, 1937.

Clark, Evans. *Dollars and Houses: An Economic Brief on Low Rent Housing in Relation to Government Subsidies and Private Capital.* New York: National Public Housing Conference, 1936.

Clark, Kenneth B. *Dark Ghetto: Dilemmas of Social Power.* Middletown, CT: Wesleyan University Press, 1965.

Clinton. *The Value of Real Estate in the City of New York, Past, Present, and Prospective: As Illustrated in a Series of Articles from the Evening Post, in 1858, 1859, and 1860 by a Retired Merchant.* New York: n.p., 1860?

Cloward, Richard, and Frances Fox Piven. "Corporate Imperialism for the Poor." *The Nation,* October 16, 1967, 365–367.

Coler, Bird Sim. "The City's Power to Incur Indebtedness." In *National Conference on City Government,* 96–103. Philadelphia: National Municipal League, December 1899.

Coler, Bird Sim. *Municipal Government: As Illustrated by the Charter, Finances and Public Charities of New York.* New York: D. Appleton, 1901.

Connolly, Maurice. "Ten Months of the New Regime." *The Queens Magazine, the Voter's Voice,* 1 (August 1912): 12.

Conyngton, Mary. "Effect of the Tax-Exemption Ordinance in New York City on Housing," *Monthly Labor Review* 12, no. 4 (1922): 23–32.

Cook, Fred J., and Gene Gleason. "The Shame of New York." *The Nation,* October 31, 1959, 261–264.

Cornick, Philip H. "The Real Estate Tax." *American Journal of Economics and Sociology* 26, no. 3 (1967): 251–262.

Cottingham, Phoebe H. "Review Symposium." *Urban Affairs Quarterly* 5 no. 4 (1970): 481–484.

Crawford, Andrew Wright. "Aspects of City Financing." *National Municipal Review* 3, no. 3 (1914): 505–516.

Davenport, H. J. "Extent and Significance of the Unearned Increment." *Bulletin of the American Economic Association* 1 (April 1911): 322–331.

David, Wilfred L. "Black America in Developmental Perspective Part I." *Review of Black Political Economy* 3, no. 2 (1973): 89–104.

David, Wilfred L. "Black America in Developmental Perspective Part II." *Review of Black Political Economy* 3, no. 4 (1973): 79–112.

Davis, Frank G. *The Economics of Black Community Development: An Analysis and Program for Autonomous Growth and Development.* Chicago: Markham, 1972.

Davis, Frank G. "Problems of Economic Growth in the Black Community: Some Alternative Hypotheses." *Review of Black Political Economy* 1, no. 4 (1971): 75–107.

Deming, George H. Review of *Metropolis 1958: An Interpretation of the Findings of the New York Metropolitan Region Study,* by Raymond Vernon. *National Civic Review* 50, no. 2 (1961): 114.

deMoll, Lane, ed. *Rainbook: Resources for Appropriate Technology*. New York: Schoken Books, 1977.

Desmond, Thomas C. "Blighted Areas Get a New Chance." *National Municipal Review* 30, no. 11 (1941): 629–640.

Driskell, Dana R. "Funding the Capital and Expense Budgets: Report of the Temporary Commission on New York City Finances." Master's thesis, Massachusetts Institute of Technology, 1979.

Durand, Edward Dana. *The Finances of New York City*. New York: Macmillan, 1898.

Ebenezer, Howard, and Frederic J. Osborn. *Garden Cities of To-Morrow*. Cambridge, MA: MIT Press, 1965.

Edel, Matthew. "Rent Theory and Working Class Strategy: Marx, George and the Urban Crisis." *Review of Radical Political Economics* 9, no. 4 (1977): 10–15.

Eisinger, Peter K. *The Rise of the Entrepreneurial State: State and Local Economic Development Policy in the United States*. Madison: University of Wisconsin Press, 1988.

Ely, Richard T. *Natural Monopolies and Local Taxation*. Boston, MA: Robinson & Stephenson, 1889.

Ely, Richard T. *Problems of To-Day: A Discussion of Protective Tariffs, Taxation, and Monopolies*. New York: T. Y. Crowell, 1888.

Ely, Richard T. *Taxation in American States and Cities*. New York: Thomas Y. Crowell, 1888.

Fecil, C. G. *New York City's Land: The Safest and Most Profitable Investment in the World*. Wilkes-Barre, PA: Reader Press, 1908.

The Finances of New York City. New York: Dun & Bradstreet, 1934.

Fisher, Robert Moore. "Public Costs of Urban Renewal." *Journal of Finance* 5, no. 2 (1962): 379–386.

Flynn, Edward J. *You're The Boss*. New York: Viking Press, 1947.

Foote, Allen Ripley. *Cost of Service to Users and Tax Payers: The Only Proper Basis for Comparisons between Private and Municipal Ownership of Water, Gas and Electric Lighting Works*. Cincinnati: R. Clarke, 1898.

Foote, Allen Ripley. *Low Fares for Public Service vs. Franchise Taxation*. Norfolk, VA: n.p., 1907.

Foote, Allen Ripley. "Taxation of Public Service Corporations." *National Conference on Taxation* 1 (May 1901): 655–661.

Ford, James. *Slums and Housing: With Special Reference to New York City*. New York: Phelps-Stokes Fund, 1936.

Ford, John. "Municipal Government in the United States." *North American Review* 172, no. 534 (1901): 751–763.

French, Fred R. *Housing in Lower Manhattan: Address by Fred R. French at Department of Economics and Social Institute at Princeton University*. New York: self-pub., 1933.

Freund, Bruce. Review of *The Fiscal Crisis of American Cities*, ed. Roger E. Alcaly and David Mermelstein. *University of Detroit Journal of Urban Law* 55, no. 3 (1978): 843–852.

Friedenberg, Daniel. "Real Estate Confidential." *Dissent* 8 (1961), 260–276.

Friedland, Roger. "Central City Fiscal Strains: The Public Costs of Private Growth." *International Journal of Urban and Regional Research* 5, no. 3 (1981): 356–376.

Friedland, Roger. *Power and Crisis in the City: Corporations, Unions, and Urban Policy*. London: Macmillan, 1982.

Friedland, Roger, Frances Piven, and Robert Alford. "Political Conflict, Urban Structure, and the Fiscal Crisis." *International Journal of Urban and Regional Research* 1, no. 3 (1977): 447–471.

Fusfeld, Daniel R. "Basic Economics of the Urban and Racial Crisis." *Review of Black Political Economy* 1, no. 1 (1970): 58–83.

Fusfeld, Daniel R. *The Basic Economics of the Urban Racial Crisis.* New York: Holt, Rinehart and Winston, 1973.

Gans, Herbert. "The Dream of Human Cities." *New Republic*, November 1969, 28–30.

George, Henry. *Progress and Poverty.* New York: Schalkenbach Foundation, 1935. First published 1879.

George, Henry. *Social Problems.* New York: Doubleday and McClure, 1900.

Gilbert, Donald W. "Cycles in Municipal Finance." *Review of Economics and Statistics* 22, no.4 (1940): 190–202.

Goldsmith, William W. "The Ghetto as a Resource for Black America." *Journal of the American Institute of Planners* 40, no. 1 (1974): 17–30.

Goodman, Percival, and Paul Goodman. *Communitas: Means of Livelihood and Ways of Life.* New York: Vintage Books, 1960.

Gordon, Harry A. *Subway Nickels: A Survey of New York City's Transit Problem.* New York: Brown, 1925.

Greer, Guy. "Getting Ready for Federal Aid in Urban Redevelopment." *American City* 58 (May 1943): 47–49.

Greer, Guy, and Alvin H. Hansen. *Urban Redevelopment and Housing.* Washington, DC: National Planning Association, 1941.

Griffin, John I. *Industrial Location in the New York Area.* New York: City College Press, 1956.

Grossman, David A. *The Future of New York City's Capital Plant: A Case Study of Trends and Prospects Affecting the City's Public Infrastructure.* Washington, DC: Urban Institute, 1979.

Grout, Edward M. *Municipal Ownership: Its Necessity Demonstrated: From Writings and Speeches of Edward M. Grout.* New York: Commonwealth, 1897.

Grout, Edward M. "New York City Should Own the Gas Supply." *Municipal Affairs* 1, no. 2 (1897): 225–243.

Grout, Edward M. *Speech Delivered before the Franchise Tax and Municipal Ownership League, New York City, January 30, 1903, on the Franchise Tax Law.* New York: Mail and Express, 1903.

Gulick, Luther, and Dick Netzer. "Municipal Income Taxes: An Economic Evaluation." *Proceedings of the Academy of Political Science* 28, no. 4 (1968): 1–18.

Haig, Robert Murray. *Major Economic Factors in Metropolitan Growth and Arrangement; A Study of Trends and Tendencies in the Economic Activities within the Region of New York and Its Environs.* New York: Arno Press, 1928.

Haig, Robert Murray. "New Sources of City Revenue." *National Municipal Review* 4, no. 4 (1915): 594–603.

Haig, Robert Murray. "Toward an Understanding of the Metropolis." *Quarterly Journal of Economics* 40, no. 2 (1926): 179–208.

Hansen, Alvin. "The City of the Future." *National Municipal Review* 68, no. 32 (1943): 68–72.

Harris, Joseph. "New York City and the Economic Crisis." *Journal of Sociology and Social Welfare* 4, no. 3 (1977): 351–365.

Harrison, Bennet. "Ghetto Economic Development: A Survey." *Journal of Economic Literature* 12, no. 1 (1970): 1–37.

Heilbrun, James, and Stansilaw Wellisz. "An Economic Program for the Ghetto." *Proceedings of the Academy of Political Science* 29, no. 1 (1968): 72–85.

Herbert, Agar. *Land of the Free.* Boston: Houghton Mifflin, 1935.

Hillhouse, A. M. *Municipal Bonds; A Century of Experience.* New York: Prentice-Hall, 1936.

Hoch, Charles, and Joel Friedman. *Radical Urban Political Economy: A Bibliographic Introduction.* Monticello, IL: Vance Bibliographies, 1980.

Hoffman, Paul. *Lions in the Street: The Inside Story of the Great Wall Street Law Firms.* New York: New American Library, 1974.

Hoguet, R. L. "The Land-Tax Illusion." *Trusts and Estates* 75 (August 1942): 115–118.

Holden, Arthur C. *Has the City Betrayed the Homeseeker?* 1930, p. 10, Box 28, Folder 1, Articles by Arthur Cort Holden, Arthur Cort Holden Papers. Princeton NJ: Princeton University Library.

Holden, Arthur C. "The Crisis in Real Estate." *Harper's Magazine*, November 1931.

Holden, Arthur C. *The Financial Plight of the City of New York: A Plea for Creative Financial Thinking Respecting the Growing Menace of Overhead Costs.* New York: self-pub., 1976.

Hopps, June G. "Ghetto Economic Corporation Theory, Reality and Policy Implications." *Review of Black Political Economy* 3, no. 3 (1973): 43–64.

Horton, Raymond D. "A Diversity Theory of Urban Development: Policy Implications for Business and Government." *Columbia Journal of World Business* 13 (Winter 1978): 72–80.

Howe, Frederic C. *The City: The Hope of Democracy.* New York: Charles Scribner's Sons, 1906.

Howe, Frederic C. *European Cities at Work.* New York: Charles Scribner's Sons, 1913.

Hoyt, Homer. "Economic Background of Cities." *Journal of Land and Public Utility Economics* 17, no. 2 (1941): 188–195.

Hoyt, Homer. "Homer Hoyt on the Development of Economic Base Concept." *Land Economics* 30, no. 2 (1954): 182–186.

Hoyt, Homer. "Urban Decentralization." *Journal of Land and Public Utility Economics* 16, no. 3 (1940): 270.

Hurd, Richard M. *Principles of City Land Values.* New York: Real Estate Record and Builders' Guide, 1903.

Hurd, George A. "Real-Estate Bonds as an Investment Security." *Annals of the American Academy of Political and Social Science* 88, no. 1 (1907): 79–94.

Huxtable, Ada Louise. "Stumbling toward Tomorrow: The Decline and Fall of the New York Vision." In *In Search of New York*, edited by Jim Sleeper, 47–56. New Brunswick, NJ: Transaction Publishers, 1987.

Hyde, Dorsey William. "The Fate of the Five Cent Fare." *National Municipal Review* 7, no. 6 (1918): 545–552.

Hylan, John. "Traction and Finance." *Forum* 65 (March 1921): 257–266.

Isard, Walter. *Location and Space-Economy: A General Theory Relating to Industrial Location, Market Areas, Land Use, Trade and Urban Structure.* London: MIT Press, 1956.

The Investment Position of Local Housing Authority Bonds. New York: R. R. Pressprich, 1942.

Invitation to Learning Radio Program. "On the Merits of Henry George's Progress and Poverty." February 28, 1943. https://cooperative-individualism.org/gideonse-harry_roundtable-on-henry-george-1943-apr-may.pdf.

Jacobs, Jane. "Downtown Is for People." *Fortune*, April 1958, 133–140.

Jacobs, Jane. "Strategies for Helping Cities." *American Economic Review* 49, no. 4 (1969): 652–656.

Jencks, Christopher. "The Perils of Pollyanna." *Working Papers for a New Society* 1, no. 1 (1973): 5–8.

Jones, Barclay Gibbs. "The Theory of the Urban Economy: Origins and Development with Emphasis on Intraurban Distribution of Population and Economic Activity." PhD diss., University of North Carolina, 1961.

Jones, Jesse H. *Real Estate's Importance in Recovery*. New York: National Capital Press, 1935.

Kennedy, Michael B. "The Fiscal Crisis of the City." In *Cities in Transformation: Class, Capital, and the State*, edited by Michael Peter Smith, 91-110. London: Sage Publications, 1985.

Kirshner, Edward M., and James Morey. "Controlling a City's Wealth: The Lessons of New Town Development." *Working Papers for a New Society* 1, no. 1 (1973): 9–19.

Klein, Henry H. *A Jew Exposes the Jewish World Conspiracy*. Arab, LA: Sons of Liberty, 1970.

Klein, Henry H. *My Last Fifty Years: An Autobiographical History of 'Inside' New York*. New York: Isaac Goldman, 1935.

Klein, Henry H. *Politics, Government and the Public Utilities in New York City*. New York: Isaac Goldmann, 1933.

Klein, Henry H. *Zionism Rules the World*. New York: Henry H. Klein, 1955.

Kropotkin, Petr Alekseevich. *Fields, Factories and Workshops: Or, Industry Combined with Agriculture and Brain Work with Manual Work*. New York: G. P. Putnam's Sons, 1904.

Kuenkle, Walter R. "A New Approach to Urban Land Valuation." *Journal of the American Institute of Real Estate Appraisers* 3 (April 1933): 193-195.

Lebenthal, Louis B. *The ABC of Municipal Bonds*. New York: Harper & Brothers, 1937.

Leinsdorf, David, and Donald Etra. *Citibank: Ralph Nader's Study Group Report on First National City Bank*. New York: Grossman Publishers, 1973.

Levey, Edgar J. *New York City's Progress towards Bankruptcy. A Communication Addressed to Hon. Martin Saxe, Member of the Joint Legislative Committee, Appointed to Examine into the Finances of New York City*. New York: Allied Real Estate Interests, 1908.

Long, Norton E. "Have Cities a Future?" *Public Administration Review* 33, no. 6 (1973): 543-552.

"'Lower Rents' as a City Slogan." *The Survey* 29, no. 24 (1913): 830–831.

MacCracken, John H. "Taxation of City Real Estate and Improvements on Real Estate as Illustrated in New York City." In *National Tax Association, State and Local Taxation First National Conference under the Auspices of the National Tax Association*, 375–397. New York: Macmillan, 1908.

Maltbie, Milo R. "The Taxation of Public Service Corporations." In *State and Local Taxation Second International Conference October 6–9, 1908*, 477–486. Columbus, OH: International Tax Season, 1908.

Maltbie, Milo R. "Transportation and City Planning." In *Fifth National Conference on City Planning*, 117–118. Cambridge, MA: Harvard University Press, 1913.

Mankoff, Milton. "Mythologies of Revolution." *Working Papers for a New Society* 2, no. 2 (1974): 74-79.

Marsh, Benjamin C. *An Introduction to City Planning: Democracy's Challenge to the American City*. New York: Benjamin C. Marsh, 1909.

Marsh, Benjamin C. *Lobbyist for the People: A Record of Fifty Years*. Washington, DC: Public Affairs Press, 1953.

Marsh, Benjamin C. *Taxation of Land Values in American Cities: The Next Step in Exterminating Poverty*. New York: Benjamin C. Marsh, 1911.

Marsh, Benjamin C. "Taxation versus Congestion." *Single Tax Review* 14 (January–February 1914): 16–20.

Massey, Doreen. "Towards a Critique of Industrial Location Theory." In *The Doreen Massey Reader*, edited by Brett Christophers, Rebecca Lave, Jamie Peck, and Marion Werner. Newcastle-upon-Tyne, 43-58. UK: Agenda Publishing, 2018.

McClellan, George B. *The Gentleman and the Tiger: The Autobiography of George B. McClellan, Jr.* New York: Lippincott, 1956.

McGoldrick, Joseph Daniel. *The Board of Estimate and Apportionment of New York City.* New York: National Municipal League, 1932.

McGoldrick, Joseph Daniel. "The New Tammany." *American Mercury* 15, no. 27 (1928): 1–12.

Meyer, Carlin. "Whose Windfall?" In *In Search of New York*, edited by Jim Sleeper, 18–22. New Brunswick, NJ: Transaction Publishers, 1987.

Miller, Stephen M., and William K. Tabb, "A New Look at a Pure Theory of Local Expenditures." *National Tax Journal* 26, no. 2 (1973): 161–176.

Millett, John D. *The Works Progress Administration in New York City.* Chicago: Public Administration Service, 1938.

Molotch, Harvey. "The City as a Growth Machine: Toward a Political Economy of Place." *American Journal of Sociology* 82, no. 2 (1976): 309–332.

Morgan, John S. *Business Faces the Urban Crisis.* Houston, TX: Gulf Publishing, 1969.

Moscow, Warren. *Politics in the Empire State.* New York: Greenwood Books, 1948.

Muller, W., and R. Rohr-Zanker, "The Fiscal Crisis and the Local State: Examination of the Structuralist Concept." *Environment and Planning A: Economy and Space* 21, no. 12 (1989): 1619–1638.

Mumford, Lewis. "Architecture and Broad Planning II. Realities vs. Dream." *Journal of the American Institute of Architects* 13, no. 6 (1925): 198–199.

Mumford, Lewis. "Botched Cities." *American Mercury* 27, no. 70 (1929): 143–150.

Mumford, Lewis. *The City in History: Its Origins, Its Transformations, and Its Prospects.* New York: Harcourt Brace & World, 1961.

Mumford, Lewis. *The Culture of Cities.* New York: Harcourt, Brace & Company, 1938.

Mumford, Lewis. "The Plan of New York." *New Republic*, June 22, 1932, 146–154.

Mumford, Lewis. *Technics and Civilization.* New York: Routledge and Kegan Paul, 1934.

Nelson, Stanley Carl. "Property Valuation in Urban Blighted Areas." PhD diss., University of California, Berkeley, 1955.

Newfield, Jack and Paul Du Bruel, *The Abuse of Power: The Permanent Government and the Fall of New York.* New York: Viking Press, 1977.

Noonan, Albert W. "Lawson Purdy's Influence on Assessment Practice." *American Journal of Economics and Sociology* 9, no. 1 (1949): 25–30.

O'Connor, James. *The Fiscal Crisis of the State.* New York: St. Martin's Press, 1973.

Odiorne, George S. *Green Power: The Corporation and the Urban Crisis.* New York: Pitman Publishing, 1969.

Olken, Charles E. "Economic Development in the Model Cities Program." *Law and Contemporary Problems* 36, no. 2 (1971): 205–226.

Olmsted, Frederick L. *Being Two Papers Read Before the American Social Science Association in 1870, Entitled, Respectively, Public Parks and the Enlargement of Towns and A Consideration of the Justifying Value of a Public Park.* Brookline, MA: n.p., 1902.

Olmsted, Frederick L. "The Future of New York." In *Frederick Law Olmsted: Writings on Landscape, Culture and Society Essential Texts*, edited by Charles Beveridge, 556–564. Washington, DC: Library of America, 2010.

Osborne, Philip B. *The War That Business Must Win.* New York: McGraw Hill, 1970.

Ott, Attiat F., and Jang H. Yoo. *New York City's Financial Crisis: Can the Trend Be Reversed?* Washington, DC: American Enterprise Institute for Public Policy Research, 1975.

Paine, Willis S. "Savings Banks That Have Failed." *Banker's Magazine* 67 (July–December 1903): 31–34.

Panuch, Anthony J. *Building a Better New York: Final Report to the Mayor Robert F. Wagner.* New York: n.p., 1960.

Peel, Roy. *The Political Clubs of New York.* New York: G. P. Putnam's Sons, 1935.

Perlo, Victor. *The Empire of High Finance.* Ann Arbor: University of Michigan Press, 1957.

Pogodzinski, J. M. "The Effects of Fiscal and Exclusionary Zoning on Household Location: A Critical Review." *Journal of Housing Research* 2, no. 2 (1991): 145–160.

Polak, Edward. "The New York Tax Exemption Law." In *Report of the National Tax Relief Convention*, 25–32. Chicago: Manufactures and Merchants Federal Tax League, 1923.

Polak, Edward. "Reduction of Tax on Buildings in the City of New York." *Annals of the American Academy of Political and Social Science* 58, no. 1 (1915): 183–188.

Post, Langdon. *The Challenge of Housing.* New York: Farrar & Rinehart, 1938.

Post, Louis F. "The Taxing Power and the Housing Problem." *Municipal Affairs* 6, no. 418 (1902): 418–430.

Powers, L. G. "Increasing Municipal Indebtedness." *National Municipal Review* 3, no. 1 (1914): 102–106.

Purdy, Lawson. "The Best Taxed City in the World: Address before the Real Estate Board of Brokers of the City of New York." Henry George School of Social Science, New York, February 24, 1906. https://hgarchives.org/historical-collections-2/new-york-tax-reform-association-1891-1924/series-one/.

Purdy, Lawson. *City Real Estate Assessment.* Columbus, OH: International Tax Association, 1908.

Purdy, Lawson. "Condemnation, Assessments and Taxation in Relation to City Planning." In *Proceedings of the Third National Conference on City Planning*, 118–130. Boston: Harvard University Press, 1911.

Purdy, Lawson. "Districting and Zoning of Cities." In *Proceedings of the Ninth National Conference on City Planning*, 170–182. Cambridge, MA: Harvard University Press, 1917.

Purdy, Lawson. "The Influence of Taxation on the Prosperity of Cities." *The Public* 9 (October 6, 1906): 639–645.

Quante, Wolfgang. *The Exodus of Corporate Headquarters from New York City.* New York: Praeger Publishers, 1976.

Ratcliff, Richard U. Review of *The Economic Status of the New York Region*, by Homer Hoyt. *Journal of Political Economy* 54, no. 3 (1947): 382–333.

Real Estate Analysis. *Real Estate Trends in New York City: With Special Emphasis on the Island of Manhattan.* Saint Louis, MO: Real Estate Analysis, 1942.

Reed, Henry E. "The True Value of Real Estate." *Journal of the American Institute of Real Estate Appraisers* 3, no. 4 (1935): 342–350.

Richards, David H. *Your Taxes: An Explanation and a Program.* New York: New York State Committee, Communist Party, 1938.

Robinson, Allan. "The Heavier Land Tax." *Annals of the American Academy of Political and Social Science* 58, no. 1 (1915): 198–201.

Rodgers, Cleveland. *New York Plans for the Future.* New York: Harper & Brothers, 1943.

Rosen, S. M. "Better Mousetraps—Reflections on Economic Development in the Ghetto." *Urban Review* 4 (1970): 14–18.

Rowdin, Lloyd. "Land Economics in the United States." *Town Planning Review* 21, no. 2 (1950): 161–179.

Sales, William W., Jr. "New York City: Prototype of the Urban Crisis." *Black Scholar* 7 no. 3 (1975): 20–30, 35–39.

Sayre, Wallace Stanley, and Herbert Kaufman. *Governing New York City: Politics in the Metropolis*. New York: W. W. Norton, 1960.

Scholz, Karl. Review of *The Valuation of Real Estate*, by Frederick M. Babcock. *Annals of the American Academy of Political and Social Science* 169 (September 1933): 219.

Schumacher, E. F. *Small Is Beautiful: Economics as if People Mattered*. New York: First Harper Perennial, 2010.

Schwab, John Christopher. "History of the New York Property Tax." *Publications of the American Economic Association* 5 (September 1890): 363–466.

Seabury, Samuel. *Municipal Ownership and Operation of Public Utilities*. New York: Municipal Ownership Publishing, 1905.

Seligman, E. R. A. "Discussion." In *The Government of the City of New York*, edited by the New York State Constitutional Convention Commission, 164–169. New York: Academy of Political Science, 1915.

Seligman, E. R. A. "The Franchise Tax Law in New York." *Quarterly Journal of Economics* 13 (July 1899): 445–452.

Shanks, Sanders, Jr. "The Extent of Municipal Defaults." *National Municipal Review* 24, no. 32 (1935): 24–32.

Shanks, Sanders, Jr. "Present State of Municipal Credit." *National Municipal Review* 23, no. 2 (1934): 92–106.

Simpson, Herbert. "Real Estate Speculation and the Depression." *American Economic Review* 23, no. 1 (1933): 163–171.

Sinclair, Upton. *The Epic Plan for California*. New York: Farrar & Rinehart, 1934.

Sisson, Francis H. "New York Real Estate as a Field for Investment." *Banker's Magazine* 75 (1907): 95–101.

Sleeper, Harold R. *A Realistic Approach to Private Investment in Urban Redevelopment Applied to East Harlem as a Blighted Area . . . under the Direction of the Manhattan Development Committee*. New York: Architectural Forum, 1945.

Sleeper, Jim. "Boom and Bust with Ed Koch," in *In Search of New York*, ed. Jim Sleeper, 31–46. New Brunswick, NJ: Transaction Publishers, 1987.

Somers, William A. *The Valuation of Real Estate for Purposes of Taxation*. St. Paul, MN: William Somers, 1901.

Smith, Chris. "In Conversation: Michael Bloomberg." *New York Magazine*, September 6, 2013.

Smith, Francis. "New York City's Fiscal Situation." *American Journal of Economics and Sociology* 29, no. 1 (1970): 49-54.

Smith, Stephen. *Methods of Improving the Homes of the Laboring and Tenement House Classes of New York*. Publisher Not Identified, Place of Publication Not Identified, April 1875.

Spengler, Edwin Harold. *Land Values in New York in Relation to Transit Facilities*. New York: Columbia University, 1930.

Spratlen, Thaddeus H. "Ghetto Economic Development: Content and Character of the Literature." *Review of Black Political Economy* 1, no. 4 (1971): 43–71.

Steffens, Lincoln. "Hearst, The Man of Mystery." *American Magazine* 63, no. 1 (1906): 3–22.

Stein, Clarence. "Dinosaur Cities." *Survey Graphic* 54, no. 1 (1925): 134–138.

Stein, Clarence. "The Housing Crisis in New York." *Survey* 44 (September 1920): 659–661.

Stein, L. K. Review of *The History of Municipal Ownership of Land on Manhattan Island*, by George Ashton Black. *Annals of the American Academy of Political and Social Science* 2 (1892): 100.

Swan, Herbert S. *The Housing Market in New York City*. New York: Reinhold Publishing, 1944.

Swan, Herbert S. "Land Values and City Growth." *Journal of Land and Public Utility Economics* 10, no. 2 (1934): 188–201.

Tabb, William K. "Perspectives on Black Economic Development." *Journal of Economic Issues* 4, no. 4 (1970): 68–81.

Tabb, William K. *The Political Economy of the Black Ghetto*. New York: Norton, 1970.

Tabb, William K. "What Happened to Black Economic Development?" *Review of Black Political Economy* 17, no. 2 (1988): 65–85.

Tanzer, Laurence Arnold. *The New York City Charter: Adopted November 3, 1936, with Source Notes, a History of the Charter and Analysis and Summary of Its Provisions, Together with Appendices*. New York: Clark Boardman, 1937.

Tanzer, Laurence Arnold. "The Work of the New York Committee on Taxation." *Bulletin of the National Tax Association* 1, no. 2 (1916): 29–37.

Thomas, Norman, and Paul Blanshard. *What's the Matter with New York: A National Problem*. New York: Macmillan, 1932.

Tiebout, Charles M. "A Pure Theory of Local Expenditures." *Journal of Political Economy* 64, no. 5 (1945): 416–424.

Tooke, C. W. "Uniformity in Municipal Finance." *Municipal Affairs* 2 (June 1898): 200–202.

Tretter, Maxwell H. "Public Housing Finance." *Harvard Law Review* 54, no. 8 (1941): 1325–1358.

Trosten, David. *The New Charter for New York City: A Digest of the Proposed Charter for New York City as Filed with the City Clerk on August 17, 1936*. New York: Oxford Books, 1936.

Tugwell, Rexford. *Housing Activities and Plans of the Resettlement Administration*. Housing Officials Yearbook. Washington, DC: National Association of Housing, 1936.

Tugwell, Rexford. "Implementing the General Interest." *Public Administration Review* 1, no. 1 (1940): 32–49.

Tugwell, Rexford. "The Real Estate Dilemma." *Public Administration Review* 2 (Winter 1942): 27–29.

Tugwell, Rexford. "The Sources of New Deal Reformism." *Ethics* 64, no. 4 (1954): 249–276.

Tugwell, Rexford. "When the USHA Buys Land." *New Republic*, October 25, 1939, 141–143.

Vietorisz, Thomas, and Bennet Harrison. *The Economic Development of Harlem*. New York: Praeger Publishers, 1970.

Vernon, Raymond. *The Changing Economic Function of the Central City*. New York: Area Development Committee of the CED, 1959.

Vernon, Raymond. *The Myth and Reality of Our Urban Problems*. Cambridge, MA: Harvard University Press, 1966.

Vernon, Raymond. "Production and Distribution in the Large Metropolis." *Annals of the American Academy of Political and Social Sciences* 314, no. 1 (1957): 15–29.

Walker, Mabel. "Property Tax Expedients in Urban Renewal." In *Proceedings of the Annual Conference on Taxation under the Auspices of the National Tax Association*, 41–51. Harrisburg, PA: National Tax Association, 1960.

Walker, Mabel. "Upheaval in Local Tax Patterns." *Challenge* 5, no. 6 (1957): 23–27.

Walker, Mabel. *Urban Blight and Slums: Economic and Legal Factors in Their Origin, Reclamation, and Prevention*. New York: Russel & Russell, 1938.

Warner, Richard F. "Profiles on the Up." *New Yorker*, May 31, 1930, 19–22.

Weimer, A. M. "A Note on the Early History of Land Economics." *Real Estate Economics* 12, no. 3 (1984): 408–416.

Wendt, Paul F. "Influence of Transportation Changes on Urban Land Uses and Values." *HRB Bulletin* 268 (1960): 95–104.

West, Max. "Municipal Franchises in New York." In *Municipal Monopolies: A Collection of Papers by American Economists and Specialists*, edited by Webster Bemis, 465–422. New York: Thomas Y. Crowell, 1899.

Wexelstein, Leon. *Building Up Greater Brooklyn: With Sketches of Men Instrumental in Brooklyn's Amazing Development*. Brooklyn, NY: Brooklyn Biographical Society, 1925.

Wheelock, William H. "The Effects of the Present Financial Situation upon Real Estate." *Harvard Business Review* 9 (April 1931): 312–318.

White, J. Austin. *An Analysis of Municipal Bonds*. Cincinnati: J. A. White, 1942.

White, John R., and Edna L. Hebard. *The Manhattan Housing Market*. New York: Brown Harris Stevens, 1960.

Whitten, Robert. "Suburban Land Speculation." *Journal of Land and Public Utility Economics* 12, no. 3 (1936): 221–227.

Wickens, David L. *Residential Real Estate: Its Economic Position as Shown by Values, Rents, Family Incomes, Financing, and Construction, Together with Estimates for All Real Estate*. Washington, DC: National Bureau of Economic Research, 1941.

Wilcox, Delos F. *The American City: A Problem in Democracy*. New York: Macmillan, 1904.

Wilcox, Delos F. "Financial and Administrative Preparation for Municipal Ownership." Address before the National Public Ownership Conference, Chicago, November 25, 1917.

Wilcox, Delos F. "Fundamental Planks in a Public Utility Program." In *Proceedings of the Conference of American Mayors on Public Policies as to Municipal Utilities* 57 (January 1915): 8–19.

Wilcox, Delos F. "The New York Subway Contracts." *National Municipal Review* 2, no. 3 (1913): 375–391.

Wood, George W. *The Growth of New York*. New York: George W. Wood, 1865.

Selected Secondary Books and Articles

Abramson, Daniel M. *Obsolescence: An Architectural History*. Chicago: University of Chicago Press, 2016.

Adésínà, Jìmí. "Return to a Wider Vision of Social Policy: Re-reading Theory and History," *South African Review of Sociology* 46, no. 3 (2015): 99–119.

Abu-Lughod, Janet L. *New York, Chicago, Los Angeles: America's Global Cities*. Minneapolis: University of Minnesota Press, 1999.

Adelstein, Richard P. "'The Nation as an Economic Unit': Keynes, Roosevelt, and the Managerial Ideal." *Journal of American History* 78, no. 1 (1991): 160–187.

Akuno, Kali, and Ajamu Nangwaya, eds. *Jackson Rising: The Struggle for Economic Democracy and Black Self-Determination in Jackson, Mississippi*. Montreal, Canada: Daraja Press, 2018.

Alperovitz, Gar. *What Then Must We Do? Straight Talk about the Next American Revolution*. White River Junction, VT: Chelsea Green, 2013.

Andelson, Robert V., and Mason Gaffney. "Seligman and His Critique from Social Utility." *American Journal of Economics and Sociology* 62, no. 5 (2003): 407–432.

Andersson, Jenny. *Between Growth and Security: Swedish Social Democracy from a Strong Society to a Third Way.* Manchester: Manchester University Press, 2006.

Baer, William C. "Is Speculative Building Underappreciated in Urban History?" *Urban History* 34, no. 2 (2007): 296–316.

Bakersville, Peter A. "Financial Capital and the Municipal State: The Case of Victoria, British Columbia, 1910–1936." *Studies in Political Economy: A Socialist Review* 21, no. 1 (January 1986): 83–106.

Balogh, Brian. *The Associational State: American Governance in the Twentieth Century.* Philadelphia: University of Pennsylvania Press, 2018.

Baradaran, Mehrsa. *The Color of Money: Black Banks and the Racial Wealth Gap.* Cambridge, MA: Harvard University Press, 2019.

Barcelona En Comu, eds. *Fearless Cities: A Guide to the Global Municipalist Movement.* Oxford: New Internationalist Publications, 2019.

Barr, Jason M. *Building the Skyline: The Birth and Growth of Manhattan's Skyscrapers.* New York: Oxford University Press, 2016.

Bartik, Timothy J. *Making Sense of Incentives: Taming Business Incentives to Promote Prosperity.* Kalamazoo, MI: W. E. Upjohn Institute for Employment Research, 2019.

Batt, H. William. "Land Value Maps Are Not New, but Their Utility Needs to Be Rediscovered." *International Journal of Transdisciplinary Research* 4, no. 1 (2009): 108–158.

Beauregard, Robert. *Voices of Decline: The Postwar Fate of US Cities.* Cambridge, MA: Blackwell Publishers, 1993.

Been, Vicki, Josiah Madar, and Simon McDonnell. "Urban Land-Use Regulation: Are Homevoters Overtaking the Growth Machine?" *Journal of Empirical Legal Studies* 11, no. 2 (2014): 227–265.

Belussi, Fiorenza, and Katia Caldari, "At the Origin of the Industrial District: Alfred Marshall and the Cambridge School." *Cambridge Journal of Economics* 33, no. 2 (2009): 335–355.

Bender, Thomas. *The Unfinished City: New York and the Metropolitan Idea.* New York: New York University Press, 2002.

Berman, Elizabeth Popp. *Thinking Like an Economist: How Efficiency Replaced Equality in U.S. Public Policy.* Princeton, NJ: Princeton University Press, 2022.

Bernstein, Michael A. *A Perilous Progress: Economists and Public Purpose in Twentieth-Century America.* Princeton, NJ: Princeton University Press, 2001.

Bivens, Josh. *The Industrial Policy Revolution Has Begun, but Another Is Still Needed.* Economic Policy Institute. May 18, 2023. https://www.epi.org/publication/industrial-policy/.

Blackmar, Elizabeth. *Manhattan for Rent, 1785–1850.* Ithaca, NY: Cornell University Press, 1989.

Blok, Fred L., and Margaret R. Somers. *The Power of Market Fundamentalism: Karl Polanyi's Critique.* Cambridge, MA: Harvard University Press, 2016.

Bloom, Nicholas Dagen. *Public Housing That Worked: New York in the Twentieth Century.* Philadelphia: University of Pennsylvania Press, 2009.

Blyth, Mark. *Great Transformations: Economic Ideas and Institutional Change in the Twentieth Century.* New York: Cambridge University Press, 2002.

Bookchin, Murray. *The Limits of the City.* New York: Harper and Row, 1974.

Booth, Douglas E. "Municipal Socialism and City Government Reform: The Milwaukee Experience 1910–1940." *Journal of Urban History* 12, no. 1 (1985): 51–74.

Booth, Douglas E. "Transportation, City Building, and Financial Crisis: Milwaukee, 1852–1868." *Journal of Urban History* 9, no. 1 (1983): 335–363.

Booth, Douglas E. "Urban Growth and Decline, Budgetary Incrementalism and Municipal Finances: Milwaukee 1870–1977." *Explorations in Economic History* 25, no. 1 (1988): 20–41.

Bosselman, Fred P. "The Commodification of 'Nature's Metropolis': The Historical Context of Illinois' Unique Zoning Standards." *Northern Illinois University Law Review* 12, no. 3 (1992): 527–588.

Bower, Lewis Lattin. "An Examination of the Emergence, Development and Current State of Urban Land Use Theory." PhD diss., Syracuse University, 1964.

Brenner, Neil. *New State Spaces: Urban Governance and the Rescaling of Statehood.* New York: Oxford University Press, 2004.

Brinkley, Alan. *The End of Reform: New Deal Liberalism in Recession and War.* New York: Vintage Books, 1996.

Brick, Howard. *Transcending Capitalism: Visions of a New Society in Modern American Thought.* Ithaca, NY: Cornell University Press, 2016.

Brocker, Michael, and Christopher Hanes. "The 1920s American Real Estate Boom and the Downturn of the Great Depression: Evidence from City Cross-Sections." In *Housing and Mortgage Markets in Historical Perspectives,* edited by Eugene N. White, Kenneth Snowden, and Price Fishback, 161–202. Chicago: University of Chicago Press, 2014.

Broxmeyer, Jeffrey. *Electoral Capitalism: The Party System in New York's Gilded Age.* Philadelphia: University of Pennsylvania Press, 2020.

Buenker, John D. *Urban Liberalism and Progressive Reform.* New York: Scribner, 1978.

Buder, Stanley. *Visionaries and Planners: The Garden City Movement and the Modern Community.* New York: Oxford University Press, 1990.

Burrows, Edwin G., and Mike Wallace. *Gotham: A History of New York City to 1898.* New York: Oxford University Press, 1999.

Buttenwieser, Ann L. "Shelter for What and for Whom? On the Route towards Vladeck Houses, 1930 to 1940." *Journal of Urban History* 12, no. 4 (1986): 391–413.

Callinicos, Ale, Stathis Kouvelakis, and Lucia Pradella, eds. *Routledge Handbook of Marxism and Post-Marxism.* New York: Taylor & Francis, 2020.

Cameron, Angus. "Turning Point: The Volatile Geographies of Taxation." *Antipode* 38, no. 2 (2006): 236–258.

Campanella, Thomas J. *Brooklyn: The Once and Future City.* Princeton, NJ: Princeton University Press, 2019.

Caniglia, Beth, Beatrice Frank, John L. Knott Jr., Kenneth S. Sagendorf, and Eugene A. Wilkerson, eds. *Regenerative Urban Development, Climate Change and the Common Good.* New York: Routledge, 2020.

Cannato, Vincent J. *The Ungovernable City: John Lindsay and His Struggle to Save New York.* New York: Perseus Books, 2001.

Caro, Robert. *The Power Broker: Robert Moses and the Fall of New York.* New York: Knopf, 1975.

Cebul, Brent. "Creative Competition: Georgia Power, the Tennessee Valley Authority, and the Creation of a Rural Consumer Economy, 1934–1955." *Journal of American History* 105, no. 1 (2018): 45–70.

Cebul, Brent. *Illusions of Progress: Business, Poverty, and Liberalism in the American Century.* Philadelphia: University of Pennsylvania Press, 2023.

Cebul, Brent. "'They Were the Moving Spirits': Local Businesspeople and Supply Side Liberalism in the Postwar South." In *Capital Gains: Business and Politics in the Twentieth Century,* edited by Richard John and Kimberly Phillips-Fein, 139–156. Philadelphia: University of Pennsylvania Press, 2016.

Cebul, Brent, Lily Geismer, and Mason B. Williams, eds. *Shaped by the State: Towards a New Political History of the Twentieth Century*. Chicago: University of Chicago Press, 2019.

Cebul, Brent, and Mason B. Williams. "'Really and Truly a Partnership': The New Deal's Associational State and the Making of Postwar American Politics." In *Shaped by the State: Towards a New Political History of the Twentieth Century*, edited by Brent Cebul, Lily Geismer, and Mason B. Williams, 96–122. Chicago: University of Chicago Press, 2019.

Ceplaire, Larry. *Anti-Communism in Twentieth-Century America: A Critical History*. New York: Bloomsbury Publishing, 2011.

Chrysopoulou, Anna, Mark Anielski, and Michael Weatherhead. *Failure Demand: Counting the Trust Costs of an Unjust and Unsustainable Economic System*. Wellbeing Economy Alliance. September 2021. https://weall.org/wp-content/uploads/FailureDemand_Finaleport_September 2021-1.pdf.

Chwalisz, Claudia, and Patrick Diamond, eds. *The Predistribution Agenda: Tackling Inequality and Supporting Sustainable Growth*. New York: I. B. Tauris, 2015.

Clark, Shannan. *The Making of the American Creative Class: New York's Culture Workers and Twentieth Century Consumer Capitalism*. New York: Oxford University Press, 2021.

Clavel, Pierre. *The Progressive City: Planning and Participation, 1969–1984*. New Brunswick, NJ: Rutgers University Press, 1986.

Cohen, Lizabeth. *A Consumer's Republic: The Politics of Mass Consumption in Postwar America*. New York: Knopf Doubleday, 2008.

Cohen, Nancy L. *The Reconstruction of American Liberalism 1865–1914*. Chapel Hill: University of North Carolina Press, 2002.

Collins, Robert M. *More: The Politics of Economic Growth in Postwar America*. New York: Oxford University Press, 2002.

Colton, Kent W. "Housing Finance in the United States: The Transformation of the U.S. Housing Finance System." Cambridge, MA: Harvard Joint Center for Housing Studies, 2002. https://www.jchs.harvard.edu/sites/default/files/media/imp/w02-5_colton.df.

Conn, Steven. *Americans against the City: Anti-Urbanism in the Twentieth Century*. New York: Oxford University Press, 2014.

Connolly, James. "Bringing the City Back In: Space and Place in the Urban History of the Gilded Age and Progressive Era." *Journal of the Gilded Age and Progressive Era* 1, no. 3 (2002): 258–278.

Connolly, James. *The Triumph of Ethnic Progressivism: Urban Political Culture in Boston, 1900–1925*. Cambridge, MA: Harvard University Press, 1998.

Connolly, N.D.B. *A World More Concrete: Real Estate and the Remaking of Jim Crow South Florida*. Chicago: University of Chicago Press, 2014.

Cowie, Jefferson. *The Great Exception: The New Deal and the Limits of American Politics*. Princeton, NJ: Princeton University Press, 2016.

Crompton, John L. "A Review of the Economic Data Emanating from the Development of Central Park and Its Influence on the Construction of Early Urban Parks in the United States." *Journal of Planning History* 20, no. 2 (2021): 134–156.

Curl, John. *For All the People: Uncovering the Hidden History of Cooperation, Cooperative Movements, and Communalism in America*. Oakland, CA: PM Press, 2009.

Currarino, Rosanne. *The Labor Question in America: Economic Democracy in the Gilded Age*. Urbana: University of Illinois Press, 2011.

Dabel, Jane E. *A Respectable Woman: The Public Roles of African American Women in 19th Century New York*. New York: New York University Press, 2008.

Daly, Herman. *From Uneconomic Growth to a Steady-State Economy*. Cheltenham, UK: Edward Elgar Publishing, 2014.

Daly, Herman. *Steady-State Economics*. Washington, DC: Island Press, 1991.

Darton, Eric. *Divided We Stand: A Biography of New York's World Trade Center*. New York: Basic Books, 2011.

Davies, Tom Adam. *Mainstreaming Black Power*. Oakland: University of California Press, 2017.

DeFillipis, James. *Unmaking Goliath: Community Control in the Face of Global Capital*. New York: Routledge, 2004.

Derrick, Peter. *Tunneling to the Future: The Story of the Great Subway Expansion That Saved New York*. New York: New York University Press, 2002.

Diamond, Andrew J., and Thomas J. Sugrue, eds. *The Neoliberal City: The Remaking of Postwar Urban America*. New York: New York University Press, 2020.

Dilworth, Richardson, ed. *The City in American Political Development*. New York: Routledge, 2009.

Dilworth, Richardson. *The Urban Origins of Suburban Autonomy*. Cambridge, MA: Harvard University Press, 2003.

Dilworth, Richardson, and Timothy P. R. Weaver. *How Ideas Shape Urban Political Development*. Philadelphia: University of Pennsylvania Press, 2020.

Doherty, Iwan. "Why Has New York Seen a Boom in New Yorker Cooperatives?" *Mutual Interest Media*, September 30, 2021. https://www.mutualinterest.coop/2021/09/why-has-new-york-seen-a-boom-in-new-worker-cooperatives/.

Dolgoff, Sam, ed. *The Anarchist Collectives: Worker's Self-Management in the Spanish Revolution*. Montreal, Canada: Black Rose Books, 1974.

Dunning, Claire. *Nonprofit Neighborhoods: An Urban History of Inequality and the American State*. Chicago: University of Chicago Press, 2022.

Dyble, Louis Nelson. *Paying the Toll: Local Power, Regional Politics, and the Golden Gate Bridge*. Philadelphia: University of Pennsylvania Press, 2009.

Einhorn, Robin L. *Property Rules: Political Economy in Chicago, 1833–1872*. Chicago: University of Chicago Press, 2001.

Einstein, Katherine Levine, and Maxwell Palmer. "Land of the Freeholder: How Property Rights Make Local Voting Rights." *Journal of Historical Political Economy* 1, no. 4 (2021): 499–530.

Ekman, Peter. "From Prophecy to Projection: The Metropolitan Region Study and the Rescaling of the Urban Future, 1956–1968." *Planning Perspectives* 36, no. 1 (2021): 147–182.

Elbaum, Max. *Revolution in the Air: Sixties Radicals Turn to Lenin, Mao and Che*. New York: Verso, 2002.

Elkin, Stanley. *City and Regime in the American Republic*. Chicago: University of Chicago Press, 1987.

England, Christopher William. "Land and Liberty: Henry George, the Single Tax Movement, and the Origins of 20th Century Liberalism." PhD diss., Georgetown University, 2015.

Erie, Steven P. "How the Urban West Was Won: The Local State and Economic Growth in Los Angeles, 1880–1932." *Urban Affairs Quarterly* 27, no. 4 (1992): 519–554.

Erie, Steven P., Vladimir Kogan, and Scott A. Mackenzie. *Paradise Plundered: Fiscal Crisis and Governance Failures in San Diego*. Stanford, CA: Stanford University Press, 2011.

Escobar, Arturo. *Encountering Development: The Making and Unmaking of the Third World*. Princeton, NJ: Princeton University Press, 2012.

Fainstein, Norman., and Susan Fainstein. "New York City: The Manhattan Business District, 1945–1988." In *Unequal Partnerships: The Political Economy of Urban Redevelopment in Postwar America*, edited by Gregory Squires, 59–79. New Brunswick, NJ: Rutgers University Press, 1989.

Fairfield, John D. *The Public and Its Possibilities: Cities and Civic Life in American History*. Philadelphia, PA: Temple University Press, 2010.

Fasenfest, David, and Laura Reese, eds. *Critical Evaluations of Economic Development Policies*. Detroit: Wayne State University Press, 2004.

Field, Alexander J. "Uncontrolled Land Development and the Duration of the Depression in the United States." *Journal of Economic History* 52, no. 4 (1992): 785–805.

Finegold, Kenneth. *Reform Challenges to Machine Politics in New York, Cleveland, and Chicago*. Princeton, NJ: Princeton University Press, 1994.

Fink, Leon. *In Search of the Working Class: Essays in American Labor History and Political Culture*. Urbana: University of Illinois Press, 1994.

Fitch, Robert. "Planning New York," in *The Fiscal Crisis of American Cities*, ed. Roger E. Alcaly and David Mermelstein, 246–285. New York: Vintage Original, 1976.

Fitch, Robert. *The Assassination of New York*. New York: Verso, 1993.

Fioramonti, Lorenzo. *Gross Domestic Problem: The Politics behind the World's Most Powerful Number*. London: Zed Books, 2013.

Flanagan, Richard M. *Robert Wagner and the Rise of New York City's Plebiscitary Mayorality: The Tamer of the Tammany Tiger*. New York: Palgrave Macmillan, 2014.

Florida, Richard. *The Rise of the Creative Class, and How It's Transforming Work, Leisure, Community, and Everyday Life*. New York: Basic Books, 2002.

Fogelson, Robert M. *Downtown: Its Rise and Fall, 1880–1950*. New Haven, CT: Yale University Press, 2008.

Fogelson, Robert M. *The Great Rent Wars; New York 1917–1929*. New Haven, CT: Yale University Press, 2013.

Fogelson, Robert. *Working-Class Utopias: A History of Cooperative Housing in New York City* Princeton, NJ: Princeton University Press, 2022.

Foster, Mark S. *From Streetcar to Superhighway: American City Planners and Urban Transportation, 1900–1940*. Philadelphia, PA: Temple University Press, 1981.

Fraser, Steve. *The Age of Acquiescence: The Life and Death of American Resistance to Organized Wealth and Power*. New York: Basic Books, 2016.

Fraser, Steve, and Gary Gerstle, eds. *The Rise and Fall of the New Deal Order, 1930–1980*. Princeton, NJ: Princeton University Press. 1989.

Frazier, Nishani. *Harambee City: The Congress of Racial Equality in Cleveland and the Rise of Black Power Populism*. Fayetteville: University of Arkansas Press, 2017.

Freeman, Joshua Benjamin. *Working-Class New York: Life and Labor since World War II*. New York: New Press, 2001.

Freund, David M. P. *Colored Property: State Policy and White Racial Politics in Suburban America*. Chicago: University of Chicago Press, 2010.

Freund, David M. P. "Marketing the Free Market: State Intervention and the Politics of Prosperity in Metropolitan America." In *The New Suburban History*, edited by Kevin M. Kruse and Thomas J. Sugrue, 11–32. Chicago: University of Chicago Press, 2006.

Fuchs, Ester. *Mayors and Money: Fiscal Policy in New York and Chicago*. Chicago: University of Chicago, 2010.

Fure-Slocum, Eric. *Contesting the Postwar City: Working-Class and Growth Politics in 1940s Milwaukee*. Cambridge: Cambridge University Press, 2015.

Gale, Dennis E. *The Misunderstood History of Gentrification: People, Planning, Preservation, and Urban Renewal, 1915–2020*. Philadelphia, PA: Temple University Press, 2021.

Galston, William A. *Liberal Purposes: Goods, Virtues, and Diversity in the Liberal State*. New York: Cambridge University Press, 1991.

Geismer, Lily. *Don't Blame Us: Suburban Liberals and the Transformation of the Democratic Party*. Princeton, NJ: Princeton University Press, 2015.

Gelfand, Mark I. "Rexford G. Tugwell and the Frustration of Planning in New York City." *Journal of the American Planning Association* 51, no. 2 (1985): 151–160.

Gerstle, Gary. "The Protean Character of American Liberalism." *American Historical Review* 99, no. 4 (1994): 143–173.

Gibson-Graham, J. K. *The End of Capitalism (As We Knew It): A Feminist Critique of Political Economy*. Minneapolis: University of Minnesota Press, 2006.

Gill, Jonathan. *Harlem: The Four Hundred Year History from Dutch Village to Capital of Black America*. New York: Grove Atlantic, 2011.

Gilman, Nils. *Mandarins of the Future: Modernization Theory in Cold War America*. Baltimore: Johns Hopkins University Press, 2003.

Glaeser, Edward L. "A Nation of Gamblers: Real Estate Speculation and American History." *American Economic Review* 103, no. 3 (2013): 1–42.

Glickman, Lawrence B. *Free Enterprise: An American History*. New Haven, CT: Yale University Press, 2019.

Goldscheid, Rudolf. "A Sociological Approach to Problems of Public Finance." In *Classics in the Theory of Public Finances*, edited by R. A. Musgrave and A. T. Peacock, 202–213. London: Macmillan, 1962.

Goldstein, Brian D. *The Roots of Urban Renaissance: Gentrification and the Struggle over Harlem*. Cambridge, MA: Harvard University Press, 2017.

Golway, Terry. *Machine Made: Tammany Hall and the Creation of Modern American Politics*. New York: Liveright Publishing, 2014.

Gordon, Colin. "Blighting the Way: Urban Renewal, Economic Development, and the Elusive Definition of Blight." *Fordham Urban Law Journal* 31, no. 305 (2004): 305–337.

Gordon, Robert J. *The Rise and Fall of American Growth: The U.S. Standard of Living since the Civil War*. Princeton, NJ: Princeton University Press, 2017.

Gotham, Kevin Fox. "Growth Machine Up-Links: Urban Renewal and the Rise and Fall of a Pro-Growth Coalition in a U.S. City." *Critical Sociology* 26, no. 3 (2000): 268–300.

Gourevitch, Alexander. *From Slavery to the Cooperative Commonwealth: Labor and the Republican Liberty in the Nineteenth Century*. New York: Cambridge University Press, 2015.

Gray, Rowena. "Inequality in Nineteenth Century Manhattan: Evidence from the Housing Market." *Social Science History* 44, no. 3 (2020): 571–582.

Green, Alix R. *History, Policy and Public Purpose: Historians and Historical Thinking in Government*. London: Palgrave Macmillan, 2016.

Greenberg, Miriam. *Branding New York: How a City in Crisis Was Sold to the World*. New York: Routledge, 2008.

Guinan, Joe, and Martin O'Neill. *The Case for Community Wealth Building*. Medford, MA: Polity Press, 2020.

Hackworth, Jason. "Local Autonomy, Bond-Rating Agencies and Neoliberal Urbanism in the United States." *International Journal of Urban and Regional Research* 26, no. 4 (2003): 707–725.

Hackworth, Jason. *The Neoliberal City: Governance, Ideology, and Development in American Urbanism.* Ithaca, NY: Cornell University Press, 2013.

Haila, Anna. *Urban Land Rent: Singapore as a Property State.* Hoboken, NJ: John Wiley & Sons, 2015.

Hammack, David C. *Power and Society: Greater New York at the Turn of the Century.* New York: Russel Sage Foundation, 1982.

Harris, Richard. *Unplanned Suburbs: Toronto's American Tragedy, 1900 to 1950.* Baltimore: Johns Hopkins University Press, 1996.

Hartog, Hendrik. *Public Property and Private Property: The Corporation of the City of New York in American Law, 173–1870.* Ithaca, NY: Cornell University Press, 1983.

Harvey, David. *A Brief History of Neoliberalism.* Oxford: Oxford University Press, 2007.

Harvey, David. "From Managerialism to Entrepreneurialism: The Transformation in Urban Governance in Late Capitalism." *Geografiska Annaler. Series B, Human Geography* 71, no. 1 (1989): 3–17.

Harvey, David. *Rebel Cities: From the Right to the City to the Urban Revolution.* London: Verso, 2013.

Haydu, Jeffrey. *Citizen Employers: Business Communities and Labor in Cincinnati and San Francisco, 1870–1916.* Ithaca, NY: Cornell University Press, 2008.

Heim, Carol E. "Who Pays, Who Benefits, Who Decides? Urban Infrastructure in Nineteenth-Century Chicago and Twentieth-Century Phoenix." *Social Science History* 39, no. 3 (2015): 453–482.

Henderson, A. Scott. *Housing and the Democratic Ideal: The Life and Thought of Charles Abrams.* New York: Columbia University Press, 2000.

Henderson, Thomas M. *Tammany Hall and the New Immigrants: The Progressive Year.* New York: Arno Press, 1976.

Hickel, Jason. *Less Is More: How Degrowth Will Save the World.* London: William Heinemann, 2020.

Hill, Laura Warren, and Julia Rabig. *The Business of Black Power: Community Development, Capitalism, and Corporate Responsibility in Postwar America.* Rochester, NY: University of Rochester Press, 2012.

Higgens-Evenson, R. Rudy. "Financing a Second Era of Internal Improvements: Transportation and Tax Reform, 1890–1929." *Social Science History* 26, no. 4 (2002): 623–651.

Higgens-Evenson, R. Rudy. *The Price of Progress: Public Services, Taxation and the American Corporate State, 1877–1919.* Baltimore: Johns Hopkins University Press, 2003.

Hirsch, Arnold R. *Making the Second Ghetto: Race and Housing in Chicago, 1940–1960.* Chicago: University of Chicago Press, 2011.

Hirt, Sonia A. *Zoned in the USA: The Origins and Implications of American Land-Use Regulation.* Ithaca, NY: Cornell University Press, 2014.

Hoffman, Alexander Von. "The Lost History of Urban Renewal." *Journal of Urbanism: International Research on Placemaking and Urban Sustainability* 1, no. 3 (2008): 281–301.

Hoffman, Joan. "Urban Squeeze Plays: New York City Crises of the 1930s and 1970s." *Review of Radical Political Economics* 15, no. 2 (1983): 29–57.

Holtzman, Benjamin. *The Long Crisis: New York City and the Path to Neoliberalism.* New York: Oxford University Press, 2021.

Hood, Clifton. *722 Miles: The Building of the Subways and How They Transformed New York.* Baltimore: Johns Hopkins University Press, 1993.

Horowitz, Daniel. *The Anxieties of Affluence: Critiques of American Consumer Culture 1939–1979*. Amherst: University of Massachusetts Press, 2009.

Horkheimer, Max. *Critical Theory : Selected Essays*. New York: Continuum, 1972.

Horowitz, Sarah. *Mutualism: Building the Next Economy from the Ground Up*. New York: Random House, 2021.

Howell-Moroney, Michael. "The Tiebout Hypothesis 50 Years Later." *Public Administration Review* 68, no. 1 (2008): 97–109.

Huddleston, Jack R. *The Intersection between Planning and the Municipal Budget*. Cambridge, MA: Lincoln Institute of Land Policy, 2007.

Huret, Romain, Nelson Lichtenstein, and Jean-Christian Vinel, eds. *Capitalism Contested: The New Deal and Its Legacies*. Philadelphia: University of Pennsylvania Press, 2020.

Hutchmacher, J. Joseph. *Senator Robert F. Wagner and the Rise of Urban Liberalism*. New York: Atheneum, 1971.

Hyra, Derek. "Conceptualizing the New Urban Renewal: Comparing the Past to the Present." *Urban Affairs Review* 48, no. 4 (2012): 498–527.

Imbroscio, David L. *Reconstructing City Politics: Alternative Economic Development and Urban Regimes*. London: Sage Publications, 1997.

Imbroscio, David L. "The Local Public Balance Sheet: An Alternative Evaluation Methodology for Local Economic Development," in *Critical Evaluations of Economic Development Policies*, edited by David Fasenfest and Laura Reese, 77–101. Detroit: Wayne State University Press, 2004.

Imbroscio, David L. *Urban America Reconsidered: Alternatives for Governance and Policy*. Ithaca, NY: Cornell University Press, 2010.

Imbroscio, David L., and Jonathan S. Davies. *Theories of Urban Politics*. London: Sage Publications, 2008.

Immelwahr, Daniel. *Thinking Small: The United States and the Lure of Community Development*. Cambridge, MA: Harvard University Press, 2015.

Isenberg, Alison. *Downtown America*. Chicago: University of Chicago Press, 2010.

Jackson, Kenneth T. *Crabgrass Frontier: The Suburbanization of America*. New York: Oxford University Press, 1985.

Jackson, Timothy. *Prosperity without Growth: Foundations for the Economy of Tomorrow*. London: Routledge, 2009.

Jacobs, Jane. *The Death and Life of Great American Cities*. New York: Random House, 2003.

Jacobson, Matthew Frye. *Whiteness of a Different Color: European Immigrants and the Alchemy of Race*. Cambridge, MA: Harvard University Press, 1998.

Jacques, Richard. *Radical Ecological Economics and Accounting to Save the Planet: The Failure of Mainstream Economists*. New York: Routledge, 2023.

Jager, Anton. "State and Corporation in American Populist Political Philosophy, 1877–1902." *Historical Journal* 64, no. 4 (2021): 1035–1059.

Jeffries, Judson L., ed. *On the Ground: The Black Panther Party in Communities Across America*. Jackson: University of Mississippi Press, 2010.

Jenkins, Destin. *The Bonds of Inequality: Debt and the Making of the American City*. Chicago: University of Chicago Press, 2021.

Jenkins, Destin. "Money and the Ghetto, Money in the Ghetto." *Journal of Urban History* 46, no. 3 (2019): 494–499.

Jensen, Nathan, and Edmund J. Malesky. *Incentives to Pander: How Politicians Use Corporate Welfare for Political Gain*. Cambridge: Cambridge University Press, 2019.

Johnson, David A. *Planning the Great Metropolis: The 1929 Regional Plan of New York and Its Environs*. New York: Routledge, 2015.

Johnson, Kimberley. "Community Development Corporations, Participation, and Accountability: The Harlem Urban Development Corporation and the Bedford-Stuyvesant Restoration Corporation." *Annals of the American Academy of Political and Social Sciences* 594 (2004): 109–124.

Johnston, Robert D. *The Radical Middle Class: Populist Democracy and the Question of Capitalism in Progressive Era Portland, Oregon*. Princeton, NJ: Princeton University Press, 2013.

Judt, Tony. "The Wrecking Ball of Innovation." *New York Review of Books*, December 6, 2007. https://www.nybooks.com/articles/2007/12/06/the-wrecking-ball-of-innovation/.

Kahn, Jonathan. *Budgeting Democracy: State Building and Citizenship in America, 1890–1928*. Ithaca, NY: Cornell University Press, 1997.

Kahrl, Andrew W. "The Short End of Both Sticks: Property Assessments and Black Taxpayer Disadvantage in Urban America." In *Shaped by the State: Towards a New Political History of the Twentieth Century*, edited by Brent Cebul, Lily Geismer, and Mason B. Williams, 189–217. Chicago: University of Chicago Press, 2019.

Kaufman, Jason. "Rent-Seeking and Municipal Social Spending: Data from America's Early Urban-Industrial Age." *Urban Affairs Review* 39, no. 5 (2004): 552–588.

Kazin, Michael. *The Populist Persuasion: An American History*. Ithaca, NY: Cornell University Press, 2017.

Keating, Ann Durkin. *Building Chicago: Suburban Developers and the Creation of a Divided Metropolis*. Columbus: Ohio State University Press, 1988.

Kessner, Thomas. *The Golden Door: Italian and Jewish Immigrant Mobility in New York City, 1880–1915*. New York: Oxford University Press, 1977.

Kioupkiolis, Alexandros. *Common Hegemony Populism and the New Municipalism: Democratic Alter-Politics and Transformative Strategies*. New York: Routledge, 2022.

Kirkpatrick, L. Owen, and Michael Peter Smith. "The Infrastructural Limits to Growth: Rethinking the Urban Growth Machine in Times of Fiscal Crisis." *International Journal of Urban and Regional Research* 35, no. 3 (2019): 477–503.

Kirschling, Kyle M. "An Economic Analysis of Rapid Transit in New York, 1870–2010." Master's thesis, Columbia University, May 2012.

Klemek, Christopher. *The Transatlantic Collapse of Urban Renewal: Postwar Urbanism from New York to Berlin*. Chicago: University of Chicago Press, 2011.

Kloppenberg, James T. *The Virtues of Liberalism*. New York: Oxford University Press, 1998.

Knewitz, Simone. *The Politics of Private Property: Contested Claims to Ownership in U.S. Cultural Discourse*. Lanham, MD: Lexington Books, 2021.

Krikelas, Andrew C. "Why Regions Grow: A Review of Research on the Economic Base Model." *Economic Review* 77, no. 4 (1992): 16–29.

Krippner, Greta R. *Capitalizing on Crisis: The Political Origins of the Rise of Finance*. Cambridge, MA: Harvard University Press, 2012.

Kruse, Kevin. *White Flight: Atlanta and the Making of Modern Conservatism*. Princeton, NJ: Princeton University Press, 2013.

Kruse, Kevin M., and Thomas J. Sugrue, eds. *The New Suburban History*. Chicago: University of Chicago, 2005.

Kurland, Gerald. *Seth Low: The Reformer in an Urban Industrial Age*. New York: Arden Media, 1971.

Land, Alan E. "Toward Optimal Land Use: Property Tax Policy and Land Use Planning." *California Law Review* 27, no. 3 (1967): 856–897.

Lands, LeeAnn. *The Culture of Property: Race, Class, and Housing Landscapes in Atlanta, 1880–1950*. Athens: University of Georgia Press, 2011.

Larson, Scott. *Building Like Moses with Jacobs in Mind: Contemporary Planning in New York City*. Philadelphia, PA: Temple University Press, 2013.

Lasch, Christopher. *The True and Only Heaven: Progress and Its Critics*. New York: W. W. Norton, 1991.

Laurence, Peter. *Becoming Jane Jacobs*. Philadelphia: University of Pennsylvania Press, 2016.

Leidenberger, Georg. *Chicago's Progressive Alliance: Labor and the Bid for Public Streetcars*. Dekalb: Northern Illinois University Press, 2006.

Leval, Gaston. *Collectives in the Spanish Revolution*. Oakland, CA: PM Press, 2018.

Lewinnek, Elaine. *The Working Man's Reward: Chicago's Early Suburbs and the Roots of American Sprawl*. Oxford: Oxford University Press, 2014.

Liat, Spiro. "Global Histories of Neoliberalism: An Interview with Quinn Slobodian." Toynbee Prize Foundation. March 21, 2018. https://toynbeeprize.org/posts/quinn-slobodian.

Link, Stefan, and Noam Maggor. "The United States as a Developing Nation: Revisiting the Peculiarities of American History." *Past and Present* 246, no. 1 (2020): 269–306.

Lipartito, Kenneth. "Reassembling the Economic: New Departures in Historical Materialism." *American Historical Review* 121, no. 1 (2016): 101–139.

Lipin, Lawrence M. "Nature, the City, and the Family Circle: Domesticity and the Urban Home in Henry George's Thought." *Journal of the Gilded Age and Progressive Era* 13, no. 3 (2014): 305–335.

Logan, John R., and Harvey Luskin Molotch. *Urban Fortunes: The Political Economy of Place*. Berkeley: University of California Press, 2007.

Looker, Benjamin. *A Nation of Neighborhoods: Imagining Cities, Communities, and Democracy in Postwar America*. Chicago: University of Chicago Press, 2015.

Lucht, Bernie. *The Lost Massey Lectures: Recovered Classics from Five Great Thinkers*. New York: House of Anansi Press, 2011.

Macekura, Stephen J. *The Mismeasure of Progress: Economic Growth and Its Critics*. Chicago: University of Chicago Press, 2022.

Maggor, Noam. *Brahmin Capitalism: Frontiers of Wealth and Populism in America's First Gilded Age*. Cambridge, MA: Harvard University Press, 2017.

Maher, Neil M. *Nature's New Deal: The Civilian Conservation Corps and the Roots of the American Environmental Movement*. New York: Oxford University Press, 2005.

Mako, Keith. *The Ecocentrists: A History of Radical Environmentalism*. New York: Columbia University Press, 2018.

Marglin, Stephen A. *The Dismal Science: How Thinking Like an Economist Undermines Community*. Cambridge, MA: Harvard University Press, 2008.

Marohn, Charles. *Strong Towns: A Bottom-Up Revolution to Rebuild American Prosperity*. Hoboken, NJ: John Wiley & Sons, 2020.

Martin, Isaac William, Ajay K. Mehrotra, and Monica Prasad, eds. *The New Fiscal Sociology: Taxation in Comparative and Historical Perspective*. Cambridge: Cambridge University Press, 2010.

Mawtree, Victoria, and Majid Rahnema, eds. *The Post-Development Reader*. London: Bloomsbury Publishing, 1997.

McCormick, Richard L. "The Discovery That Business Corrupts Politics: A Reappraisal of the Origins of Progressivism." *American Historical Review* 86, no. 2 (1981): 247–274.

McDonald, Terrence J. "Building the Impossible State: Toward an Institutional Analysis of Statebuilding in America, 1820–1930." In *Institutions in American Society: Essays in Market,*

Political, and Social Organizations, edited by John Edgar Jackson, 217–140. Ann Arbor: University of Michigan Press, 1990.

McDonald, Terrence J. "The Burdens of Urban History: The Theory of the State in Recent American Social History." *Studies in American Political Development* 3 (Spring 1989): 3–29.

McDonald, Terrence J. "The History of Urban Fiscal Politics in America, 1830–1930: What Was Supposed to Be versus What Was and the Difference It Makes." *International Journal of Public Administration* 11, no. 6 (1988): 679–712.

McDonald, Terrence J. *The Parameters of Urban Fiscal Policy: Socioeconomic Change and Political Culture in San Francisco, 1860–1906.* Berkeley: University of California Press, 1986.

McDonald, Terrence J., and Sally K., eds. *The Politics of Urban Fiscal Policy.* Beverly Hills, CA: Sage Publications, 1984.

McDonough, Ryan P., Paul J. Miranti, and Michael P. Schoderbek. "The Search for Order in Municipal Administration: Herman A. Metz and the New York City Experience, 1898–1909." *Accounting Historians Journal* 47, no. 1 (2020): 55–74.

McGirr, Lisa. *Suburban Warriors: The Origins of the New American Right.* Princeton, NJ: Princeton University Press, 2015.

McKee, Guian A. *The Problem of Jobs: Liberalism, Race, and Deindustrialization in Philadelphia.* Chicago: University of Chicago Press, 2019.

Meadows, Donella H., Jorgen Randers, and Dennis L. Meadows, eds. *Limits to Growth: The 30-Year Update.* London: Earchscan, 2004.

Mehrotra, Ajay K. *Making the Modern American Fiscal State: Law, Politics, and the Rise of Progressive Taxation, 1877–1929.* Cambridge: Cambridge University Press, 2013.

Méndez, Pablo F., Jaime M. Amezaga, and Luis Santamaría. "Explaining Path-Dependent Rigidity Traps: Increasing Returns, Power, Discourses, and Entrepreneurship Intertwined in Social-Ecological Systems." *Ecology and Society* 24, no. 2 (2019).

Merrifield, Andy. *Metromarxism: A Marxist Tale of the City.* New York: Routledge, 2002.

Meyers, Andrew A. "Invisible Cities: Lewis Mumford, Thomas Adams, and the Invention of the Regional City, 1923–1929." *Business and Economic History* 27, no. 2 (1998): 292–306.

Michelmore, Molly C. *Tax and Spend: The Welfare State, Tax Politics, and the Limits of American Liberalism.* Philadelphia: University of Pennsylvania Press, 2014.

Midgley, James. *Social Development: The Developmental Perspective in Social Welfare.* Thousand Oaks, CA: Sage Publications, 1995.

Miller, Kenneth E. *From Progressive to New Dealer: Frederic C. Howe and American Liberalism.* University Park, PA: Penn State University Press, 2014.

Mills, Edwin S. "A Thematic History of Urban Economic Analysis." *Brookings-Wharton Papers on Urban Affairs*, 2000, 1–38.

Mintz, Frank. *Anarchism and Worker's Self-Management in Revolutionary Spain.* Oakland, CA: AK Press, 2013.

Moehring, Eugene P. *Public Works and the Patterns of Urban Real Estate Growth in Manhattan, 1835–1894.* New York: Arno Press, 1981.

Mollenkopf, John. *A Phoenix in the Ashes: The Rise and Fall of the Koch Coalition in New York City Politics.* Princeton, NJ: Princeton University Press, 1992.

Monkkonen, Eric H. *America Becomes Urban: The Development of U.S. Cities and Towns, 1780–1980.* Berkeley: University of California Press, 1988.

Monkkonen, Eric H. *The Local State: Public Money and American Cities.* Stanford, CA: Stanford University Press, 1996.

Monkkonen, Eric H. "What Urban Crisis? A Historian's Point of View." *Urban Affairs Quarterly* 20, no. 4 (1985): 429–447.

Moody, Kim. *From Welfare State to Real Estate: Regime Change in New York City to the Present.* New York: New Press, 2007.

Moore, J. Wayne. "A History of Appraisal Theory and Practice: Looking Back from IAAO's 75th year." *Journal of Property Tax Assessment and Administration* 6, no. 3 (2009): 23–50.

Morris, Charles R. *The Cost of Good Intentions: New York City and the Liberal Experiment, 1960–1975.* New York: W. W. Norton, 1980.

Moskowitz, Marine. "Zoning the Industrial City: Planers, Commissioners, and Boosters in the 1920s." *Business and Economic History* 27, no. 2 (1998): 307–317.

Mudge, Stephanie. *Leftism Reinvented: Western Parties from Socialism to Neoliberalism.* Cambridge, MA: Harvard University Press, 2018.

Murray, Robin. "London and the Greater London Council: Restructuring the Capital of Capital." *Institute of Development Studies Bulletin* 16, no. 1 (1985): 47–55.

Nasaw, David. *The Chief: The Life of William Randolph Hearst.* Boston, MA: Houghton Mifflin, 2000.

Needham, Andrew. *Power Lines: Phoenix and the Making of the Modern Southwest.* Princeton, NJ: Princeton University Press, 2017.

Nembhard, Jessica Gordon. *Collective Courage: A History of African American Cooperative Economic Thought and Practice.* University Park, PA: Penn State University Press, 2015.

Netzer, Dick. *Real Property Tax Policy for New York City.* New York: New York University Graduate School of Public Affairs, 1980.

Neumann, Tracy. *Remaking the Rust Belt: The Postindustrial Transformation of North America.* Philadelphia: University of Pennsylvania Press, 2019.

Nickerson, Michelle, and Darren Dochuk, eds. *Sunbelt Rising: The Politics of Space, Place and Region.* Philadelphia: University of Pennsylvania Press, 2011.

Nicolaides, Becky M. *My Blue Heaven: Life and Politics in the Working-Class Suburbs of Los Angeles, 1920–1965.* Chicago: University of Chicago Press, 2002.

Novak, William J. "Public-Private Governance: A Historical Introduction." In *Government by Contract: Outsourcing and American Democracy,* edited by Jody Freedman and Martha Minow, 23–40. Cambridge, MA: Harvard University Press, 2009.

O'Connor, James. *Natural Causes: Essays in Ecological Marxism.* New York: Guilford Press, 1998.

O'Donnell, Edward T. *Henry George and the Crisis of Inequality: Progress and Poverty in the Gilded Age.* New York: Columbia University Press, 2017.

O'Donnell, Edward T. "Henry George and the 'New Political Forces': Ethnic Nationalism, Labor Radicalism, and Politics in Gilded Age New York." PhD diss., Columbia University, 1995.

O'Donnell, Edward T. "'Though Not an Irishman': Henry George and the American Irish." *American Journal of Economics and Sociology* 56, no. 4 (1997): 407–419.

Ottman, Tod M. "Government That Has Both a Heart and a Head: The Growth of New York State Government during the World War II Era, 1930–1950." PhD diss., State University of New York at Albany, 2001.

Osman, Suleiman. *The Invention of Brownstone Brooklyn: Gentrification and the Search for Authenticity in Postwar New York.* New York: Oxford University Press, 2011.

Osman, Suleiman. "'We're Doing It Ourselves': The Unexpected Origins of New York City's Public-Private Parks during the 1970s Fiscal Crisis." *Journal of Planning History* 16, no. 2 (2017): 162–174.

Page, Max. *The Creative Destruction of Manhattan, 1900–1940.* Chicago: University of Chicago Press, 2008.

Parilla, Joseph, and Sifan Liu. "Examining the Local Value of Economic Development Incentives: Evidence from Four U.S. Cities." Metropolitan Policy Program at Brookings. March 2018. https://www.brookings.edu/wp-content/uploads/2018/02/report_examining-the-local -value-of-economic-development-incentives_brookings-metro_march-2018.pdf.

Patton, Terry K., and Paul D. Hutchison. "Historical Development of the Financial Reporting Model for State and Local Governments in the United States from Late 1800s to 1999." *Accounting Historians Journal* 40, no. 2 (2013): 21–53.

Peck, Jamie. *Variegated Economies.* Oxford: Oxford University Press, 2023.

Perloff, Harvey S. "The Development of Urban Economics in the United States." *Urban Studies* 10 (1973): 289–301.

Peterson, Paul E. *City Limits.* Chicago: University of Chicago Press, 2012.

Phillips-Fein, Kim. *Fear City: New York's Fiscal Crisis and the Rise of Austerity Politics.* New York: Henry Holt, 2017.

Phillips-Fein, Kim. "The History of Neoliberalism," in Brent Cebul, Lily Geismer, and Mason Williams, eds., 347–62. *Shaped by the State: Toward a New Political History of the Twentieth Century.* Chicago: Chicago University Press, 2019.

Phillips-Fein, Kim, and Richard R. John, eds. *Capital Gains: Business and Politics in Twentieth Century America.* Philadelphia: University of Pennsylvania Press, 2017.

Picciotti, Antonio, Andrea Bernardoni, Massimo Cossignani, and Luca Ferrucci. "Social Cooperatives in Italy: Economic Antecedents and Regional Distribution." *Annals of Public and Cooperative Economics* 85, no. 2 (2014): 165–325.

Porter, Michael E. "The Competitive Advantages of the Inner City." *Harvard Business Review,* May–June 1995. https://hbr.org/1995/05/the-competitive-advantage-of-the-inner-city.

Postel, Charles. *The Populist Vision.* Oxford: Oxford University Press, 2009.

Pritchett, Wendell E. *Brownsville, Brooklyn: Blacks, Jews, and the Changing Face of the Ghetto.* Chicago: University of Chicago Press, 2002.

Pritchett, Wendell E. "The 'Public Menace' of Blight: Urban Renewal and the Private Uses of Eminent Domain." *Yale Law and Policy Review* 2, no. 1 (2003): 1–52.

Przeworski, Adam. *Capitalism and Social Democracy.* New York: Cambridge University Press, 1986.

Prosterman, Daniel O. *Defining Democracy: Electoral Reform and the Struggle for Power in New York City.* New York: Oxford University Press, 2013.

Rabig, Julia. *The Fixers: Devolution, Development, and Civil Society in Newark, 1960–1990.* Chicago: University of Chicago Press, 2017.

Radford, Gail. *Modern Housing for America: Policy Struggles in the New Deal Era.* Chicago: University of Chicago Press, 1996.

Radford, Gail. *The Rise of the Public Authority: Statebuilding and Economic Development in Twentieth Century America.* Chicago: University of Chicago Press, 2013.

Rast, Joel. "Critical Junctures, Long-Term Processes: Urban Redevelopment in Chicago and Milwaukee, 1945–1980." *Social Science History* 33, no. 4 (2009): 393–426.

Raworth, Kate. *Seven Ways to Think Like a 21st Century Economist.* White River Junction, VT: Chelsea Green Publishing, 2017.

Reaven, Marci. "Neighborhood Activism in Planning for New York City, 1945–1975." *Journal of Urban History* 46, no. 6 (2020): 1261–1289.

Reider, Jonathan. *Canarsie: The Jews and Italians of Brooklyn against Liberalism*. Cambridge, MA: Harvard University Press, 1985.

Reitano, Joanne. *The Restless City: A Short History of New York City from Colonial Times to the Present*. New York: Taylor & Francis, 2010.

Revell, Keith D. *Building Gotham: Civic Culture and Public Policy in New York City, 1898–1938*. Baltimore: Johns Hopkins University Press, 2005.

Robertson, Thomas. *The Malthusian Moment: Global Population Growth and the Birth of American Environmentalism*. New Brunswick, NJ: Rutgers University Press, 2012.

Rocco, Roberto, ed. *Jane Jacobs Is Still Here: Jane Jacobs 100, Her Legacy and Relevance in the 21st Century*. https://issuu.com/robertorocco/docs/jane_jacobs_report (accessed June 10, 2023).

Rockman, Seth. "What Makes the History of Capitalism Newsworthy?" *Journal of the Early Republic* 34 (Fall 2014): 439–466.

Rodgers, Daniel T. *Atlantic Crossings: Social Politics in a Progressive Age*. Cambridge, MA: Harvard University Press, 2009.

Rosenof, Theodore. *Economics in the Long Run: New Deal Theorists and Their Legacies, 1933–1993*. Chapel Hill: University of North Carolina Press, 2000.

Rowan, Jamin Creed. *The Sociable City: An American Intellectual Tradition*. Philadelphia: University of Pennsylvania Press, 2017.

Rutland, Ted. "The City Is an Apartment House: Property, Improvement, and Dispossession in Early Twentieth-Century Halifax, Nova Scotia." *Urban Geography* 36, no. 3 (2015): 359–384.

Satter, Beryl. *Family Properties: Race, Real Estate and the Exploitation of Black Urban America*. New York: Henry Holt, 2013.

Savini, Federico, António Ferreira, and Kim Carlotta von Schönfeld, eds. *Post-Growth Planning: Cities beyond the Market*. London: Routledge, 2022.

Sbragia, Alberta M. *Debt Wish: Entrepreneurial Cities, US Federalism, and Economic Development*. Pittsburgh, PA: University of Pittsburgh Press, 1996.

Schlesinger, Arthur M. *The Coming of the New Deal*. Boston: Houghton Mifflin, 1958.

Schlichting, Kara Murphy. *New York Recentered: Building the Metropolis from the Shore*. Chicago: University of Chicago Press, 2019.

Schmelzer, Matthias. *The Hegemony of Growth: The OECD and the Making of the Economic Growth Paradigm*. Cambridge: Cambridge University Press, 2016.

Schmelzer, Matthias, and Iris Borowy, eds. *History of the Future of Economic Growth: Historical Roots of Current Debates on Sustainable Degrowth*. London: Routledge, 2018.

Schmelzer, Matthias, Andrea Vetter, and Aaron Vansintjan. *The Future Is Degrowth: A Guide to a World beyond Capitalism*. London: Verso, 2022.

Schneider, Mark. "Undermining the Growth Machine: The Missing Link between Local Economic Development and Fiscal Payoffs." *Journal of Politics* 54, no. 1 (1992): 214–230.

Schoenberger, Erica. "From Fordism to Flexible Accumulation: Technology, Competitive Strategies, and International Location." *International Journal of Urban and Regional Research: Environment & Planning* 6, no. 3 (1988): 245–262.

Schragger. Richard C. "Rethinking the Theory and Practice of Local Economic Development." *University of Chicago Law Review* 77, no. 1 (2010): 311–339.

Schubert, Dirk, ed. *Contemporary Perspectives on Jane Jacobs: Reassessing the Impacts of an Urban Visionary*. New York: Routledge, 2014.

Schulman, Bruce J. "Post-1968 U.S. History: Neo-Consensus History for the Age of Polarization." *Reviews in American History* 47, no. 3 (2019): 479–499.

Schwartz, Joel. *The New York Approach: Robert Moses, Urban Liberals, and Redevelopment of the Inner City*. Columbus: Ohio State University Press, 1993.

Schwartz, Joel. "Tenement Renewal in New York City in the 1930s: The District-Improvement Ideas of Arthur C. Holden." *Journal of Planning History* 1, no. 4 (2002): 290–310.

Scobey, David. "Boycotting the Politics Factory: Labor Radicalism and the New York City Mayoral Election of 1884." *Radical History Review* 28, no. 30 (1984): 280–325.

Scobey, David. *Empire City: The Making and Meaning of the New York City Landscape*. Philadelphia, PA: Temple University Press, 2002.

Sebastian, Berger. *The Social Costs of Neoliberalism: Essays on the Economics of K. William Kapp*. Nottingham, UK: Spokesman, 2017.

Self, Robert O. *American Babylon: Race and the Struggle for Postwar Oakland*. Princeton, NJ: Princeton University Press, 2003.

Sellers, Charles. *The Market Revolution: Jacksonian America, 1815–1846*. New York: Oxford University Press, 1991.

Sewell, William H., Jr. *Logics of History: Social Theory and Social Transformation*. Chicago: University of Chicago, 2005.

Shapiro, Edward S. "Decentralist Intellectuals and the New Deal." *Journal of American History* 58, no. 4 (1972): 938–957.

Shefter, Martin. *Political Crisis/Fiscal Crisis: The Collapse and Revival of New York City*. New York: Columbia University Press, 1992.

Shenk, Timothy. "Inventing the American Economy," in *Capitalism Contested: The New Deal and Its Legacies*, edited by Romain Huret, Nelson Lichtenstein, and Jean-Christian Vinel, 42–58. Philadelphia: University of Pennsylvania Press, 2020.

Shkuda, Aaron. "Housing the 'Front Office to the World': Urban Planning for the Service Economy in Battery Park City, New York." *Journal of Planning History* 13, no. 3 (2013): 234–246.

Siodla, James. "Debt and Taxes: Fiscal Strain and US City Budgets during the Great Depression." *Explorations in Economic History* 76 (April 2020). https://www.sciencedirect.com/science/article/abs/pii/S0014498320300140?via%3Dihub (Accessed April 4, 2020).

Smith, Jason Scott. *Building New Deal Liberalism: The Political Economy of Public Works, 1933–1956*. Cambridge: Cambridge University Press, 2006.

Soffer, Jonathan. *Ed Koch and the Rebuilding of New York*. New York: Columbia University Press, 2010.

Soja, Edward W. "The Socio-Spatial Dialectic." *Annals of the Association of American Geographers* 70, no. 2 (1980): 207–225.

Sorenson, Andre. "Taking Path Dependence Seriously: An Historical Institutionalist Research Agenda in Planning History." *Planning Perspectives* 30, no. 1 (2015): 17–38.

Soyer, Daniel. *Left in the Center: The Liberal Party of New York and the Rise and Fall of American Social Democracy*. Ithaca, NY: Cornell University Press, 2022.

Spence, Mark David. *Dispossessing the Wilderness: Indian Removal and the Making of the National Parks*. New York: Oxford University Press, 1999.

Speth, James Gustave, and Kathleen Courrier, eds. *The New Systems Reader: Alternatives to a Failed Economy*. New York: Routledge, 2021.

Stanfield, J. Ron. *The Economic Thought of Karl Polanyi: Lives and Livelihood*. New York: St. Martin's Press 1986, 56.

Stein, Judith. *Pivotal Decade: How the United States Trade Factories for Finance in the Seventies*. New Haven, CT: Yale University Press, 2010.

Stern, Robert A. M., David Fishman, and Thomas Mellins. *New York 1960: Architecture and Urbanism between the Second World War and the Bicentennial.* New York: Monacelli Press, 1997.

Stevens, Sara. *Developing Expertise: Architecture and Real Estate in Metropolitan America.* New Haven, CT: Yale University Press, 2016.

Stigltiz, Joseph, Amartya Sen, and Jean-Paul Fitoussi. *Mismeasuring Our Lives: Why GDP Doesn't Add Up.* New York: New Press, 2010.

Stivers, Camilla. *Bureau Men Settlement Women: Constructing Public Administration in the Progressive Era.* Lawrence: University Press of Kansas, 2000.

Stone, Geoffrey R. *Perilous Times: Free Speech in Wartime from the Sedition Act of 1798 to the War on Terrorism.* New York: W. W. Norton, 2004.

Stone, Michael. *Shelter Poverty: New Ideas on Housing Affordability.* Philadelphia, PA: Temple University Press, 2010.

Sugrue, Thomas J. *The Origins of the Urban Crisis.* Princeton, NJ: Princeton University Press, 2014.

Sugrue, Thomas J. "All Politics Is Local: The Persistence of Localism in Twentieth-Century America." In *The Democratic Experiment: New Directions in American Political History,* edited by Meg Jacobs, William J. Novak, and Julian E. Zelizer, 301–326. Princeton, NJ: Princeton University Press, 2003.

Sullivan, Joseph Patrick. "From Municipal Ownership to Regulation: Municipal Utility Reform in New York City, 1880–1907." PhD diss., Rutgers University, 1995.

Sussman, Carol. *Planning the Fourth Migration: The Neglected Vision of the Regional Planning Association of America.* Cambridge, MA: MIT Press, 1977.

Tanaka, Adam. "Private Projects, Public Ambitions: Large-Scale, Middle-Income Housing in New York City." PhD diss., Harvard University, 2018.

Taylor, Keeanga-Yamahtta. *Race for Profit: How Banks and the Real Estate Industry Undermined Black Homeownership.* Chapel Hill: University of North Carolina Press, 2019.

Teaford, Jon C. *The Rough Road to Renaissance: Urban Revitalization in America, 1940–1985.* Baltimore: Johns Hopkins University Press, 1990.

Thomas, Curlew O., and Barbara Boston Thomas. "Blacks' Socioeconomic Status and the Civil Rights Movement's Decline, 1970–1979: An Examination of some Hypotheses." *Phylon* 45, no. 1 (1984): 40–51.

Trebeck, Katherine, and Jeremy Williams. *The Economics of Arrival: Ideas for a Grown-Up Economy.* Bristol, UK: Policy Press, 2019.

Tribe, Keith. *Constructing Economic Science: The Invention of a Discipline 1850–1950.* New York: Oxford University Press, 2022.

Vale, Lawrence. *From the Puritans to the Projects: Public Housing and Public Neighbors.* Cambridge: Harvard University Press, 2007.

Vitiello, Domenic. "Machine Building and City Building Urban Planning and Industrial Restructuring in Philadelphia, 1894–1928." *Journal of Urban History* 34, no. 3 (2008): 399–434.

Vitiello, Domenic. "Monopolizing the Metropolis: Gilded Age Growth Machines and Power in American Urbanization." *Planning Perspectives* 28, no. 1 (2013): 71–90.

Walker, Christine Corlet, Angela Druckman, and Tim Jackson. "Growth Dependency in the Welfare State: An Analysis of Drivers in the UK's Adult Social Care Sector and Proposals for Change." *Ecological Economics* 220 (June 2024). https://www.sciencedirect.com/science/article/pii/S0921800924000569#ab0005 (accessed June 3, 2024).

Wallace, Mike. *Greater Gotham: A History of New York City from 1898 to 1919.* Oxford: Oxford University Press, 2018.

Wallis, John Joseph. "American Government Finance in the Long Run: 1790–1990." *Journal of Economic Perspectives* 14, no. 1 (2000): 61–82.

Wallis, John Joseph. "The Birth of the Old Federalism: Financing the New Deal, 1932–1940." *Journal of Economic History* 44, no. 1 (1984): 139–159.

Warner, Sam Bass. *Streetcar Suburbs: The Process of Growth in Boston, 1870–1900.* Cambridge, MA: Harvard University Press, 1962.

Warren, Joyce W. *Women, Money, and the Law: Nineteenth-Century Fiction, Gender, and the Courts.* Iowa City: University of Iowa Press, 2005.

Weaver, Timothy. *Blazing the Neoliberal Trail: Urban Political Development in the United States and the United Kingdom.* Philadelphia: University of Pennsylvania Press, 2016.

Weber, Joe. "Yesterday's Freeway Network of Tomorrow." *Geographic Review* 106, no. 1 (2016): 54–71.

Weir, Margaret. *Politics and Jobs: The Boundaries of Employment Policy in the United States.* Princeton, NJ: Princeton University Press, 1993.

Weir, Robert. "A Fragile Alliance: Henry George and the Knights of Labor." *American Journal of Economics and Sociology* 56, no. 4 (1997): 421–439.

Weiss, Marc A. "Real Estate History: An Overview and Research Agenda." *Business History Review* 63, no. 2 (1989): 241–282.

Weiss, Marc A. "Richard T. Ely and the Contribution of Economic Research to National Housing Policy, 1920–1940." *Urban Studies* 26 (1988): 115–126.

Weiss, Marc A. "The Real Estate Industry and the Politics of Zoning in San Francisco, 1914–1928." *Planning Perspectives* 3, no. 3 (1988): 311–324.

Weiss, Nancy J. *Charles Francis Murphy, 1858–1924.* Northampton, MA: Smith College, 1968.

White, Eugene N. *Lessons from the Great American Real Estate Boom of the 1920s.* Cambridge, MA: National Bureau of Economic Research, 2009. https://www.nber.org/papers/w15573.pdf.

Williams, Daniel W. "Measuring Government in the Early Twentieth Century." *Public Administration Review* 63, no. 6 (2003): 643–659.

Williams, Mason. *City of Ambition: FDR, La Guardia, and the Making of Modern New York.* New York: John Wiley & Sons, 2014.

Winling, LaDale C., and Todd M. Michney. "The Roots of Redlining: Academic, Governmental, and Professional Networks in the Making of the New Deal Lending Regime." *Journal of American History* 108, no. 1 (2021): 42–68.

Woodsworth, Michael. *Battle for Bed-Stuy: The Long War on Poverty in New York City.* Cambridge, MA: Harvard University Press, 2016.

Wortel-London, Daniel. "All's Fare: Subways and the Transformation of Metropolitan Politics in New York City, 1904–1934." In *Urban Infrastructure: Historical and Social Dimensions of an Interconnected World*, edited by Joseph Heathcott, Jonathan Soffer, and Rae Zimmerman, 147–164. Pittsburgh, PA: University of Pittsburgh Press, 2022.

Wortel-London, Daniel. "Building a People's Economy in London." *Tribune*, September 25, 2022. https://www.tribunemag.co.uk/2022/09/glc-gleb-robin-murray-economics-socialism-london-thatcher.

Wortel-London, Daniel. "Progress and Authenticity: Urban Renewal, Urban Tourism, and the Meanings of Mid-Twentieth Century New York." *Journal of Tourism History* 5, no. 2 (2013): 172–184.

Wortel-London, Daniel. "The Tax Trap." *Dissent* 68, no. 1 (2021): 125–134.

Wortel-London, Daniel. "Worker Co-Ops Have a Role to Play in Socialist Strategy." *Jacobin*, May 5, 2024. https://jacobin.com/2024/05/cooperatives-dsa-left-strategy-solidarity.

Wunderlin, Clarence E. *Visions of a New Industrial Order: Social Science and Labor Theory in America's Progressive Era*. New York: Columbia University Press, 1992.

Yarrow, Andrew L. *Measuring America: How Economic Growth Came to Define American Greatness in the Late Twentieth Century*. Amherst: University of Massachusetts Press, 2010.

Yearley, Clifton K. *The Money Machines: The Breakdown and Reform of Governmental and Party Finance in the North, 1860–1920*. Albany: State University of New York Press, 1972.

Yin, Jordan S. "A Review of Alternative Economic Base Study Methods for Community Economic Development," in *Critical Evaluations of Economic Development Policies*, edited by David Fasenfest and Laura A. Reese, 101–113. Detroit: Wayne State University Press, 2004.

Zipp, Samuel. "The Roots and Routes of Urban Renewal." *Journal of Urban History* 39, no. 3 (2012): 366–391.

Zipp, Samuel, and Michael Carriere. "Introduction: Thinking Through Urban Renewal." *Journal of Urban History* 39, no. 3 (2012): 359–365.

Zunz, Olivier. *The Changing Face of Inequality: Urbanization, Industrial Development, and Immigrants in Detroit, 1880–1920*. Chicago: University of Chicago Press, 1982.

Index

Abrams, Charles: on federal aid, 264n63; on Jacobs, 177; on profit potential, 116; on taxes, 94, 131, 162; on transportation and communication technology, 150; and urban redevelopment in 1930s, 131, 142

accessibility and land values, 57, 58, 66

Ackerman, Frederick, 100, 102, 110, 134

Adams, Herbert, 24–25

Adler, Felix, 39

Advisory Commission on Taxation and Finance, 68

Agar, Herbert, 156

Agee, James, 103

Agriculture Adjustment Administration, 105

Allen, Robert, 186

Allen, William Harvey, 126

Allied Real Estate Interests, 56, 68

Amalgamated Clothing Workers of America, 116

Amazon, 223

American Real Estate Company, 66

Anderson, Martin, 167

anti-colonialism and Black economic development, 182, 184

anti-discrimination laws, 132

anti-growth paradigm, 211–12

Architect's Renewal Committee, 191

Ascher, Charles S., 154

assessments: after 1970s financial crisis, 216; and 1970s financial crisis, 202; bankers on, 126; based on structures, 35; and central-city speculation, 112; federal aid's effect on, 135; and race, 94; and service franchises, 46–47; special assessments, 19, 87–88, 139; and subway development, 68; and urban redevelopment, 265n64; and white homeownership in outer boroughs, 85, 86, 92, 93, 123, 126, 128, 138, 139, 209; and

white-collar work focus, 162–65, 199. *See also* confiscatory property taxes

Association for the Public Control of Franchises, 29

Association of Long Island and Queens Property Owners, 69

Baltimore: probusiness focus, 221; rehabilitation vs. renewal in, 179

Bankers Trust, 190

banking. *See* finance industry

bankruptcies, 23, 103

Bankrupting a Great City (Klein), 30, 44–45, 50, 74

Battery Park City Authority, 216

Bauer, Catherine, 8, 99, 102, 120, 137, 156, 157

Beame, Abraham, 202

Bedford Park Taxpayers Association, 56

Bell, Daniel, 166, 176

Bender, Thomas, 139

Benedict Taxpayer Association, 87

Berle, Adolf, 105

Berry, Charles White, 140

Beverly Hills, land-use controls in, 212

Bird, Frederick, 107, 138

Black, George Ashton, 13

Black citizens: and community economic control, 8, 169, 170, 182–92, 206, 211; homeownership rates, 95; and landownership restrictions, 16; and mutual aid societies and cooperatives, 33; poverty, and Jacobs, 178; and segregation, 119–20, 132; as subsidizing white homeownership in outer boroughs, 79, 80–81, 92–96, 182–83, 185, 226; as tenants, 119–20; and urban redevelopment criticism, 168, 169–70. *See also* race

Black Freedom Movement, 184, 191

Black Power, 6, 169, 182

Printed and bound by CPI Group (UK) Ltd, Croydon, CR0 4YY

12/11/2025

14771393-0001